# The Disappearance of Objects

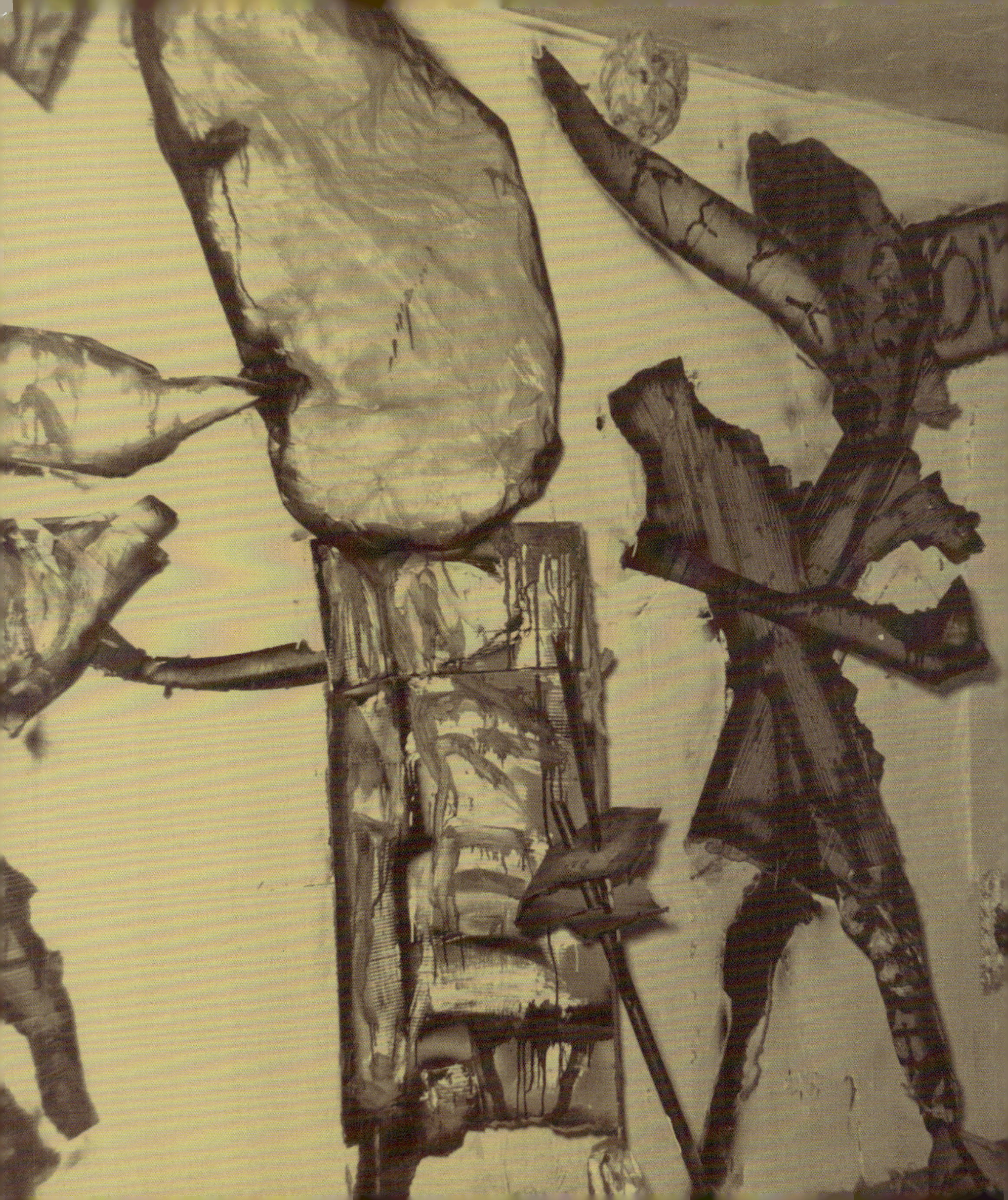

Joshua Shannon

# The Disappearance of Objects

## NEW YORK ART AND THE RISE OF THE POSTMODERN CITY

YALE UNIVERSITY PRESS
NEW HAVEN AND LONDON

Publication of this book has been aided by a grant from the Wyeth Foundation for American Art Publication Fund of the College Art Association.



**Designed by**
HVADesign, NY
Henk Van Assen and Yuko Kawashimo
**Typeset by**
HVADesign, NY
**Set in**
Whitney + Galaxy Polaris
**Printed in**
Singapore by Tien Wah Press

Library of Congress Cataloging-in-Publication Data

Shannon, Joshua, 1972–
    The disappearance of objects : New York art and the rise of the postmodern city / Joshua Shannon.
        p.  cm.
    Includes bibliographical references and index.
    ISBN 978-0-300-13706-4 (cloth : alk. paper)
    1.  Postmodernism—New York (State)—New York. 2.  Art, American—New York (State)—New York—20th century. 3.  Art and society—New York (State)—New York—History—20th century. I. Title.
    N6512.5.P65S53 2009
    709.747'109046—dc22                    2008039276

A catalogue record for this book is available from the British Library.

This paper meets the requirements of ANSI/NISO Z 39.48-1992 (Permanence of Paper).

10  9  8  7  6  5  4  3  2  1

TITLE PAGE: Claes Oldenburg, *The Street* installation, 1960 (detail of fig. 1.6)
COVER: (front) Robert Rauschenberg, *Black Market,* 1961 (fig. 3.45); (back) Union Carbide Building, c. 1957, 270 Park Avenue, New York. Collection of Mayor Robert F. Wagner, NYC Municipal Archives

# CONTENTS

*For my parents*

*and in memory of Robert Rauschenberg*
*and his love for New York*

# Acknowledgments

This book began as a Ph.D. dissertation at the University of California, Berkeley, and it would have been impossible without the guidance of T. J. Clark and Anne Wagner. Both advisers left a deep impression on my thinking with their own published work, too, for which I extend sincere thanks. In the long course of revision, the book has also benefited immeasurably from close readings by Kevin Chua, Benjamin Grant, Michael J. Kramer, Rona Marech, Christopher Nealon, Alex Potts, Jennifer L. Roberts, and Jason Weems. The first chapter appeared in the *Art Bulletin* 86, no. 1 (2004), published by the College Art Association; I thank H. Perry Chapman, Robert E. Haywood, Lory Finkel, and an anonymous reader for their responses. Others who have offered important suggestions and encouragement at various stages include Jennifer Bethke, Huey Copeland, John Davis, Alexander Dumbadze, Hannah Feldman, Suzanne Hudson, Jonathan D. Katz, Howard Lay, James Luria, Steven Mansbach, Janine Mileaf, Sally Promey, Christine Schick, Matthew Witkovsky, Bryan Wolf, and Rebecca Zurier. The book of course also owes its fruition to the hard work of Patricia Fidler, John Long, Daniella Berman, and many others at Yale University Press, and to the Press's readers.

Several audiences and reading groups responded generously to my ideas at various stages, and I particularly thank those at the City University of New York, the George Washington University, Harvard University, Northwestern University, the Phillips Collection Center for the Study of Modern Art, the Royal Netherlands Academy of Arts and Sciences, the University of Manchester, the University of Washington, and at meetings of the College Art Association and the American Studies Association.

I appreciate the financial support offered by the General Research Board and the Department of Art History and Archaeology at the University of Maryland; the Andrew W. Mellon Postdoctoral Research Fellowship at the University of Michigan; the Patricia and Phillip Frost Fellowship at the Smithsonian American Art Museum; and the University of California, Berkeley, and its History of Art Department. I could never have written the book without the time offered by these grants. I owe thanks, too, to my colleagues and students at these institutions, whose thoughts proved integral to the development of the project.

For their help with my research, I extend appreciation to staff members at the Archives of American Art, the Chinati Foundation, the Getty Research Institute, the Hartman Center at Duke University, the Judd Foundation, the Judson Memorial Church, the Library of Congress, the Museum Ludwig in Cologne, the Museum of Contemporary Art in Los Angeles, the Metropolitan Museum of Art, the Museum of Modern Art, and the New York Public Library. I would also like to thank Richard Bernstein, Jim Dine, Jasper Johns, Jeffrey Kopie, Patty Mucha, Claes Oldenburg, and Anita Reuben Simons for kindly offering their recollections. Above all, I thank my friends and family—and especially my wife, Rona—for their unfailing generosity and support.

# Materiality in New York, 1960

IN OCTOBER 1958, "The Legacy of Jackson Pollock," which Allan Kaprow had written shortly after Pollock's fatal crash two years earlier, appeared in *Artnews*. There, it caught the attention of a legion of New Yorkers interested in the direction of avant-garde art, among them the twenty-eight-year-old Claes Oldenburg, who worked shelving books downtown, and who had been making sketches of street scenes since before he moved, in 1956, from Chicago. Kaprow's essay argued that Pollock's legacy was an art that eschewed expression and representation for a literalist emphasis on material fact. The art of the next several years, Kaprow predicted, would offer a literal presentation not just of paint but of all kinds of things from the everyday world. "Objects of every sort," he declared, "are materials for the new art: paint, chairs, food, electric and neon lights, smoke, water, old socks, a dog, movies, a thousand other things." All these ordinary things were to be presented as they were, untransformed by transcendental or even metaphoric impulse: "Only their real meaning," Kaprow wrote, "will be stated."[1]

Oldenburg was so excited by Kaprow's manifesto that he sought out the author in person. Other New York artists, meanwhile, were already making the art Kaprow described. Robert Rauschenberg, for example, working even farther downtown, had been using stuffed animals, clothing, and electric lights in his works for several years.[2] Jasper Johns picked up a common flashlight in 1958 and coated it in Sculp-Metal, as part of a new series of sculptures of ordinary objects. Within a few years, the painter Donald Judd would begin scavenging asphalt pipes and discarded warehouse pallets to build what he termed "specific objects." Other local artists making assemblages from found objects included Lee Bontecou, George Brecht, John Chamberlain, Jim Dine, Jean Follett, Marisol, Lucas Samaras, Richard Stankiewicz, and Kaprow himself. Some of their new

exhibition spaces—the major venues were the Castelli, Green, Jackson, Judson, and Reuben galleries—soon became prominent to curious members of New York's art-going public.

The literalist appropriation of common objects in art began to emerge as the unanticipated successor to Abstract Expressionist painting. In addition to the work in New York, there were common object assemblages being made in California (by artists including Bruce Conner, Jess, and Edward Kienholz) and in Paris (by Arman, Niki de Saint Phalle, Daniel Spoerri, and Jean Tinguely, among others). In New York, there was also quite a bit of nonvisual art in a similar vein: John Cage was using ordinary sounds in avant-garde music, Stan Brakhage was making movies that drew attention to the film stock itself, and the choreographers Merce Cunningham and Yvonne Rainer were crafting new, literalist kinds of dance. ("I am more interested in the *facts* of moving," Cunningham said, "rather than in my feelings about them."[3]) Many of the painters and sculptors, too, were dabbling in theater, directing the nonnarrative performances that came to be called happenings. Dine, Kaprow, and Oldenburg all organized such performances, as did Red Grooms, Richard O. Tyler, Robert Whitman, and others. Like the sculptures and assemblages of the period, these pieces were "preoccupied with objects" and characterized by nonnarrative "fragments of action."[4]

All of these gestures and investigations belonged to a longer history of modernism, which had for a century been dwelling on the opacity of representation, on the tensions between the act of picturing and the material facts of the art object itself. In 1963, Dore Ashton observed that, while the new work was unique, much of modernist art had already been working with "the solid simple object which resists everything—interpretation, incorporation, juxtaposition, transformation."[5] Indeed the archetypical account of modernism asks us to remember Édouard Manet's flat impasto as a signal of the failures of picturing, of the inevitable material *otherness* of the artwork from any thing it might propose to represent. For its part, modernist literature, although not precisely materialist, had been resisting narrative much as visual art had been resisting pictoriality. The mid-century manifestations of these literalist strains included concrete poetry in Brazil, the *nouveau roman* in France, Neorealist cinema in Italy, and Gutai performance art in Japan.

The avant-garde painters and sculptors in New York around 1960, however, formed a unique case. For a time, they worked intensively with specific kinds of objects: not just the ordinary materials of art but also the street signs, consumer objects, and building fragments of New York City itself. In their work with these things, the dialectic between image and object turned sharply to one side, developing into an extreme materialism that nearly refused representation altogether. Regarding his assemblages of street detritus, Rauschenberg said, "I don't want a picture to look like something it isn't. I want it to look like something it is," while Judd, maker of iron boxes, declared, "I'd like work that didn't allude to other things and was a specific thing in itself."[6]

There was considerable confusion about how to group and name these materialist art objects. Billy Klüver called several of the artists "Factualists." Walter Hopps named a show at the Pasadena Art Museum simply *New Paintings of Common Objects*. A 1962 show at Sidney Janis helped popularize the term *New Realists*, which was borrowed from Pierre Restany's characterization of the Paris avant-garde as "Le Nouveau Réalisme." In a brief essay he wrote in 1960 for the *New Media—New Forms* show at the Martha Jackson Gallery, Lawrence Alloway announced a movement he called "New York junk culture."[7] The term *Neo-Dada*,

stressing some works' debts to an earlier moment of collage (and eventually referring to early Pop art as well), appeared in a variety of sources in the press—ranging from *Art International* and *Arts Magazine* to *Newsweek*.[8]

Some of the best early criticism recognized that this art focused on certain kinds of objects in particular. Alloway noted, for example, that much contemporary art took special interest in detritus of an urban kind. The "source," of this art, he wrote, was "obsolescence, the throwaway material of cities, as it collects in drawers, closets, attics, garbage cans, gutters, waste lots, and city dumps."[9] Alloway noted further that all these material bits were, as Kaprow had wanted, "assembled factually, [with] their original identity stolidly kept." Alloway placed special emphasis on this point: "Essential to junk culture is retention of the original status of the objects . . . their first function grittily resisting incorporation into a smooth esthetic whole." It was their fragmentary, noncombinatory, and gritty resistance to wholeness (whether aesthetic, metaphoric, or narrative) that defined these works. This art was preoccupied with the material remainders it found everywhere around it, obsessed with bits of the city failing to match up with the meanings inevitably laid over and through them.

The purpose of this book is to uncover the historical significance of these struggles with the nature and limits of representation. New York City in this period was undergoing one of the most rapid and thoroughgoing transformations in its history. I argue here that this art, engaged as it was with problems of meaning, offered a uniquely revealing understanding of that transformation, and of its place in the history of capitalism. These works, attending to the changing nature of the everyday environment, can allow us to see clearly the texture of New York's first waves of postmodernization—the transition by which the city's economy, together with its very buildings and objects, seemed to be becoming dramatically more abstract.

Around 1960 New York's economy was rapidly shifting, and the direction of its architectural character was bitterly contested. At the heart of the change was the fact that the city was rapidly losing its industrial base: manufacturers were departing for larger, highway-accessible sites in the suburbs, taking many thousands of industrial jobs with them. The city's financial sector, meanwhile, was booming, breaking ground on countless International Style office towers. At the same time, New York's great period of urban renewal was under way, with the city's master planner, Robert Moses, seizing whole neighborhoods for the largest "slum clearance" program in the nation.[10] Moses and many other city officials believed that wholesale destruction and rebuilding were necessary to bring order and clarity to the urban environment. To ease and simplify the flow of traffic in these years, they also set to work demolishing some of the city's oldest streets, replacing them with a new network of highways, one-way avenues, and street-level expressways. With all these changes, the landscape of New York—and especially of lower Manhattan—seemed to lose its material specificity: aging tenements were demolished, small shops were shuttered, and industrial lofts were abandoned by the hundreds. In the place of an old urban texture of chaotic streets and neoclassical detail, there appeared a new downtown of widened roadways, light-colored housing blocks, and glass-faced towers.

Much of this urban redevelopment came in for harsh critique from such figures as Jane Jacobs, Lewis Mumford, and William H. Whyte Jr. Local activists founded a "Save the Village" movement, meanwhile, and the Mayor's Committee on Slum Clearance was charged with corruption. This book repositions the scraps of urban detritus in the period's art within these vitriolic fights over the transformation of the city. It identifies in the art a concern over the degree of abstract order desirable—or even possible—in the urban environment.

As the city's architecture and urban design were rapidly changing, so, too, were its everyday objects. Indeed the debates over the shape of New York were contemporaneous with a transformation of American consumerism—one that was noticeably changing the relationships between human beings and their things. Per capita consumption in America was increasing rapidly around 1960, while the nation's spending on advertising was growing even faster. At the same time, several marketing shifts—including more frequent use of plastics, the rise of "soft-sell" image advertising, and the advent of television's ethereal pictures—made consumer goods seem less substantial. A crop of popular critiques appeared, questioning the new rapidity and immateriality of consumption. Prominent among these were John Kenneth Galbraith's *Affluent Society*, Vance Packard's trio of best sellers (*The Hidden Persuaders, The Status Seekers, and The Waste Makers*), and Daniel Boorstin's critique of the increasingly abstract nature of American culture, *The Image; or, What Happened to the American Dream*.[11] Simultaneous with the rebuilding of the city, the shift in consumerism was perhaps especially noticeable in New York. Home of Madison Avenue (and therefore also of popular representations of the advertising industry), the city was also the site of a rapid decline—under deindustrialization and suburbanization—of some kinds of small-scale retail. In its everyday objects as much as its buildings, New York's traditional palpability seemed to be evaporating.

Although the essential nature of the transformation facing New York was largely inarticulable at the time, the new avant-garde, steeped in the literalism of recent painting, recognized this transformation as a dematerialization of the everyday landscape. The new art invented in these years—an odd art of illegible street signs, outmoded flashlights, discarded architectural scraps, and useless machinery—exaggerated the visual vocabulary of a disappearing New York. Acutely conscious of what Johns called "the loss, destruction [and] disappearance of objects," these artists produced a uniquely sensitive cogitation on the process of abstraction that was then remaking their city.[12]

The book proceeds by means of four case studies, focused, respectively, on tightly bounded bodies of work by Claes Oldenburg, Jasper Johns, Robert Rauschenberg, and Donald Judd. These are by no means the only cases that I could have chosen; they are, however, especially complex (even self-contradictory) examples of their movement. They also deeply embody—in their literalist, often illegible appropriation of everyday materials—the traits at the heart of this avant-garde. I closely track the artists' immersion in the city's changes throughout: all four lived amid demolition sites, decrepit hardware stores, and abandoned factories. Using close visual analysis, I argue that this art's obsession with urban detritus was both a willful resistance to New York's transformation and a grudging acknowledgment of the new urban texture of flow and sleek homogeneity.

A word, then, on each of the chapters as they engage these issues. The first chapter examines Claes Oldenburg's *Street*, an installation mounted twice in Greenwich Village in 1960. The work represented the city with a chaotic—and at times unintelligible—collection of cardboard, newspaper, and wood. Just as Oldenburg was assembling the work, Moses was promoting plans in the neighborhood for large-

scale clearance and a four-lane expressway through Washington Square Park. Pointing out that *The Street*'s untidy image of the city was contemporaneous with bitter public debates over these projects, the chapter sees the work as a representation—in the face of official efforts to systematize the city—of the abiding, unincorporable materiality of urban space.

Chapter 2 treats the series of sculptures of small consumer objects that Jasper Johns executed in 1958 and 1960. I understand these works here as an inquiry into the transformation of urban consumerism in the period, taking note of contemporary changes in the designs of many of Johns's subjects (beer cans, flashlights, even the American flag), and pointing out that the artist frequently based his sculptures on just-outmoded designs. I also trace the decline of hardware stores in Johns's neighborhood, as well as the rapid ascendancy in the period of "soft-sell" advertising techniques, by which goods were associated with abstract values (such as femininity or sophistication), rather than being sold for specific material advantages. Seeing the sculptures in relation to popular books and periodicals critical of such developments, I argue that Johns's works were weighty fragments of a nostalgic utopia, where consumer goods existed as pure material, as natural forms outside of use or meaning.

Robert Rauschenberg's "combines" of 1961 and 1962 are the focus of chapter 3. These works—assembled from scraps the artist picked up from vacant lots—have a complicated, dialectical relationship to meaning, seeming at times to be rebuslike puzzles, and at others to be pointless collections of junk. Noting the works' preoccupations with both the city and consumer detritus, I examine such contemporary developments as the rebuilding of lower Manhattan to support International Style banking towers, and the concern in the press over the problem of waste. The chapter contends that these works offered a critical investigation of the hope, endemic to New York at this moment, of transforming the material environment into an abstract system of legibility, order, and frictionless exchange.

Donald Judd's sculpture, the subject of the final chapter, is now usually understood as a claim for literalism in art, rather than expression or metaphor. In this chapter, I recover what critics acknowledged at the time—that Judd's works manipulated a visual vocabulary of architecture and machinery—to argue that the artist's literalist project was also a means of thinking about the changing nature of New York City. As Judd was developing his sculpture, industrial lofts in his neighborhood were being abandoned, New York's shipping was being containerized, and the new office buildings of Wall Street were being filled with cubicles. The chapter considers early works (which included bits of aging building materials) in addition to the Minimalist boxes begun in 1965. I argue here that Judd's Minimalist sculptures—stubbornly asserting their own autonomy even while distilling the systematic look of late capitalism—imagined an alternative version of the new city, one that just held onto the uniqueness of its things.

The conclusion briefly considers the later 1960s, as New York artists began rapidly to abandon the materialism of the preceding years. Addressing the ongoing development of Pop and the rise of Conceptual art, I argue that this period indeed constituted, as Lucy Lippard had it, "The Dematerialization of the Art Object."[13] While acknowledging that this dematerialization was a perfectly logical move for New York artists—at last relinquishing grit in order to track the new direction of their world—I end by arguing that even some of the most immaterial works remained critically engaged in the culture's transformation.

This book sees the art it analyzes in the context of a cultural tension between an abstract aesthetic of smoothness and clarity (systematic administration, simple towers, speedy expressways, and symbolic goods) and a material aesthetic of specificity (small-scale industry, chaotic tenements, crowded streets, and trash). That is, it diagnoses a split in New York around 1960 between a vision of the world as (potentially) seamlessly negotiable and communicative and a vision of it as forever particular and obdurate. For the most part, the art treated here lingered around the older, material city, dwelling in the failures of representation—its cracks and clumsy groundedness. Part of the complexity and richness of this art, however, comes from its ambivalence: all four of these artists demonstrated some interest in flat, immediately apprehensible images, and all of them made a turn in their work, sometime between 1962 and 1965, toward pictoriality, smoothness, or lucidity.[14] Their later work, and that of the artists who followed them, came to follow far more closely the abstract direction of their culture. This book is about the odd position articulated in these years, transitional in the art world as in the city at large; it is about an art that grappled with and represented the dematerialization of everyday life around it.

It bears stating outright here that this book's conceptual work operates frequently along a continuum, or within a dialectic, between abstraction on the one hand and materiality on the other. I use the word *abstraction* here not to refer to nonfigurative art but rather, in a broader sense, to denote the realm of meaning, the order of ideas, which we impose upon or draw from the material world. (In this sense, representation is humankind's fundamental act of abstraction; it uses things to convey meaning.) As is no doubt already apparent, I pay a great deal of attention to the literal nature of this art, by which I mean its presentation of its material qualities "as they are," as if drained of narrative and meta-phor, even at times as if drained of meaning altogether. I say *as if* because, in art, materiality and abstraction of course always exist together—there can be no object without ideas attached. The literalness in these works is nevertheless a pushing of art toward its material facts and away from the (apparently) second-order function of representation, of adding up, of meaning something. It is in the realm of this materiality that this book does its historicizing work.

I should state explicitly here, too, that I view the remak-ing of New York in this period as the city's first major shift toward postmodernity. Postmodernization has taken many different forms; I use the notion here to emphasize that the change in the shape and texture of New York was bound up with an economic transformation—one in which a relatively material economy based largely in manufacturing was replaced by a more abstract one increasingly dominated by the exchange of financial services. As David Harvey has put it, in an uncommonly powerful synthesis, postmodernity is an especially nimble and fluid stage of capitalism, one marked by the globalization of commerce, the predomi-nance of salable events over hard products, and the rise of dematerialized "paper entrepreneurialism."[15] It was this historical condition of abstraction—both new and continu-ous with modernity—to which these artists responded. My argument that this art was contemplating the local rise of postmodernity, I should add, does not lead me to claim that these artists were themselves postmodernists. On the con-trary, it seems to me that much of this art really constituted one of the last waves of modernism—a materialist confron-tation with a world becoming more abstract.

We should remember that New York's shift was far from total; the tactile objects of the city certainly did not vanish altogether. For a time, in fact—much to the fascina-tion of these four artists—the city's reconstruction made parts of it even denser with trash. Meanwhile, New York's postmodernization was also complicated by the fact that it drew on earlier innovations. Most notably, the International Style, developed decades before as a critique of traditional authority, proved a perfect match to a revised capitalist ide-ology—one that vested power less in any historical mantle than in a pretension to irrefutable logic. It was in the early postmodern city, finally, that modernist architecture be-came the lingua franca of corporate construction. Similarly, urban planning philosophies developed in Europe between the world wars (and often therefore termed modernist) became dominant only in the postwar period, as the classic stage of industrial modernity itself was fading.[16]

The art in this book represents for us the lived qualities of a transition in the history of capitalism. It is far from a uni-formly critical art, admitting to the necessity and even the appeal of abstraction, while struggling to understand the new conditions and to propose possible subjective relation-ships to them. The art helps us to see in the period not only a disappearance of objects but also an erosion of place. It makes apparent a weakening of the individual human subject's palpable connection to her environment. I do not wish to propagate a romanticized vision of life in New York before World War II. I hope rather to show that some artists imagined in these years a halting alternative to the world of the steel carton, the glass wall, and the smooth plastic push button.

Finally, I should add a note about method. It is not now fashionable in contemporary art history to pay espe-cially close attention to the details of individual works of art, or to the smaller facts of history. Such a reluctance has its reasons: art history has at times marshaled close attention only to fetishize art and to ignore larger historical conditions. It seems to me, however, that some purely theoretical analyses of art have had to relegate themselves to rediscovering historical forces already identified elsewhere. Here, close, contextualized looking is brought to bear precisely in hopes of yielding a fresh and fuller understanding of the rise of postmodernity—a condition too easily totalized as instrumentalization, atomization, and spectacularization. By recovering the texture of an early moment of postmodernization, this book aims to remind us that the global economy—however much it seems to abstract and systematize our built environment—is forever problematically entangled with material diversity, confusing urban spaces, and junk.

# 1 A Neo-Dada City

## OLDENBURG

PEDESTRIANS WALKING down Thompson Street off Greenwich Village's Washington Square Park in the winter of 1960 were beckoned, by means of a messily painted sign and mural, into the basement of the Judson Church House (fig. 1.1). The building was the center of the social programs of the progressive Judson Memorial Church, which had presided over the south side of the square for more than a century (figs. 1.2, 1.3). The basement of the church house had been converted in the late 1950s into living and studio space for a handful of the neighborhood's many artists, and by the beginning of 1960, it had become the Judson Gallery, a public venue for the new urban and quotidian art working to counter the hegemony of Abstract Expressionism. Those curious enough to descend the stairs that winter found themselves in an exhibition called *Ray Gun*. The first room had been converted into an environment called *The Street* by Claes Oldenburg, a thirty-year-old neighborhood artist.[1]

*The Street* was a visual cacophony of cardboard, paper, newsprint, wood fragments, and black paint (figs. 1.4–1.7). Scraps of trash covered the floor from corner to corner, strips of newspaper hung from the light fixture, and the walls were covered with a brown and sooty-looking cardboard relief. A few freestanding sculptures shared the viewer's own space in the middle of the scrap-strewn floor. Across the whole work, which Oldenburg described as a three-dimensional mural, were marks of black paint, in places seeming only to give the installation a sullied look, but in others forming letters of the alphabet, defining scorched-looking contours, and identifying facial features.[2] In fact, the careful tearing and cutting of the cardboard, the nailing together of a broad variety of braces and sculptural supports, and the particular—if untidy—application of paint all worked, in their clumsy way, to make a readable representation of an urban environment. Over a period of

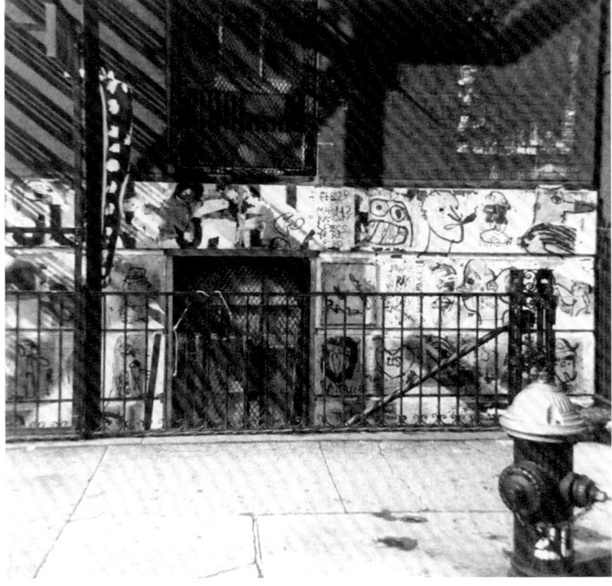

**FIG. 1.1**
Entrance to the *Ray Gun* exhibition at the Judson Gallery, 1960

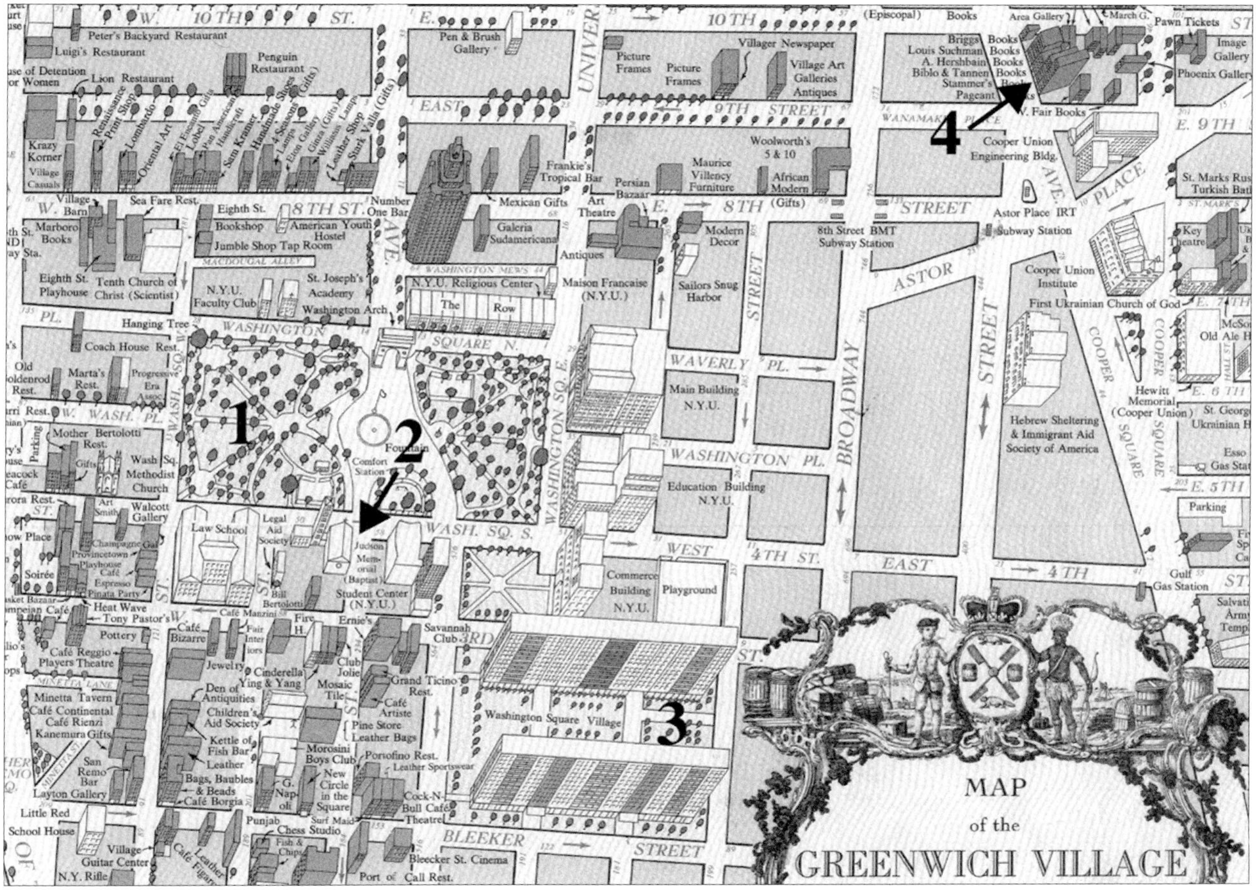

FIG. 1.2

**Lawrence Fahey**

*Map of the Greenwich Village Section
of New York City* (detail), 1960.
Major buildings are indicated;
privately owned buildings are
shaded. Numbers added by author:
(**1**) Washington Square Park; (**2**)
Judson Gallery; (**3**) Washington
Square Village; (**4**) Reuben Gallery.
New York Public Library

FIG. 1.3

**André Kertész**

*Washington Square and the Judson
Memorial Church*, 1953

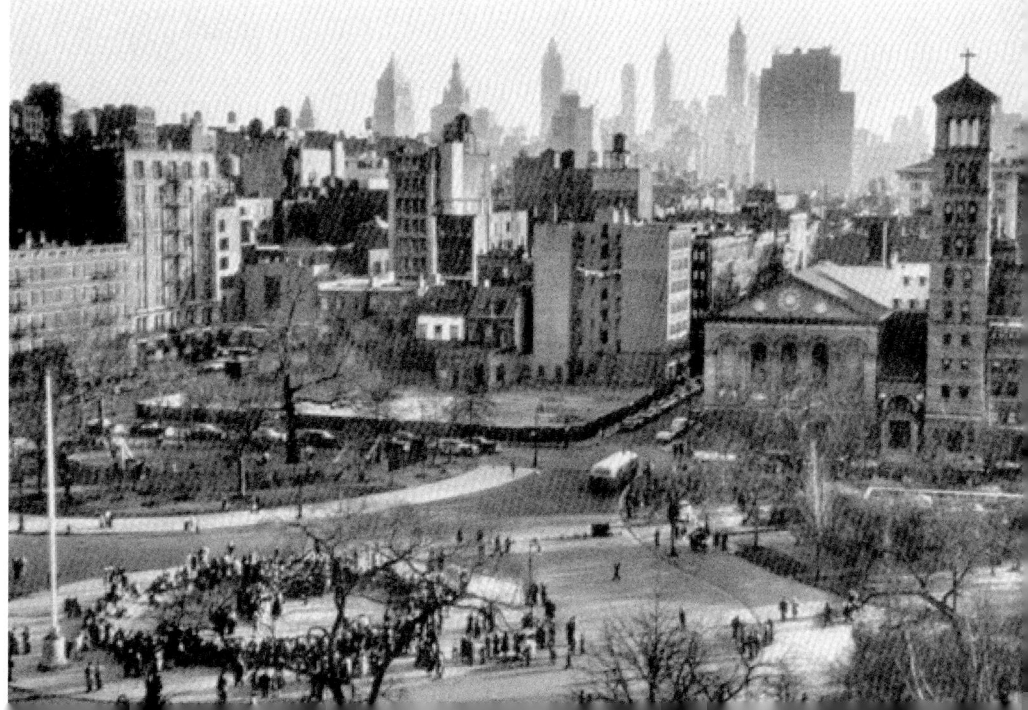

FIGS. 1.4 and 1.5
Claes Oldenburg
The Street, installation at the Judson Gallery, 1960

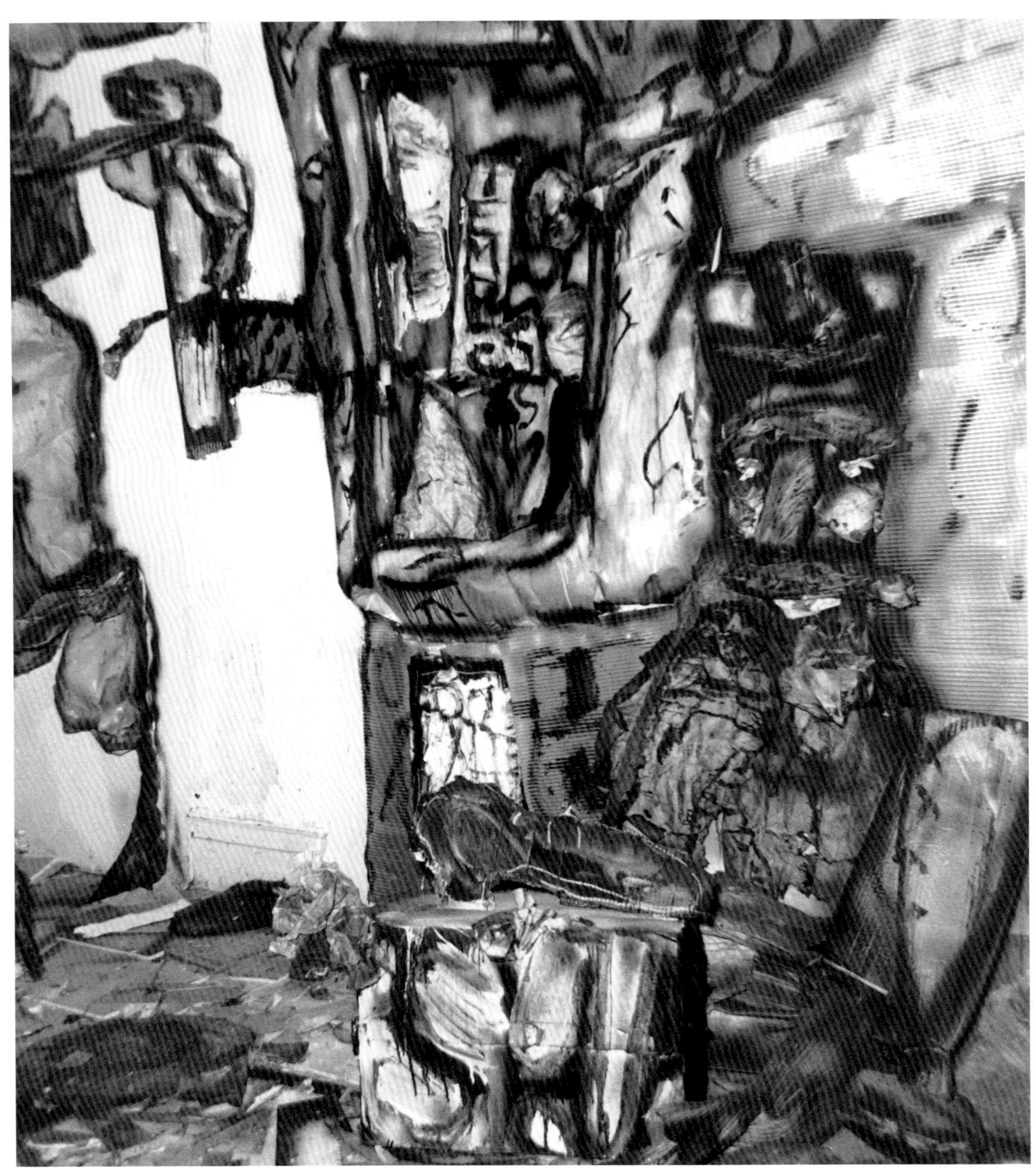

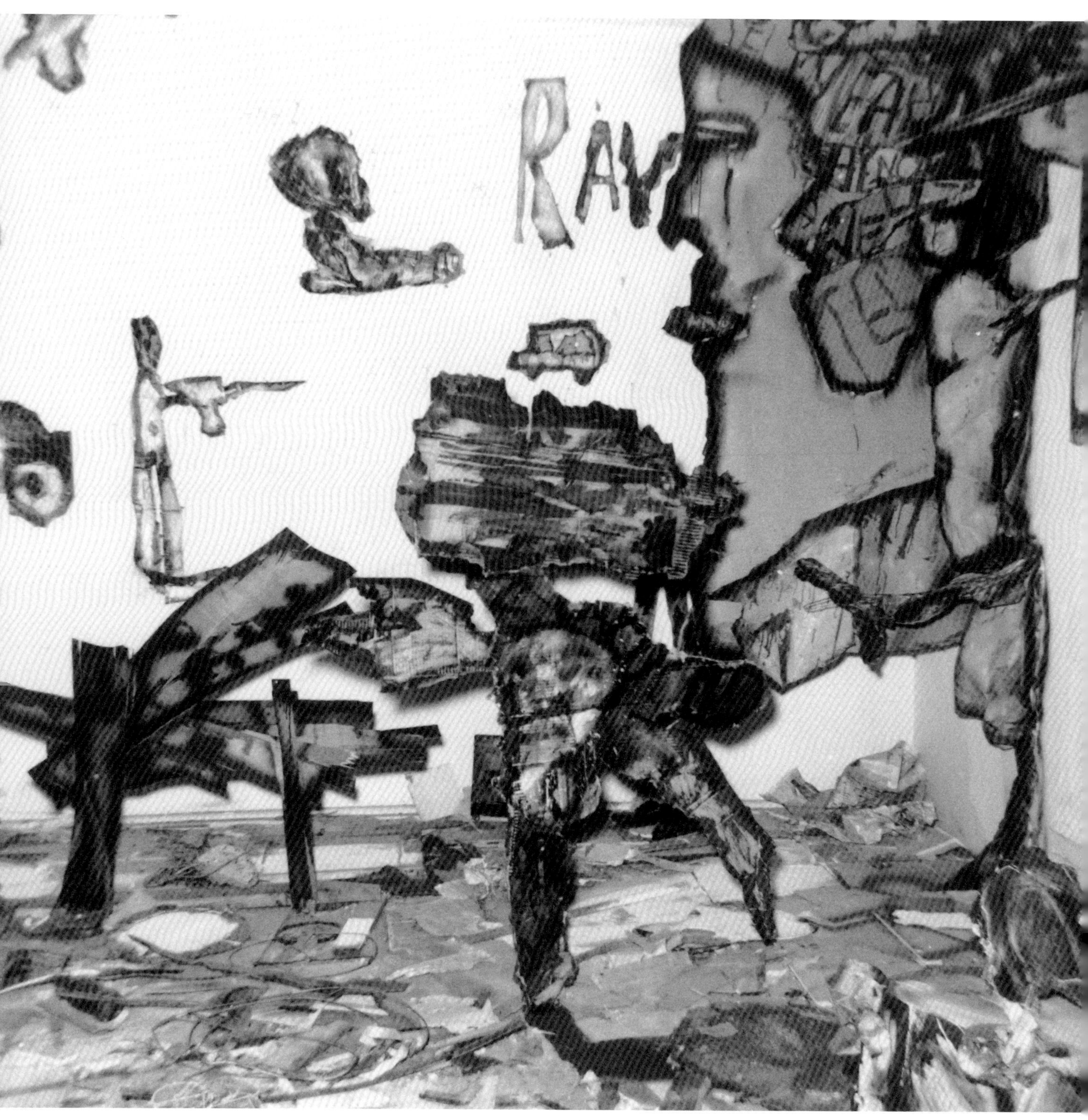
RAV

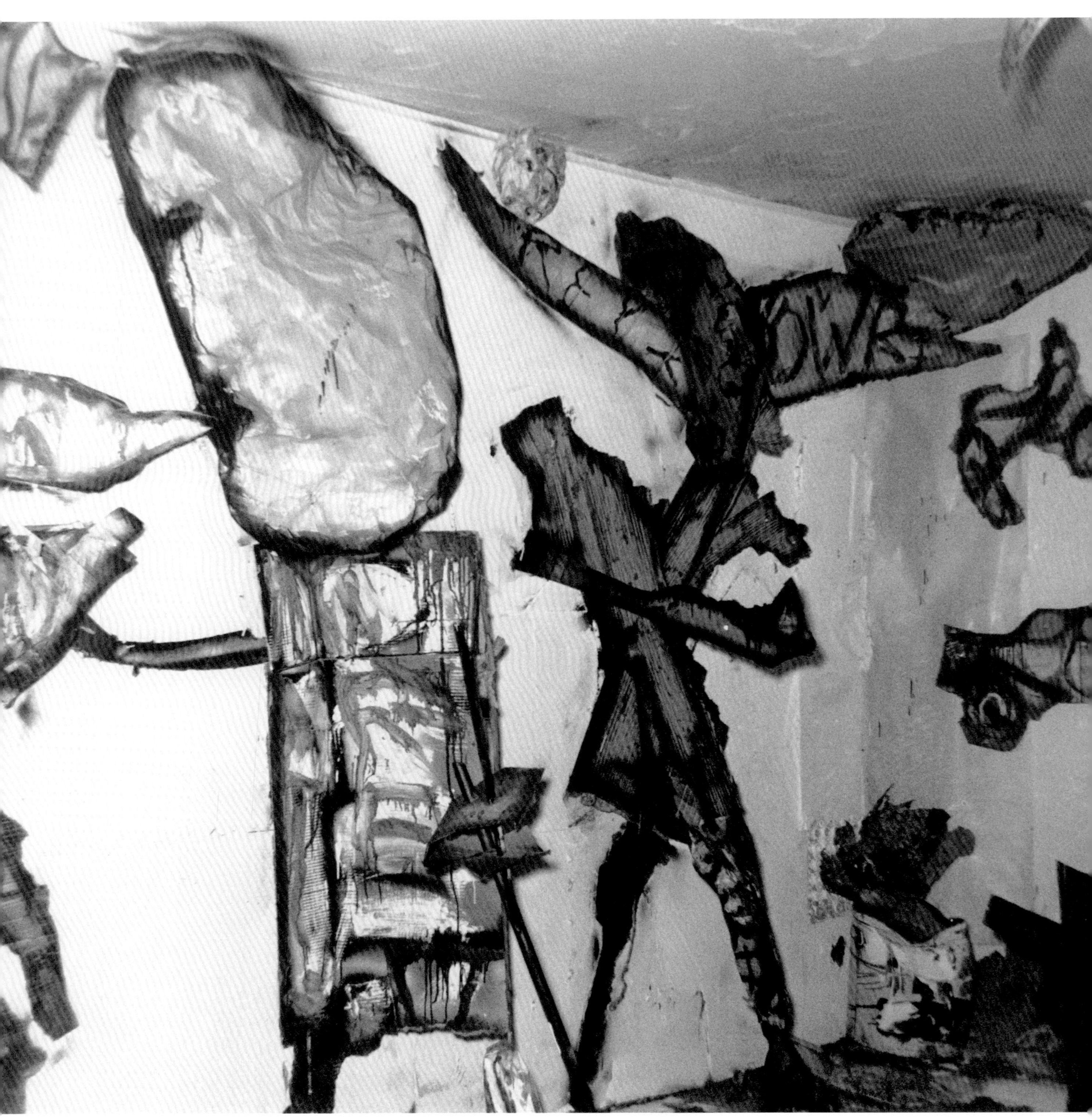

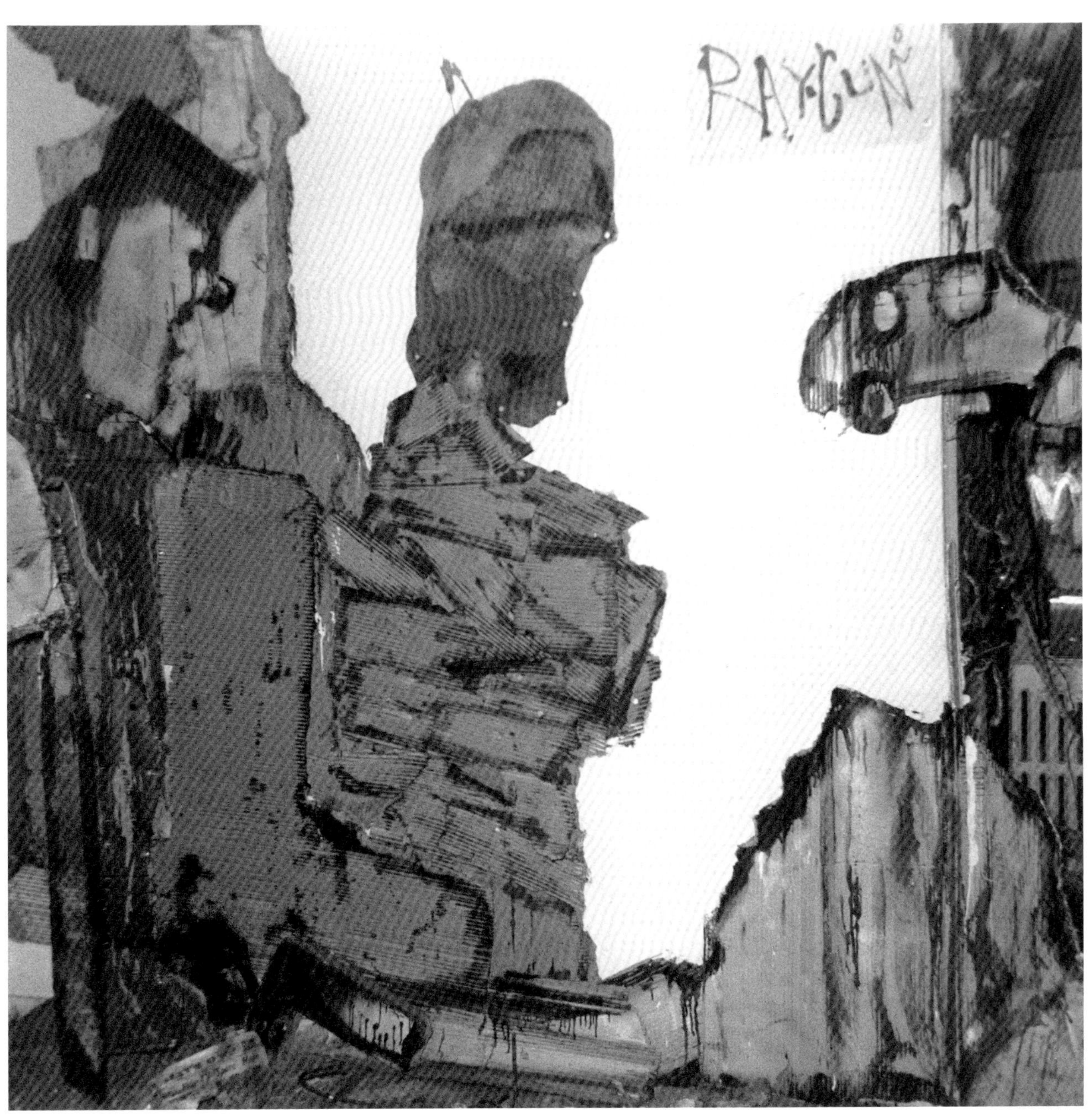

FIGS. 1.6 and 1.7

**Claes Oldenburg**

*The Street*, installation at the Judson Gallery, 1960

close looking, viewers would have been able to make out at least nine major human figures and four small automobiles, among other forms.

Most of the historical and critical literature on *The Street* has focused on its innovative use of banal materials or its dark representation of human suffering.[3] By contrast, I seek here to understand Oldenburg's odd streetscape as a cogitation on the changing shape of New York City. In particular, this chapter considers *The Street* as a means of thinking about the possibilities for and limitations upon the city, in view of the giant urban renewal program then under way. I argue that *The Street*, by carrying the problems of recent painting and sculpture into a representation of New York, identified some of the logic hidden within renewal. Specifically, the work responds to renewal's central effort—through the promotion of order, negotiability, and legibility—to render a newly abstracted city.[4] A close look at *The Street* now allows us to recognize the ways in which the debate over the city was fundamentally a debate (at the center of an economic and epistemic shift) over the degree of abstraction desirable in everyday life. *The Street*'s reflection on this transformation was chiefly a negative one, insisting on the obdurate materiality of the city, but it was also complicated, and far from single-minded.

The surviving exhibition photographs, flash-bleached though they are, allow a fairly thorough reconstruction of the original installation (as we shall see, Oldenburg would install it again, a few blocks away, in the spring). Entering the room and facing right, the visitor would have confronted a bearded man in a top hat, slumping behind a shoe-shine stand (see fig. 1.4, at right). At the shoe-shine man's shoulder was a shop window displaying indefinite goods and a small, illegible sign.[5] Farther to the left, but along the same wall, there stood another figure, perhaps holding a gun in

outstretched arms (see fig. 1.4, at left, and fig. 1.5, at right). As the viewer turned to her left—negotiating the floor's muck of discarded shoes, empty bottles, and scraps of wood and wire—she would have approached a huge silhouetted face looming in the corner, and its hair of scrawled-out words (see fig. 1.5, at right). Her passage would have been obstructed, however, by two sculptures standing on the floor of the installation: a striding figure and, beside it, a similarly rendered prominent traffic barricade. Nevertheless, our viewer would have seen a few small forms floating in the undefined pictorial space on the far wall, some describing cars and figures (one, it seems, with another gun), some more ambiguous. Turning left again to face back toward the entrance, the viewer would have seen four major figures populating the remaining walls. Two of these (see fig. 1.6), although talking, were facing away from each other and rendered quite differently—one in round bulges of paper, the other in angular swaths of cardboard. The last two, on the wall by the entryway, had indistinct bodies that seemed to merge together (see fig. 1.7). Just beside these were another automobile and, below that, a large illegible form, painted with the contours and indistinct splotches that ran across the entire installation.[6]

A proper understanding of *The Street* will require us to consider the work both in its installations, as well as in its various contexts; first of all, it will involve us in a recovery of the earliest clamorous death throes of New York's classic period of urban renewal.

**Renewal in New York City**

From the 1930s, American urban planning had been shaped by the hegemonic European modernism of Le Corbusier. In his books *The City of Tomorrow* and *When the Cathedrals Were White*, Le Corbusier had proposed the wholesale

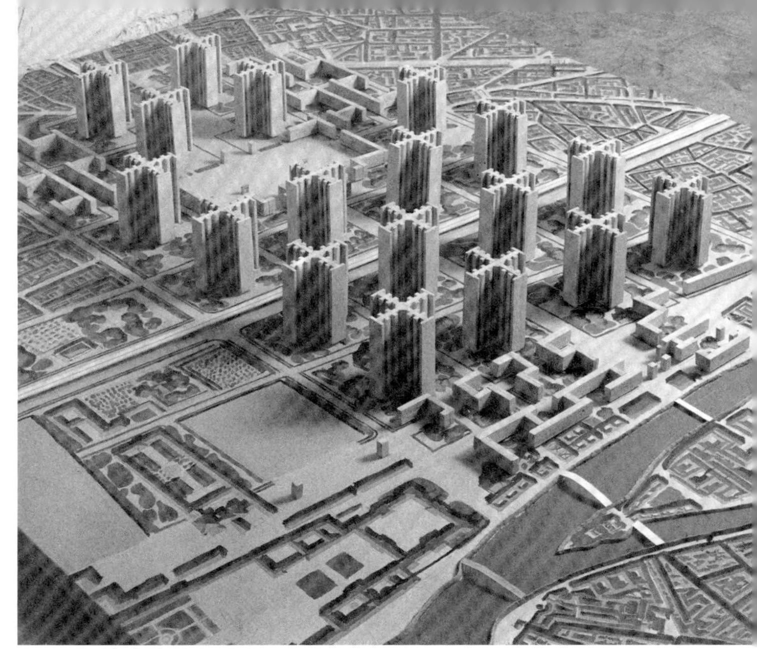

destruction of chaotic, dirty old cities such as Paris and New York.[7] In their place would rise gleaming new cities of uniform towers, surrounded by parks and connected by ribbons of high-speed automobile expressways (fig. 1.8). This sort of urban planning became a kind of official program among Europe's leading architects when, in 1933, the Congrès Internationaux d'Architecture Moderne (CIAM) adopted the Athens Charter, a manifesto for the new city. Meanwhile, in the United States, the means of engineering the new trafficways were being worked out by the German immigrant Fritz Malcher, whose 1935 *Steadyflow Traffic System* proposed soft curves, dedicated turn lanes, median strips, and separated parking areas to promote the ceaseless, signal-free flow of cars across cities.[8] His book, which began by excluding any discussion of sidewalks, formed the foundation of American urban traffic engineering. The tower-in-the-park program and the expressway program became the two chief principles of postwar urban planning.

Although the sheer scale of Le Corbusier's plans meant that they were virtually impossible to adopt completely, at mid-century many governments found ways to incorporate aspects of the Athens Charter in their urban plans. Brasília is the ultimate example of this kind of planning, but it was constructed from scratch. If existing cities were going to adopt the modernist model, they needed laws of eminent domain allowing them to dynamite existing blocks to make way for the new towers and greenery.[9] In the United States, such a possibility was opened by Title I of the Housing Act of 1949, which appropriated $1 billion to initiate a national program of urban renewal, and which allowed governments, for the first time, to seize private property in order to offer it, below cost, to private developers. (Often developers, who stood to profit neatly when areas were declared blighted, were not under obligation to provide affordable housing in

these new buildings.) In New York City alone, $267 million had been spent on Title I housing reconstruction by 1957, twice as much as in all other American cities combined.[10] Alongside this private development were the public projects of the New York City Housing Authority, which, by 1960, had completed fully a third of multiple-dwelling construction in the city since World War II—virtually all of it razing old brick and stone tenements in order to put up neo-Corbusian towers (fig. 1.9).[11]

Meanwhile, the Federal Aid Highway Act of 1956 established the interstate system, guaranteeing federal money to cover 90 percent of the cost of its construction, and initially committing $25 billion. Despite confusion at the highest levels of government about whether the interstates were meant to continue within city limits at all, seven thousand miles of urban highways were planned as part of the system, an amount that would more than quadruple total city highway mileage.[12] Greater New York's urban highway boom was particularly robust, with 899 miles existing or under construction by 1964, twice as many as in the runner-up, metropolitan Los Angeles.[13] A plan adopted in 1951 called for the easing of street traffic as well, and by 1960 Manhattan had converted nearly all of its avenues to one-way flow. Over roughly the same period, the borough narrowed sidewalks on over 450 of its streets.[14]

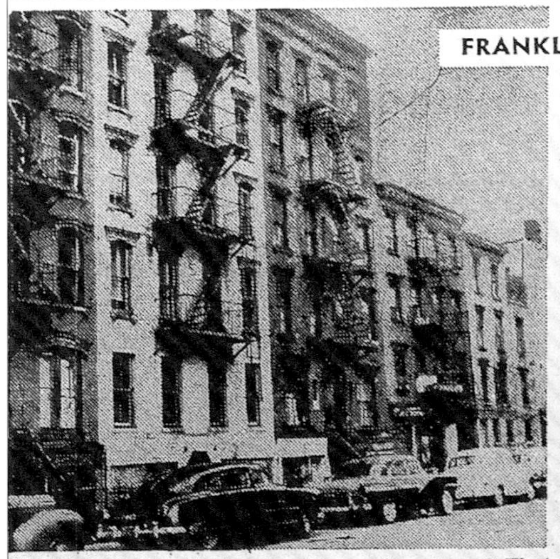

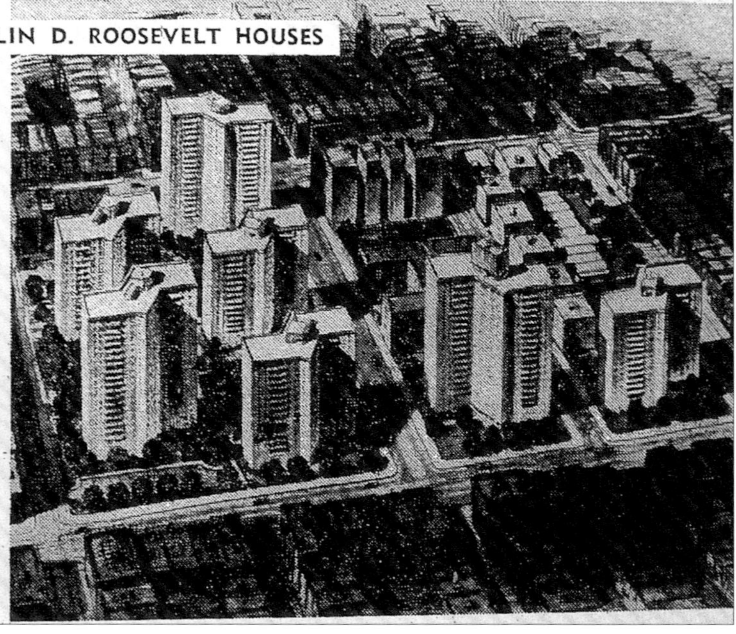



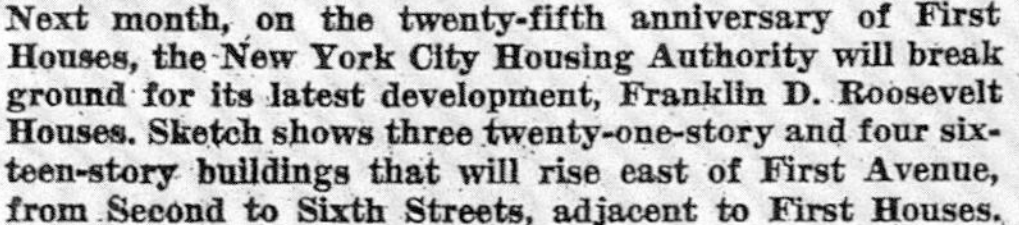

Next month, on the twenty-fifth anniversary of First Houses, the New York City Housing Authority will break ground for its latest development, Franklin D. Roosevelt Houses. Sketch shows three twenty-one-story and four sixteen-story buildings that will rise east of First Avenue, from Second to Sixth Streets, adjacent to First Houses.

At the head of virtually all of New York's rebuilding efforts was Robert Moses, who simultaneously held jobs as a city planning commissioner, chairman of the Mayor's Committee on Slum Clearance, and commissioner of parks, among other positions. As director of the extremely lucrative and autonomous Triborough Bridge and Tunnel Authority, Moses bullied governors and mayors—from the 1930s to the mid-1960s—into letting him realize his plans for New York City and its suburbs. His biographer estimates that, counting only the projects executed directly under his authority, Moses built public works costing $26 billion (in 1968 dollars) and displacing a stunning half million people.[15] He oversaw the building of the Long Island, Gowanus, Brooklyn-Queens, and Major Deegan expressways, among many others, as well as the construction of towering housing projects from Brooklyn to the Bronx.

The realization of a new vision of the city through renewal and highway construction was accompanied by subtler methods of controlling urban chaos. One front in the war for more ordered streets was formed by an effort to clean the city of litter. Begun in 1956, the Big Sweep was an annual campaign for cleaner streets. In 1959, the campaign was to be "longer and more intense than ever before," with "very rigid enforcement" imposed throughout spring, summer, and fall. A twenty-foot trash-basket sign was displayed that year in Times Square, Herald Square, and Harlem, and in the fall the Sanitation Department made the largest purchase of new bins in its history, nearly doubling the number on the streets. By one measure, sidewalks in New York were nearly *seven times* cleaner in 1959 than they had been just four years earlier.[16]

At the same time, New York City also launched a major anti-jaywalking campaign to promote safety, traffic flow, and order. The city had experimented with an anti-jaywalking law briefly in 1929, but after its hasty withdrawal, there were no regulations of pedestrian behavior until the summer of 1958, when special signals (the soon ubiquitous Walk/Don't Walk lights) were introduced at many intersections. New Yorkers were then prohibited from crossing against these lights and from otherwise interfering with

FIG. 1.9
Projected Franklin D. Roosevelt Houses (now Village
View Houses), bordered by First Avenue, Avenue A, East
Second Street, and East Sixth Street, *New York Times*,
20 November 1960

the flow of traffic; by the end of that year, the city's police had issued nearly 20,000 citations to pedestrians. In June 1959 Mayor Wagner declarec a Pedestrian Safety Month, and launched a public awareness campaign that included radio and newspaper ads, stickers on taxis and buses, and 100,000 anti-jaywalking posters hung on the city's lampposts.[17]

For decades, Moses and the city's renewal campaign had enjoyed the approbation of both the press and the public—at least the powerful white public that imagined itself benefiting from the changes. Indeed, many officials in New York and around the world shared the commissioner's vision of the city. However, in the late 1950s, the fortunes of renewal in New York began to change. In 1956, a group of well-connected citizens defeated Moses's plans for a new parking lot in Central Park. In 1958 *Tne Exploding Metropolis*—a collection of irate essays about renewal, sprawl, and urban trafficways—appeared in mass-market format, echoing arguments that had been available in publications from *Architectural Forum* to the *New Yorker* and *Fortune* for several years.[18] By the spring of 1959 John Lindsay, then the U.S. representative from New York City, had introduced legislation to diminish the secrecy under which Title I renewal was planned, and in the summer, the *New York Times* ran a series accusing the Mayor's Committee on Slum Clearance (which Moses chaired) of corruption. The *Times* reported conflicts of interest on the committee, unfair b dding processes, and profit-motivated delays in development.[19]

Even excepting scandal, however, arguments against renewal were becoming vociferous. In one contribution to *The Exploding Metropolis*, for example, Jane Jacobs—soon to be famous for her invective *The Death and Life of Great American Cities*—argued that cities needed old buildings and small blocks in order to flourish. In Jacobs's view, good planning required "leaving room for the incongruous, or the vulgar, or the strange." She was direct in naming the linchpin of a successful city: "The best place to look at first is the street. One had better look quickly, too; not only are the projects making away with the noisy automobile traffic of the street, they are making away with the street itself. In its stead will be open spaces with long vistas and lots and lots of elbowroom." William H. Whyte Jr. called special attention to this point in his introduction to the anthology: "In laying out the superblocks of the huge urban redevelopment projects [many of the people who are redesigning the city] banish the most wonderful of city features—the street." Indeed the elimination of the street was, in the words of one major proponent of modernist planning, the "first necessity" of future cities.[20] The street, a narrow space used for many purposes, made the city a place of chaos. In its stead, a system of parks and expressways would guarantee order and steady flow in the urban fabric. This hostility toward complex, mixed-use urban space was perhaps nowhere more apparent in 1960 than on Thompson Street, just south of Washington Square Park, in New York City's Greenwich Village.

## Greenwich Village

For over a century and a half, Washington Square Park, in addition to being the unofficial front yard of the Judson Church, had served as the heart of Greenwich Village. Its famous plazas provided "the refuge, the summer vacation place of those who cannot afford to leave the city's heat . . . a meeting place for the elderly men who enjoy their chess and checkers under the great tree[, and] above all . . . the children's playground."[21] Since 1900, a modicum of traffic—primarily the occasional bus—had run across the otherwise tranquil square. During the mid-century renewal and roadway boom, however, the park's open space attracted the eye of civic planners, including Moses, who wanted to ease the flow of downtown traffic. In 1946 and again in 1952, plans to build a more substantial trafficway across the park had been pushed, but they were delayed by local opposition. In 1958, however, the Board of Estimate and the City Planning Commission both preliminarily approved a proposal to extend Fifth Avenue—which terminated at the north end of the Park—across the square, joining it with an existing street to be widened and renamed Fifth Avenue South (fig. 1.10).

Residents, neighborhood groups, and architecture critics were outraged, fearing the loss of the square. Some believed that Moses, who had advocated a roadway broader than the one approved, had covert plans to use the park as part of a major conduit for carrying traffic right through Manhattan and across to New Jersey.[22] Lewis Mumford called the road an "almost classic example of bad city planning," and the Judson's own Reverend Howard Moody spoke out against it, in testimony and in public letters to both Mayor Robert F. Wagner Jr. and Tammany boss Carmine DeSapio.[23] Although the roadway seemed inevitable, two rallies, a torrent of published letters and opinions, and a petition of 30,000 signatures also appeared to protest the plan. Finally, at a dramatic Board of Estimate hearing, the mayor "brought down the house" when, in consideration of the objections, he canceled his plans to travel to Albany that evening and declared, "It is much more important to me to be here."[24] The board that night voted to delay a final decision, and when it met again in late October, it ordered a temporary closing of even the small existing road in Washington Square. The study was a success: in the spring of 1959, the board voted to close the park permanently to all traffic. Villagers held a celebration that June, burning a mock car in effigy.[25]

During the long battle, the press had often called the project an expressway, while Moses objected that it was merely a "wide avenue."[26] Whatever it was, it was certainly not a street. Indeed, the very point of the project had been to upgrade the trafficways in the neighborhood, mitigating the complexity and obstructions caused by the diverse uses of true streets. Had the project gone ahead, circulation in the area would have been defined not by multiuse public spaces fringed with sidewalks and old facades, but rather by a constant flow of automobiles through a freshly widened roadway. The symbolic outcome of the Washington Square battle was a triumph for traditional paved public space over efficiency of travel. "Progress" was stopped, and to this day the square blocks and fractures the flow of traffic at the foot of Fifth Avenue.[27]

Despite their victory over the Washington Square roadway, opponents of renewal in Greenwich Village were not so fortunate in other respects. A slum-clearance construction project that the roadway had been intended to support, for example, went ahead. Built one block from the Judson Gallery between 1957 and 1960, Washington Square Village is a mammoth Title I development that demolished "191 old stores and lofts" and replaced them with a superblock (now Greenwich Village's biggest block) of privately owned "luxury" apartments (fig. 1.11; see fig. 1.10).[28] The project comprises two seventeen-story buildings (three were originally planned), each running the entire length of what had been three blocks. Between them is a large courtyard with trees, benches, and—of course—parking. The project's addresses deny any relationship to the surrounding neighborhood, refusing ordinary street numbers. In a Herculean achievement of Corbusian order, 148 distinct street addresses on seven separate streets were replaced simply by numbers 1 through 4, Washington Square Village.[29]

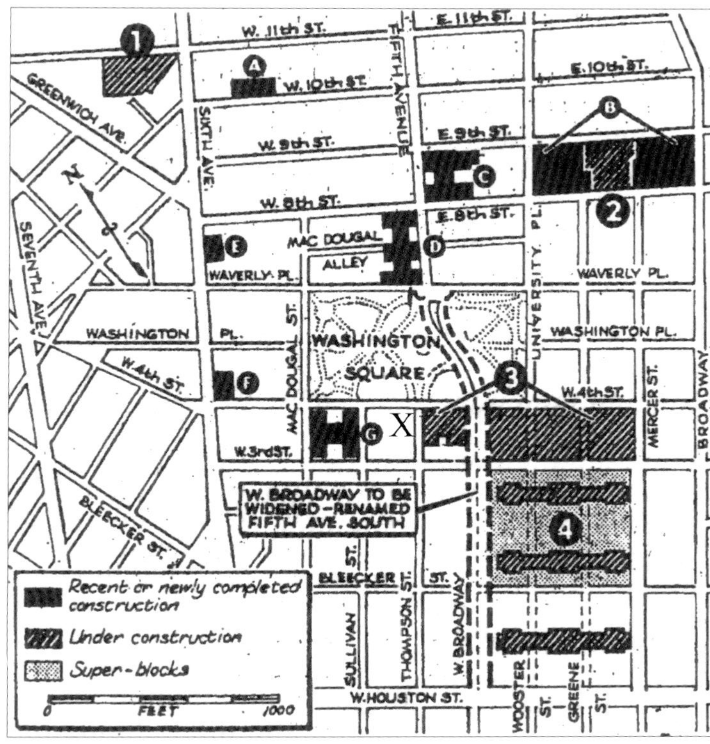



FIG. 1.10

Map of the Washington Square area,
showing construction projects and
the proposed Washington Square roadway
*New York Times*, 8 December 1957.
(**3**) New York University Title I renewal;
(**4**) Washington Square Village.
Added by author: (**X**) Judson Memorial Church

And Washington Square Village was only one of many major new building projects in the neighborhood; at the end of 1957, the *New York Times* counted ten active construction sites within about 1,500 feet of Washington Square (see fig. 1.10).[30] New York University's Title I renewal, for example, razed several of the blocks along the south side of the square. These developments included even the property directly facing the entrance to the Judson Gallery, which remained an open lot during the run of *Ray Gun*. When one of the new NYU buildings was nearing completion, the *Voice*, barely veiling its contempt, charged that the building, "with its rigorously modern, glassy look, has dramatically changed the aspect of the Square" (fig. 1.12).[31]

This local rebuilding faced criticism throughout the late 1950s, but it was in the spring of 1959, with Washington Square Village mostly complete and the roadway battle over, that local opinion decidedly turned against the new construction. John Lindsay argued in March that Wash-ington Square Village would never have been built if the public had known more about it in advance.[32] In April, the *Voice* ran an editorial asserting that Greenwich Village was threatened by the current building boom; in July the paper bemoaned the neighborhood's "vanishing local color"; and in August it ran a lengthy letter charging that the "orgy of destruction" was neutralizing the physical character that attracted artists and intellectuals to the neighborhood.[33] The letter ended imperatively: "Save the Village!" By October, the Save the Square Committee had been formed to "preserve the present architectural character and scale of Greenwich Village," and a "Save the Village" petition had been launched "to preserve the character of the area 'from obliteration by spreading apartment projects.'"[34]

Of course, there were many reasons for this backlash in the Village against renewal. Corruption and high rents were prominent among them. But what is striking about the objections is how often they centered on rhetorical claims that the simplicity and uniformity of the new buildings threatened

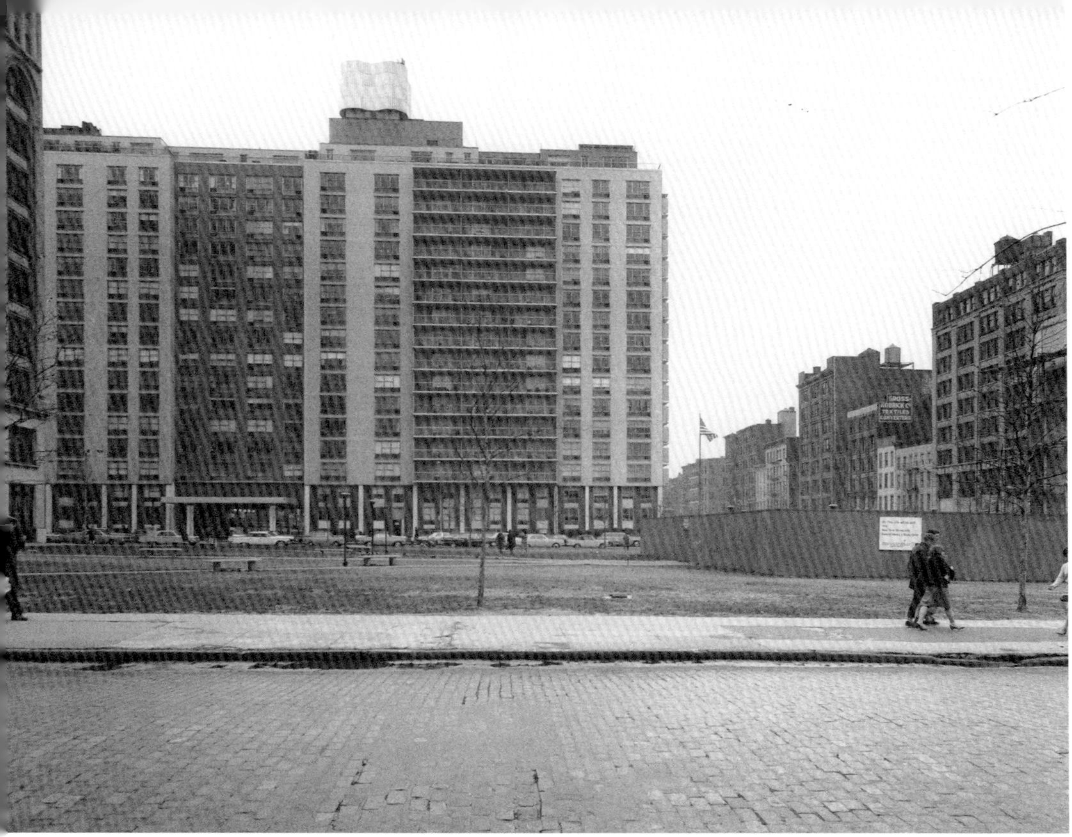

FIG. 1.11
Washington Square Village,
completed, 1959, from West
Fourth Street, looking across
undeveloped property of
New York University

FIG. 1.12
Loeb Student Center, 1960, Judson
Memorial Church, and Washing-
ton Square Park, photographed
after the 1963 completion of New
York University's Catholic chapel,
between the Loeb Center and the
Judson Church


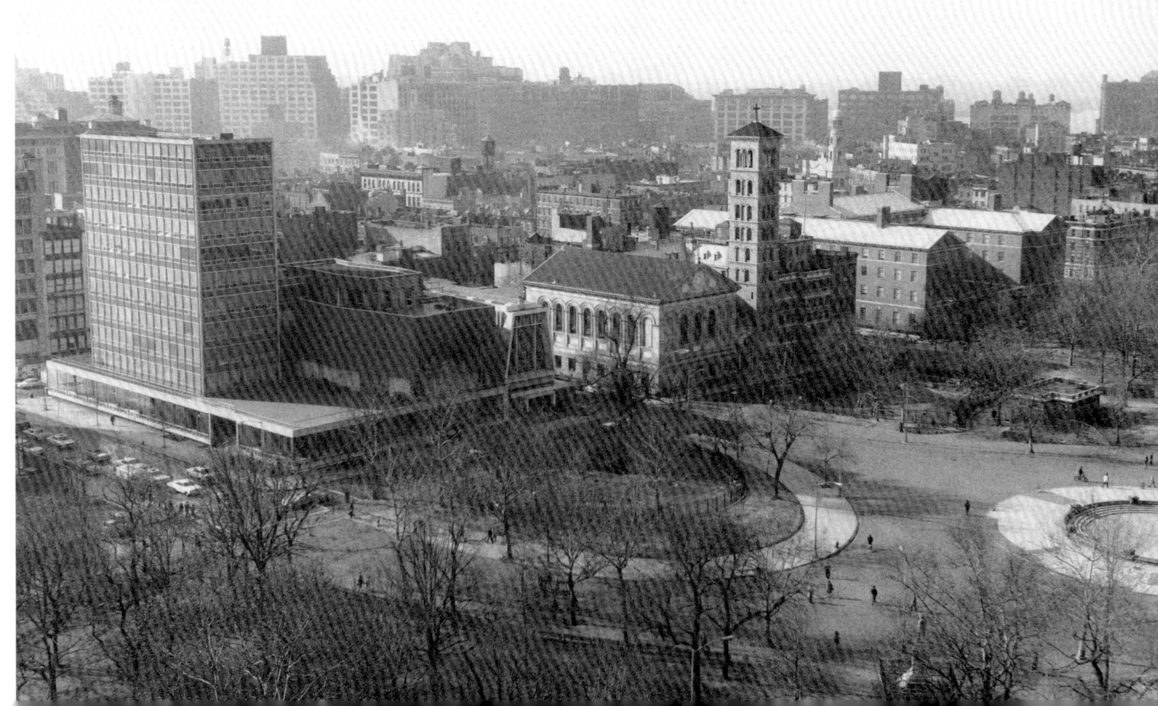

the cultural fecundity of the neighborhood. Again and again it was claimed that the Village's artists and bohemians would be driven out, not so much by higher rents as by the loss of some particular quality of the neighborhood. Perhaps the most sustained example came very early, in the eulogistic article that appeared on the front of the *New York Times* real estate section on 8 December 1957: "New Projects Will Change the Face—and the Character—of the Washington Square Area: Bohemian Flair Fades in Village."

The article mentions rising rents and the arrival of the bourgeoisie, but the real threat to writers and artists, it would seem, came from the new "curtain of blue-green glass" punctuating the neighborhood. In the article's final paragraph, its author, Ira Henry Freeman, describes in vivid terms what about the Village is disappearing: "There are now under construction, or soon will be, in the Village at least eight modern apartment buildings where crooked studios with smoky fireplaces used to huddle. There won't even be an ailanthus tree and a broken fountain in the back yard."[35] This is a particular kind of nostalgia, leaning heavily on terms such as *huddle, smoky,* and *crooked.* The denotative accuracy of these terms is questionable—Can studios really be "crooked"? How many of the old buildings had broken fountains in their yards?—but their force is clear. The nostalgia is for disorganization, irrationality, and excess matter in the face of the plans for an ordered and sensible new city.

## Oldenburg and the Judson Gallery

Soon after arriving in New York, in 1956, Claes Oldenburg moved into an apartment on East Ninth Street, a few blocks northeast of Washington Square. Asked in 1973 about these quarters, he stressed one salient quality: "At that time they were tearing down a big building there called Bible House so that in my room I could only see the flames and the wreck-

age that they were tearing down. It's where Cooper Union has now built a new building."[36] The artist soon moved to an apartment at 330 East Fourth Street, just east of Greenwich Village. He offered very similar recollections of this place, where he lived while making *The Street:* "When I lived in the Lower East Side there was a great deal of tearing down going on, especially between where I lived and where I worked. So I could pass through all these ruins all the time."[37]

Oldenburg's keen awareness of the urban renewal surrounding him turned, in at least one case, to harsh critique. In an absurdist poem he wrote at the time, renewal is associated with class-based oppression, as a public official shouts: "Civic improvement, plazas, malls, centers, ports, projects, projects, projects. Got two heads full! Cut the folks up, cut up the plain folks, trim em like trees, saw em to size, make bricks of em, beams, pile em up, seal em to each other by their juices. Build Build Bld [*sic*]."[38]

With "plain folks" literally sacrificed to urban building projects, this is grim satire indeed. Taken as a whole, however, Oldenburg's thoughts about renewal were complicated and even contradictory. He seems, for example, to have had an aesthetic appreciation of "the flames and the wreckage" around him, as well as a satisfaction in the fact that he "could pass through all these ruins all the time." At around the time of *The Street*, he wrote delightedly in one of his notebooks, "The city is a landscape well worth enjoying— damn necessary if you live in the city. Dirt has depth and beauty. I love soot and scorching."[39]

Oldenburg was clearly attentive to the changing form of the city around 1960, but his investment was not that of a partisan in the political battles. Rather, the changes in New York formed the environment in which the artist viewed his own creative production. The new slabs everywhere supplanting lower Manhattan's tenements, the recent roadway fight—these were symptoms of the postwar vision of an ordered, negotiable, and legible city. This dream (and its active antonyms) deeply interested Oldenburg: *Ray Gun* and *The Street* were, among other things, his complicated response. "A new definition of NY is needed you see," Oldenburg wrote, "and that is why New York will be renamed Ray-Gun."[40]

The installation of *The Street* at the Judson Gallery was a carefully constructed mess. Its discards and other banal materials covered every surface, and even the grandest sculptures in the installation were made of trash—cardboard, crumpled package paper, and broken slats of wood. Oldenburg had liberally dirtied the whole scene with black paint. Scale and representational mode were inconsistent, and the parts floated in an unordered pictorial space, with tiny cars jostling against giant silhouetted heads. It was not only in *The Street,* however, that *Ray Gun*'s aesthetic of disorder was at work. The whole exhibition was conceived and directed by Oldenburg as a festival of sorts for a new post–Abstract Expressionist art form.[41] The other fixture of the show was Jim Dine's similarly chaotic installation *The House* (fig. 1.13), which was made from newspaper, children's paintings, a ripped umbrella, and other scraps of trash, and overpainted with nonsensical expressions such as "Yes eggs" and "Goo." The exhibition also hosted several happenings, or "Ray Gun Spex": one performance each by Oldenburg, Dine, Red Grooms, Al Hansen, Dick Higgins, Allan Kaprow, and Bob Whitman.[42] These, like most happenings, were characterized by a conspicuous lack of narrative sense.

All the untidy abjection at the *Ray Gun* exhibition made at least some viewers recoil sharply, sensing an attack on

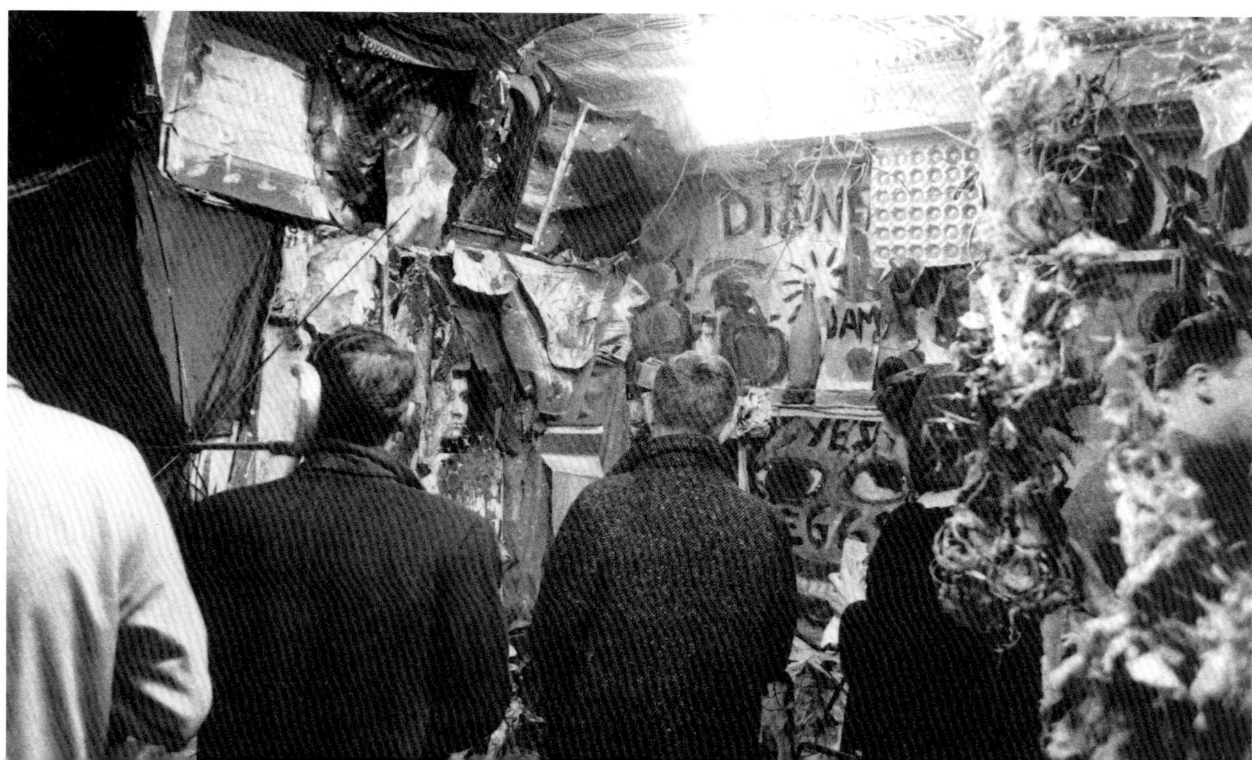

order and logic. Perhaps the *Village Voice* critic stretched slightly in claiming that some people—square uptowners, presumably—"feel that [*Ray Gun*] must be stamped out or that civilization will be in peril," but the show did certainly garner efficient dismissals in the mainstream publications that deigned to review it.[43] The tiny review in *Artnews* described *Ray Gun* as "varied junk," and *Time* magazine, discussing the happenings, concluded sarcastically: "It was beat, man, though up-beat, and it was, like, existential. Real children might do it better."[44]

These are easy, and empty, clichés. But *Time*'s invocation of children, even in sneering disapproval, speaks to something of *Ray Gun*'s deliberate refusal of logic, its carnivalesque delight in disorder and nonsense. Notice, for example, the hair of that imposing silhouette in the far corner of *The Street* (see fig. 1.5): the ambiguous words YEAH, WELL, and TELL join, in a Dada nursery rhyme, with the nonsense expressions HYNO and GURB. Look, too, at the careful ambiguity of the form to the left of the silhouette, suspended beside the word RAY.[45] Here we have the most illegible of objects, representing, we might guess, a human figure, an automobile, or even an airplane. If any art in New York in this period deserved the label Neo-Dada, *The Street* is it—a kind of Merzbau of the sidewalk, rendered in trash.

Predictably, *Snapshots from the City*, the happening Oldenburg staged in *The Street*, offered no more order or sense. Instead, the medium's potential for narrative seems only to have compelled a further refusal of these terms. *Snapshots* was performed three times for live audiences (who, Oldenburg reported, could hardly see it) and separately recorded in 16mm for a film version directed by Stan Vanderbeek almost identically entitled *Snapshots of the City*. Aside from a few documentary photographs (fig. 1.14), this film is the only formal record we have of the happening, which was performed by Oldenburg and Pat Muschinski, whom he was soon to marry.[46]

The film, no longer than five minutes, devotes itself chiefly to brief shots of Oldenburg and Muschinski writhing in exaggerated, jerky motions. These are separated by periods of blackness, created by Lucas Samaras, who turned the light on and off "when he felt like it."[47] Meanwhile, sounds of sirens, car horns, and rumbling traffic alternate at random with periods of monosyllabic yelping and apelike grunts. Visually, Oldenburg is tied to *The Street* by his costume of large sackcloth boots, white underwear, and a dirtied shirt, open to the chest. Strips of cloth also hang from his head, neck, shoulders, and wrists. Muschinski wears a newspaper mask, marked with simple outlines of empty eyes and a frowning face, and a set of bloated hair braids, made of stuffed rags.

Eventually, Oldenburg's character shoots himself several times with a gun of cutout cardboard.[48] The character seems to recuperate each time, however, until someone offscreen slowly but fatally pushes a dark, barely legible cardboard car at his shoulder, causing him to crumple. The camera then pans across Oldenburg's lifeless body and holds a final close-up of his upturned hand, deathly still and dirtied as if with gun soot or the effects of poverty.

Of course *Snapshots*, both as happening and as film, has elements of social realism, representing characters of urban abjection, whose formal similarity to their garbage-strewn surroundings articulates their position under the heel of New York's capitalist wealth. And it is not just an agonizing poverty that is on show here, but a pedestrian world bombarded by the sounds, soot, and mortal effects of automobiles. All of this could be read as a desperate representation of the poor of lower Manhattan, those perhaps most adversely affected by luxury renewal projects and

FIG. 1.14
Pat Muschinski and Oldenburg in Oldenburg's
happening *Snapshots from the City*,
at the Judson Gallery, 1960


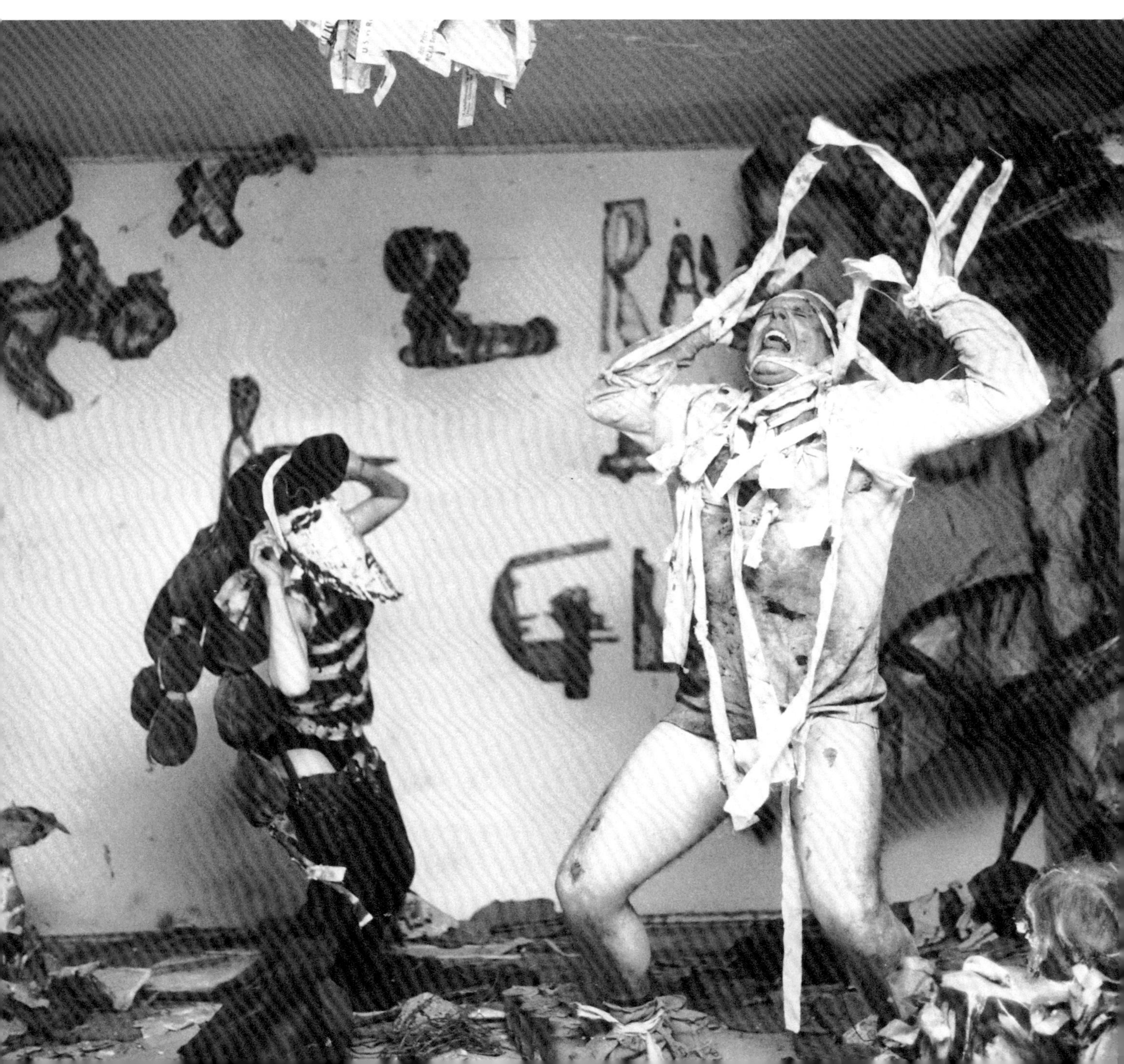

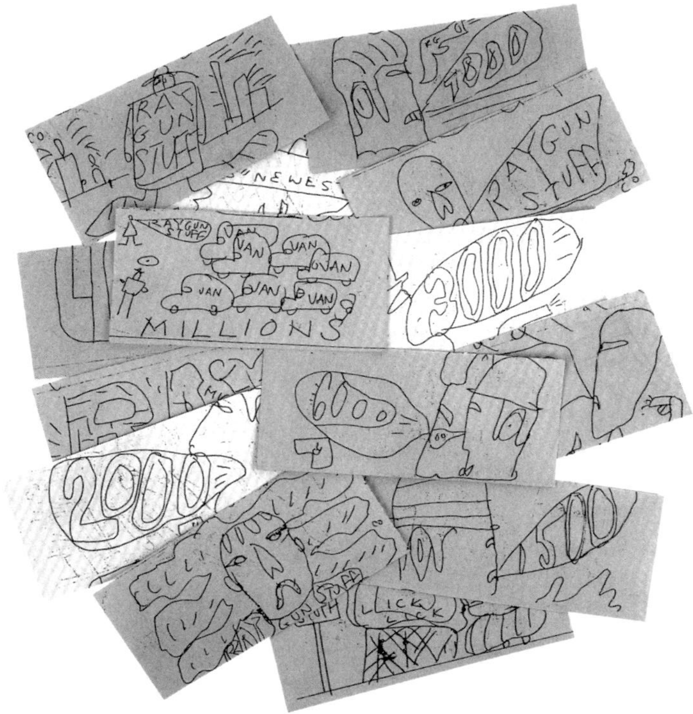



**FIG. 1.15**
**Claes Oldenburg**
Ray Gun money, 1960
Mimeographed paper

increased traffic. On one level, this is certainly right. But the performance clearly had other commitments as well. The dirty bandages, for example, not wrapped as if for a specific wound but rather winding around much of Oldenburg's upper body, evoke Egyptian mummification, and Muschinski's African-style mask is clearly intended as a manifestation of the "contemporary primitivism" that Oldenburg had mentioned in 1959 as one of his aspirations as an artist.[49]

Michael Leja has observed that the primitivism in Abstract Expressionism served as an instance of Barthesian "inoculation": an injection of a small amount of disorder within the "Modern Man discourse," functioning to make contemporary American society seem all the more ordered and secure.[50] The primitivism of *Snapshots from the City* does not offer itself as such an ideological prophylactic. On the contrary, the primitivism here—which runs alongside pervasive filth and moaning, general darkness, and overall inscrutability—is anything but contained or sanitized. This is part of the show, remember, that, unchecked, would help to put "civilization . . . in peril." It was the work of a group of artists "determined to be offbeat, off-Broadway, and off their rockers."[51]

For the Ray Gun Spex series, Oldenburg also minted a special Ray Gun currency (fig. 1.15). Members of the audience, each given $1 million, used the money to buy junk that was gathered from surrounding streets and sold from carts at intermission.[52] The words and images on the money epitomize both the violence and the nonsense of *Ray Gun*: traffic swarms menacingly, a man is seen licking or kissing a form that seems at once "ice crym kon" and woman, and a jet is emblazoned with the words "Kill 'Miss' Newest." The buying of trash with counterfeit money was itself—as Robert E. Haywood has pointed out—a Dada-like parody of consumption.[53] That Oldenburg was reading something "incomprehensible" during the sale must only have furthered the sense of *Ray Gun*'s attack on civilized sensibilities.[54]

In part, *The Street*—along with the performances and printed ephemera made with it—was an attack on sense and order; in the place of logic and legibility, it offered a kind of passionate insanity. In discussing this work recently, Oldenburg described it—affirmatively and respectfully—as "my ravings." In an earlier comment the artist emphasized the serious representational project running through his work's absurdism: "It sounds too crazy when you speak the truth. The truth is too crazy."[55] In a notation probably made in 1961, Oldenburg suggested that this crazy truth might have been intended as quixotic attack on mainstream culture, including even the received notion of art itself: "This country is all bourgeois down to the last deathtail [*sic*] and most of the criticism is an exhortation to observe art and justice and good sense and humanity, which are also bourgeois values, so there is no escaping bourgeois values in America. The enemy is bourgeois culture nevertheless."[56]

Of course, Oldenburg was not alone in aiming Dada-like nonsense at Eisenhower culture. The Beats—whom Oldenburg disdained as themselves bourgeois, partly because "they would never think f. ex. of making the city a value of good"—had also lauded irrationality and even in-sanity in the face of a conformist mainstream. The figure of the madman prophet appears repeatedly in *On the Road*, for example, and Dean Moriarty (the Neal Cassady stand-in) is praised as "the Idiot, the Imbecile, the Saint of the Lot . . . the HOLY GOOF."[57] This rejection of the logic, of the "good sense" as Oldenburg had it, of mainstream culture was endemic to Greenwich Village around 1960. A 1959 *Village Voice* adver-tisement soliciting subscriptions pictured a figure holding a sign reading: "Help To Stamp Out Mental Health!" When the Judson Gallery launched *Exodus*, its own journal, the *Voice* ran a warm news piece about the publication, citing its inclusion of entries called "The Insanity Bit," and "Poem of Holy Madness," as well as Bud Scott's description of it as "a way-out magazine."[58]

The struggle over the Washington Square roadway and the shape of Greenwich Village was itself cast as a struggle between logic and nonsense. In a statement about the expressway plans published both in the *New York Times* and the *Village Voice*, Robert Moses twice invoked "common sense" in defense of the project, saying that the result of not building it would be a "mess" and an "absurdity." An essay in the *Voice* satirically urged support for Moses and every "right thinker" under him. Another piece run in the same publication argued against the new campaign of issuing tickets for littering: "It seems to take us all one giant step nearer to that ideal society envisaged by the prophets of pure order."[59]

The value of Greenwich Village itself was said to depend on the illogic of its landscape. An essay about the character of the neighborhood linked "a magic in Greenwich Village" to the fact that "West 11th Street crosses West 4th." A prominent New York politician remarked in a similar vein that "city planners who would probably straighten out Morton and Gay Streets or widen MacDougal Alley . . . have shown no appreciation for what a community is." And a letter in the *Voice* argued that the Village's "community" and the fact of its housing "the most creative theatre in the country" depended on its being a "holdout from the nineteenth century," a "crazy patchwork of streets and buildings."[60]

It would be easy, then, to see *Ray Gun*'s celebration of illogic as a volley in a war between the reason of post-war planning and a culturally motivated refusal of order. Certainly this is part of what was going on. But to simplify the exhibition as an attack on the new vision of urban order would mean covering up the violence and destitution every-where bound to the show's chaos. *The Street,* after all, does not picture the delightfully quirky city of Jane Jacobs. It con-tinually emphasizes dirt, poverty, and violence. Remember, for example, the patina of soot covering the figure slumped behind the shoe-shine stand, as well as the unhappy ploy for respectability signaled by his anachronistic facial hair and top hat (see fig. 1.4). As Barbara Rose has noted, Oldenburg associated *The Street* with *Guernica*, the century's most conspicuous painting of misery, even noting that his subject was "everyday agony."[61]

The double-edgedness of disorder in *The Street* is nowhere more apparent than in its ambiguous evocation of gun violence. In addition to the gun carried by Oldenburg in *Snapshots of the City,* there are the guns in the hands of two of the figures on and near *The Street*'s back wall (see fig. 1.5). The name of the exhibition, however, suggests that these guns, like those of science fiction, might not be purely deadly. As Oldenburg has said recently: "The idea was Ray Gun was shooting something other than a lethal blast." At the time, Oldenburg wrote in his notebook, "When Ray Gun shoots, noone [*sic*] dies."[62] Oldenburg and Dine had also written that the "slogan" for the *Ray Gun* exhibition was "Annihilate-Illuminate," a phrase that appeared in the show's advertisement in the *Voice* (fig. 1.16), the Judson Gallery's spring calendar, and Oldenburg's own notebooks, among other spots.[63] The phrase bespeaks *The Street*'s two-sided nature as a city of both fecundity and destruction.

The postwar planners envisioned an open, airy, and peaceful city—a clean and ordered system of smooth, white walls and seamlessly flowing traffic.[64] *The Street*, by contrast, is a hyperbolic representation of the city as it had been (and—despite the incursions of renewal—as it continued to be); it exaggerates not only the exciting disorder and density of the existing city but also its dirt, desperation, and confusion. Above all, *The Street* offers an image of the city as a place of unruly matter, of obdurate stuff refusing to be abstracted into order or legibility. It is these qualities we need to understand, if we are to make sense of this conflicted representation of New York.

The chaos of *The Street* made it very difficult to "read" in any conventional sense. Recall the visual and interpretive opacity that marks our first experiences of the work. Look again, for example, at the wall to the right of the doorway—the one with the two large standing figures (see fig. 1.6). Although we can be fairly certain that we see two human figures here, we cannot be sure what that form might be against the ceiling in the far corner, or what is on the floor below it. Also, we are not certain if the long horizontal forms extending from the head of the large figure on the right are ears, hair, speech bubbles, or perhaps somehow all three. Even where there is clearly a speech bubble—attached to the figure at left—its only content is a dripping squiggle of paint. The unclear identities of the triangular form in the figure's hand and of the odd stick at its side further underline this illegibility in *The Street*, this blockage of interpretation.



Advertisement for the *Ray Gun* exhibition, *Village Voice*, 27 January 1960

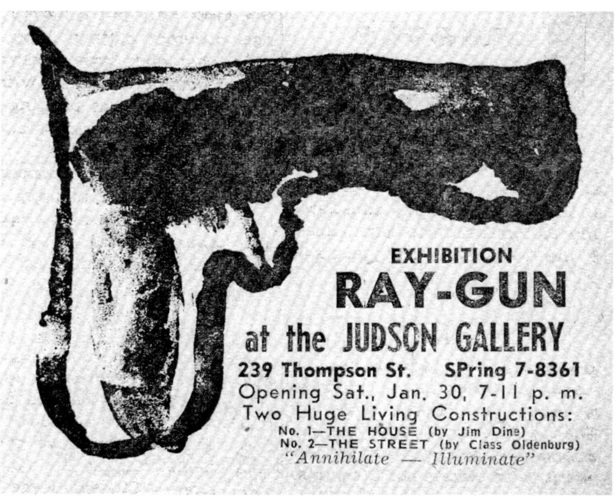

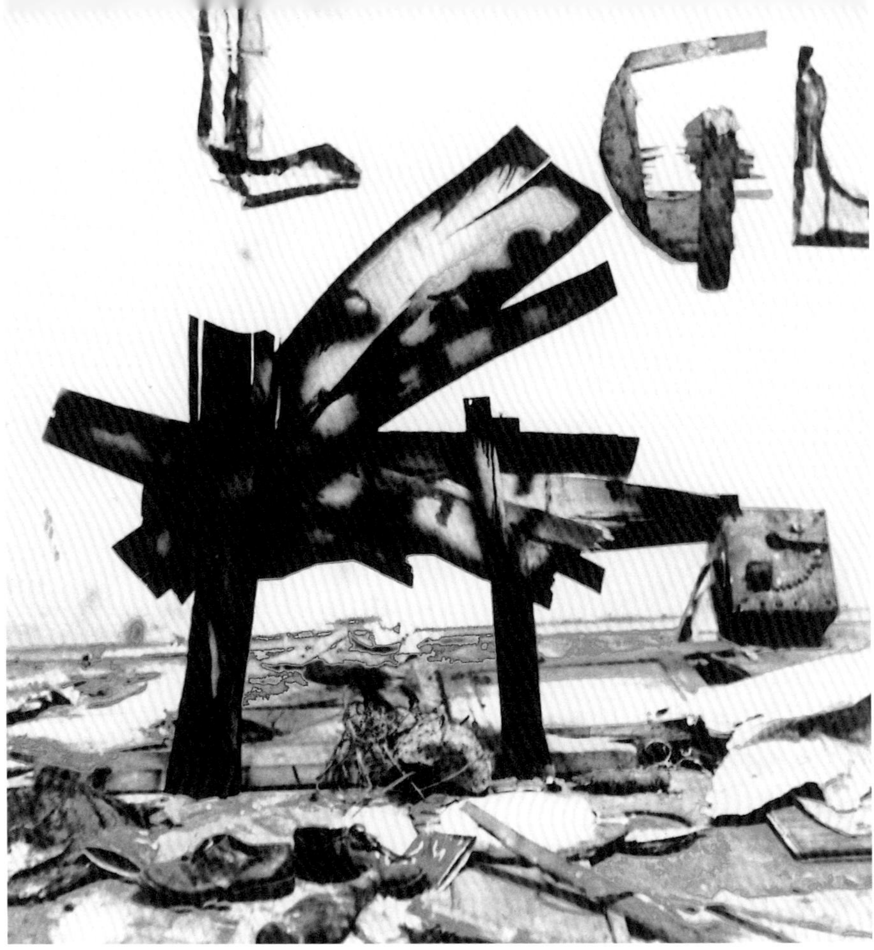



Look also at the biggest nonfigurative element in the installation, that freestanding sculpture of the scorched traffic barricade (fig. 1.17). Much of *The Street*'s account of urban experience is condensed into this one apparently senseless tool of blockage. An ordinary barricade depends for its utility on the legibility of its bright colors, bold lettering, and deliberate placement, but Oldenburg's version is dark and sooty, without clear history or institutional authority. It seems pointlessly dense with renegade and overlapping wood slats, all cracked and sullied. Its awkward placement at the center of this odd streetscape leaves even its very purpose ambiguous: is it meant to stop the flow of automobile traffic, or—by blocking pedestrians—to foster it? Then there is also the ambiguity of the sooty finish. Has this barricade been darkened by the dirt of the old city? By the fires of renewal? All these difficulties of interpretation cue us to what these boards really do insist upon, namely their identity as trash, as materiality beyond or at the fringes of representation. What is blocked by the particular material excess here, therefore, is not simply physical movements, but also meaning.[65]

The rhetoric in the "Battle of Washington Square" had explicitly pitted "flow" against a kind of blockage. One activist attacked the notion that "we must accommodate everything else to easing [traffic's] flow." An architectural critic, too, had said that Greenwich Village was "inhabitable" only because of "its jaywalkers, who slow up a confused and intermittent traffic," and Washington Square Park Committee chair Shirley Hayes had argued that the neighborhood depended on the fact that traffic "winds" around the square—emphasizing that "winding is a good word for it."[66]

The barricade does a lot to make *The Street* a place where traffic (both corporeal and intellectual) must do a lot of "winding." There is no easy flow here; our experience and understanding of this work might well be characterized as "confused and intermittent." The sense of diversion, blockage, and fracture (of viewers' paths in the space, of our interpretations of the work) imitate very closely the ways traffic might be diverted, blocked, or fractured at a barricade line or around a city park. For Oldenburg, one of the effects of his work was specifically a blockage of meaning. He typed a note about this effect a few years later: "My art is the constant enemy of meaning . . . or you could say I have aimed at neutralizing meaning (which is unexpungable). . . . To eliminate appearances seems to me impossible and therefore artificial. . . . Simply grasp them and show how little they mean."[67] *The Street* shows the city locked in a stunted transformation, where paper, cardboard, wood, and trash are used literally, as street debris, at least as much as they are used in service of representation. The obdurate matter of the city clogs up renewal, traffic, and representation itself.

**The Reuben Installation**

Although it opened only a few weeks after the Judson show came down, the Reuben Gallery incarnation of *The Street* was vastly different (figs. 1.18, 1.19).[68] In fact, the whole of the Judson show's chaos seems to have been jettisoned for a quality of finish. The floors are bare, and each piece of the new installation is mounted separately, surrounded with sufficient space for individual contemplation. In this second version of *The Street,* Oldenburg has allowed himself to make several individual characters with their own titles (*Lorraine*, for example, occupies the center of figs. 1.18, 1.19). He hangs the figures, now untethered from their back-

grounds, in the viewer's space, creating a scene in which viewers can imagine a kind of belonging to this streetscape, a correspondence between their own bodies and the stuffed burlap of the odd pedestrians around them. This crystallization of *The Street* into discrete sculptures evolved over a series of sketches the artist seems to have made between the two shows. From the first, these drawings suggest a desire to try out making more legible units. Oldenburg writes on one sheet, for example, "FACES against black floor ea. a picture."[69] After all the resistance to representation at the Judson, Oldenburg is having a try at making pictures.

Oldenburg emphasized the new particularization of *The Street*'s components in a description quoted in the Reuben press release: "There will be men and women and heroes and bums and children and drunks and streetchicks . . . and trucks and cars . . . and shadows and cats and doggies . . . cockroaches and mornings and evenings and guns . . . and cops and mamagangers and a lot more." The artist's stringing together of all these elements, and his joining of them all with the repeated "and," levels their differences; it is as if "shadows" and "mornings" were material pieces of the streetscape, just like "cars," "cockroaches," and even "drunks." Of course Oldenburg does not really include most of these things. Whatever they might look like, there are no sculptures of shadows or mornings here. Even many of the material things listed are red herrings; there are no cockroaches, not even any guns. In fact almost all the sculptures we do see at the Reuben very clearly represent either human beings or street signs of some sort. In this description, Oldenburg wants to emphasize the discrete and material qualities of the installation's various units, as well as the overall aim—despite the continued inscrutability of such imagined elements as the nonsensical "mamagangers"— to make a legible representation of the city.[70]

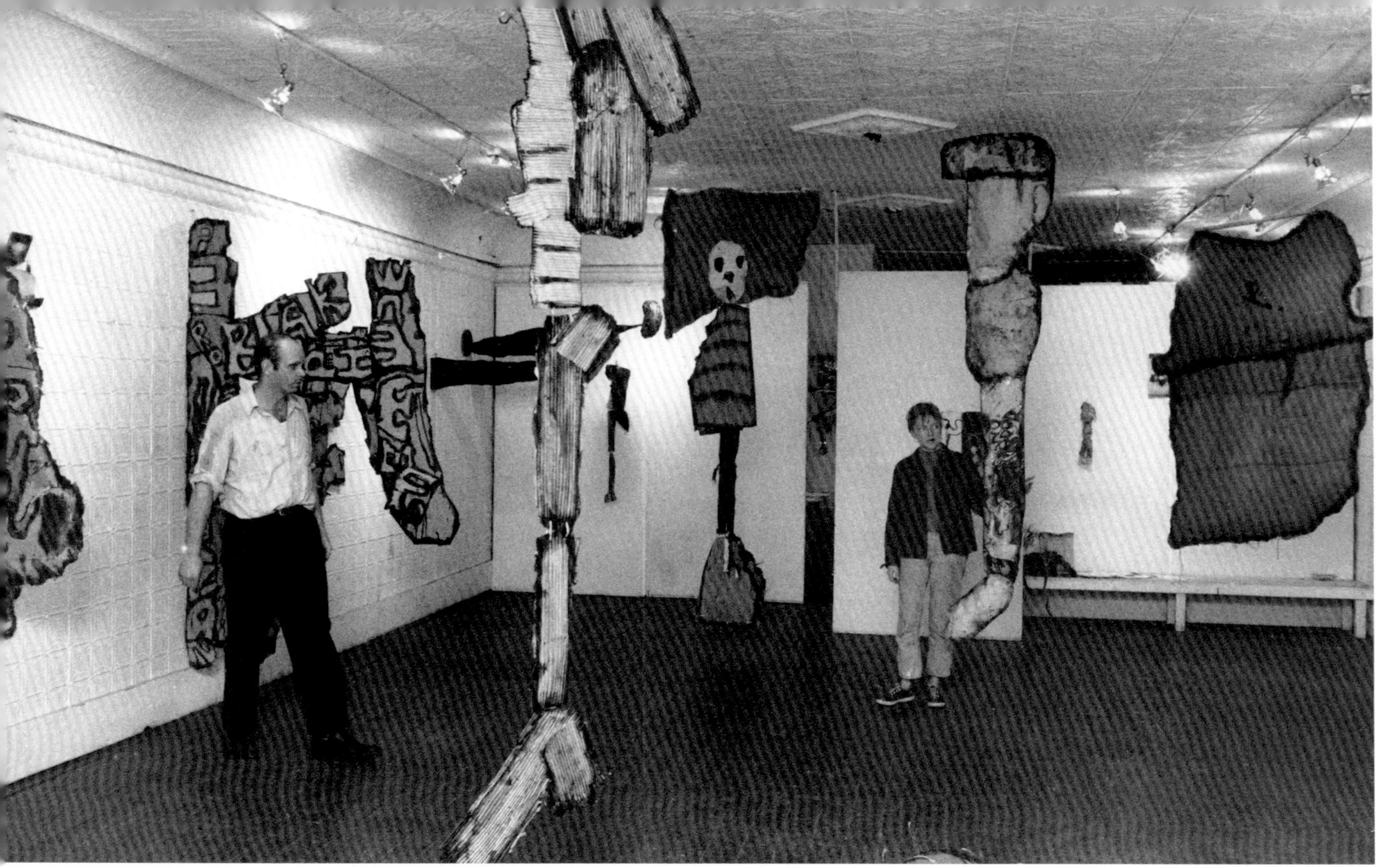

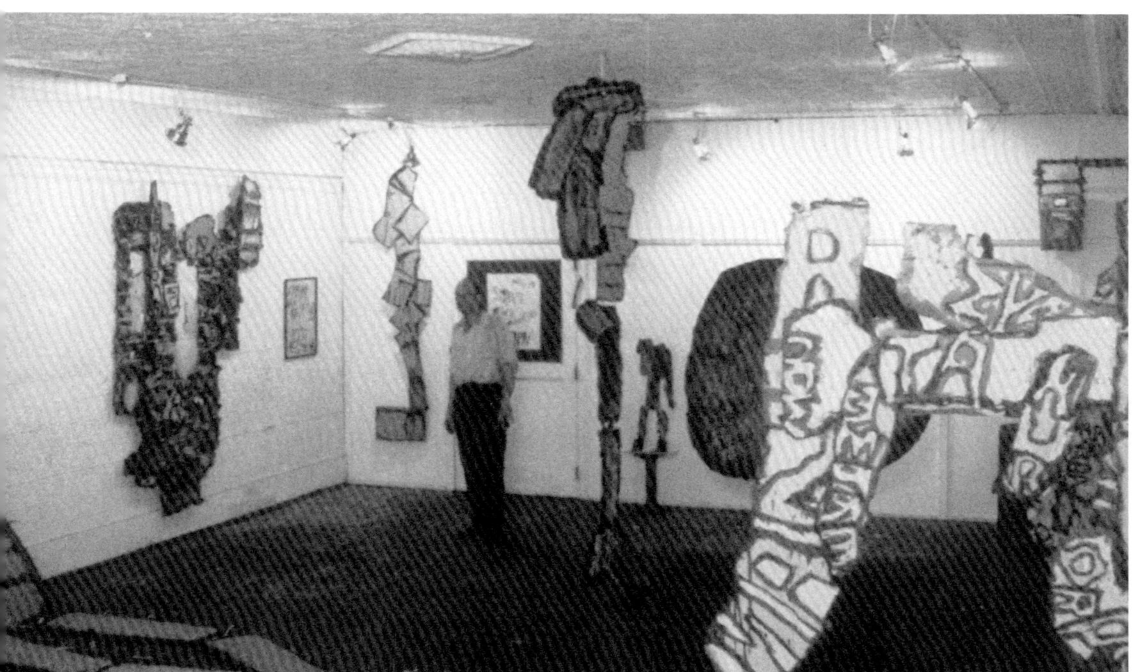

FIGS. 1.18 and 1.19
Claes Oldenburg
*The Street*, installation at
the Reuben Gallery, 1960

For all its new order, however, the Reuben installation of *The Street* is still very much an image of the old city, emphasizing its trash and poverty and confusion. Like the Judson version, it is rendered all in brown and black, a reduced color scheme evocative both of city pavement and of aging social documentary photographs. The figures' lack of arms and their ragged clothes (see, for example, the repaired shoes worn by *Street Chick [Big]*, at rear, fig. 1.18) also communicate a general desperation. As at the Judson, the whole work here is executed in plain materials, including paper, muslin, burlap, and at least two types of cardboard. And here, too, there is a confusing scattering of scales; the figures vary in height from about sixteen inches (*Street Chick [Small]*) to over fifteen feet (*Big Man [Big Guy]*). At the same time, a more definitive flatness—expressive of the unforgiving planarity of the old city, its hard walls and sidewalks—has entered the work, so that even though they share the viewer's space, the sculptures are all but two-dimensional.

Another quality shared with the Judson installation is the look of singeing on everything: many of the works have sooty washes across them, and all are outlined with a scorched-looking contour line. Oldenburg, remember, was drawn to the destructive force of fire ("I love soot and scorching"), a force he associated with the "wreckage" of renewal. The singeing throughout the Reuben installation of *The Street* suggests that the work is a snapshot of renewal just at the moment when it actually adds to the dirt and chaos of the city, just at the moment when the seams and the material excess it aims to eliminate are most visible. This moment in the process of renewal was everywhere manifest in Greenwich Village in the winter of 1960; look, for example, at the unfinished southern section of

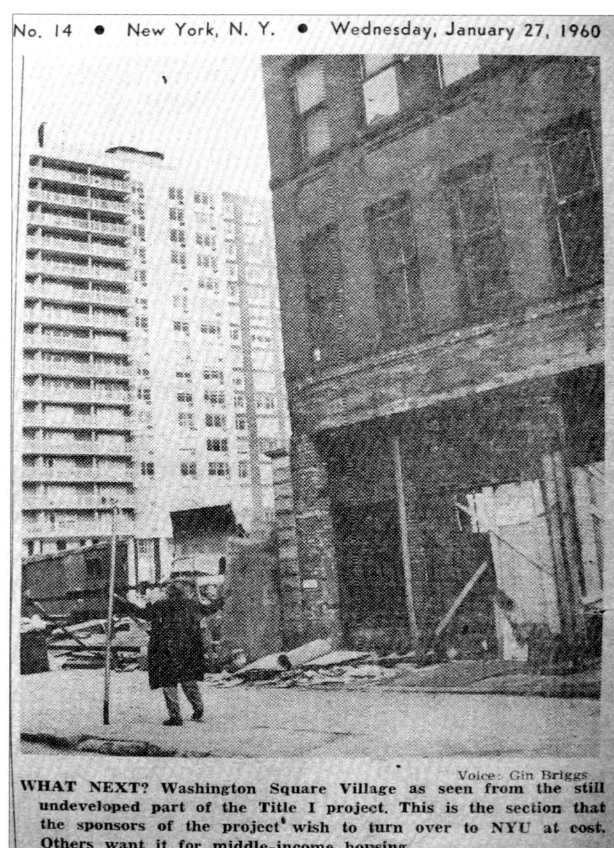



Washington Square Village, as it appeared in the *Village Voice* on January 27 (fig. 1.20).[71]

At first appearance, of course, the Reuben *Street* seems far easier to read than its predecessor. In the place of that continuum of chaos, we have newly discrete objects. But one effect of this change is that the work offers neatly framed studies of varying degrees of legibility. Representation nearly evaporates altogether, for example, in works such as the enormous and ambiguous *Street Head I ("Big Head"; "Gong")* (see fig. 1.19, against the back wall, and fig. 1.21), in which the title underscores the interpretive flexibility of the form. In fact, the childish stick-figure quality of the whole installation might be understood as a careful rendering of the streetscape in a language of reduced symbolism, where the pieces threaten not to cohere, not to mean.

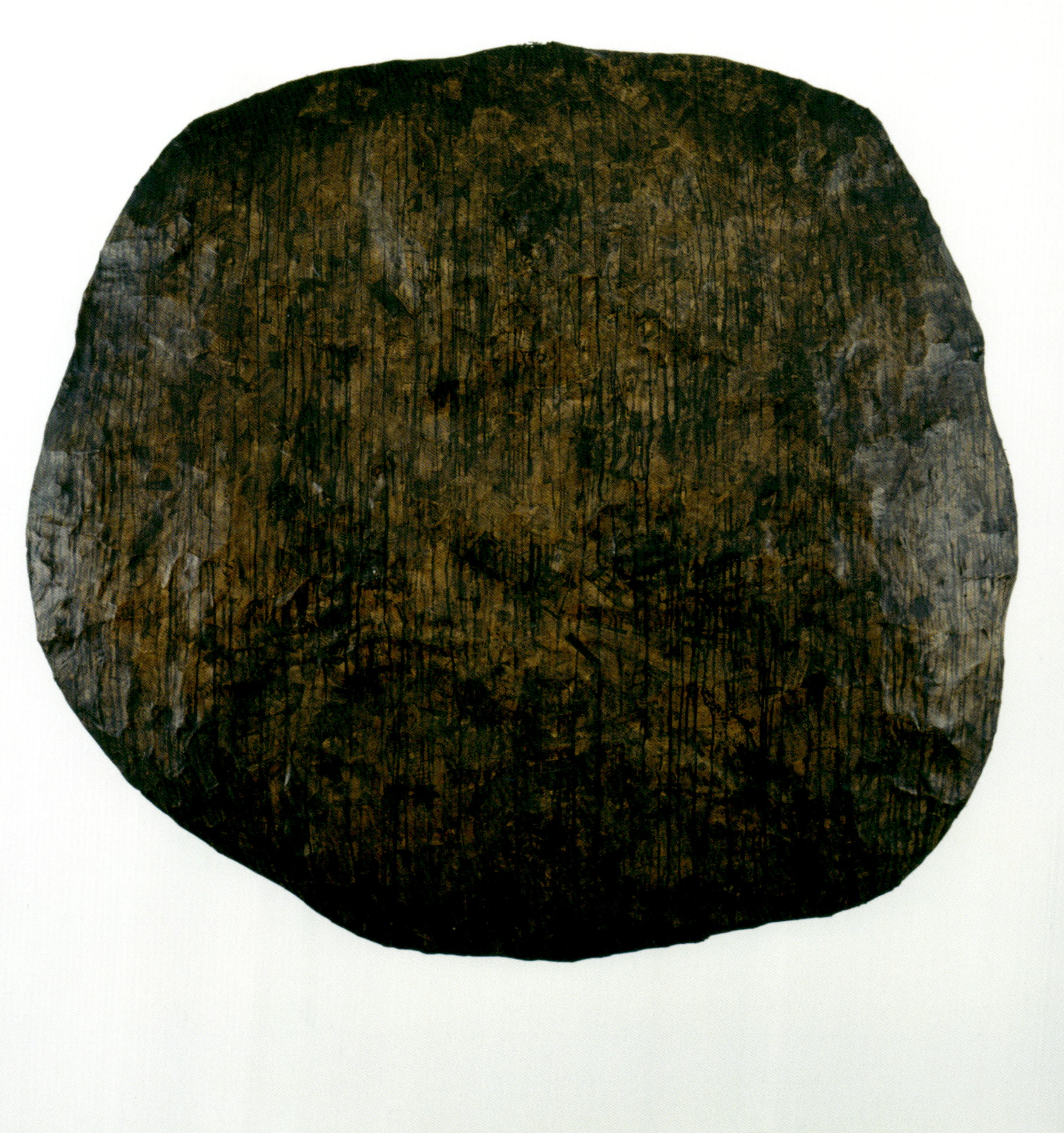

FIG. 1.21
**Claes Oldenburg**
*Street Head I ("Big Head"; "Gong"),* 1959
Newspaper soaked in wheat paste over wire frame
painted with casein, 61 x 64 x 14 in. (155 x 163 x 36 cm)
Museum Moderner Kunst Stiftung Ludwig, Vienna

One of the most significant differences between the two installations is the inclusion, at the Reuben, of several prominent signs, occupying as much space as the figures and surrounding them on all sides. *Street Sign I* (see fig. 1.18, behind Oldenburg, and fig. 1.19, at right) and *Street Sign II* (fig. 1.22)—which, like most of the other works from this installation, survive in the Ludwig Collection in Cologne— were accompanied by at least two similar works visible in the installation photographs. An untidy black lettering crawls all over these signs, overpacking them with percussive, ambiguous syllables. The variety of forms taken by the letters of the alphabet stresses their materiality: some are merely painted, others are in pasted or nailed-on cardboard, and still others are defined by scraps attached as negative space. Orientation is insecure, so some forms resolve alternatively as Z or N or as E or M. A few expressions are generally emphatic (YA, NOW), while others seem simply nonsensical (ZY, KIG); some passages fail to resolve into letters at all. In a notation that seems to address the Street Sign works, Oldenburg made explicit his interest in noncommunicative lettering: "Where I use writing, I should like to provoke a physical effect of enunciation . . . certain letters are missing . . . the writing loses its sign character. There is a way to physicalize the sign . . . the word . . . to do this through the eyes."[72] The signs in *The Street* are made so as to short-circuit communication in favor of an insistence on their own materiality and their own occupation of space in the city. If "physical," however, these signs still offer an "effect of enunciation," an emphatic call for the possibility of representation.

In particular, careful scrutiny reveals that most of the letters in the Street Sign works do in fact function as fragments of one of two words: ORPHEUM (which appears as ORPHM, ORPH, HEUM, EUM, and HUR ) and EMPIRE (EPRIRE,

EMPIRIS, EM, and EMPIRS). It seems likely that Oldenburg was drawn to *Orpheum* as a term for the Street Signs by the fact that it recalls Orpheus, a figure of both artistic power and failure. But he might also have been drawn to it because it was the name of three corset shops, a Greenwich Village playhouse, and two movie theaters in Manhattan alone.[73] EMPIRE had even more associations, evoking the nickname of New York State (and its most famous building), and naming over a full page of businesses in the Manhattan phone books between 1958 and 1961. The Empire Theater was joined by the downtrodden Empire Diner as well as hairdressers, printers, parking garages; packing, oil, and shipping companies; and four separate listings for the Empire Mfg. Co.[74] (By 1961, Oldenburg had invented Ray Gun Mfg. Co., host of his next installation, *The Store.*) Also listed were both an Empire Display Co. and an Empire Display Mfg. Co. In the Street Signs, then, urban representation is frustrated not only by heaping, nonsensical forms, but also by constant multiplication of meanings and ambiguities of reference.

Even the most legible of the Street Head works, the giant burlap *Street Head III* (*Profile with Hat*) (see fig. 1.18, at right, and fig. 1.23) is a far more ambiguous object than its title would suggest. Many of the black marks across both sides of it, for example, seem randomly and meaninglessly applied; it is only after a comparison of front and back that we can clearly recognize the eyes, mouth, and sideburns indicated on both sides. And, even though expressive content emerges immediately (the lips appear pursed, almost cute), these legible marks remain at the brink of meaninglessness, quite small compared even with marks (such as those across the back of the hat) that really are haphazard and nonspecific.

That this work may have had implications specifically for *The Street*'s consideration of the urban landscape is

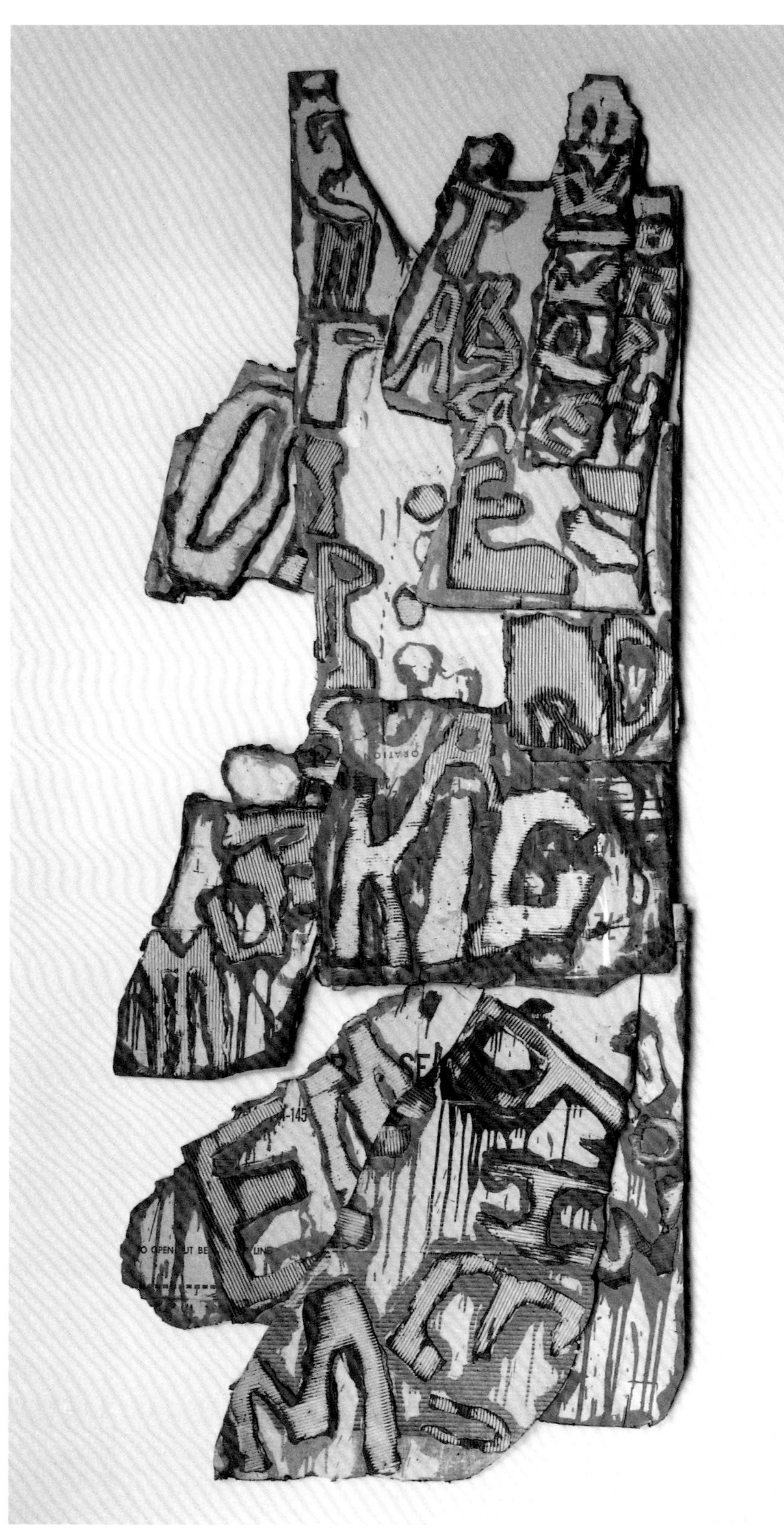



FIG. 1.22
**Claes Oldenburg**
*Street Sign II*, 1960
Wood, cardboard, casein, nails,
102 x 40 x 2 in. (259 x 102 x 5 cm)
Museum Ludwig, Cologne

FIG. 1.23 (opposite and following)
**Claes Oldenburg**
*Street Head III (Profile with Hat)*, 1960
Stuffed burlap, casein, wire,
79 x 48 x 5 in. (201 x 122 x 13 cm)
Museum Ludwig, Cologne

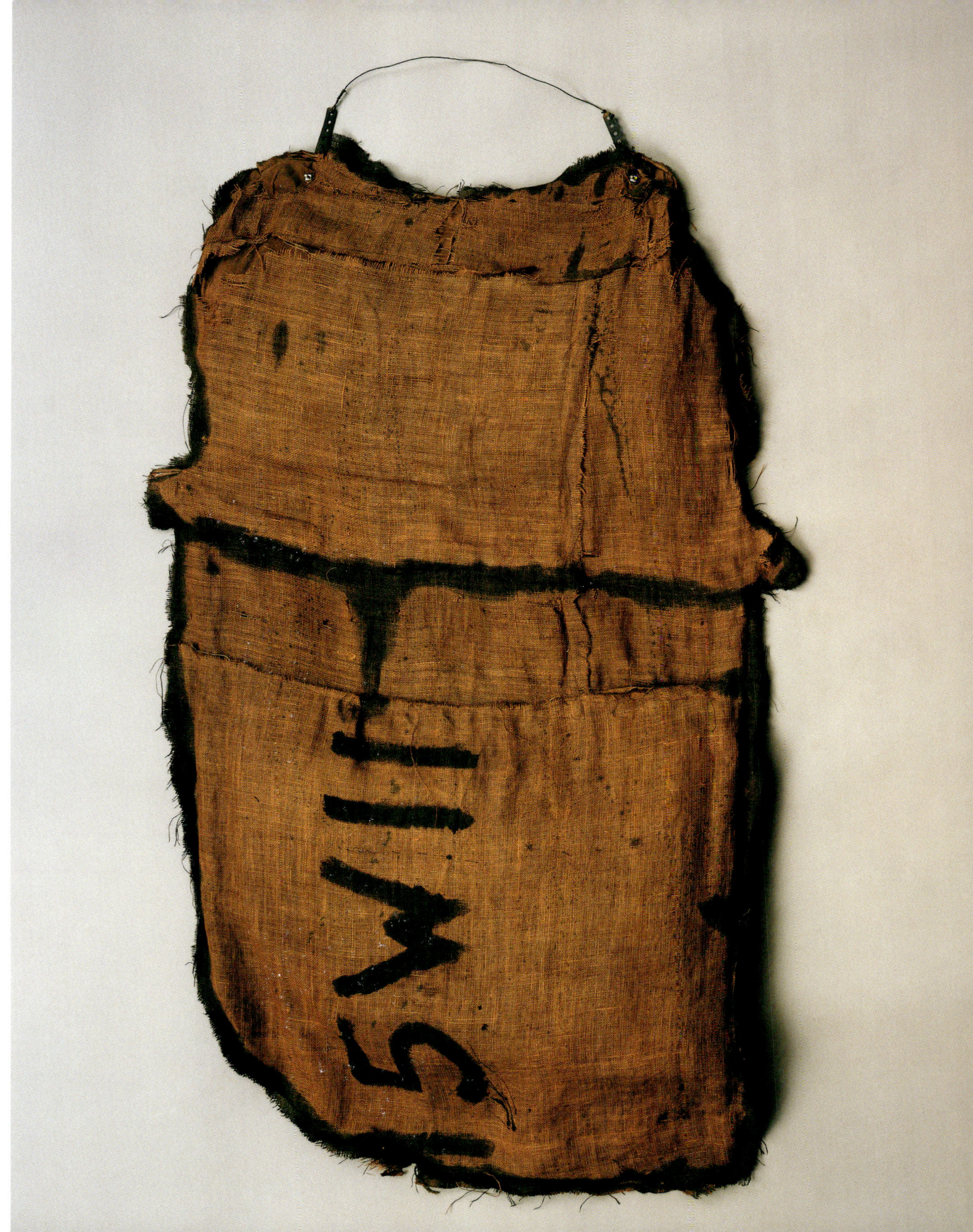

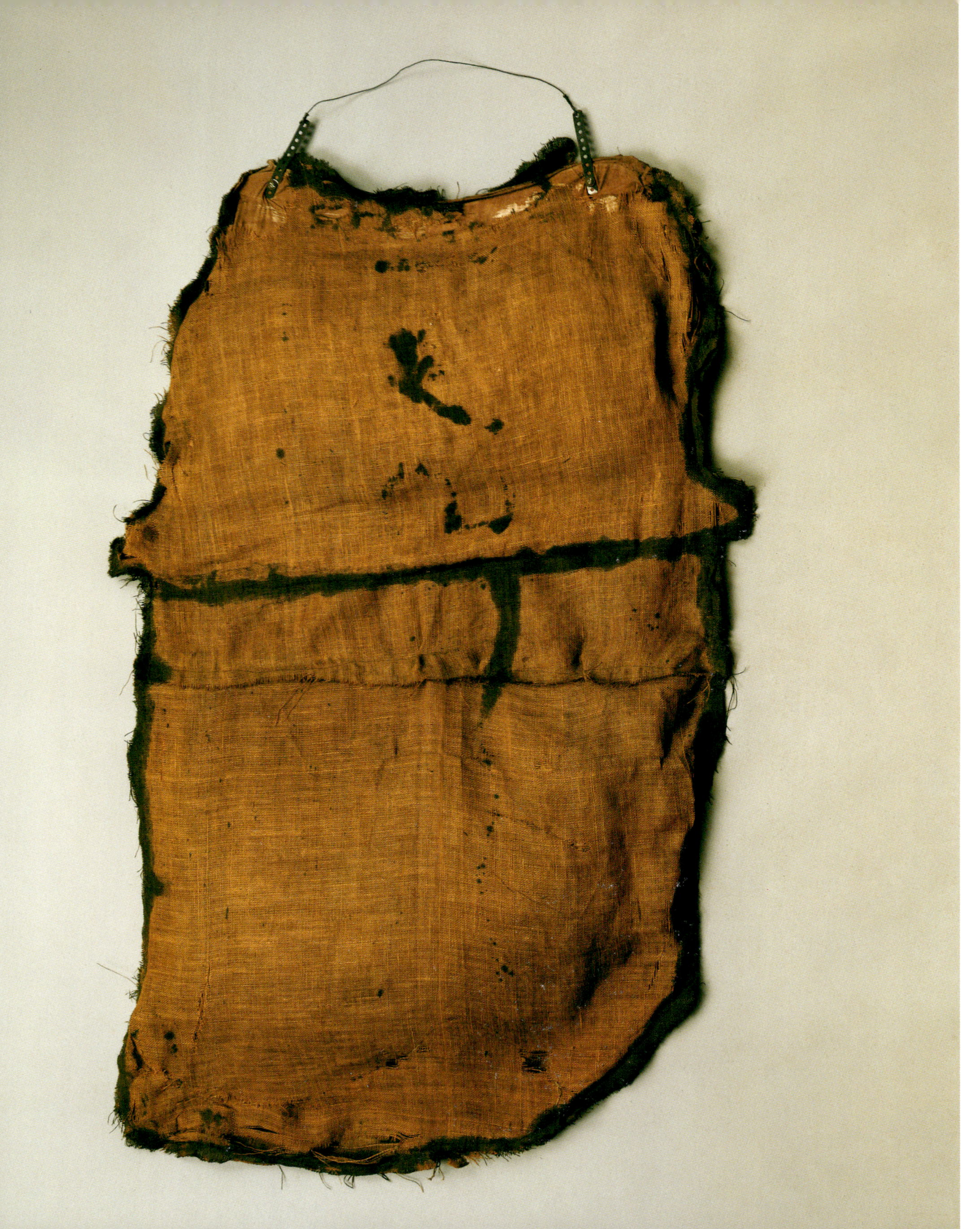

emphasized by Oldenburg's careful painting of a Manhattan street address right across the face of this sculpture. Barbara Rose suggests that *Street Head III* was made from a "burlap garbage bag," and Oldenburg has recently repeated this assertion, adding that "5 w 11" was painted on the bag when he found it, indicating that it belonged to 5 West Eleventh Street.[75] However, the color, texture, and width of the brushstrokes in the address match those of the sculpture's outlines so closely that it seems more probable that Oldenburg added the address himself. This possibility seems all the more likely when one considers that there is no 5 West Eleventh Street in Manhattan and that there has not been since at least 1893.[76]

If Oldenburg did in fact paint on this address, one can imagine that he selected the address he did for the ambiguity of its figures: the number five looks like the letter S, the number eleven could be mistaken for two Ls or Is. Perhaps—West Eleventh Street is less than a five-minute walk from the Judson—Oldenburg even selected 5 w 11 specifically because he knew it was a sign with a phantom referent. In any case, the doubt about his account of the address also calls into question the claim that he collected the burlap from the streets at all. It seems at least as likely that Oldenburg purchased the burlap, which he might have done six blocks from his home in the Lower East Side, at a business called the Empire Burlap Bag Company.[77]

*Street Head III* does not merely stress its own materiality at the expense of particular readings. It also enacts elaborate failed representation—communications begun but stalled. Its marks might or might not form facial features. Its lettering might or might not signify an address. Representation is not merely obstructed here; it is performed as ever-present possibility followed by slippage,

meaninglessness, failure. Meaning is always suggested but then bungled by particular material fact.

Early in 1960, the Reuben Gallery was no less surrounded by rebuilding than the Judson was. The gallery, on the block of Fourth Avenue between East Ninth and East Tenth streets, was bordered on the south and the west by whole-block construction projects (fig. 1.24), both of which were completed that year. The project to the south was Cooper Union's engineering building, the very site Oldenburg had observed being cleared a few years earlier, from one of his first homes in New York. The artist would have known this development particularly well because, even after moving farther east, he retained a day job at the library of the Cooper Union Museum through November 1961.[78] The other project was a gargantuan upscale apartment building (fig. 1.25). This site, which faced the gallery directly, had housed Wanamaker's Department Store until 1956.[79] The new building shunned the street in the typical modernist fashion, with a fence lining Fourth Avenue and a virtually unbroken wall along the entire length of Wanamaker Place.

The Reuben Gallery was, by contrast, a third-floor walk-up in a small, aging building. Not only the ceilings but even the walls on which the art was hung were made of stamped metal, a hallmark of New York prewar construction (see figs. 1.18, 1.19). With an awkwardly exposed utility meter plainly visible in the room and even an old heating stove, the space would have registered as an antiquated antonym to the development of the neighborhood. It might just have qualified as one of the "crooked studios" Ira Henry Freeman had eulogized in the *New York Times*.

In its second incarnation, then, *The Street* again appeared in the context of competing visions of the city. It is

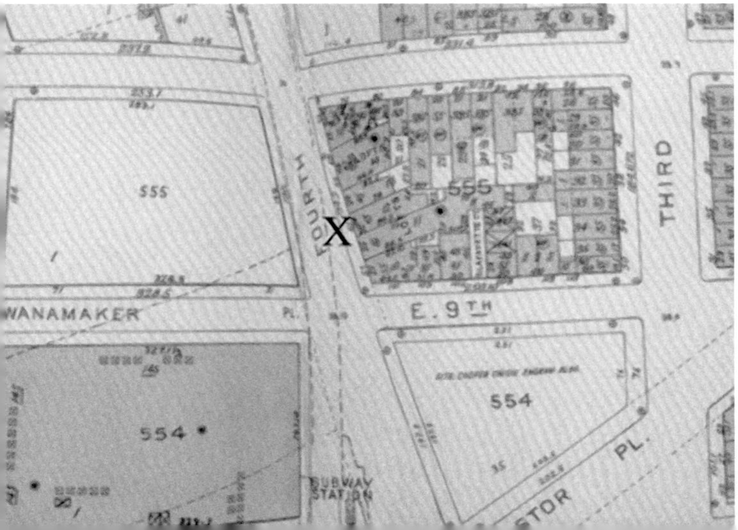

Reuben Gallery, at 61 Fourth Avenue, and adjacent construction sites, as mapped in the *Atlas of the City of New York: Borough of Manhattan*, vol. 1: *Battery to 14th Street.* New York: G. W. Bromley, 1959. Added by author: (**X**) Reuben Gallery

specifically in this context that Oldenburg again represented the city with a collection of carefully rendered but emphatically unruly and illegible detritus. The installation at the Judson had presented a city refusing order, negotiability, and legibility. The city presented in the Reuben reinstallation—now superficially tidied—appeared to offer these values a potential foothold. Instead, the Reuben *Street* offered only elaborately bungled gestures at communication—an excess of saying, with little clearly said. If this was an urban space imagining the possibility of coherent abstraction, its material particularity frustrated that possibility at every turn.

### "The Legacy of Jackson Pollock"

Oldenburg helped to host a symposium at the Judson Church in 1959 called "New Uses of the Human Image in Painting," which seems now like the seminal moment in an art history that never happened. At the symposium, Oldenburg, along with Dine, Allan Kaprow, Lester Johnson, and others, offered up plenty of 1950s masculine avant-garde bombast (Oldenburg: "To be concerned with man's relationship to the universe"; Kaprow: "I would like to see

people dig my vision"), but the artists also claimed—more specifically and more defensively—that theirs was an honest attempt to develop art's means of representation in the wake of Abstract Expressionism. Here again is Oldenburg, in the clipped language of the typescript, which was clearly made without the help of a recording: "[My art is an] instance of the human image which has a strong formal guise. Carries art definitely forward." Later in the meeting, Oldenburg again stressed this hybridity of figural representation with the formalist concerns of the art of the preceding decade, saying he wanted to create "a combination of the formal and human image." Oldenburg clearly felt that his art ("This art that I am trying to set up") would be a way of developing the claims and investigations of Abstract Expressionism into an environment he saw as more human: "They want everything to happen on the picture plane. My impulse is to make it come to life—to be an actual living thing."[80]

Quite a lot in Oldenburg's work up to 1960 was driven by this imperative to make art "be an actual living thing." For much of the late 1950s, this meant working specifically to develop a post–Abstract Expressionist language for figure painting.[81] Note, for example, his large *Self-Portrait* of 1959 (fig. 1.26), in which a vocabulary of flowing lines serves at once to depict (for example) the recession of the artist's left shoulder, and also to mark the flatness of the canvas, the materiality of paint. In this period, Oldenburg was particularly drawn to subjects of urban misery, perhaps feeling that images of suffering offered an even stronger ("living") corrective to nonobjective painting than did ordinary figure painting. See, for example, *Street Event—Woman Beating Child* of 1958 (fig. 1.27). Oldenburg's desire to make a living art, however, seems not to have been satisfied by his work in charcoal, watercolor, and oil; as early as 1957, he was beginning to sculpt in non-art materials. In *Lady* (fig. 1.28), wood

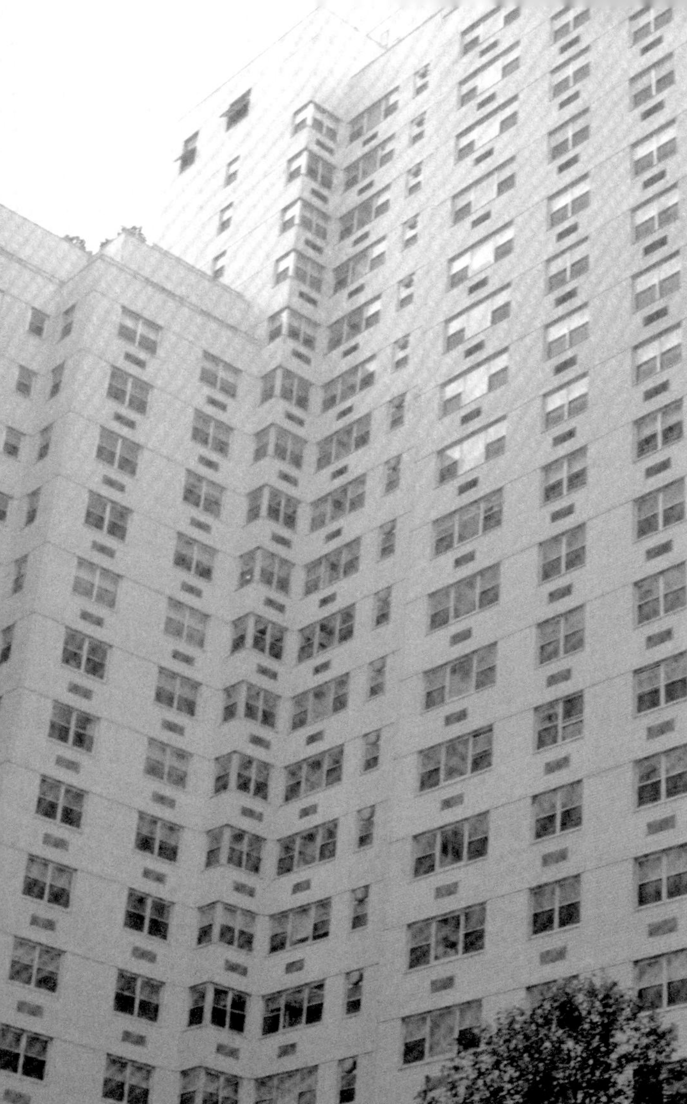



scraps are used sculpturally, and, while they still offer—with the help of their title—something of pictorial illusion, it is their own banality, their own identity as detritus, that is most conspicuous.[82] Oldenburg must have felt, by the end of the 1950s, that a fully living work of art would necessarily use ordinary materials, and that it would use them literally—that is, as themselves—at least as much as it would use them for representational ends. (In both the Judson and the Reuben installations, Oldenburg seems to have felt that he could just about get away with picturing a street, so long as he used real objects from the street to do it.)

Of course, much of this materialist impulse was inherited directly from a certain understanding of Abstract Expressionism. It seems that Oldenburg, even while trying to push art back toward optical representation, wanted to hold on to the flat, worldly literalness that some viewers had been championing in the work of recent painters. Here, for example, is the typical Clement Greenberg of the 1950s: "The picture has now become an object of literally the same spatial order as our bodies, and no longer the vehicle of an imagined equivalent of that order. . . . The spectator can no longer escape into it from the space in which he himself stands; on the contrary, the abstract or quasi-abstract picture returns him to that space in all its brute literalness."[83]

For Greenberg, as is now well known, modernist "brute literalness" was a means for investigating the essentials of visual art, the limits of representation. Oldenburg's concerns were similar, but—as we saw in the introduction—they owed a special debt to the brand of materialism that Allan Kaprow had advocated in his 1958 essay "The Legacy of Jackson Pollock." There, Kaprow characterized the previous seventy-five years of painting not as a high modernist effort (per Picasso or Mondrian) to question and sharpen *representation*, but rather as a gradual (but ultimately Pollockian) move toward materiality: "Strokes, smears, lines, etc. became less and less attached to represented objects and existed more and more on their own, self-sufficiently." Kaprow then argued that the contemporary situation required an investigation of quotidian experiences and substances: "The young artist of today," he declared, "will discover out of ordinary things the meaning of ordinariness."[84]

The legacy of Pollock, in Kaprow's view, was an inclusiveness of the world, a retraining of formalist literalism onto the banal materials of everyday life.[85] On these points, Oldenburg followed Kaprow closely, writing in his notebook,

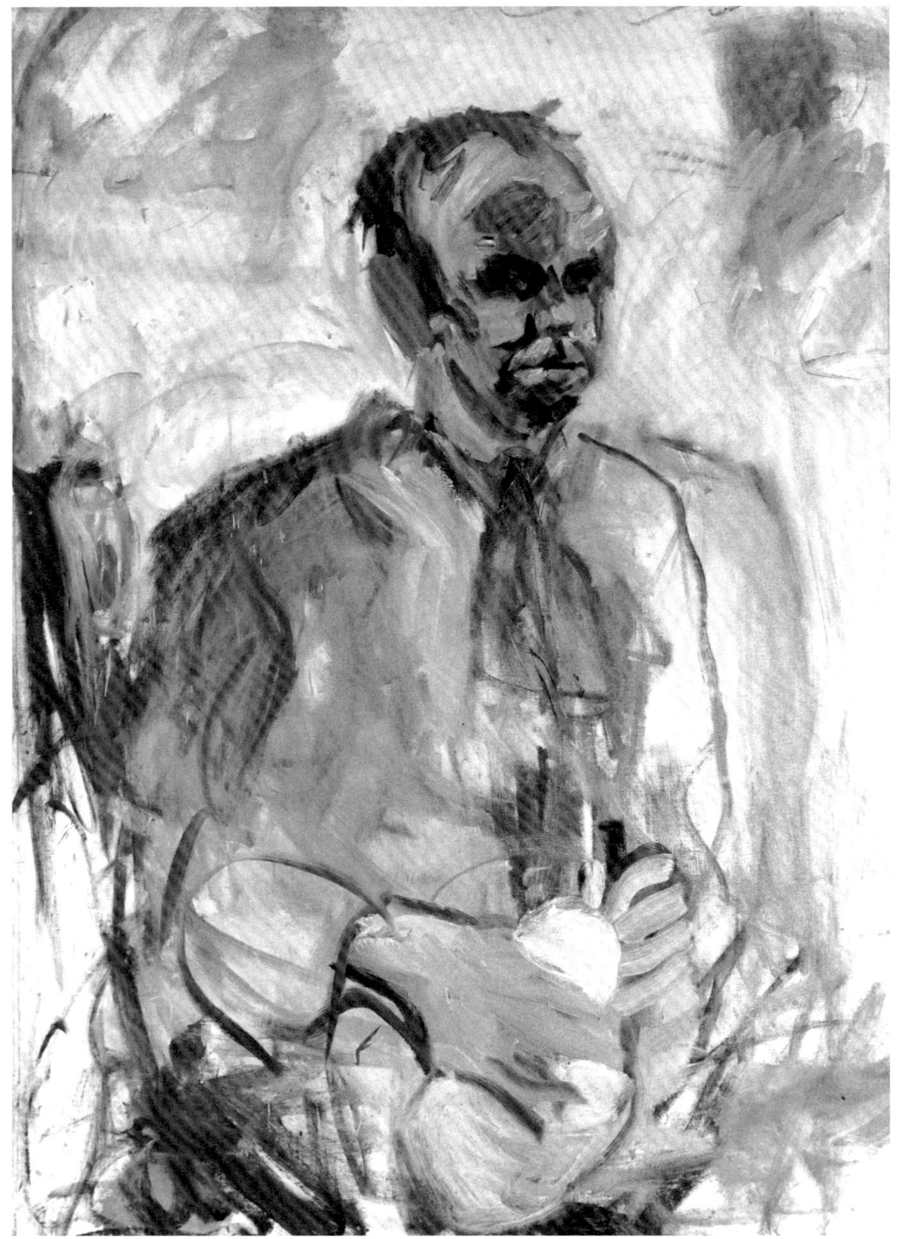

FIG. 1.26
**Claes Oldenburg**
*Self-Portrait*, 1959
Oil on canvas,
68 x 47 ½ in.
(173 x 121 cm)
Collection of the artist

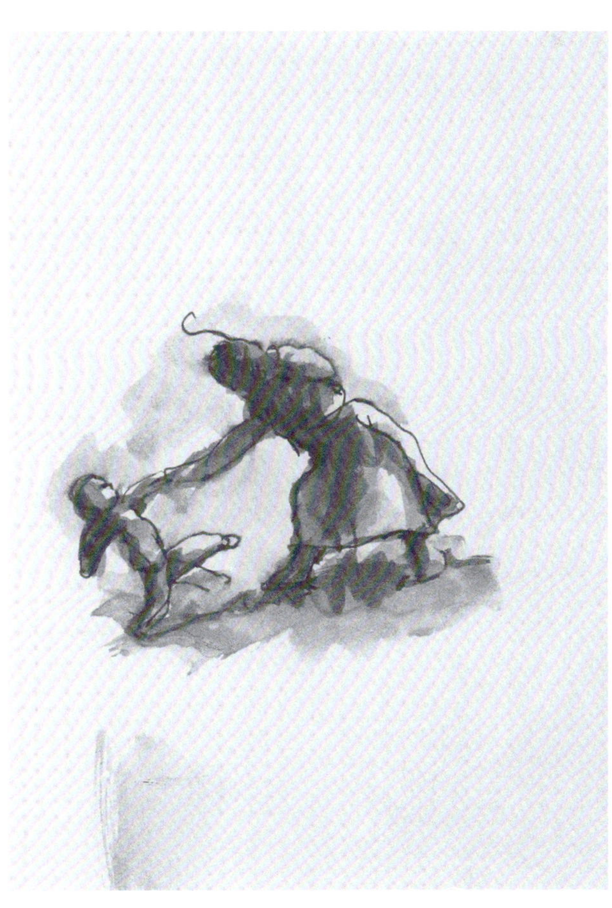

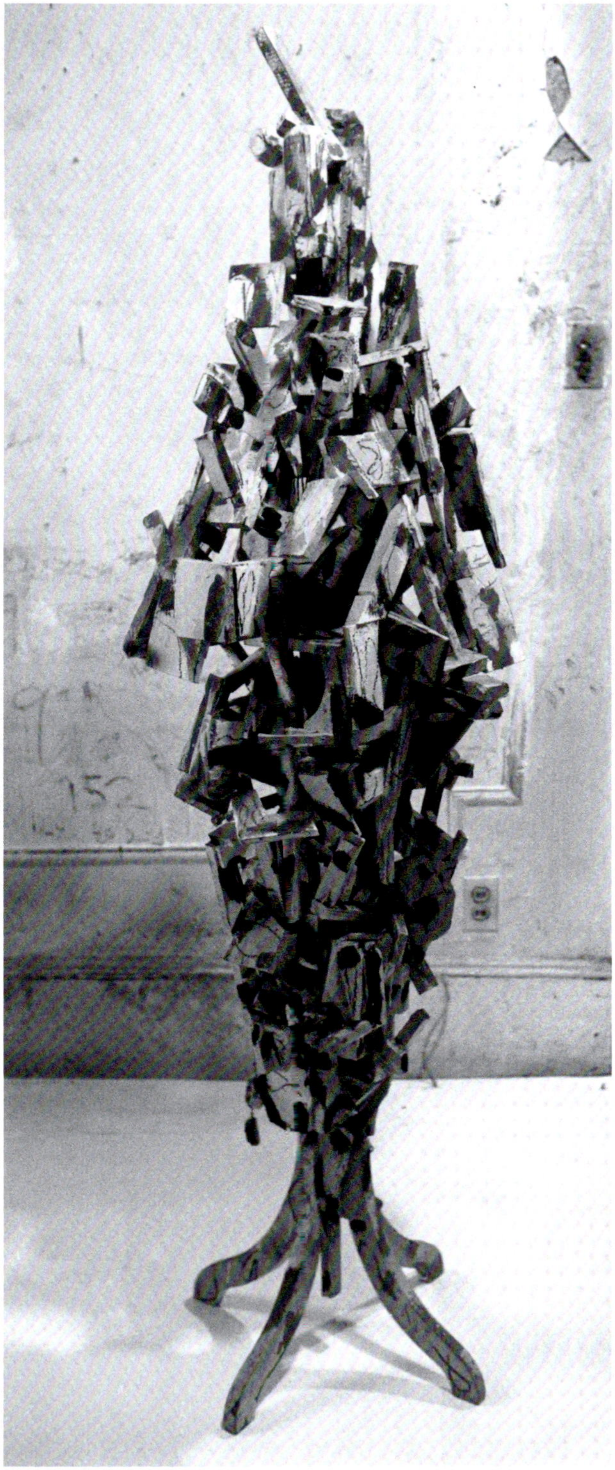

FIG. 1.27
Claes Oldenburg
*Street Event—Woman Beating Child*, 1958
Pen and watercolor, 7 ½ x 5 in. (19 x 13 cm)
Collection of the artist

FIG. 1.28
Claes Oldenburg
*Lady*, 1957
Wood on casein
Destroyed

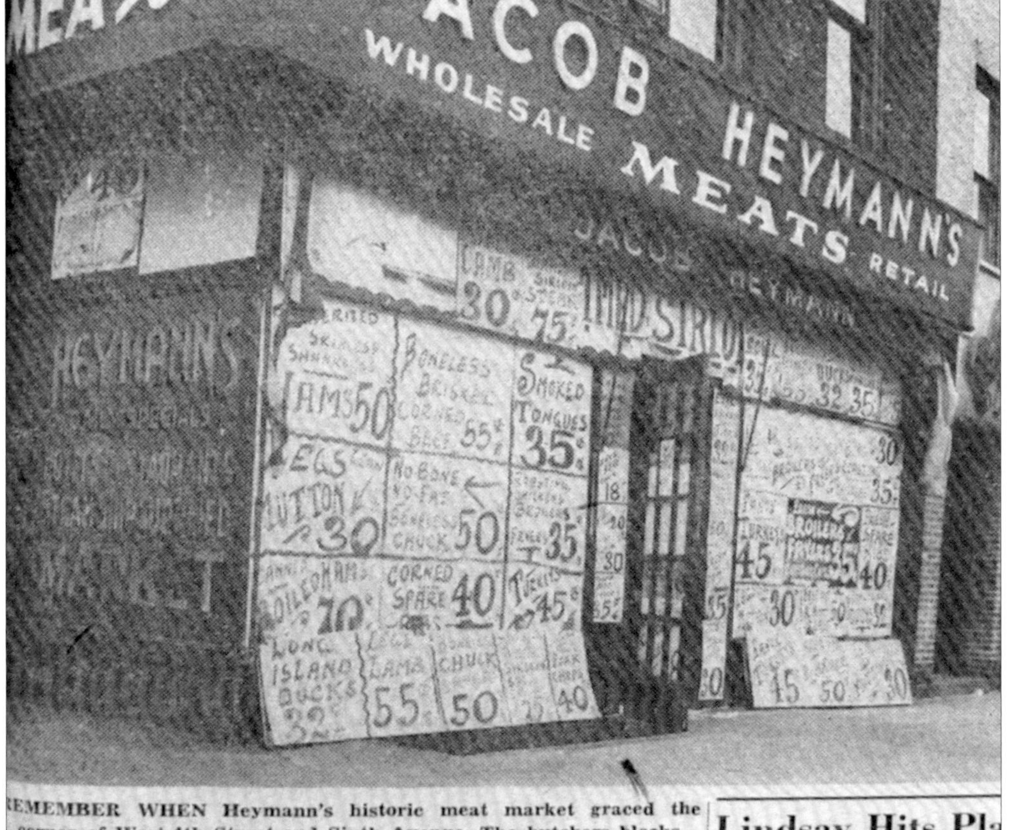


REMEMBER WHEN Heymann's historic meat market graced the corner of West 4th Street and Sixth Avenue. The butchers blocks and the uniforms remain, but the decor is different. The considerably more discreet sign on the window now reads: O. Henry's. The new restaurant, with/its turn-of-the-century elegance, was inspired in a modest way by its meat-dispensing predecessor.

Lindsay Hits Pla
To Switch Title
Property to NYl



"Art should literally be made of the ordinary world; its space should be our space; its time our time; its objects our ordinary objects."[86] *The Street* (think of the talking pair at the Judson, for example, or *Street Head III*) was meant to let in the world in two registers simultaneously: the pictorial and the material. Driven by twin imperatives to represent and to offer up untransformed ordinary matter, *The Street* was insistent both about picturing and about resisting that picturing with an excess of untidy, interpretation-resistant substance.[87]

The emphatic materiality of *The Street* (and the corollary cost to easy legibility) was not especially new in avant-garde art. Some thought it had been Pollock's defining feature. Dada, too, had gathered ordinary scraps in works that frustrated or deflected meanings. Jean Dubuffet, whose work Oldenburg discovered in 1959, had piled on extraordinarily thick impasto in his own primitivist, faux-naïf art.[88] What was particular to Oldenburg was his use of this emphatic materiality (and its resistance to legibility) to consider the nature of the urban environment. Oldenburg's materiality—in a complicated, even self-contradictory way—was marshaled against postwar renewal's aims of abstracting the city.

### The Street and the City

One day in the middle of *Ray Gun*'s run at the Judson, the *Village Voice* published a photograph of an old butcher shop (fig. 1.29). The caption read: "Remember when Heymann's historic meat market graced the corner of West 4th Street and Sixth Avenue. The butchers [sic] blocks and the uniforms remain, but the decor is different. The considerably more discreet sign on the window now reads: O. Henry's."[89] One in a periodic and informal series of front-page pictures about changes in the neighborhood (captions in the previous weeks included "Remembrance of Things Past," "The Walls are Tumbling Down," and, under the photograph of the lot slated for the extension of Washington Square Village, "What Next?"), this picture eulogized Heymann's vibrantly cacophonous and unruly signs. In the photograph, blaring numbers and letters cover the shop's every vertical surface, even plastering the door and reaching to the sidewalk. This kind of overloaded urban signage was becoming less fashionable at mid-century, in favor of a more efficient and ordered kind, the kind that would not deflect easy reading with too many material particularities to take in. (It was this change that J. B. Jackson, editor of *Landscape* magazine, lamented in a short commentary called "Signs of Life." Jackson defended "raucous billboards" over the ideal of "the discreet, non-hortatory sign . . . [the] whispered . . . neatly lettered 'Please!'")[90]

Also in the year of *Ray Gun* and the *Voice* photograph, Kevin Lynch, an MIT theorist of urban design, published his landmark study *The Image of the City*. Reporting on the accuracy of residents' mental maps of Boston, Jersey City, and Los Angeles, Lynch argued that cities were successful insofar as they lent themselves to strong mental images that could diminish unpleasant feelings of disorientation and chaos.[91] Three years later, the author led a graduate seminar with Donald Appleyard specifically about urban signage. The professors published the work of their students as a book called *Signs in the City*, which they introduced with a photograph of a too-chaotic Boston streetscape and a statement of their goal: to find ways to augment the "clarity, congruence, and visible meaning of the environment." One team of graduate students proposed legislation encouraging "food smells . . . during the lunch hour, flower smells at springtime," and went so far as to add, in earnest, "Pedestrians would be encouraged to display symbols of their occupation or affiliation."[92] Lynch, Appleyard, and their students were hardly apologists for postwar renewal, but they shared its conviction that the city had to be made less chaotic, more negotiable and legible as a whole.

All planning is of course a form of representation, an attempt to get the city to hew to an image of itself. Modernist planning in particular, however, is distinguished largely by its abstraction, its drive to make the entire city cohere as a single giant sign. Particularity is eliminated in favor of a hope that city dwellers (or at least planners, with their bird's-eye views) might be able to read the ordered system of the whole city all at once. (Consider Le Corbusier's city [see fig. 1.8] or the relative clarity of Washington Square Village in aerial photographs [fig. 1.30, at lower right], or the reduction of those 148 street addresses to the simply legible 4. The French art and architecture critic Françoise Choay rightly calls this kind of planning "monosemic."[93])

Although it may seem to us at first, then, that Lynch's seminar represents the limit case in the drive at mid-century for urban sense and order, it really occupied a middle position between the systematized legibility of the new city on the one hand, and the wild, material particularity of Heymann's signs (or of McReynolds's "crazy patchwork," or of Jacobs's "incongruous, . . . vulgar, [and] strange") on the other. In fact Jackson, defender of the raucous, even praised the Lynch and Appleyard book, because he saw it as an alternative to "the dream of many an urban reformer" of a "community without any signs at all."[94]

In exploring the connections between legibility in the city and legibility in art, *The Street*—at least as we look at it in retrospect—also helps us to understand why urban renewal was such a terrible failure.[95] The complexity of city life (its particularities, its disorder, even its nonsense) cannot be made to fit within a unified, abstract scheme of order. It is partly for this reason that single-style, high-rise public housing was dynamited in the 1990s (notably in Chicago and San Francisco) for more varied, low-rise developments. Nevertheless, it must also be remembered that *The Street* was not made simply as a polemic against the flow of the

Washington Square Park roadway or against the monosemic new construction projects. It certainly could not be said to be valorizing its image of the chaotic city, nor to be blaming its depravity wholly upon renewal. On the contrary, the dirt, violence, and poverty in *The Street* all beg for some ordering of chaos, just as the unruly cardboard and burlap beg for pictorial readings. In *The Street*, a dialectic always buzzes between the need for order, negotiability, and legibility (even the *inevitability* of them) and the material facts that seem always to escape or exceed them.

Oldenburg's *Street* was not so much a protest against the abstraction of the city as an insistence that no such effort could ever be entirely successful. It shows the city forever "los[ing] its sign character." Its insistence on disorder, blockage, and illegibility ought to be understood as an equivocal negation of a material environment apparently becoming ever more abstract. (We shall see very different but equally complicated representations of this situation in the chapters below.) The work responded to the growth of an ordered, negotiable, and legible system of exchange, which seemed more and more to be trumping the world of material particularities.

*The Street* both follows Jackson Pollock's refusal of legibility and also prefigures Oldenburg's own later fantasies of an obstructed city (fig. 1.31). It prefigures, too, the work of many artists who, in the subsequent decades, have groped for a way to understand, or even to imaginatively reinvent, the postmodern urban environment. Consider, for example, Gordon Matta-Clark's attraction to the uselessness of abandoned buildings, or Valie Export's hopeless search for a biologically appropriate city, or, indeed, Martha Rosler's attention to the loss of particularized places in service of networks of roadways.[96] The artistic practice most directly

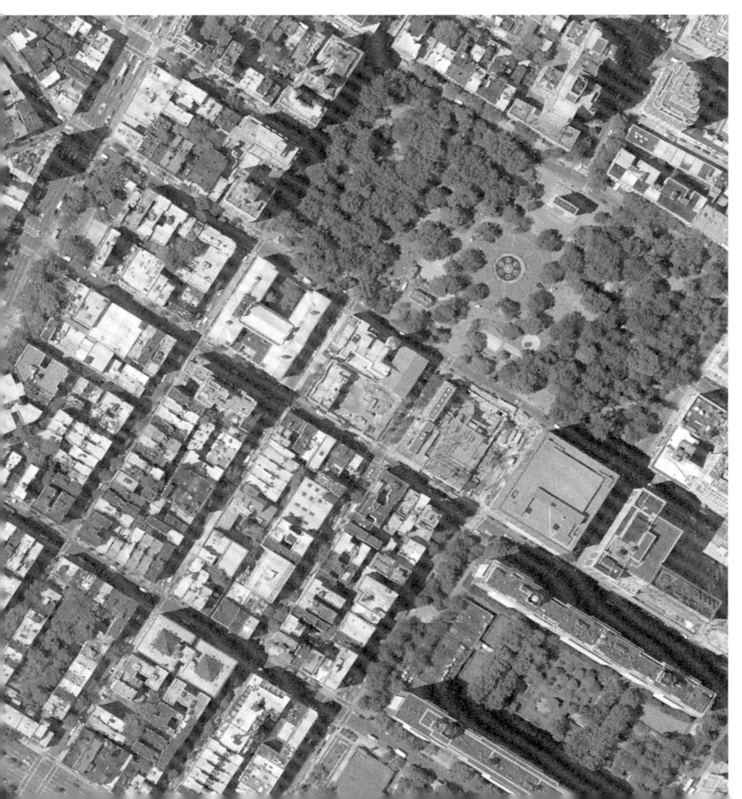

comparable to *The Street*, however, was probably the early
efforts of the Situationist International, at the end of the
1950s. Take, for example, Guy Debord's *Naked City* of 1957
(fig. 1.32), which presents, in the words of Tom McDonough,
a "fragmenting of the most popular map of Paris, the *Plan
de Paris*, into a state of near-illegibility."[97] This is an image of
micro-neighborhoods, torn free of the totality of their city.
The red arrows reconnecting them suggest a new system of
playful, illogical connections, ones that might exploit—rather than hide—the true fissures of the city. A text published
with *The Naked City* argued that it showed where a person
might go "in disregard of the useful connections that ordinarily govern his conduct."[98]

What the Situationists shared with Oldenburg was
an interest in the city as a place of possible blockage and
chaos, a place where instrumental flow might be slowed by
diverse particularities. Debord's associate Henri Lefebvre
described the city, in a similar understanding, as "the last
barrier" to a world of limitless exchange: "For two centuries
industrialization has been promoting commodities—which
although they pre-existed, were limited by agrarian and
urban structures. It has enabled the virtually unlimited
extension of exchange value. It has shown how merchandise
is not only a way of putting people in relation to each other,
but also a logic, a language, and a world. Commodities
have swept away barriers. And this process is not over: the
car, the current pilot-object in the world of commodities,
is overcoming this last barrier—the city."[99] In Lefebvre's
understanding, capitalist industrialization breaks down the
obstructions of the city, replacing them with an abstracted
universe of salability and exchange. The particularities of
the city had to be marshaled, to recast it as a place of utility
rather than alienation.

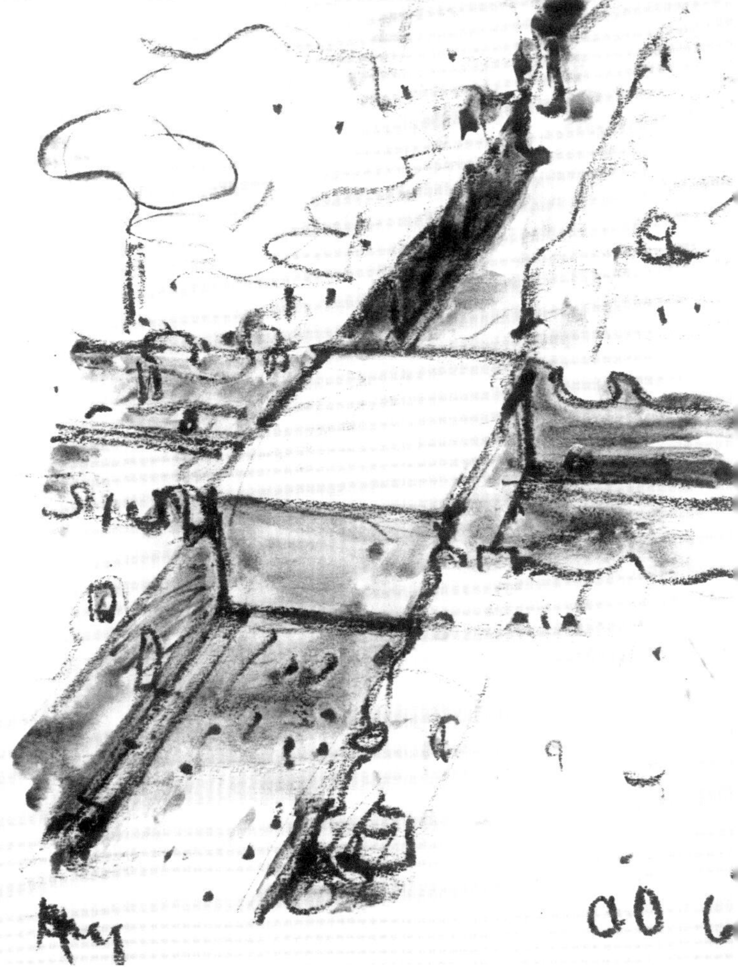

FIG. 1.31
**Claes Oldenburg**
*Proposed Monument for the
Intersection of Canal Street and
Broadway: Block of Concrete
Inscribed with the Names of
War Heroes*, 1965
Crayon and watercolor on paper,
19 x 12 in. (48 x 30.5 cm)
Private collection

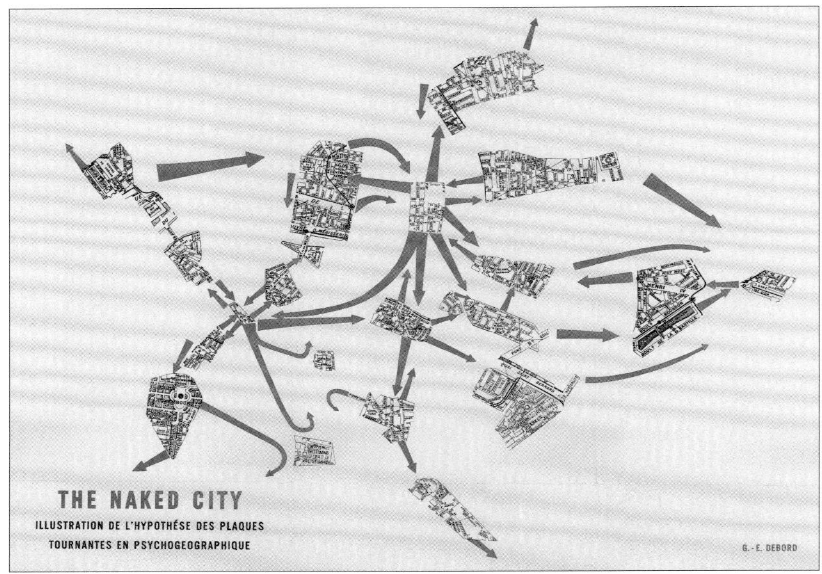



**FIG. 1.32**
**Guy Debord**
*The Naked City*, 1957
Screen print, 13 x 18 ½ in. (33 x 47.5 cm)
Rijksbureau voor Kunsthistorische
Documentatie

Certainly this is a powerful analogue to the thinking of *The Street.* The Situationists and Lefebvre, like Oldenburg, were highly conscious of the ways in which postwar renewal—prevalent in Paris as it was in New York—was transforming the city. In these French cases, as in Oldenburg's, the city was represented as a place of continuing particularity, of resistance to coherent, exchange-oriented abstraction. Oldenburg, however, was never properly a Marxist, and in contrast to Lefebvre's or Debord's thinking, *The Street* shows little interest or faith in retrieving the use value of the city. Instead Oldenburg, the American and the post–Abstract Expressionist, seems to have insisted only on the fundamental materiality of the city, its being first and foremost a set of (only partially abstractable) material facts.

*The Street* documents the changes in the city around it, lingering on the moment in which the effort to bring order and legibility to all that material chaos seemed to cause only more particularity and more chaos. This hyperbolic documentation suggests that the fight about the future of New York was fundamentally a fight about the limits and possibilities of abstracting the material city—of making it cohere in an ordered and flowing system. *The Street* at once begs for that impulse and insists that such an impulse must (and should) allow for the inherent disorder of material fact, for the inevitability of blockage and chaos. If Abstract Expressionism had been animated by doubt over the legibility or abstractability of matter (if, we might say, it had been a negative response to earlier modernists' quests for seamless representation), then Oldenburg brought that same doubt to bear on the urban terrain. In *The Street*, the planner's desire to systematize the city—like the modernist painter's desire to perfect representation—inevitably gives way, at least partially, to failure.

# 2 The Disappear-ance of Objects

JOHNS

IN 1959, JASPER JOHNS bought a cheap, spring-loaded window shade and affixed it to a large canvas. After pulling the paper down and tacking it in place, he painted the whole object—in stony black, gray, and white—with his newfound vocabulary of jagged starbursts, broad horizontals, and long drips (fig. 2.1). The result, which the artist straightforwardly titled *Shade*, was an evident nod to Abstract Expressionism and its materialist rejection of illusion. Note, for example, the large black form that monolithically dominates the left side of the work: it is applied heavily enough to help bind the shade to the canvas, foreclosing access to any three-dimensional world beyond. But note, also, the points at which the canvas and the shade are more subtly connected, as with the sharp (but lightly broken) horizontal line of black at lower right, or the folded line of white that just barely touches the shade's bottom edge. At these spots, the painting and the everyday object seem gingerly to borrow each other's flat materiality, both becoming ever more literal in the process.

Even more important to this effect of the picture is the delicate way in which the roll of the shade is painted so as to be at once continuous and discontinuous with the painting around it. At left, for example, one of the black starbursts beneath the roll creeps up onto it, while at right, a dripping white line is neatly tucked under the roll, without touching it. It is as if Johns wants us to see the petrified quality of this object both as something he applied only through dint of his own painterly will and also as a quality inherent to the shade, on the roll when he bought it and ready to be pulled out.

Like *Shade*, *Coat Hanger* (fig. 2.2) insists on a stolid materiality inherent both to paint and to common objects. Indeed these 1959 works thematize a muteness that had characterized all of Johns's paintings to date, including those exhibited at his iconically successful debut the year before: enigmatic works such as *Target with Four Faces* (fig. 2.3) and *White Flag* (fig. 2.4). These paintings quoted familiar symbols, and they were received warmly, but they also made critics grapple with their resistance to interpretation. Although John Ashbery, for example, called Johns the "hope of American painting" in 1962, it was because of the "strength of the ambiguity" in his works. Of the huge *White Flag*, Ashbery wrote, "It has tremendous—though silent—impact. It is *there*, though for what purpose it would be hard to say." Another avid fan of Johns's works, Fairfield Porter, also dwelled on their lack of clear meanings: "He looks for the first time, like a child, at things that have no meanings to the child, yet, or necessarily. . . . Johns' paintings compel your attentiveness: they bring you back to what art is in itself, before its meaning, before its usefulness." When others received the work less enthusiastically, it was sometimes also for reasons of their uncommunicative literalism. Stuart Preston, reviewing the first show for the *New York Times*, concluded simply: "All very puzzling."[1]

Starting with Leo Steinberg's 1962 article on the artist, the academic literature on Johns has been preoccupied with this reluctance to communicate.[2] Scholars have obsessively pondered the works' "refusal of meanings," their taciturn "tactile reality," and their "concealment of that which signifies."[3] In recent years, Fred Orton has understood the relative illegibility of Johns's work (the fact that "meaning is always veering off the surface") as an expression of the instability of contemporary identity, a critique of the modernist "originary 'I.'" Kenneth E. Silver and Jonathan D. Katz, meanwhile, have each understood Johns's shunning of communication as a representation of the necessity, for a gay artist in the period, of foreclosing access to the self.[4]

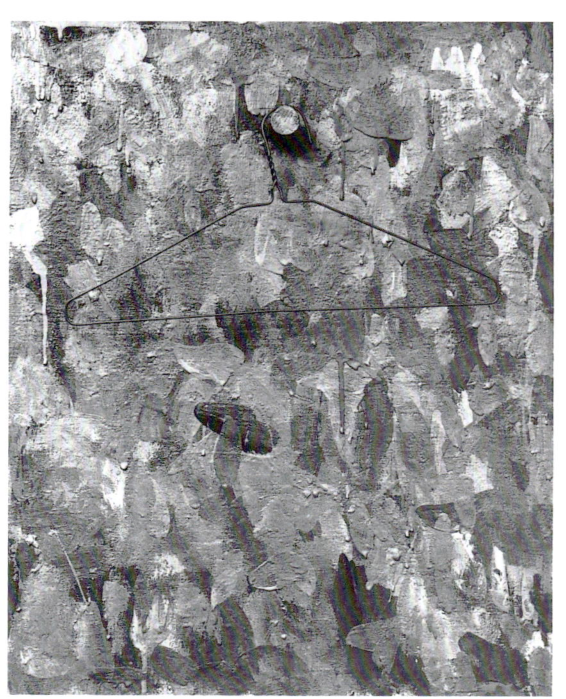

FIG. 2.2

**Jasper Johns**

*Coat Hanger*, 1959

Encaustic on canvas with objects, 27 ³/₄ x 21 ¹/₄ in.

(70.5 x 54 cm)

Private collection, Switzerland

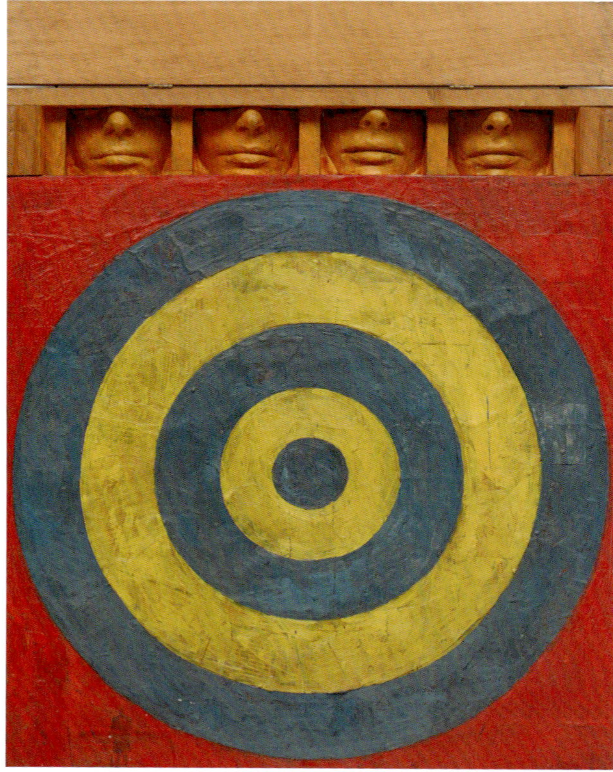

FIG. 2.3

**Jasper Johns**

*Target with Four Faces*, 1955

Encaustic on newspaper and collage on canvas with

objects, 26 x 26 in. (66 x 66 cm), surmounted by

four tinted plaster faces in wood box with hinged front,

overall, box open, 33 ⁹/₁₆ x 26 x 3 in. (85.3 x 66 x 7.6 cm),

box, closed, 3 ³/₄ x 26 x 3 ¹/₂ in. (9.5 x 66 x 8.9 cm)

Museum of Modern Art, New York, Gift of Mr. and

Mrs. Robert C. Scull

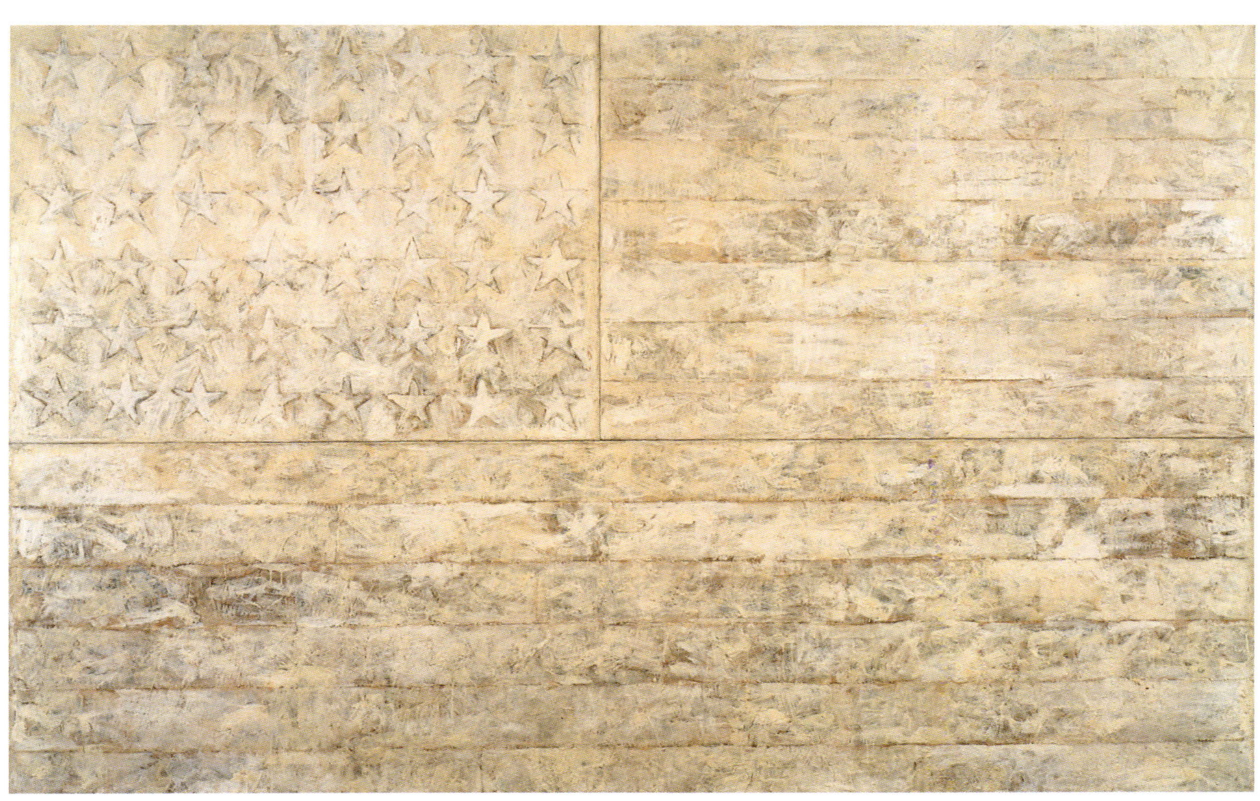

FIG. 2.4

**Jasper Johns**

*White Flag*, 1955

Encaustic, oil, newsprint, and charcoal on three
canvases, 78 ¼ x 120 ¾ in. (198.8 x 304.8 cm)
Metropolitan Museum of Art, New York

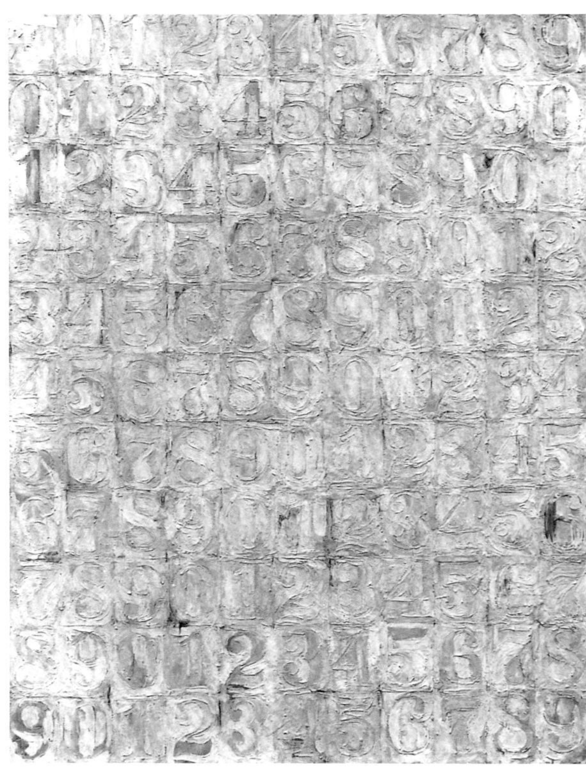



A primary aim of this chapter is to argue that Johns's early art had involvements more particular than the investigations of perception or subjectivity. It seems to me that the literature has ignored the specificity of Johns's subjects, seeing a deferral of meaning, but not looking at the objects whose meanings are deferred. Why, I want to ask, did Johns's resistance to representation take up the particular subjects and forms it did? Were flags, ale cans, and flashlights—Johns's hallmark subjects—simply chosen because they were impersonal and readily available in the visual culture, as almost all the literature on the artist has maintained?[5] And why were these subjects rendered in the labored and particular ways they were? A close look at this art in its historical context can serve to reveal its involvement in a broader concern over the state of the everyday material environment.

With an eye on the broader culture, then, this chapter asks what was at stake in these works' resistance to signification, and in the emphatic materiality that seemed always the source of that resistance. The chapter takes as its focus Johns's sculptures—a small body of essaylike objects in which these qualities of muteness and materiality were most intensively performed and worked through. It aims to understand the sculptures afresh by tracing for the first time their relationship to the dynamic and controversial context they were always addressing, at varying levels of explicitness: America's postwar consumer objects. To this end, the chapter follows the destabilization of those objects, and, especially, their apparent dematerialization. It argues for an understanding of Johns's works both as a resistance to that dematerialization and as an admission of the inevitability of the growing abstraction.

Before turning to look closely at Johns's work and the environment of its making, however, it bears mention that one art historian has tried, in quite a brief passage, to link the labored difficulty of signification in Johns's art to the historical condition of objects more generally. In his essay "The Passion of the Sign," Hal Foster views much of American art since 1955 as expressive of a postmodern crisis in signification, whereby (and he quotes Fredric Jameson here, whom he follows closely) "pure or literal signifiers are freed from the ballast of their signifieds, their former meanings."[6] Foster's quick mention of Johns, early in the essay, argues that the artist's beloved symbols (such as letters and numerals lined up in repetitive rows, fig. 2.5) are put on display without their signifieds. For Foster, this tendency in Johns (and in other artists working after him and Rauschenberg) is a symptom of our stage in the evolution of capitalism, at which all things are reduced to a single series of exchangeable signifiers. Johns's works, then, are metonymic representations of all the things in our world: exchangeable objects whose only meaning is their very exchangeability.

This passage is the best attempt we have so far to understand the historical embeddedness of Johns's art around 1960. Its generalizing approach, however, leaves the argument rather exaggerated. The notion of a postmodern condition in which signifieds are dropped in service of totalized exchangeability fails to account for the deep and real ways in which meanings (complicated, partial, and contradictory as they usually are) still very much accrue, unavoidably, to objects.[7] It is not that Johns's numbers *do not* mean (although they do not mean in the way that numbers in a price tag or a checkbook do); it's that what they *do* mean is not very clear. It should already seem obvious that they at least have meanings about representation itself.

## Johns as Sculptor

I feel that what I am doing is quite literal.

—JASPER JOHNS, C. 1960

What we see is precisely the thing in front of us.

—ANDREW FORGE, OF *PAINTED BRONZE (ALE CANS)*, 1964

In a fifty-year career as a painter, Johns has made sculptures very rarely. There are fewer than fifty such objects, treating no more than a dozen subjects. Most were produced in two spurts of activity early in his career, in 1958 and 1960. Nevertheless, Johns's sculptures are, as three magazines observed in 1964, among his best-known works.[8] Indeed, the sculptures have often been pressed into service as representations of Johns's oeuvre as a whole—in 1977, for example, the artist designed a poster for his Whitney Museum retrospective based chiefly on *Painted Bronze (Savarin)* (see fig. 2.28). Despite their special celebrity, however, the sculptures were not popular with critics early on. "Johns's bronze beer cans are pretty dumb objects," wrote Stuart Preston in the *New York Times,* "and his sculpture of a flashlight is a flashlight is a flashlight." Clement Greenberg—who was sympathetic to Johns's paintings—claimed that Johns's "'sculptures'" were "nothing more than what they really are: cast reproductions of man-made objects." *Time* magazine similarly dismissed *Painted Bronze (Ale Cans)* (see fig. 2.21) as "apparently just two Ballantine ale cans on a pedestal," and Fairfield Porter wrote of it in *Artnews*, "They do not seem to transcend the obvious reference. . . . A used beer can had a function but his casting has none."[9]

In these objections, critics seem to dislike Johns's sculptures for what might be termed their literalness, their apparent self-exhaustion in revealing their own identities as flashlights, lightbulbs, and beer cans. This complaint is a rather odd feature of the criticism, in view of the fact that it was something like this sort of literalism ("It is *there*, though for what purpose would be hard to say") that made the paintings seem so delightfully inscrutable. Indeed, Johns seems to have been intent on making sculptures for the very reason that they allowed him to hyperbolize the literalness he had been pursuing in painting. He remarked later to Grace Glueck, "The painting I was doing at the time had to do with certain literal qualities and that's what I wanted to do in sculpture."[10]

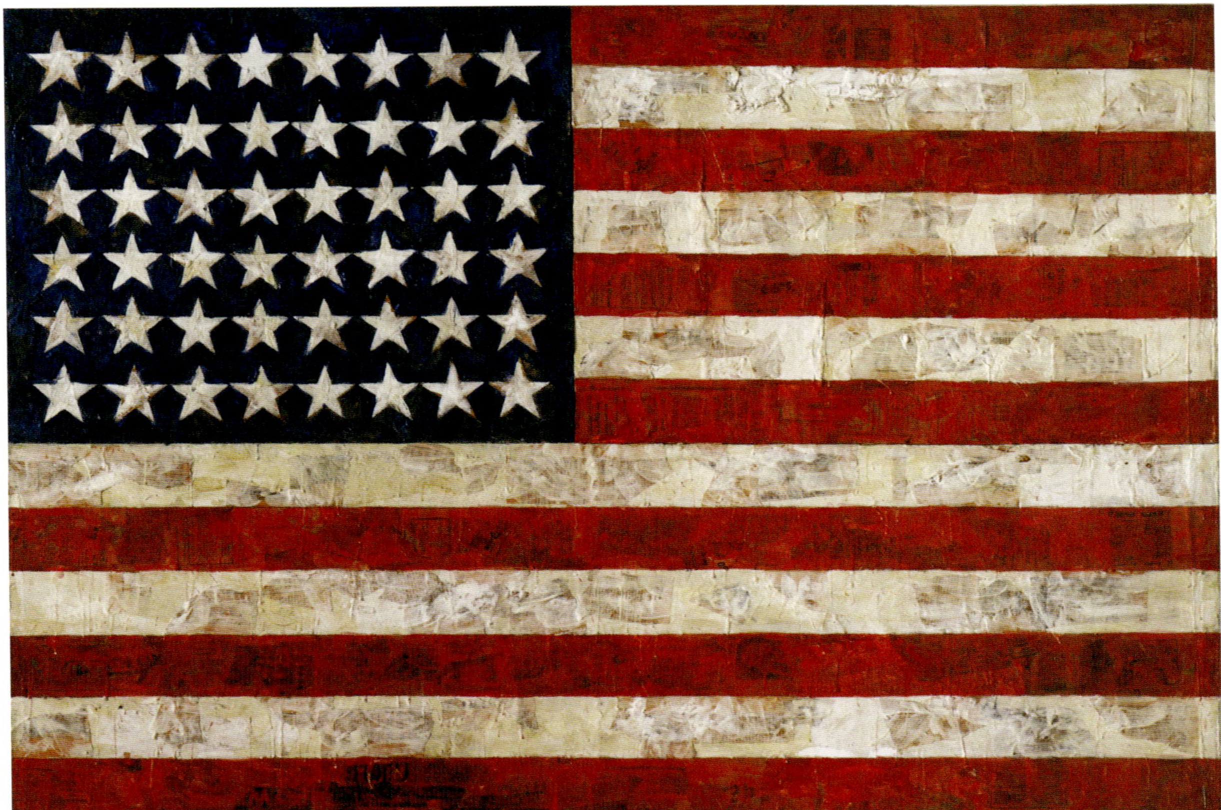

It is worth being careful about what we mean in characterizing Johns's art as literal. Johns has given hints about his intentions in several interviews. He remarked on one occasion, for example, "I personally would like to keep the painting in a state of 'shunning statement' . . . to leave the situation as a kind of actual thing." On another, the artist said, more elliptically, "I decided that looking at a painting should not require a special kind of focus like going to church. A picture ought to be looked at the same way you look at a radiator."[11] In these remarks, Johns suggests that, at least in the early years, art-making was for him a project of object creation—of making things, first and foremost, rather than making signs. This is why meanings are so problematic in Johns's art: in the place of representation (or in the place, we might more accurately say, of traditional metaphoric representation) Johns's art appears as a set of material facts. This is a rather complicated literalism, however, partly

because it operates through two mechanisms that seem to labor against each other. First, there is the process (as seen above) by which many of the works seem to signify nothing but their own identities: "his sculpture of a flashlight is a flashlight is a flashlight is a flashlight." Then there is the nearly contradictory process by which, rather than indulging the abstract act of signification (of referring, that is, to something itself not materially present), Johns's objects present themselves as material facts, particular things for which even names are unjustly abstract.[12] As much, for example, as *Flag* (fig. 2.6) is famously, literally a real flag (while seeming to represent one), it is also even less than that. It is so many dripping bits of cloth, dipped in pigmented wax. What these two processes have in common, however, is their resistance to abstraction, their producing art objects as a set of things.

**Jasper Johns**

*Flag*, 1954–55

Encaustic, oil, and collage on fabric mounted on three panels of plywood,

42 ¼ x 60 ⅝ in. (107.3 x 154 cm)

Museum of Modern Art, New York,

Gift of Philip Johnson in honor of Alfred H. Barr Jr.



The artist's first successful attempt at sculpture, *Light Bulb I* (fig. 2.7), is a dull gray object.[13] It is made in Sculp-Metal, a cheap compound synthesized from aluminum powder and plastics, and marketed to amateurs in the back pages of art magazines.[14] The resulting finish gives the object an indeterminate appearance, somewhere between that of metal and that of stone. Although the first impression is indeed of the sculpture's near-precise imitation of real lightbulbs, one soon becomes aware of the thing's infinite particularities. Notice, for example, the thin nicks across the bulb's threading, or the excess blotches of material speckling the crown. Notice, too, the hundreds of tiny holes throughout—actually the traces of air bubbles trapped as Johns layered on the Sculp-Metal, but looking exactly like tiny wormholes scattered across antique wood. Then there are the vague lines running along the length of the object (but especially apparent where the bulb begins to narrow); they subtly betray Johns's gentle application of the material by hand. Certainly it is a misshapen object, especially at the center of the bulb, where a soft dimple looks like a tiny spot crushed on a flower stem.[15]

The various effects of this sculpture are typically Johnsian ones. It is a mute object, coated in gray silence. In the place of any clear representational ends, it is literal, both about its identity as imitated lightbulb (fodder, we might even say, for Greenberg's "nothing more than what they really are") and, especially, about its own materiality. Look, for example, at the base; it is a wavy and lumpy mass, like a block of wet clay. It is large, too, more massive in fact than the bulb it was built to support. Indeed, the whole sculpture looks heavy enough that it might be taken for a colorless fossil, a prehistoric bulb stuck forever in its brick of monochrome mud.[16] It seems to speak of a fictive civilization, electrified but long lost.

And it is not just *Light Bulb I* that seems a fragment of an old civilization. Johns's early critics again and again made reference to the ancient qualities of his sculptures—a particularly striking fact when one considers the manifest modernity of their subjects: flashlights, lightbulbs, and beer cans. Harold Rosenberg, for example, simply called the sculptures "parodies of antique sculptural fragments." Irving Sandler colored the same observation very differently, writing of one of the lightbulb works, "It possesses the same sense of high art as a fragment of classical sculpture." Fairfield Porter, who, as we have seen, derided Johns's sculptures for failing to "transcend the obvious reference," nevertheless went on immediately to say that "they are often as deathly as the castings made from the holes in the lava and ash of Herculaneum and Pompeii." Andrew Forge similarly evoked antiquity and death alike in his characterization of the Painted Bronze works (see figs. 2.21, 2.28), declaring them to "have a dignity like that of certain Roman funeral portraits . . . [drawn] from death masks."[17]

I want to linger a bit on this characterization of the sculptures as deathly fragments sent down from antiquity. Fossils, casts from Pompeii, and classical sculpture fragments share a single paradox: they are small, synecdochical tokens of something now lost. Although they are themselves present, their value is in speaking for cultures or sets of objects that are absent. Perhaps it was this quality that Johns wanted to document, or to will into his art, when he wrote in his notebook, sometime around 1960, "An object that tells of the loss, destruction, disappearance of objects. Does not speak of itself. Tells of others."[18] Johns seems to have maintained the feeling for years that their "loss, destruction, [and] disappearance" constituted some kind of crisis for objects. As late as 1965, he remarked to David Sylvester: "I think the object itself is a somewhat dubious

FIG. 2.7
**Jasper Johns**
*Light Bulb I*, 1958
Sculp-Metal,
4 ¹/₂ x 6 ³/₄ x 4 ¹/₂ in. (11.4 x 17.1 x 11.4 cm)
Collection of the Museum of Contemporary Art
San Diego, Gift of Mrs. Jack M. Farris

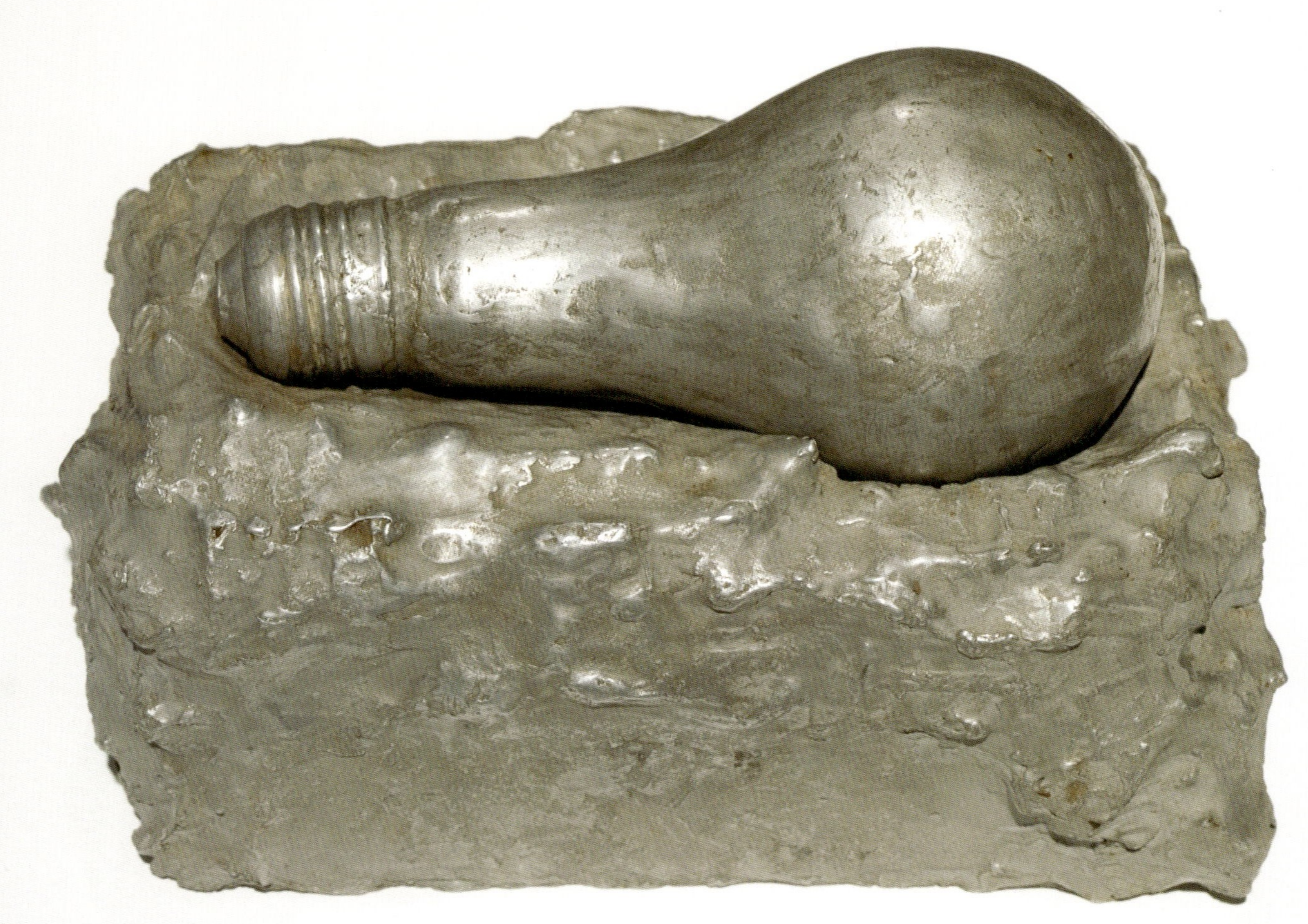

FIG. 2.8

Illustration by Edward Frascino
published with John A. Kouwenhoven,
"Waste Not, Have Not,"
*Harper's Magazine*, March 1959, 72

concept. . . . I think the object itself is perhaps in greater doubt than the illusion of an object. . . . I think one is now able to question the object itself, whether it has any real body or any real use—what we call reality, I guess." Johns appears to suggest in this remark that a doubt, in modernism, about the faith of representation has given way to a concern about the integrity of things themselves. In the same interview, he obliquely referred to this situation as a "tragedy."[19]

The ancient, fossil-like quality of *Light Bulb I,* then, may have something to do with some kind of loss the artist (and perhaps others) perceived in or around objects in the years around 1960.[20] Like a fossil or death mask, it may have been lamenting a reality lost, if a rather contemporary reality, and one only recently missing.

## The Discourse of Waste

The decade of the 1950s is the paradigmatic era of American consumerism, and not without reason. The bombast possible in the period was unrestrained, as one early example can remind us: "Automobiles, radios, television sets, washing machines and so many other wonderful things are pouring off our production lines by the thousands—daily. Never before in the history of the world have so many labor-saving, time-saving, miracle-working devices been made for the comfort and convenience of any people. . . . Our American system is the best, the most thrilling, ever devised."[21] It was in the 1950s that the president of the United States teamed up with Detroit to launch a "You 'Auto' Buy" campaign. Consumption was often promoted as an obligation to country: one slogan exhorted, "Buy, buy, buy; it's your patriotic duty," and even *Harper's Magazine* ran an article in 1959 that telegraphed its argument in its title: "Waste Not, Have Not" (fig. 2.8).[22] After America's cold-war disappoint-

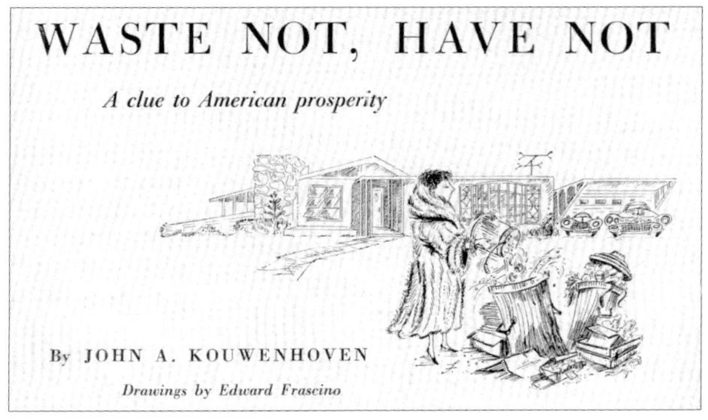


ment at the success of *Sputnik*, the proliferation of consumer goods in the United States was cited as a major point of American superiority over the Soviet Union. In 1959 Vice President Nixon debated Soviet leaders in both New York and Moscow (the confrontation in Russia famously came to be called the "kitchen debate"), citing on both occasions America's advantage in the production and consumption of consumer products.[23] Indeed, the consumption of goods was so central to American discourse in the 1950s that one popular book, David Potter's *People of Plenty,* went so far as to name material abundance as the defining quality of the "American character."[24]

Americans were in fact consuming more than ever. According to a government report, per capita consumption expenditures in 1960 were nearly 150 percent of what they had been just twenty years before, even after adjusting for inflation.[25] Other sources reported even more startling figures. Two best-selling books about American consumerism indicated that the average American had, by the middle of the 1950s, "five times as many discretionary dollars as he had in 1940," and that consumption had doubled since just before World War II.[26] In 1956, *Fortune* magazine reviewed the situation as follows, in an article called simply "What a Country!": "In the exhilarating process of exchanging cash (or a signature) for goods and services, [Americans] even seem to be laying to rest, at least temporarily, the twin spectres of 'saturation' and 'oversaving.' The electric iron market, for example, has been more than 90 per cent 'saturated' for over twenty-five years, but Americans go right on buying more electric irons than any frugally calculated replacement table would justify." In a section called "Through the Roof with Appliances," the *Fortune* article credited recent marketing tactics for the boom. "Appliance manufacturers and retailers," it concluded, were "the heroes of this success story."[27]

A writer profiling Jasper Johns for the German magazine *Das Kunstwerk* noted the artist's (inevitable) immersion in this environment of money and material acquisition: "Jasper Johns paints in a studio near the waterfront. . . . But just as close is the metropolitan turmoil of the Money world, drugstores, shops, restaurants and the lunch hour rush and the masses of the office employees streaming out of giant buildings into the canyons of the streets. During the lunch interval all those people are buying 'things' in the thousands of shops. Things everywhere! Merchandise everywhere! Money everywhere! All that Jasper Johns sees intensively. . . . To the found 'things' he tries to give an artistic reality."[28]

If Johns's stance toward his country's increasingly purchase-driven economy was a contemplative one, he was not alone; the 1950s produced a surfeit of critical reflections. David Riesman, author of *The Lonely Crowd*, criticized and lampooned the new consumerism throughout the decade; his essay "The Nylon War," for example, exposed a fictional "Operation Abundance," through which the U.S. military

was dropping excess watches, curling kits, and washing machines into the USSR. Vance Packard published three best-selling critiques of consumerism at the end of the 1950s: *The Hidden Persuaders* (1957), *The Status Seekers* (1959), and *The Waste Makers* (1960). And John Kenneth Galbraith's *Affluent Society,* published in 1958, attacked the widely held notion that consumption was the best support of a healthy economy. It criticized America's excessive attention to private needs, at the expense of public ones, and singled out advertising as a product of decadence and a spur of unnecessary desire.[29]

Indeed it was advertising that grabbed the focus of this crop of writing on consumerism in the 1950s, and with good reason. The new consumption was buoyed largely by an explosive growth in the industry: through most of the 1950s, in fact, advertising revenue grew at a rate far outstripping that of the GNP.[30] Between 1950 and 1956, American expenditures on advertising rose 75 percent, and by the end of the decade, advertisers were spending roughly six times what they had in 1939, for a total of about $12 billion annually.[31] Americans became curiously fascinated by the techniques of advertising and the people who practiced them, even as they were buying. Following the success of Frederic Wakeman's 1946 novel *The Hucksters* (which Hollywood offered in filmic version the next year), American publishers brought out no fewer than forty-three fictional books concerning advertising in the 1950s.[32] John G. Schneider's *The Golden Kazoo* (1956) and George Panetta's *Viva Madison Avenue* (1957) were among the most popular. Meanwhile, nonfiction accounts of the advertising industry also flourished, including Martin Mayer's *Madison Avenue, U.S.A.* (1958), James Playstead Wood's sympathetic *Story of Advertising* (1958), and Walter Goodman's critique, *The Clowns of Commerce* (1957).

The fascination with advertising did not lie solely in its increasing prominence. Advertising—along with its correlate, industrial design—was changing, developing new techniques to stimulate still further buying. Most conspicuous at the end of the decade were two strategies that were having visible effects on consumer goods themselves: first, a rise in the disposability of products, and, second, a new frequency of redesign.[33] Together, these changes aimed to stimulate consumption by encouraging waste—old products would be thrown away and new ones purchased to replace them. Many of the consumer critics were particularly troubled by this development, but none more conspicuously than Vance Packard, whose 1960 volume *The Waste Makers* was explicitly devoted to the topic.

The book's fifth chapter, satirically called "Progress through the Throwaway Spirit," characterized the period as "the disposable era"—an epoch epitomized by the success of the Standard Packaging company, which, Packard pointed out,

> tripled its sales in four years to become a hundred-million-dollar corporation. This company makes trays that can be cooked, bags that can be boiled, bowls and other eating utensils that can be discarded to eliminate dishwashing. Its hard-running young boss, R. Carl ("Hap") Chandler, explained happily: "Everything that we make is thrown away." *Sales Management* sought to analyze the secrets of StanPak's phenomenal success. One of its headlines offered this clue: "Stan-Pak's Research Exploits Laziness." It went on to explain that as the company conceived the future, "Tomorrow, more than ever, our life will be 'disposable.'"

Packard's other examples of needless waste included such developments as breakable plastic toys, the now-familiar disposable razor, and even "steaks and other meats . . . in disposable aluminum frying pans. When the steak is done,

just throw away the pan along with the nasty old grease." He also cited a 1960 television advertisement for a deodorant pad, in which a voice chanted, "You use it once and throw it away. . . . You use it once and throw it away."[34]

Packard focused not only on disposability but also the other of the newly dominant waste-inducing techniques, redesign. One cause of this development was the demise of the sales clerk, as Joseph J. Seldin, an advertising executive and critic of the industry, pointed out: "As the retail sales clerk began to follow the cracker barrel, the butter tub, and the sugar bag into oblivion, the package began to emerge as a dominant, and sometimes only, selling force in the store. Whereas the prewar package was considered to be nothing much more than the carrier for the product, to the postwar package was entrusted the vital mission of charming the housewife into buying." Indeed, a study conducted by the Better Packaging Advisory Council in the late 1950s found that more than half of the 1,200 advertisers surveyed were then undergoing a change in package design.[35] If it was spurred in part by the need to grab consumers' attention, however, Packard pointed out that redesign, at least when turned on products themselves, was also a means to hasten obsolescence. Packard called the strategy "planned obsolescence of desirability," asserting also that "the recent fascination of many businessmen with 'planned obsolescence' has been one of the major developments of the postwar period."[36]

Packard indicated that gratuitous redesign was learned from the fashion industry, pointing out that automobile designers had been raising and dropping tail fins like hemlines. Kitchen appliances, too, were being made alternately blocky and (pointlessly) aerodynamic: "In 1960, Consumer Reports quoted a Westinghouse official on the need of a 'new look' every year in order to assist sales. Complete redesign each year, he said, would be too costly. 'But changes only in decorative trim will satisfy the dealer, please the customer, and effectively "obsolete" the previous year's model.' "[37]

This phenomenon of product redesign did not escape the attention of Jasper Johns, who associated it even with recent changes in the American flag (of which more later) during a 1965 interview with David Sylvester:

> And one also thinks of things as having a certain quality, and in time these qualities change. The flag for instance: one thinks it has forty-eight stars and suddenly it has fifty stars; it is no longer of any great interest. The Coke bottle which seemed like a most ordinary, untransformable object in our society, suddenly some years ago appeared quart-sized: the small bottle had been enlarged to make a very large bottle which looked most peculiar except the top of the bottle remained the same size—they used the same cap on it. The flashlight: I had a particular idea in my mind what a flashlight looked like—I hadn't really handled a flashlight since, I guess, I was a child—and I had this image of a flashlight in my head, and I wanted to go and buy one as a model [for the flashlight sculptures]. I looked for a week for what I thought looked like an ordinary flashlight, and I found all kinds of flashlights with red plastic shields, wings on the sides, all kinds of things, and I finally found the one I wanted. And it made me very suspect of my idea, because it was so difficult to find this thing that I had thought was so common. And about that old ale can which I thought was very standard and unchanging, not very long ago they changed the design of that.[38]

In this remark, Johns directly associates the redesign of consumer goods with the series of sculptures he was working on at the end of the 1950s. He names no fewer than three subjects of his own sculpture (the flag, the flashlight, the ale can) in addition to the Coke bottle, a staple in the work of his partner, Robert Rauschenberg. In particular, Johns suggests he was drawn to the older versions of things—the

new flag is "no longer of any great interest"; he looked long and hard for a flashlight like the ones from his childhood. Although he claims the changes made him "very suspect of my idea," it is apparent that he found the changes worthy of interest. His motivations for making his sculptures—far from clear in this remark—seem to have been riven with contradiction.

*Flashlight I* (fig. 2.9) is almost a readymade. It is the size and shape of an ordinary flashlight, plainly supported by thin wires over the most basic of pedestals. A simple drawing preceded it (fig. 2.10), and although the artist directed himself in the sketch to make the object in bronze or papier-mâché, this first flashlight sculpture was made in fact from a store-bought flashlight and a block of wood, carefully coated in Sculp-Metal. For all its verisimilitude, the object's surface is oddly unlike that of real flashlights: all nicks and blobs and pockmarks. In places, the grooves of the lined body are quite clearly defined, even through the layered material, but in others—look, for example, at the passage extending back from beneath the switch mechanism— the Sculp-Metal is thicker, filling the lines as if with soil or corrosion. Note especially the fine threading along the head: most of it is treated quite clearly, but one section is obscured completely by a prominent gob of Sculp-Metal. It is difficult to imagine working the flashlight, as the switch's button and slide lock look frozen in the thick, metallic patina that has built here into another gob. Indeed, the whole look of *Flashlight I* is again that of an ancient archaeological object, one preserved for the visitor to the dusty back wings of a fictive natural-history museum. It appears as if forged naturally, grown and crystallized in rock. Or perhaps these divots and blurry passages are just the marks of wear, the traces of imagined centuries of use and corrosion since this flashlight tumbled off some ancient assembly line.

FIG. 2.9

**Jasper Johns**

*Flashlight I*, 1958

Sculp-Metal over flashlight and wood,

5 ¼ x 9 ⅛ x 3 ⅞ in. (13 x 23 x 10 cm)

Sonnabend Collection

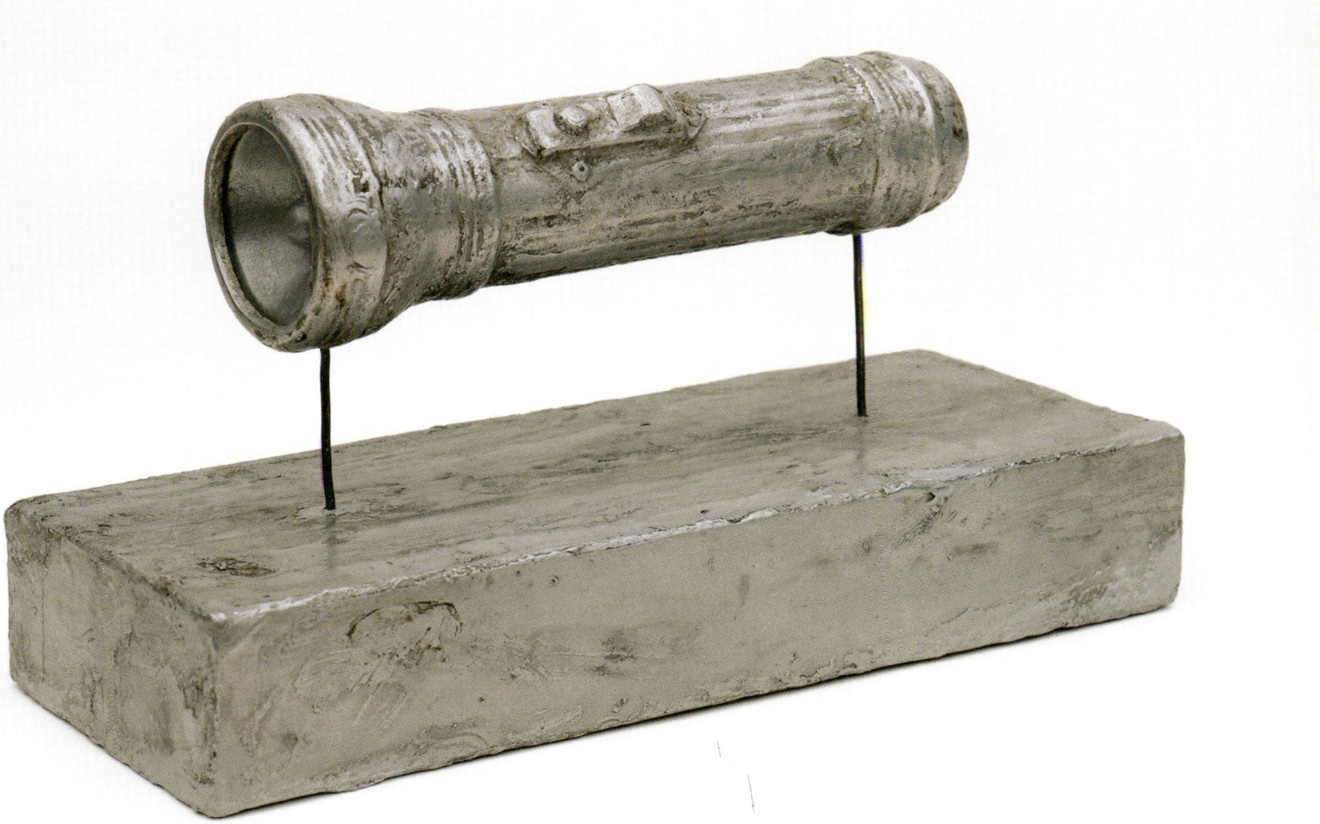

FIG. 2.10

**Jasper Johns**

Sketch for flashlight sculptures, 1958

Pencil on envelope, 4 ¼ x 9 ½ in. (11 x 24 cm)

Sonnabend Collection

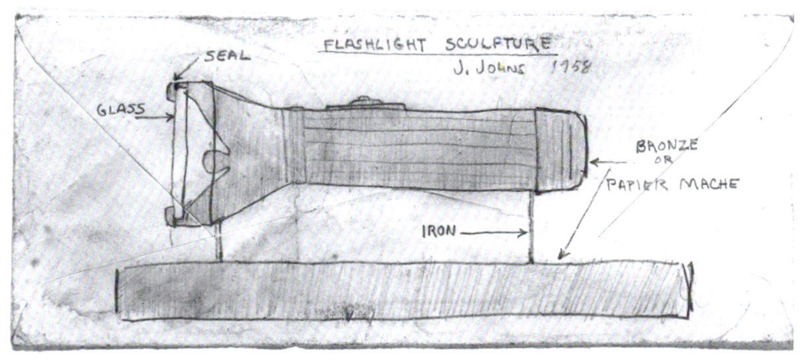

64

Johns's remark to Sylvester about flashlights offers some help in understanding this sculpture's pretensions to age and nature. Consider again the artist's recollection of his specific mental image: "I had a particular idea in my mind what a flashlight looked like—I hadn't really handled a flashlight since, I guess, I was a child—and I had this image of a flashlight in my head." Indeed, the flashlight encased in this sculpture, like the one in the sketch, was a generic, even classic type (and one that Johns repeated exactly in his three other renderings of this subject). Similar models had been produced by a variety of manufacturers starting in Johns's Depression-era childhood (fig. 2.11). For this reason, it is difficult to identify beyond doubt the specific model that Johns, in his hardware-store search, actually settled on. However, a careful look through the models available at mid-century reveals that Johns's choice was almost certainly a Usalite (fig. 2.12): note the curves around its rivet-mounted switch mechanism, its tapered body, and its thin fluting.[39] These particularizations, however, are subtle. What is remarkable about Johns's choice—it is free of any brand name or logo—is the very fact of its generic appearance.

It might seem strange, then, that Johns also remarked that this model was "so difficult to find" that he had to search for a week to get it. But the appearance of flashlights had indeed changed radically in just the three or four years previous to Johns's decision to make this sculpture. Plastics were becoming much more prevalent, and the old metal models were being replaced by a new crop of designs with red lens housings that, purportedly for road safety, allowed the lights to be seen glowing from the side.

A look at the flashlights offered in Sears, Roebuck and Co. catalogues in the 1950s can serve as an index of the changes. In 1950, all the flashlights offered in the catalogue

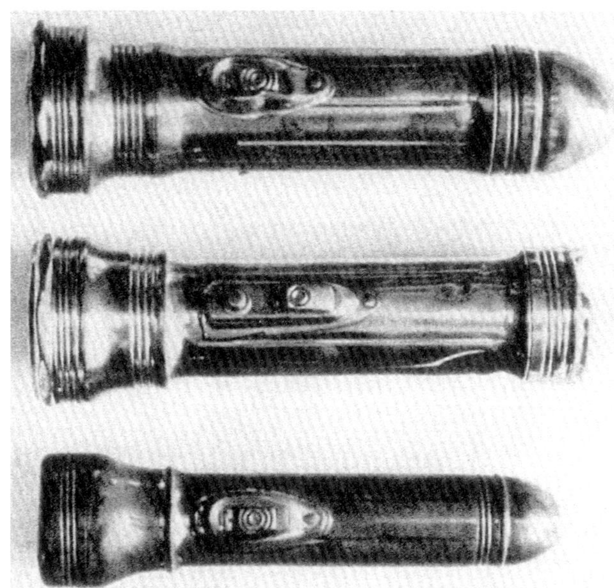

FIG. 2.11

Three Winchester flashlights, c. 1930

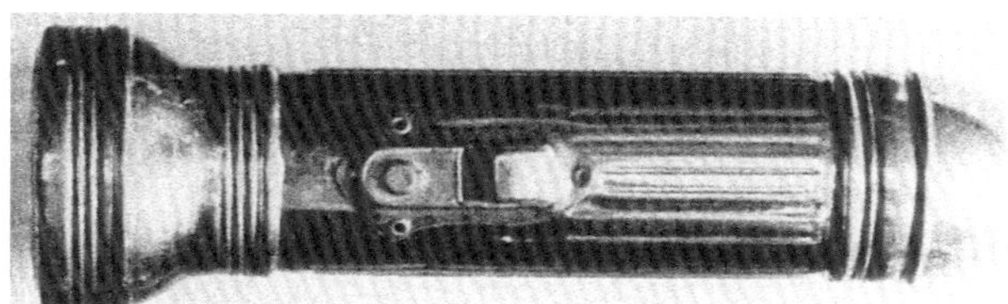

FIG. 2.12

Usalite aluminum flashlight, 1954

were made entirely of metal. They were advertised with such phrases as "solid brass" and "copper-plated steel case" (fig. 2.13). In 1955, one new model was available with a glowing red lens casing, and as soon as two years later most Sears models had "red plastic lens rings" and the group was described as the "most feature-packed we've ever offered!" (fig. 2.14). By early 1961, the classic kind was only one of a new diversity of designs, including several models made largely of plastic (fig. 2.15).[40] The plastic caps were common enough (and new enough) in 1959 that a hardware-industry periodical ran a cartoon showing a burglar at a store counter complaining, "I want one without the red signal you can see for a mile!" (fig. 2.16).[41]

FIG. 2.13 (right)
Flashlights from Sears,
Roebuck & Co. catalogue,
Philadelphia ed., Spring–
Summer 1950, 997A

FIG. 2.14 (below, top)
Flashlights from Sears,
Roebuck & Co. catalogue,
Philadelphia ed., Spring–
Summer 1957, 1053

FIG. 2.15 (below, bottom)
Flashlights from Sears,
Roebuck & Co. catalogue,
library ed., 1961, 1411

FIG. 2.16 (below right)
Boserman cartoon
from *Hardware Age*,
26 February 1959, 98

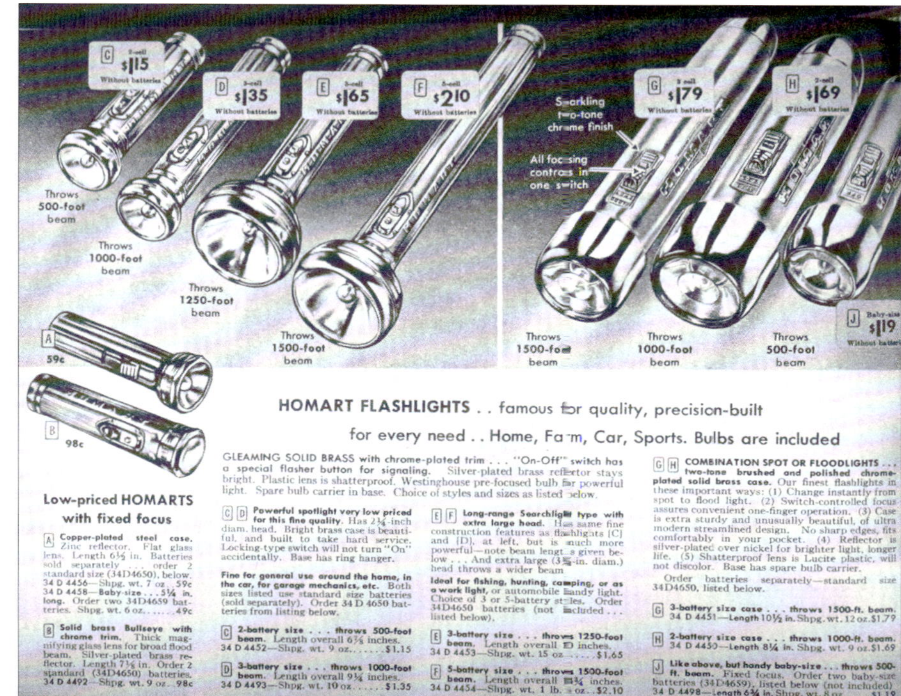


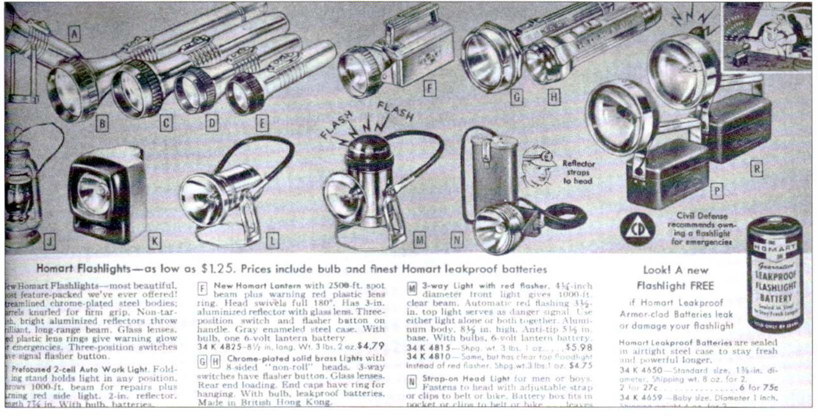


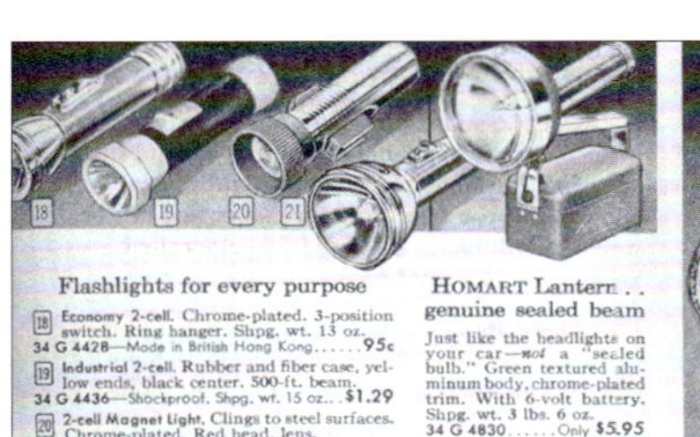


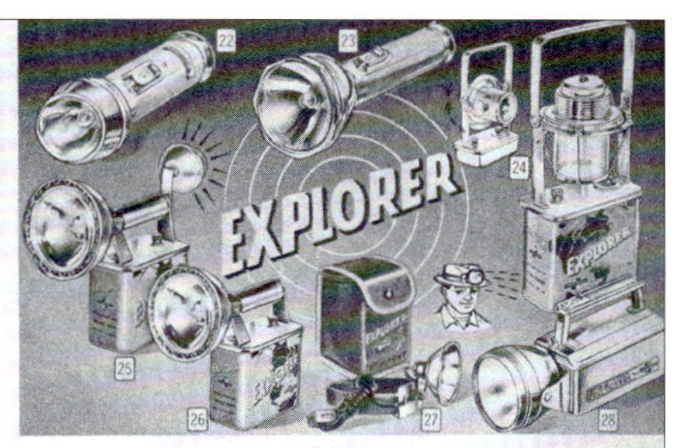


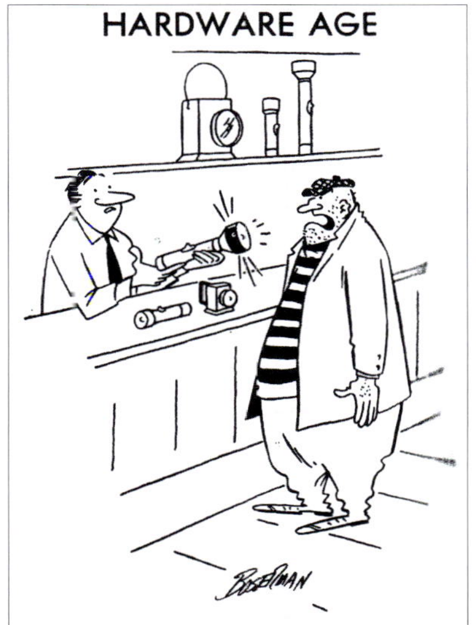

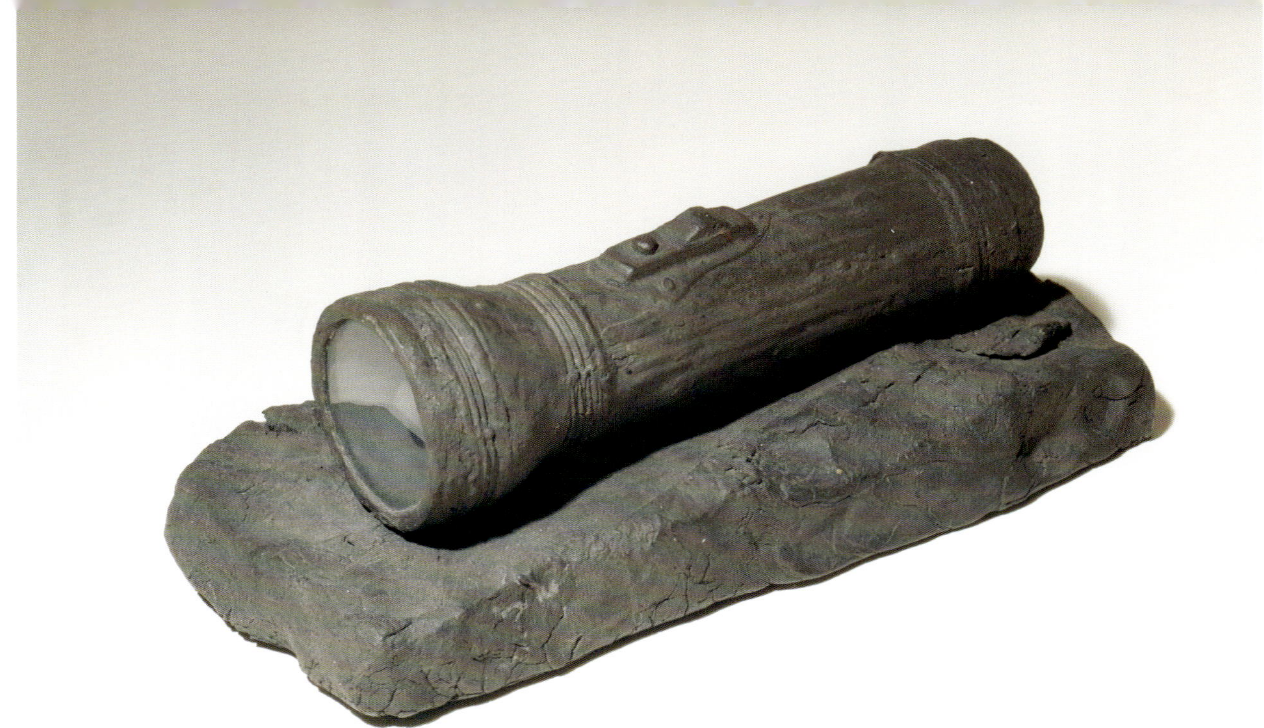

It is nearly impossible to imagine Johns sculpting a plastic flashlight, and it is no mistake that he did not. Everything in *Flashlight I* is driven toward the (hyperbolized) antiquity of the object, its almost natural inevitability or givenness. In building it up from the classic Usalite flashlight, Johns made this sculpture into a form of consumer object far more stable and traditional (if only imaginatively so) than even the outmoded flashlight inside it. However fruitlessly, each speckle of fictive rust or petrifaction speaks against the contemporary consumer environment of novel appearances and hasty expedience. Indeed, Johns's next two tries at this subject, also undertaken in 1958, seem only to assert more insistently the rhetoric of fossil-like age and material solidity. Look at the earthy cracking of the (now contiguous) base of *Flashlight II*, his papier-mâché version (fig. 2.17). Note the increased blobbiness of its body, as well as the overlapping and beautifully particular seams of Johns's efforts, where he combed lines in to describe the threading around the head. *Flashlight III,* made in plaster, is the most archaeological of all (fig. 2.18). The base (in fact a complicated structure made of various parts and strength-ened with coat hanger wire) has been built up to cradle the flashlight, and the oil rubbed over the surface has made this unified object appear less metallic than its predecessors and more like stone.[42]

Johns says that he spent a week combing hardware stores to find a flashlight for his sculptures. While not them-selves yet difficult to find, hardware stores were, like the metal flashlights within them, rapidly disappearing from Manhattan in the 1950s. The exodus of industry from the borough, together with the continued suburbanization of shopping, caused Manhattan to lose a net total of 161 hardware businesses (including wholesalers and manufacturers) between 1950 and 1961, a decline of 22 percent. In the district where the artist was living, below Canal Street, the hardware industry was especially hard hit, losing perhaps a third of its businesses.[43] Among those shuttered in the 1950s were two stores within three blocks of the artist's home on Front Street and a renowned store nearby—its passage lamented by the *New York Times* as "the ending of another New York retail institution" (fig. 2.19)—which had operated for over a century on Park Row.[44]

FIG. 2.17

**Jasper Johns**

*Flashlight II*, 1958

Papier-mâché and glass,

4 x 8 ¾ x 3 in. (10.2 x 22.2 x 7.6 cm)

Rauschenberg collection

FIG. 2.18

**Jasper Johns**

*Flashlight III*, 1958

Plaster and glass,

5 ¼ x 8 ¼ x 3 ¾ in. (13.3 x 21 x 9.5 cm)

Collection of the artist

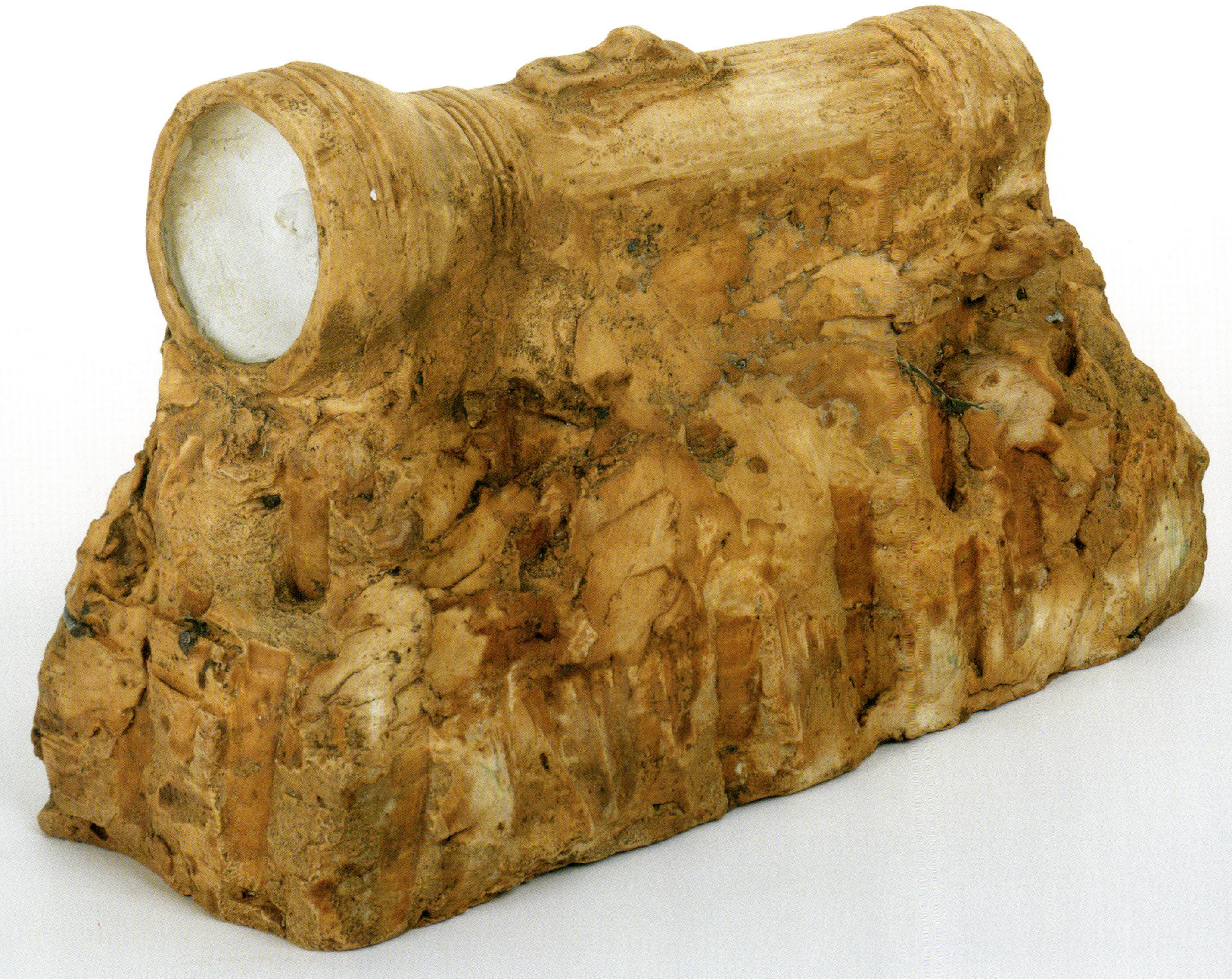

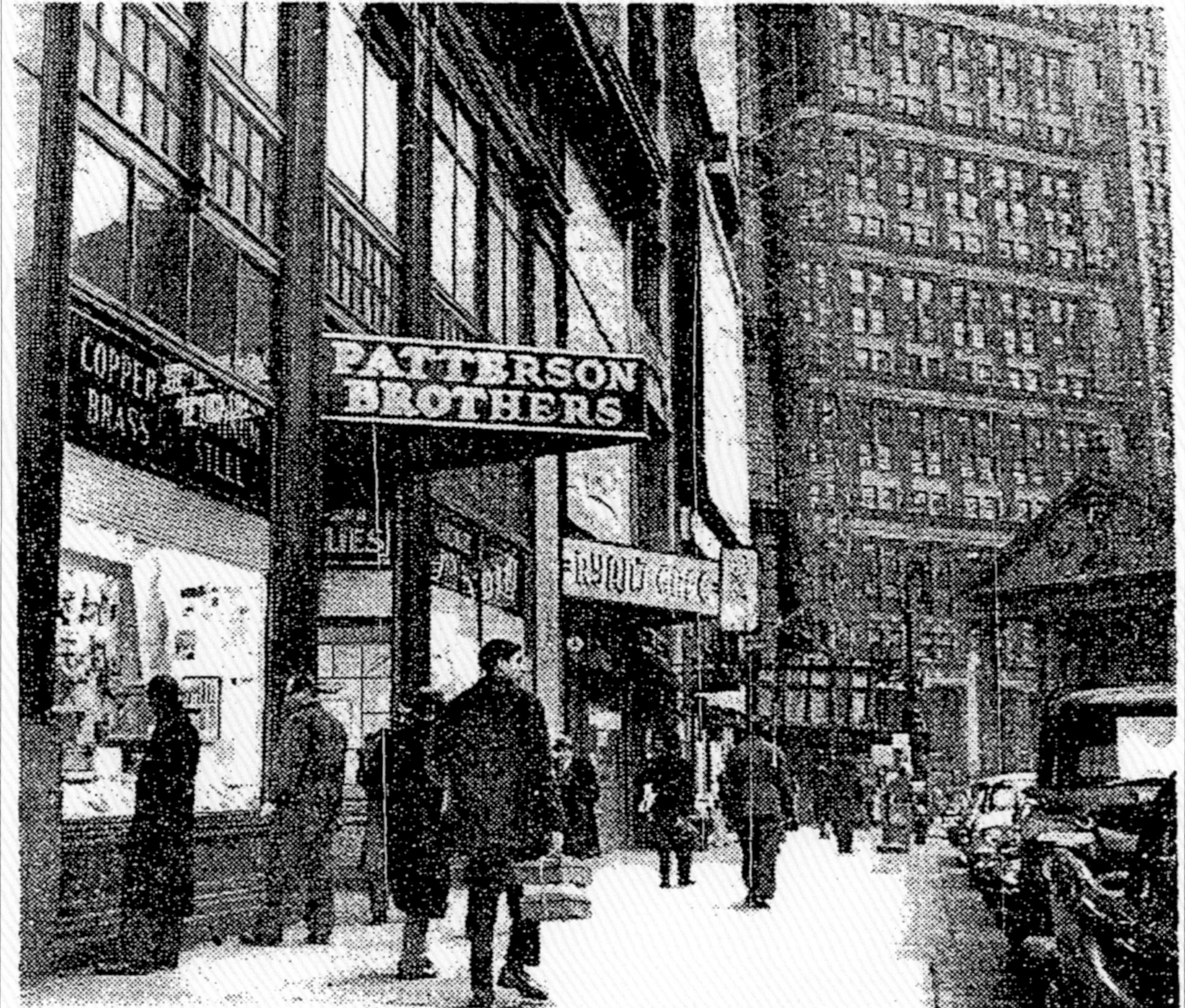


This Patterson Brothers hardware store has been at 15 Park Row since 1938. Original store was established on the Bowery in 1848 and moved to 27 Park Row ten years later.

These declines in Manhattan transpired even as the number of hardware stores nationwide was blossoming; according to one report, the United States had fully 20 percent more hardware stores in 1960 than it had had in 1940.[45] It is no surprise, then, that the New York metropolitan hardware business was becoming increasingly concentrated in the suburbs and outer boroughs. (The percentage of hardware listings in the *Manhattan Yellow Pages* for businesses outside the borough more than doubled between 1950 and 1961, to a total of 11 percent, with some firms by then included from as far away as Bridgeport, Connecticut, and Watervliet, New York.[46])

In 1956, *Fortune* ran a pair of articles describing a transformation, then just beginning, of the financial district. Called "Wall Street's Other Boom" and "'Downtown': A Last Look Backward," the articles eulogized the area's dying character, while heartily welcoming the coming wave of corporate rebuilding. Hardware stores figured prominently in their characterization of what was about to disappear. "New York's financial district has changed very little in the last quarter-century—in appearance. Its cacographic towers; its peeling lunch joints; its meek little Morgan Bank looking like a fairly respectable Indianapolis branch office; its ubiquitous hardware shops glutted with sleazy pliers—all this familiar furniture looks almost exactly the way it looked thirty years ago." This lush description focused on the small scale, dirt, and illegibility (even the aging skyscrapers are "cacographic") of the old downtown. A portfolio of Walker Evans photographs, commissioned for the feature, told a similar story (fig. 2.20). The magazine went on to extol the coming changes, for the relatively smooth and open texture they would bring the district. "In the next five years, almost a score of sleek, air-conditioned office buildings are going to transform the dark, old look of the financial section of

Manhattan," the magazine declared. "Gray stone will give way to shining metal and glass. Setbacks, open plazas, and widened streets will open the area to the sun." The reason for the rebuilding, the magazine noted, was that corporate mergers had created the need for "large, consolidated office space."[47] As early as 1956, *Fortune* knew that the old hardware stores, stuffed with little metallic objects, were giving way to an airier new architecture of abstract corporate administration.

For Johns, then, living at the heart of the financial district, the difficulty of locating a classic metal flashlight was a symptom not only of the new, lighter construction of that appliance but also of a change in the scale and texture of his own neighborhood. Given this rich context of its making, it is tempting to see *Flashlight I* and its rearticulations as Packardian fantasy objects, material counterweights to an increasingly ethereal world. Such a reading, it seems to me, is partly right. But consider again the terms of Packard's objections. The problem with the recent developments was that they promoted a new profligacy of consumerism, wasteful purchasing not in service of material needs (however advanced) but fostered instead exclusively for profit. If postwar suburban families wanted cars, televisions, or even flashlights, that had been well enough justified, but now they were going to have to replace items they already owned, because their styles had become outmoded or because they had prematurely broken down. In concluding his book, Packard declared that, instead of offering "pleasures, possessions, and trivialities," American industry ought to "devote more energy and more money to searching for brand new kinds of innovation for the consumer that would fill a genuine need."[48] The moral weight of Packard's argument, then—despite the author's conspicuously moderate politics—was not unlike a straightforward Marxist

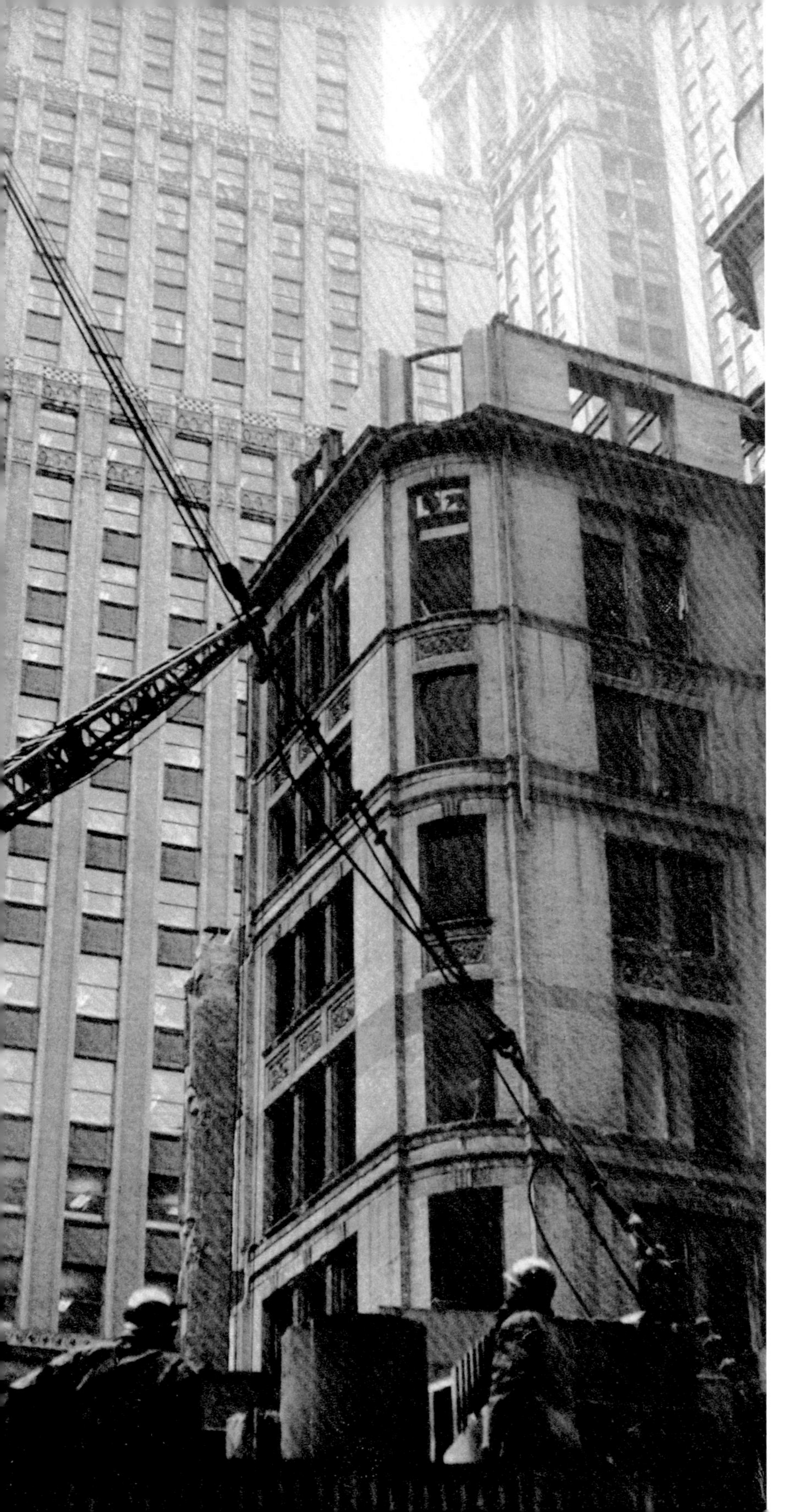



FIG. 2.20

Three Walker Evans photographs from
"'Downtown': A Last Look Backward,"
*Fortune*, October 1956, 157–62

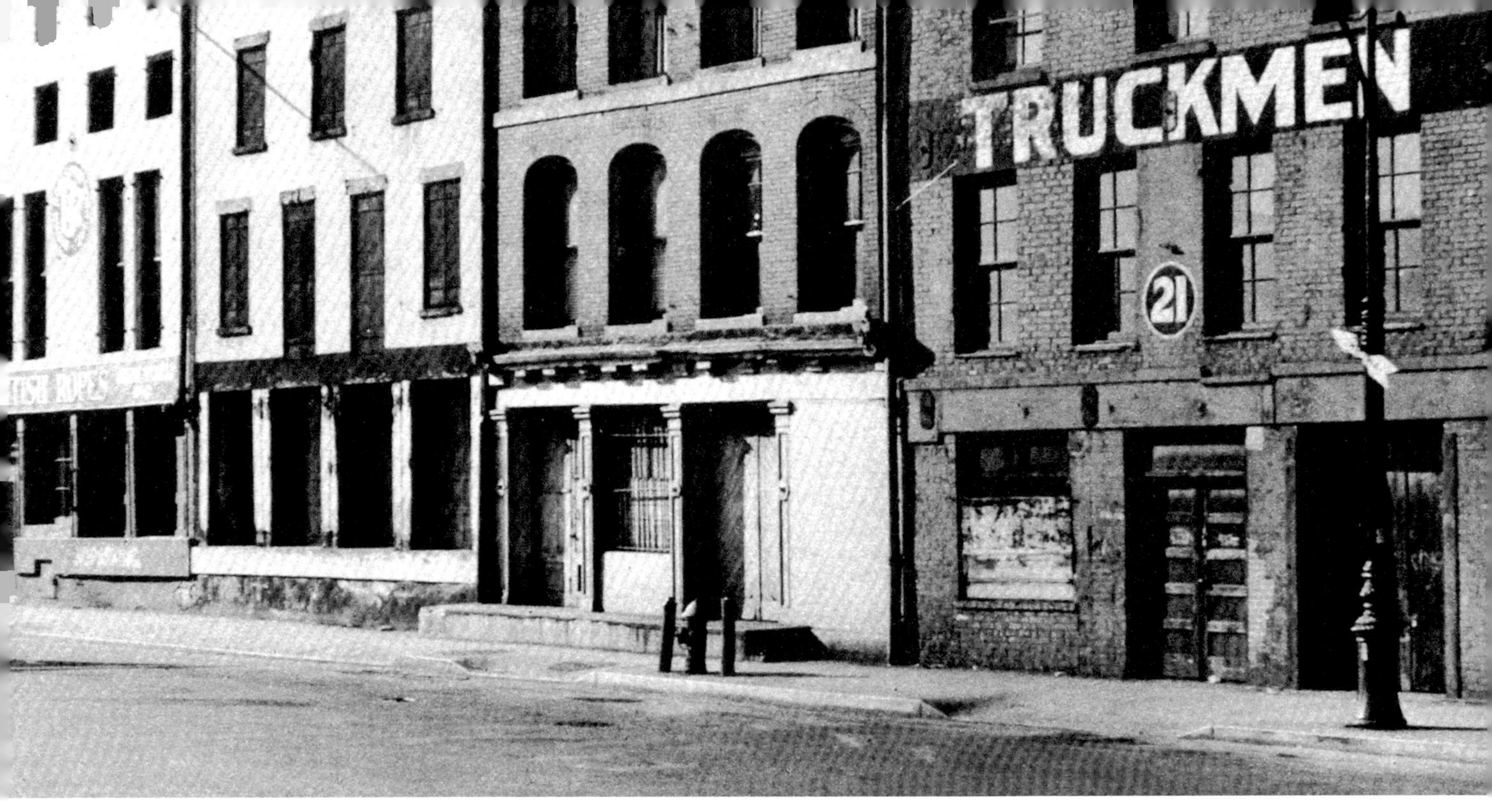

TRUCKMEN
21

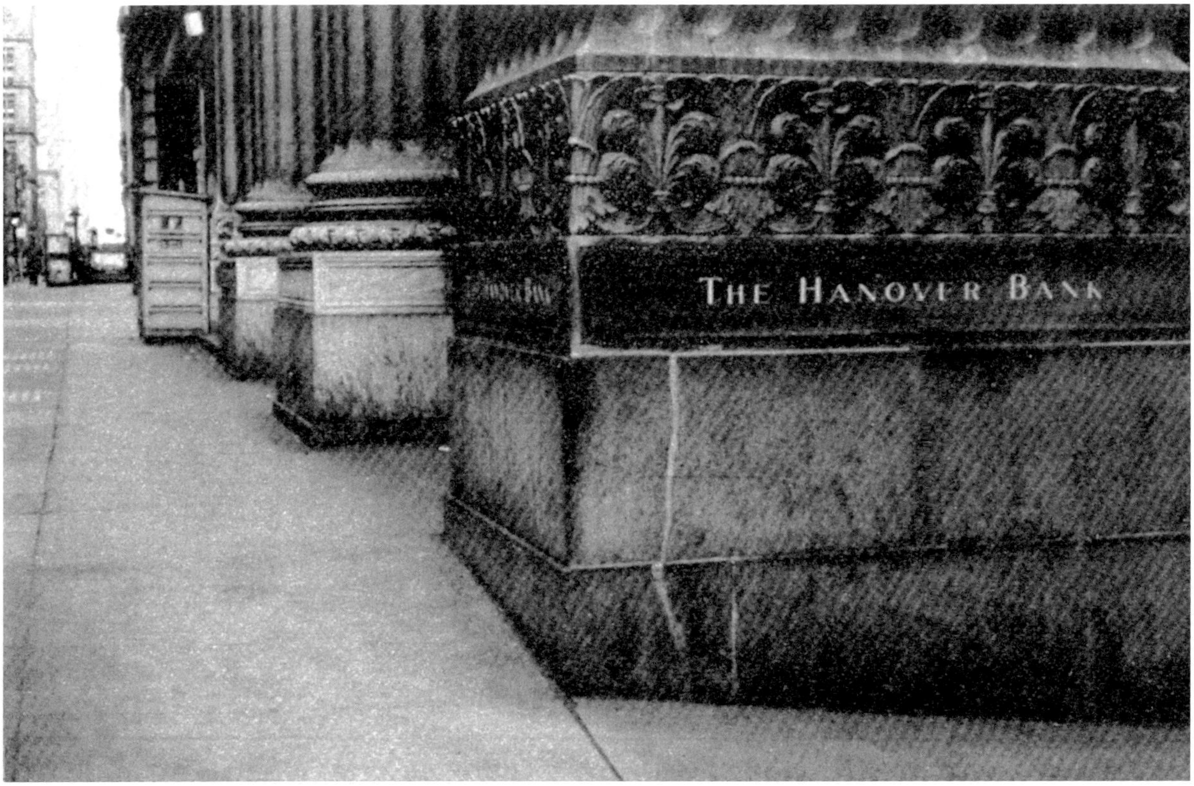

THE HANOVER BANK

materialism: his case could almost be reworded as an argument that use value, and not exchange value, ought to govern the economy.[49]

*Flashlight I, Flashlight II,* and *Flashlight III* seem not to be pursuing this materialism of utility. For all their materiality, these objects offer nothing of use value, no investment in filling "a genuine need." Indeed, the flashlights—even their bulbs are encrusted with earthy substance—are manifestly useless. Rather than use, Johns's impulse in making these objects seems to have been toward particularity, and especially toward a conspicuous material presence. If we are to understand what was at stake in this nonutilitarian materialism, we will have to look at another of Johns's sculptures, and at another of the shifts in the consumer landscape.

### *Painted Bronze (Ale Cans)* and "The Image Builders"
Given his interest in outmoded flashlights, it is no surprise that Jasper Johns, when he returned to sculpture two years later, in 1960, should have been drawn to the subject of beer cans. Just as Johns was planning *Painted Bronze (Ale Cans)* (fig. 2.21), the beer can was developing into the epitome of America's new wastefulness.[50] Cans had become a popular means of packaging beer partly for the very reason that they were used once and thrown away, unlike bottles, for which stores usually collected a deposit. They had become steadily more prevalent throughout the 1950s, too, accounting for only one-third of beer sales for the home in 1949, but a majority of that market nine years later.[51] The very substance of the container itself changed in this period as well with the arrival, in 1958, of cans made from aluminum: the new material meant that cans, previously manufactured in steel, were suddenly seamless and nearly half as heavy as they had been.[52]

As a result, the beer can became a prominent symbol in the discourse of ephemerality and waste. John Kouwen-

hoven, for example, used "beer cans by the highway" as the paramount example of the new American wastefulness in his 1959 *Harper's Magazine* article "Waste Not, Have Not," even later republishing the essay in an anthology he called *The Beer Can by the Highway: Essays on What's 'American' about America.* Although Kouwenhoven argued against those who decried waste, asserting instead that "a commitment to democracy—and a certain indifference to waste and untidiness—are prerequisites to abundance," he used the beer can to epitomize Americans' increasingly prodigal relationship to the consumer objects around them. He wrote, "We are what Dennis Brogan calls a people 'who go away and leave things' because we have enough to spare. If we did not, we would take those cans home with us, cut out their ends, slice the remaining tubes lengthwise, and roof our houses with them as the citizens of the depression's Hoovervilles did."[53]

It wasn't just Kouwenhoven who saw the can as the epitome of the new expedience of things. In *The Waste Makers,* Vance Packard noted that the average American family threw away 750 metal cans a year, and he chafed sarcastically at an advertisement for canned drinks: "And a steel company, in a television commercial, showed a pleased housewife dropping a metal can that had contained soft drinks into the wastebasket. No fussing with returns!"[54] When *The Waste Makers* was republished as a Pocket Books paperback in 1963, the cover design was dominated by a single image: a crushed steel can (fig. 2.22).

The beer can had been invented in 1935, and, like many other breweries, P. Ballantine and Sons had begun offering its beer and ale in cans right away. From the first, Ballantine's two products were sold in containers of more or less the same design; both were marked with simple elliptical labels on bronze-colored cans (fig. 2.23). That initial design almost immediately won a gold medal in *Modern*

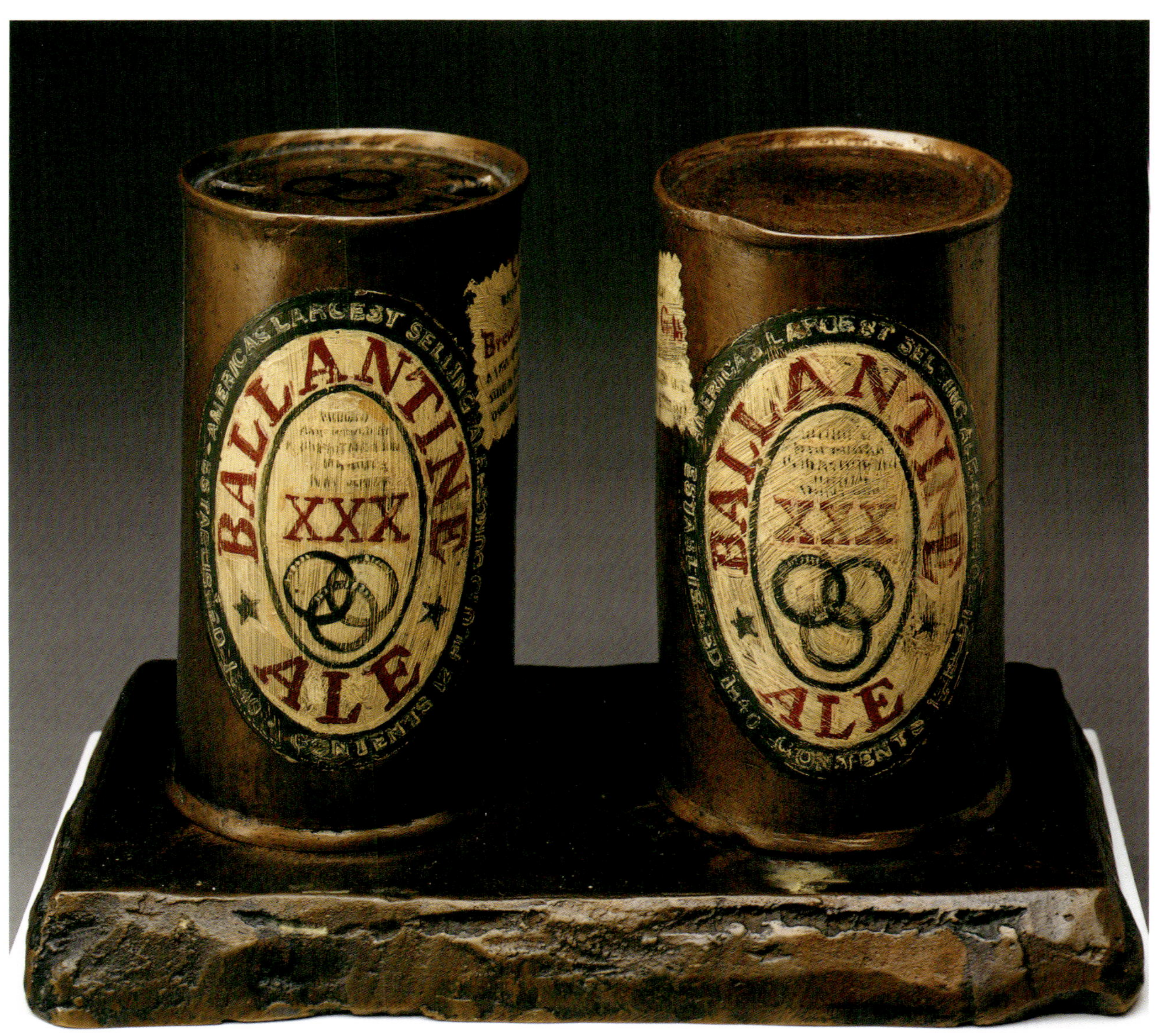


**Jasper Johns**

*Painted Bronze (Ale Cans)*, 1960

Oil on bronze, 5 ½ x 8 x 4 ¾ in. (14 x 20.3 x 12.1 cm)

Museum Ludwig, Cologne

*Packaging*'s All-America Package Competition, and it was then reproduced on every can of Ballantine Beer and Ale for decades.[55] In advertisements, the two products often appeared side by side, and in at least one image from the 1930s, the cans appeared together on a pedestal about the size and shape of the one that Johns would use in his sculpture nearly twenty-five years later (fig. 2.24).[56]

Johns seems to have known that the design of the Ballantine cans had persisted unchanged for most of his lifetime; recall that in 1965 he characterized "that old ale can" as "very standard and unchanging." His whole sentence was, "And about that old ale can which I thought was very standard and unchanging, not very long ago they changed the design of that." What is curious about this remark is that it is not strictly accurate. The ale can, which is the can Johns sculpted (in duplicate), had not undergone a significant change in design (it remained in fact almost entirely unchanged until at least 1973); it was the beer can that had changed.[57] And this change, which happened in several stages over a few years, began not after Johns had made his sculpture, as he implies, but a few years before— first with a subtle change in 1951, and then with a major redesign completed sometime between 1955 and 1958. At that time, the company narrowed and flattened the outer ring of the label and adopted a new typeface with extended serifs (fig. 2.25).[58] It seems also that in 1960—the year in which Johns made his sculpture— Ballantine compounded the changes by introducing a new product, Ballantine Draft, in a very different, white can (fig. 2.26). In the same year, the company also redesigned the label of another variety, Ballantine Bock, that had itself only been introduced as the brewery's third product around 1954. The two new drinks (which no doubt were developed in a race to claim more shelf space), along with

the modifications in design, signaled the first major departure from Ballantine's long tradition of offering just its ale and beer in their classic cans.[59]

As a model for his sculptures, then, Johns seems to have selected—from within a company undergoing rapid marketing changes—a brand that was atypically "standard and unchanging."[60] It might have been a more obvious choice, in a sculpture of two Ballantine cans, to have made one of ale and one of beer. Johns, however, chose the only contemporary can that still appeared almost exactly as it had in advertisements a quarter-century before. By rendering it in bronze, Johns further emphasized his subject's solidity and substance, its resistance to the ephemerality and expedience that it nevertheless whispered all the while.

One way to understand this weighty bronze, then, is as an imagined counterweight to an environment of expedient waste and redesign. While real cans seemed increasingly light, ephemeral, and forever changing, Johns fabricated alternatives that were heavy, substantial, and traditional. We might find further evidence of Johns's impulse in the fact that he kept for decades not only the real cans he used as models but also the plaster construction from which the sculpture was ultimately cast (fig. 2.27). This plaster object, we could note, looks like a Periclean fragment, its columnar whiteness all cracked and crumbling. Recall that *Painted Bronze (Ale Cans)* was one of the works to which Andrew Forge ascribed a "dignity like that of certain Roman funeral portraits," concluding that "nothing could be more timeless or more secure than these pieces."[61]

All this cant of antiquity does indeed circulate in *Painted Bronze (Ale Cans)*, as it had in the lightbulbs and flashlights. But we should be careful not to oversimplify the case; in coming back to sculpture in 1960, Johns seems to have wanted to reconsider his efforts of two years earlier.

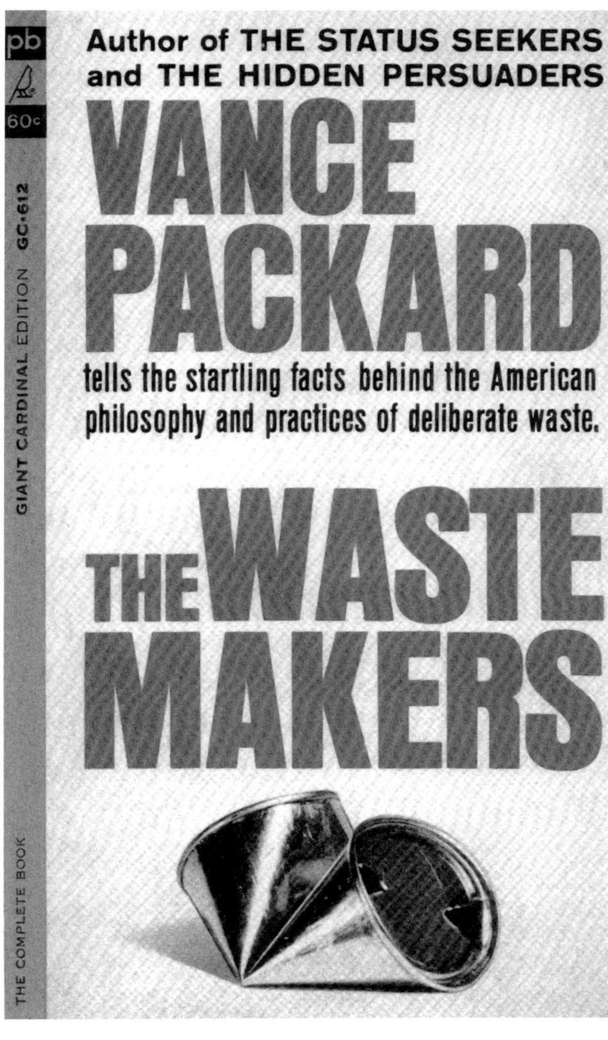


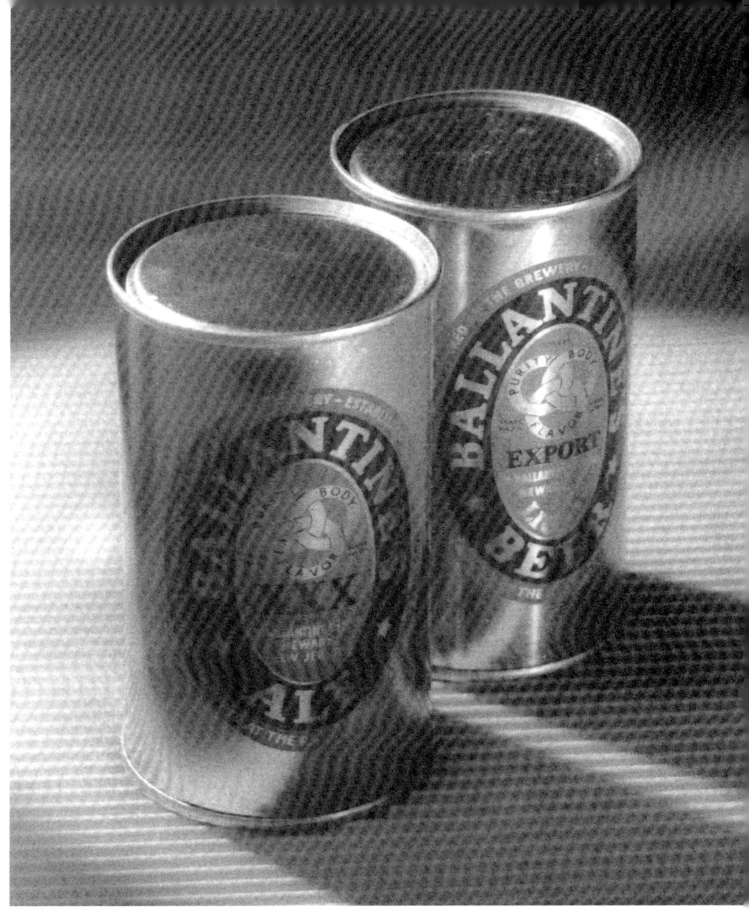

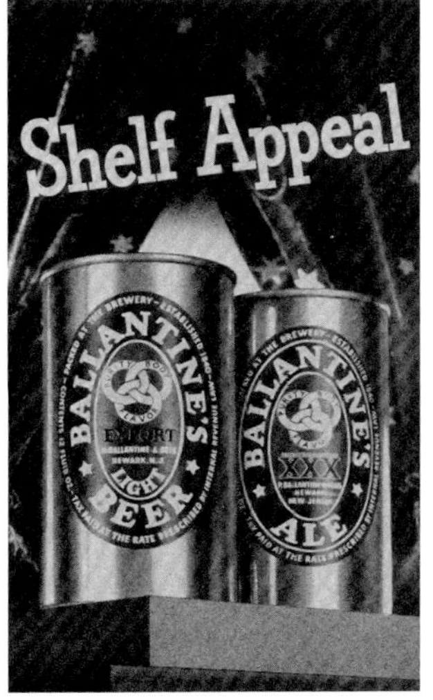


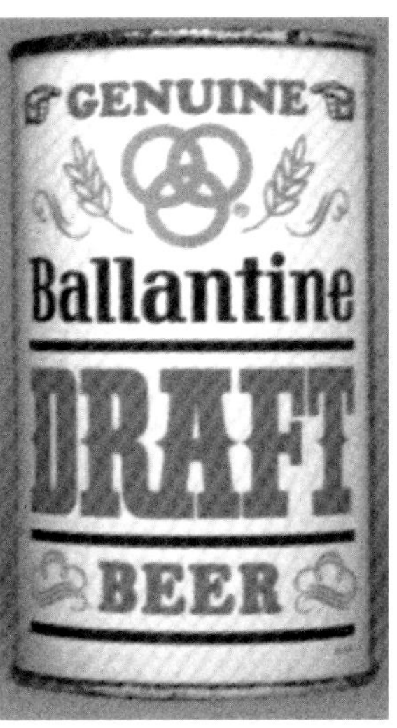


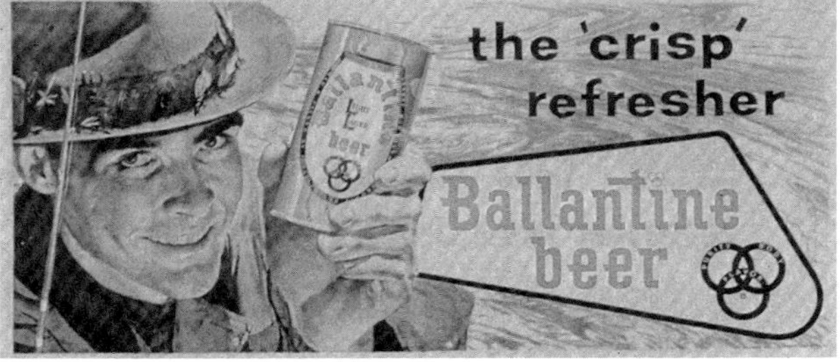


**FIG. 2.22** (above left)
Cover of reprint of Vance Packard,
*The Waste Makers* (New York:
Pocket, 1963)

**FIG. 2.24** (far left)
"First among 2,000 in Shelf
Appeal," advertisement
for the J. Walter Thompson
Company, *Printer's Ink*,
27 February 1936, 9

**FIG. 2.23** (above, top)
Ballantine cans, 1935
Gold medal winner, metal
containers, 1935 All-America
Package Competition,
from *Modern Packaging*,
February 1936, 98

**FIG. 2.25** (above, bottom)
Billboard for Ballantine Beer,
March 1958

**FIG. 2.26** (left)
Ballantine Draft can, c. 1960

FIG. 2.27
**Jasper Johns**
*Ale Cans*, 1960
Plaster, 5 ³⁄₄ x 8 ¹⁄₈ x 4 ³⁄₄ in. (14.6 x 20.6 x 12.1 cm)
Collection of the artist

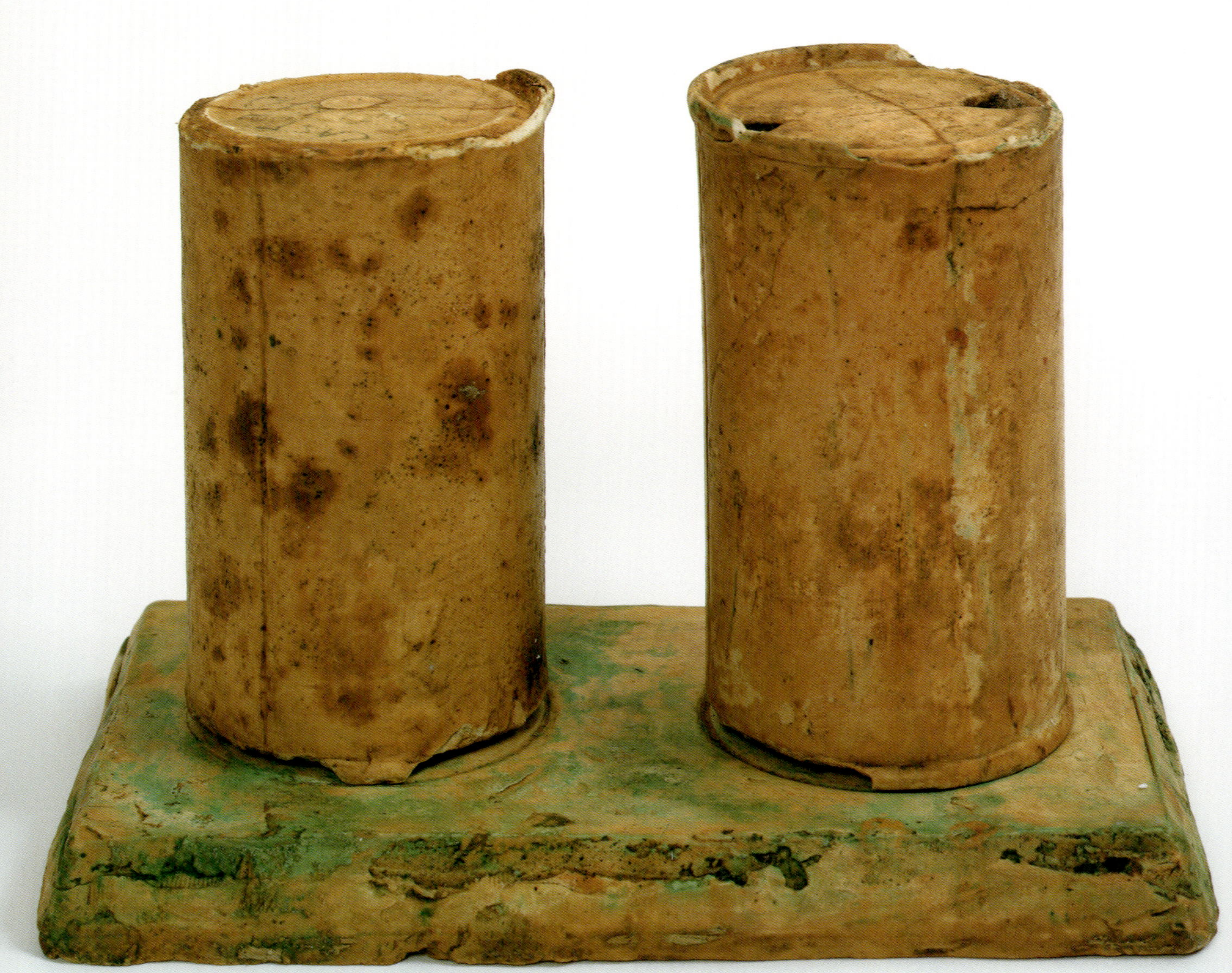

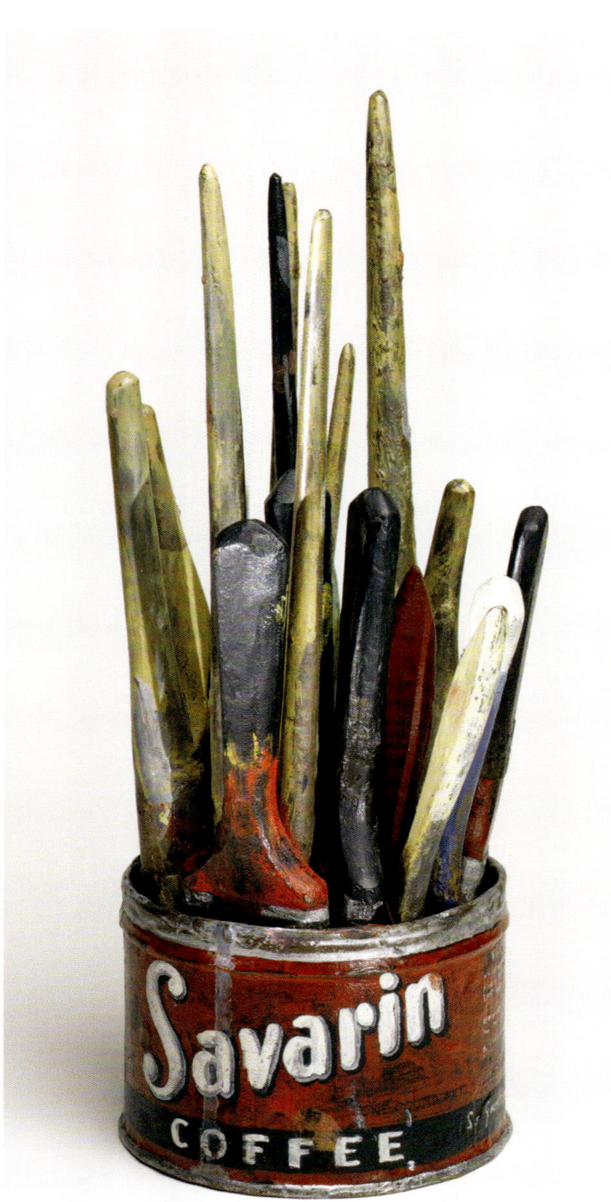



**Jasper Johns**
*Painted Bronze (Savarin)*, 1960
Painted bronze, 13 ½ x 8 in. (3±.3 x 20.3 cm)
Philadelphia Museum of Art,
Collection of the artist

Note, for example, that the bronze gives the ale cans a far smoother and less geological appearance than any of the 1958 works. Also, the beer cans—at least in their finished, painted version—prominently display a specific brand name, something it seems Johns had endeavored to exclude from his first group of sculptures. In the newer group, brand names were prominent not only in this work and in *Painted Bronze (Savarin)* (fig. 2.28) but also in the words GENERAL ELECTRIC, which the artist painted on a bronze lightbulb in 1962 (fig. 2.29).[62] Unspoken subjects of the early sculptures, advertising and brand names seem, by 1960, to have become topics the artist wanted to engage more directly.

In addition to increases in disposability and redesign, American marketing was transformed at the end of the 1950s by the introduction of a new, and vastly popular, technique in advertising: the soft sell. The new approach, rather than arguing for the specific benefits of products, aimed to associate goods with abstract and appealing images. One advertising historian writing in the period, Joseph J. Seldin, summarized the shift in this way: "The multiplication of products, brands, and packages made the art of consumership increasingly difficult to practice in the postwar period. Increasingly, the marketplace was dominated by symbolic buying and selling, with the sellers of goods engaged in selling the symbols of goods rather than the goods themselves, and the consumers buying these symbols over the inherent product values."[63]

The change had roots in poo-Freudian "motivational research" that the industry had been undertaking since the late 1940s to uncover, for example, consumers' unconscious color preferences. The more significant and lasting shift, however, would not come until the 1950s, when, as

FIG. 2.29
**Jasper Johns**
*Light Bulb,* cast 1960, painted 1962
Painted bronze, 4 ¼ x 6 x 4 in. (10.8 x 15.2 x 10.2 cm)
Philadelphia Museum of Art, Collection of the artist

FIG. 2.30
Comparison of automobile advertisements, from Larry Dobrow,
*When Advertising Tried Harder: The Sixties, the Golden Age of Advertising*
(New York: Friendly Press, 1984), 8–9


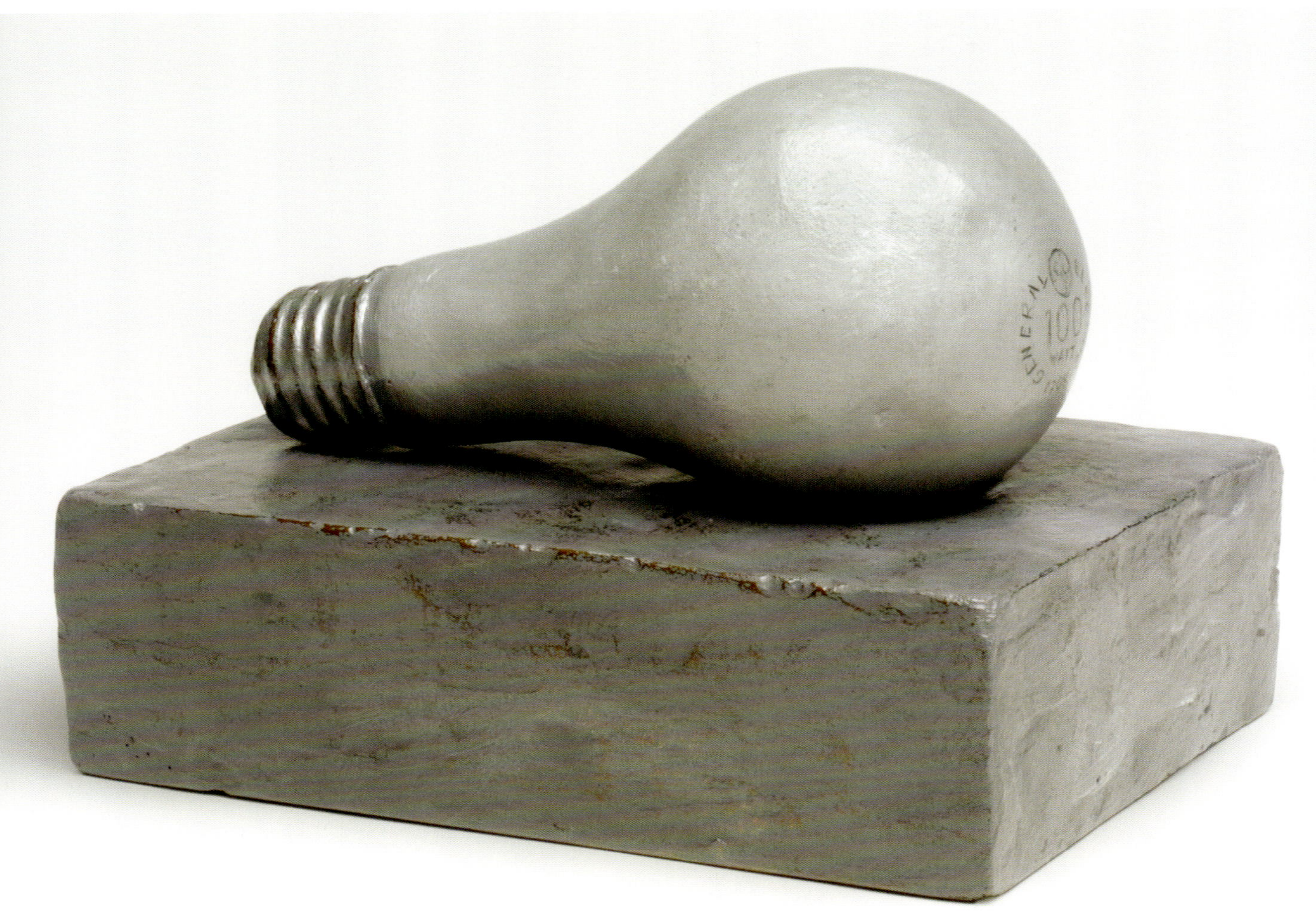

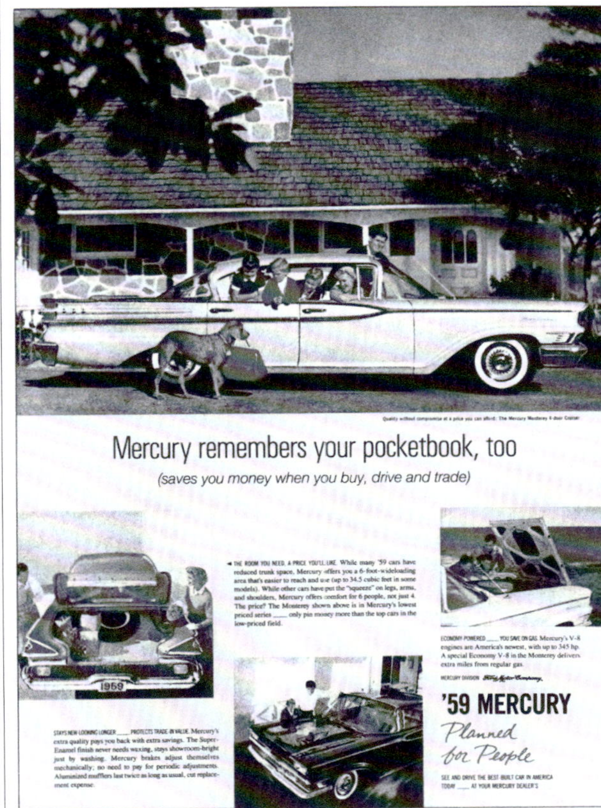



**1958** All car ads, even good ones like this for Mercury, were pure fantasy—before the creative revolution. Flattering illustrations or heavily retouched photographs were used to distort the look, length and lines of the car being advertised. This glitzy, glamorous imagery was accompanied by glib and often meaningless copy claims.

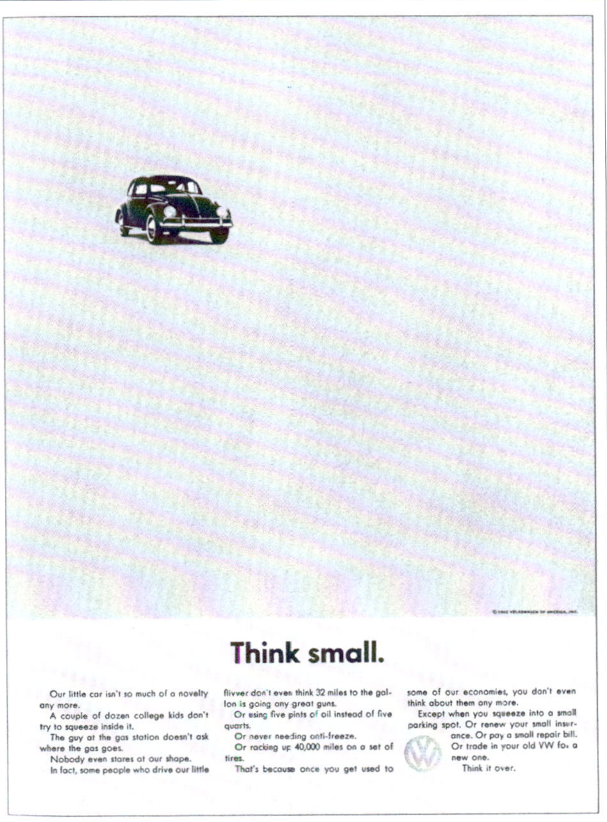



**1960** Then, along came the now legendary VW campaign, considered by most experts to be the best in the history of advertising. Gone were the lush settings, the artfully elongated automobiles, the beautiful models. In their place stood the "Beetle," unadorned and unretouched, and almost always in black and white. Most important, ads like "Think small" were achieving record readership scores. Simplicity was proving to be a virtue and relevance a far more powerful persuader than empty flights of fancy.

Seldin points out in a chapter called "The Image Builders," the soft sell took off: "The terms 'corporate image' and 'product image,' freshly minted in the fifties, received wide currency in the trade press. Scores of articles and editorials made the point that a favorable image of a corporation, or of its product, or both, gave the consumer an extra reason to buy an item, without which today's product is marked for oblivion."[64]

Larry Dobrow, a more recent advertising historian (and, like Seldin, once an advertising executive), has written about the "creative revolution" in advertising that followed the widespread adoption of the soft sell. He illustrates the change by comparing a 1958 automobile ad, in which the car's various advantages are touted in detail, to a 1960 ad, in which the emphasis is very much on the image of the product (fig. 2.30).[65] One of the major effects of the soft sell was indeed the adoption of simpler, more abstract visual language for advertising, as Vance Packard noted: "A fairly simple, straightforward use of nonrational symbolism in image building was Louis Cheskin's transformation of the Good Luck margarine package. The package originally contained several elements, including a picture of the margarine. In one corner was a little four-leaf clover. Mr. Cheskin found from his depth probing that the four-leaf clover was 'a wonderful image' so in three successive changes he brought it into more prominence until finally he had a simple foil package completely dominated by a large three-dimensional four-leaf clover. Mr. Cheskin reports that sales rose with each change."[66]

Packard was the most prominent of the many critics who responded specifically to the development of the soft sell. In fact it was his treatment of the new image advertising (together with critiques of the Freudian approaches and other pernicious Madison Avenue tactics) that had been the subject of his first great best seller, *The Hidden Persuaders* of 1957. One of Packard's many examples concerned the ways in which different brands of soap, manufactured by the same company, were sold under different images. "Procter and Gamble's image builders," he wrote, "have charted a living personification for each of their cakes of soap and cans of shortening. Ivory soap is personalized as mother and daughter on a sort of pedestal of purity. They exude simple wholesomeness. In contrast the image charted for Camay soap is of a glamorous, sophisticated woman."[67]

Packard specifically addressed the topic of beer in several places, since beer (like soap) could make especially good use of images to create distinctions among materially indistinguishable brands. He pointed out, for example, that some breweries had been experimenting with shifting the class identities for their products and told the story of an unnamed Chicago brand that, "having always appealed to the men in the taverns," tried a new approach. "In their billboard and other advertising," Packard wrote, "they began showing people in dinner jackets drinking the beer, men in fox-hunting garb sipping it after a strenuous hunt, and they even had a famed pianist, in white tie and tails, tell how he always drank it to relax after a concert." He noted that the change resulted in the beer's fall "from first to nineteenth place on the market."[68]

For Packard, what made these approaches (and the need to practice them well) so lamentable was again his utility-oriented materialism. Although he observed that many ads were still "tasteful, honest works of artistry," too many others departed speciously from the essential qualities of the goods they were promoting, arbitrarily attaching abstractions to indistinguishable products.[69]

Another popular writer, Daniel Boorstin, saw the ads as part of a broader, pernicious abstraction that had begun to develop into a "thicket of unreality [standing] between us and the facts of life." His 1961 book was called *The Image; or, What Happened to the American Dream,* and it took on the soft sell at length: "There was a time when if you wanted a lady to buy a hat you would ask her to do so, or if you wanted a man to buy a cognac you would describe the virtues of your cognac. Now persuasion is more indirect. . . . Products have become props for images into which the seller confidently assumes we will try to fit ourselves."[70]

Boorstin noted that the advertisers' confidence was justified. "More important than what a Buick really is," he wrote, "is our image of it. We are sold it and we buy it and enjoy it for its image and how we fit into the image."[71] Like Packard, Boorstin lamented the apparent irrelevance of utility in the new advertising methods, but for Boorstin, the crisis was deeper, even epistemic. Americans had adopted a new relationship to their world, one in which materiality had lost its primacy in favor of signification. One symptom was the changing nature of brand names: "The Brand Names Foundation (established in 1943) by 1959 had almost a thousand members. . . . Brand names became household words. . . . The obvious next step, so recent it has only begun to enter our dictionaries, was from the 'Brand Name' to the 'Name Brand.' The use of 'brand' as a synonym for trademark had entered the English language as early as 1827. . . . But the much newer expression 'name brand' makes the name and not the product the center of attention."[72]

It is not just advertising, newly devoted to images and brands, that was the subject of Boorstin's book. He catalogued, too, the ascendancy of abstraction in news reporting, the arts, and even Americans' sense of place. And although Boorstin did not much focus on television, the new preponderance of TVs—almost 65 percent of American homes had sets by 1953—contributed irrevocably to the centrality of fluid images in American life.[73] In Boorstin's view, this dematerialized situation (in which "people talk not of things themselves, but of their images") had been set in motion centuries before, but its most serious effects were new, and drastic: "Now, in the height of our power in this age of the Graphic Revolution, we are threatened by a new and a peculiarly American menace. It is not the menace of class war, of ideology, of poverty, of disease, of illiteracy, of demagoguery, or of tyranny, though these now plague most of the world. It is the menace of unreality." Boorstin was describing a cultural shift in which the material world was becoming detached from the ballooning sphere of representation. Focusing on phenomena we can now see as endemic to postmodernity, he worried less about decreasing utility than about the new primacy and arbitrariness of abstraction. Boorstin did not make explicit what was at stake in his lament of this development (in fact he wrote that he was hobbled by his inability to define the "reality" that Americans had lost), but his text might nevertheless help us to understand what it might have meant for an artist in the period to have rendered two beer cans as an oddly particularized bronze.[74]

It is not entirely without cause that one of Johns's hastier critics responded to *Painted Bronze (Ale Cans)* as "apparently just two Ballantine ale cans on a pedestal."[75] At first glance, the sculpture does almost seem a replica of two mass-produced consumer objects (see fig. 2.21). The bronze surface of the cans, although marked with countless tiny nicks, was brushed to match the shiny copper color of real Ballantine cans, and the artist dutifully replicated the appearance of the labeling, down to the logo and text on top of one can that identify it as a kind sold in Florida.[76] Johns has been laconic about just how he made the sculpture (and there has been a resultant lack of specificity on this topic in the literature), but it has been suggested that he built up the original plaster positive for the work entirely by hand. A recent statement of the artist's, however, suggests that the mass-produced look of *Painted Bronze (Ale Cans)* may have been achieved partly through casting from real cans. Writing about both *Painted Bronze* works, the artist has indicated that, although some parts of the original plasters were "modeled or fabricated from odds and ends," other parts "came from molds that I made."[77]

That Johns used both casting and hand modeling suggests the double-edgedness of his aims in *Painted Bronze (Ale Cans)*. He clearly wanted the sculpture to achieve a divided appearance—a look both of mass production and of hand facture. An examination of the neat cylinders of the plaster original—from which the rims have largely crumbled—suggests that Johns in fact cast his cans from real models and then knifed off the rims so he could rebuild them by hand (see fig. 2.27). Indeed, the rims in the finished bronze are manifestly particular and unmachined. Note, for example, the asymmetrical pitch in the lip of the can on the left, and the blunt flattening in the one on the right (see fig. 2.21).[78] And these are hardly the only traces of Johns's work-

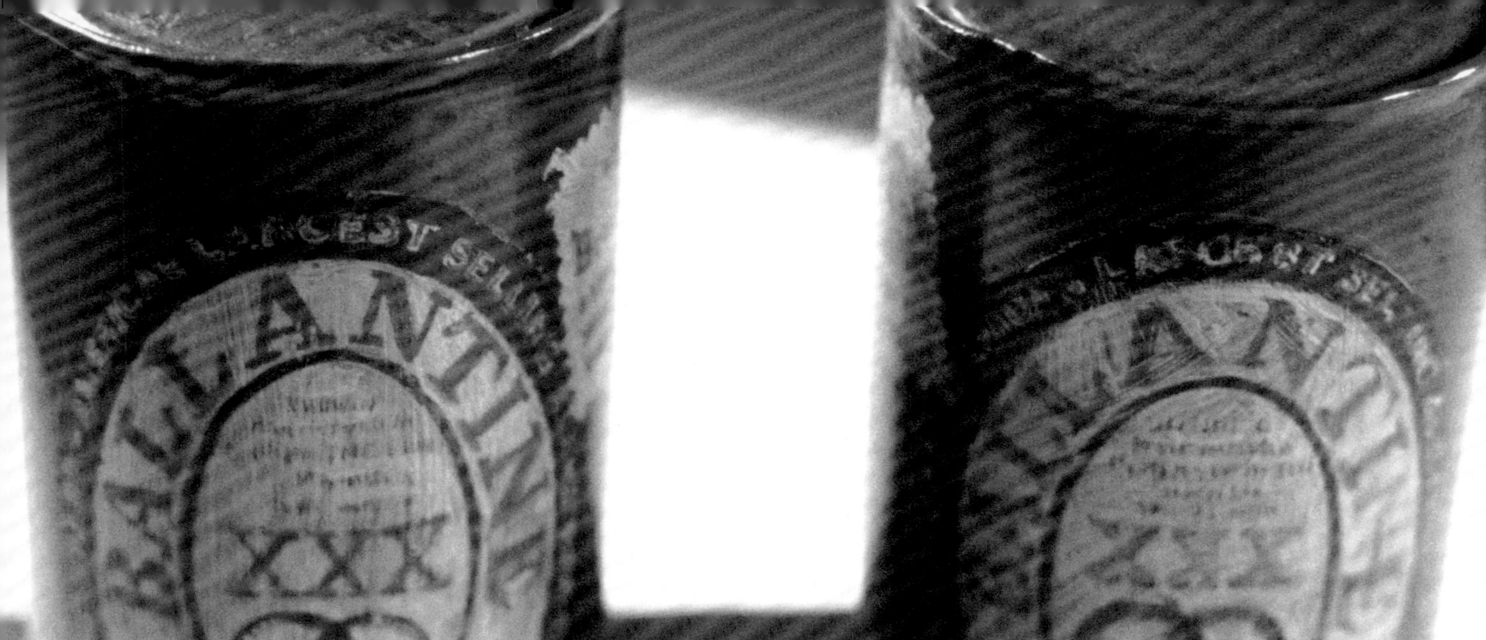



Fig. 2.31

ing by hand. The color of the labels, for example, is uneven; look at the darker patch painted just under the N of the can on the left (fig. 2.31). The whole of the label on the other can, meanwhile, is faintly obscured by a thin overpainting of dry, yellow brushwork. Note also the tactile specificity of the base—the thick, organic ridges along its vertical rise, and the two yellow marks (one fingerprint, one vague paint splotch) that Johns carefully applied to its horizontal surface (fig. 2.32, and see fig. 2.21). Indeed, the pedestal is a lexicon of carefully reproduced accident; the asymmetrical rings in which the cans snugly fit, along with the mottled black marks around them, are like the seeping ink stains made by a wet can left, between sips, on an artist's sketch.

As we might expect, each can is its own object, independent of the base. The unopened can is solid right to its core; picking it up, one finds it shockingly—even dangerously—heavy. Although the other can is hollow, it, too, is quite unwieldy. This weight belongs not to the imagined beer cans but to the sculpture itself. *Painted Bronze (Ale Cans)*, after all, is named not for what it represents but for what it is, its representational function appended as a subtitle. We are reminded here that Johns's materialism is not one of utility: these are not cans reoriented to their proper function of holding liquid for drinking. Rather, Johns seems to have

wanted to make a consumer object that could, as if for its own sake, weight down the abstraction that was increasingly circulating through the real, mass-produced goods everywhere around it.

Other factors contribute further to the work's concreteness. The labels' legibility is strained by that dry brushwork crossing the already indistinct lettering on one of the cans, as well as by the meaningless marks that Johns carefully painted in, underneath the words "Brewer's Gold," on the sides (fig. 2.33). Note, too, how Johns emphasized the cans' seams; he must have used a sharp object, while working with the plaster, to incise the deep lines that exaggerate the joints (fig. 2.34). The seams, the illegibility, the massiveness, all are on show here as part of an emphatically particular and material object, one that resists fungibility and abstraction.

Again, however, we must be careful not to oversimplify the case. Unlike Boorstin's book, the sculpture expresses some doubts about whether the materialist world it proposes is in fact possible. For example, Johns, using the language of his numeral paintings, carefully painted serial numbers on the bottom of the cans: 97843, and, less distinctly, what is probably 98148 (fig. 2.35). Johns must have known that very few viewers would ever see the numbers (and, to my

FIGS. 2.31–2.35
**Jasper Johns**
*Painted Bronze (Ale Cans)*
(details)

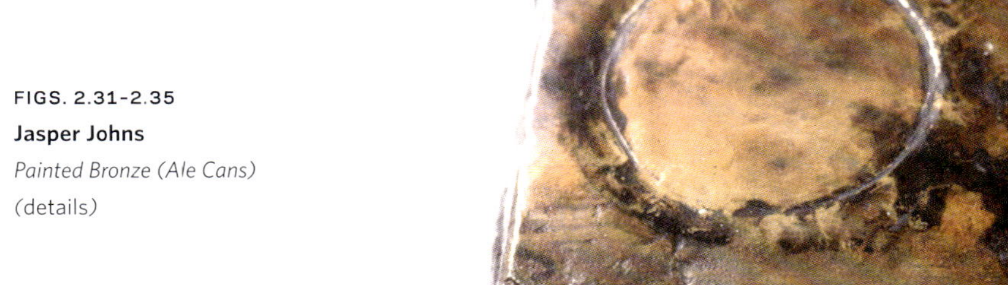

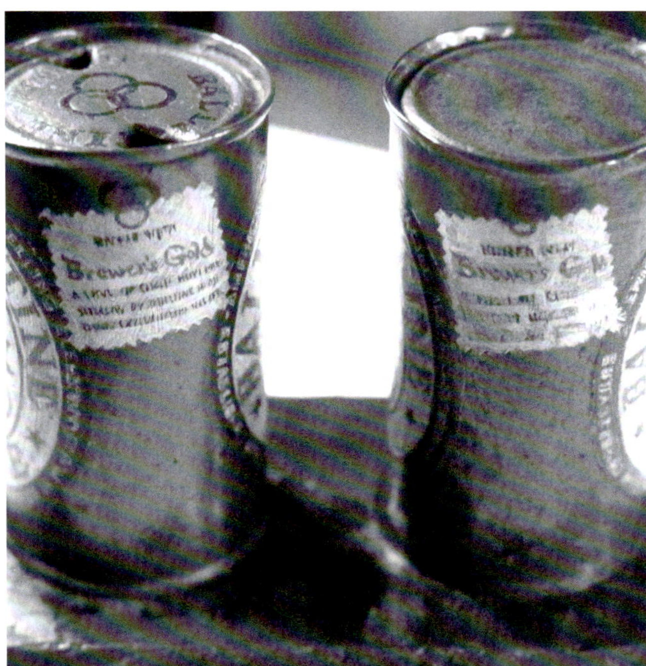

Fig. 2.32

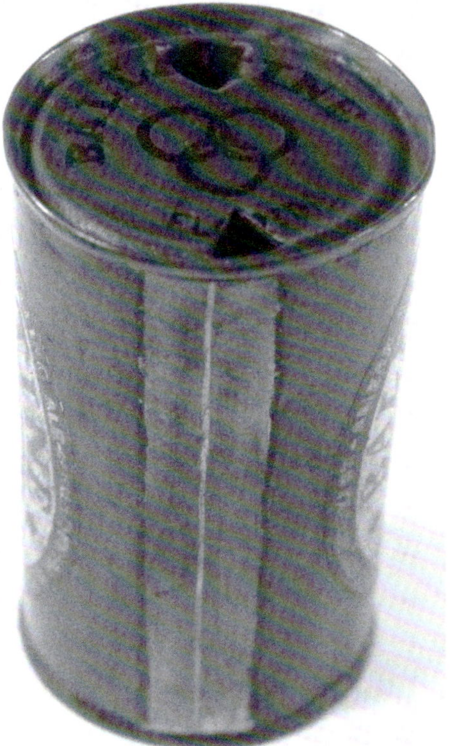

Fig. 2.33

Fig. 2.34

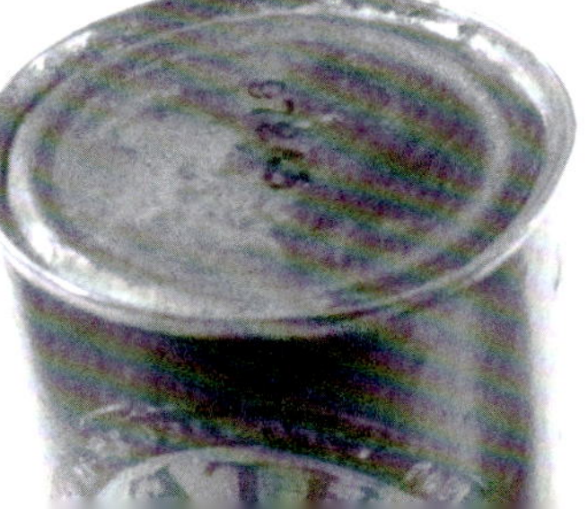
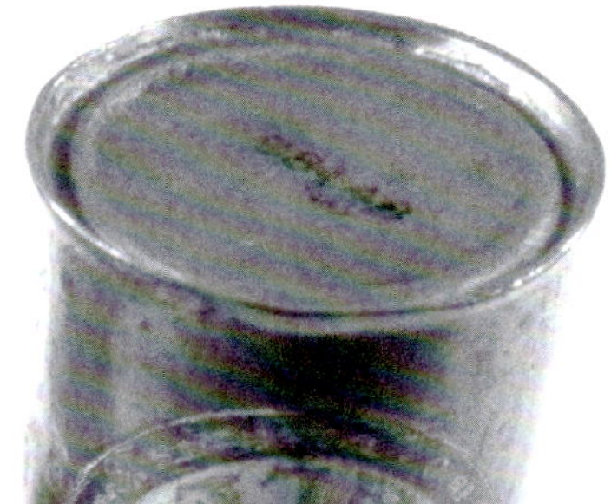

Fig. 2.35

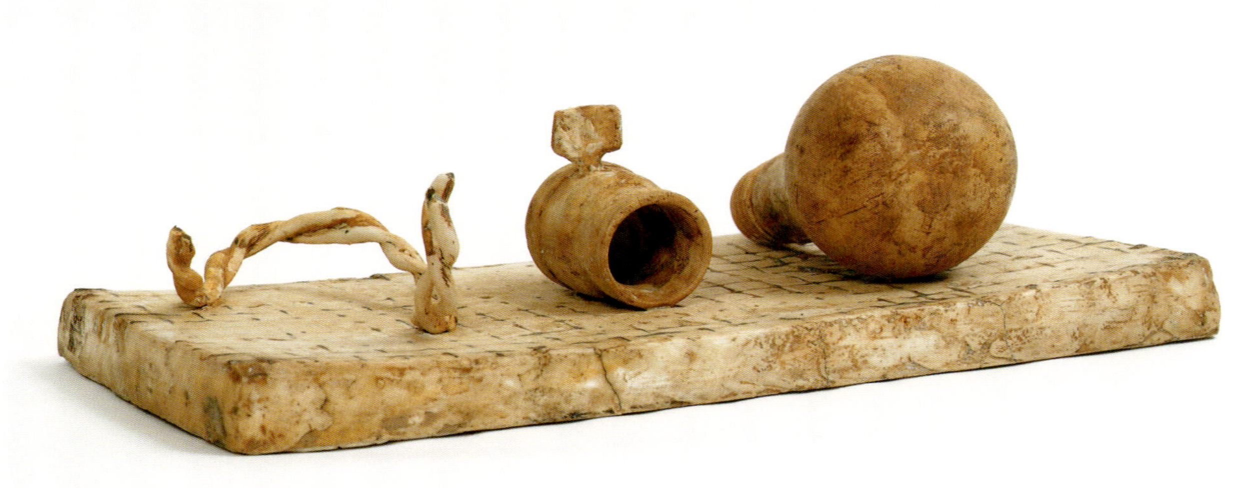

knowledge, they have never been discussed), but his hiding them here suggests that he wanted to restage the sculpture's central dialectic. On one level, certainly, the numbers help to particularize the cans, both through their smudgy, uneven painting and through the very act of their uniquely identifying each one. In tension with such effects, however, is the fact that the numbers are the trace of seriality; they point to the cans' abstract type and to the irrelevance of any particular material token.

The brand names that appeared when Johns returned to sculpture, we might also say, are a recognition of the impossibility of total materialization and particularity. They acknowledge the inevitability of signification, of the abstract ordering of things. Consider *Light Bulb* (1960), especially the version of it that Johns painted in 1962 (see fig. 2.29). This reworking of the bulb, aside from cloaking it in a logo and brand name, also renders it a far smoother object. The nicks in the threading are fewer and finer than they were, say, in *Light Bulb I* (see fig. 2.7), and the base now has been manifestly tooled. The painting makes this sculpture nearly an illusion—an *image*, even—of something it is not. In articulating a tension, then, between abstract image and material specificity, this sculpture finds a spot far closer to

abstraction. It may even be the most transparently representational work (and the one least encumbered by its own materiality) that Johns has ever executed.[79]

Johns, remember, claimed that even in 1958, when he was looking for a model for his first flashlight, the new diversity of plastic designs had made him "very suspect of my idea." Johns went ahead that year with his sculptural materializations, and he tried them again in 1960 and the years right after. In this latter group, however, he seems to have been less certain that an object could be made into a thing somehow below, or counter to, abstraction. Asked at the end of the 1960s about his 1959 remark that "a picture ought to be looked at the same way you look at a radiator," Johns responded, "I thought at the time that a radiator is a radiator. . . . Originally I meant the radiator was a secure object one didn't have to bring any special psychological relationship to. Now I'm not so sure."[80] Johns's alternating conviction and insecurity that objects could be made to resist the forces of abstraction probably got its most explicit articulation in *Untitled* (fig. 2.36). Here the lightbulb's parts, laid out on a scientific grid, look smooth and mass-produced. But Johns has also broken them apart from each other, materializing the system by which the abstract power

**Jasper Johns**

*Untitled*, 1960–61

Plaster and wire,

3 ¼ x 12 x 6½ in. (8.3 x 30.5 x 16.5 cm)

Collection of the artist

of light is brought—braided wire, twist-key socket, and bulb—into a room.[81] The result is a group of little things for the hands, means for grasping the phenomenon of light.

## Nation of Abstraction

It was far more than advertising, remember, that occupied Daniel Boorstin's account of the new hegemony of the image. Journalism (through the reporting of orchestrated "pseudo-events"), literature (through cross-media adaptations), and geography (through the homogenization of the landscape)—all were losing their old material particularity and supplanting it with a new kind of experience in which "we hide reality from ourselves." The resulting "Age of Contrivance" was a "peculiarly American menace," the product of "the whole gargantuan paraphernalia of the American economy."[82] Johns also seems to have felt that the problems of materiality and abstraction circulated through a larger terrain. In 1960, he turned his sculptural practice on the American flag, thereby addressing not only the United States as a whole but also the symbolic itself—the basic abstracting act of representation. The series included six sculptural versions of the flag: one in Sculp-Metal, one in plaster, and four in bronze. All these were related to the hyperbolically material and particularized version of the American flag that the artist had famously made in 1954 and 1955 (see fig. 2.6), and all seemed (at least in some capacities) to press that materiality and particularization still further. Note in the bronze version, for example, the long tail swinging off the thick blob of metal far in the upper left-hand corner (fig. 2.37), or the thick bands of material in the topmost stripe, folding and pocketing like icing spread across a cake. Look, too, at the broad bulges obscuring so many of the stars, and the little swatches, such as at bottom right, that stand out sharply as needless additions, almost

but never quite violating the lines between the stripes.[83] In places, these details are so particular as to strain the object's very legibility as flag.

It is not difficult to see this bronze flag as another negation of the shifting material landscape. Treating Johns's use of the American flag as a subject, John Yau has observed that "typically a flag is a symbol that helps citizens believe they stand outside time and change. . . . It is a palpable symbol which proposes that the world will go on being the same."[84] At the end of the 1950s, however, the American flag—as Johns himself pointed out in his remark about changing consumer goods—underwent two rapid transformations. Unchanged since 1912, the flag was redesigned in 1959 to accommodate a forty-ninth star, representing Alaska. A year later, it was changed again, on the admission of Hawaii, to the fifty-star design still in use today. In the early 1960s, Johns claimed that "I stopped painting flags when they changed the number of stars" ("Since then," he said, "the design doesn't interest me anymore"), but this claim was flatly false.[85] In fact, the artist's interest in the motif seems to have been particularly intense precisely in the period right after the changes. In 1960 alone—the second consecutive year in which the flag had been redesigned—Johns completed at least two major drawings and three series of lithographs, in addition to his six sculptures of the subject. Predictably, every one of these works lacked the two new stars. Even in 1962, when Johns made an eight-foot painting of two American flags, both were rendered in the outmoded design.

The flag sculptures, then, might be understood partly as compensatory objects, in which the shifting material facts of the real American flag are again and again disavowed, using heavy materials and the familiar design. This negation, in being turned on the national symbol,

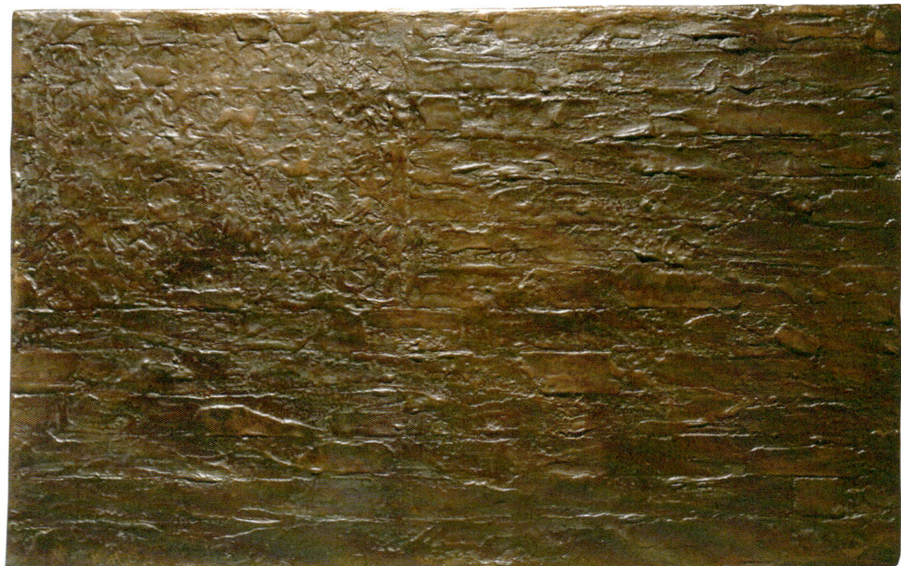

FIG. 2.37
Jasper Johns
*Flag*, 1960
Bronze, 4 casts,
12 1/8 x 18 5/8 x 1/4 in.
(30.5 x 47.3 x 0.64 cm)
Collection of the artist

FIG. 2.38
Jasper Johns
*Flag*, 1960
Sculp-Metal and collage
on canvas, 13 x 19 3/4 in.
(33 x 50.2 cm), with frame
Rauschenberg collection

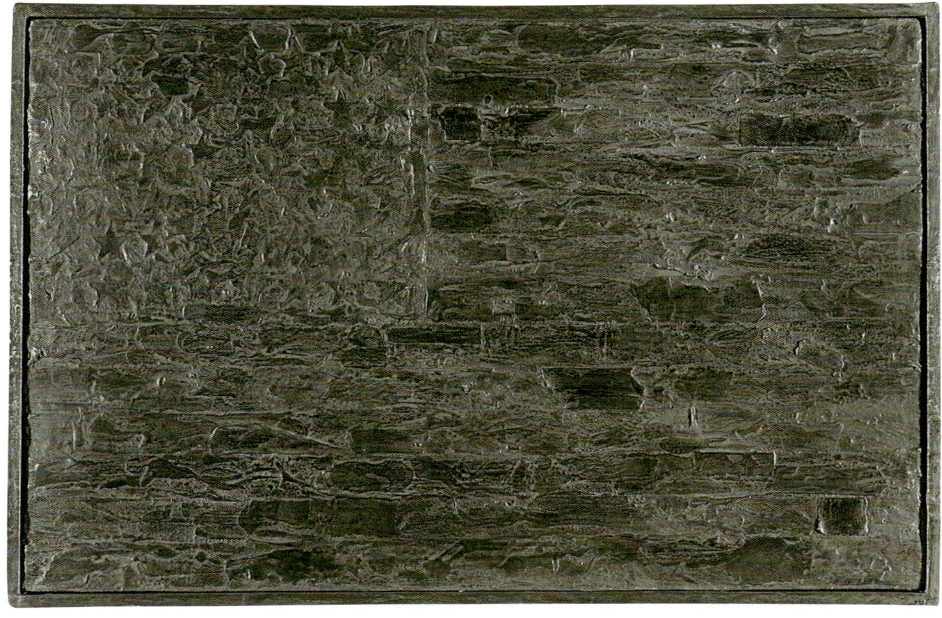

speaks also to the United States as the apparent source (as Boorstin also had it) of a new universality of abstraction. The works appear as if to redeem America, and all its objects, from the postmodern forces of etherealization. Because the flag is a symbol, these sculptures also address the most basic abstracting act: the act of representation. (Indeed, the flag's referent—the United States—is itself an abstraction, a fact newly highlighted by the addition of two noncontiguous states.) Thus, in its effort, as Irving Sandler put it, "to make [the flag] more substantial than it actually is," the bronze flag proposes a refuge from the immateriality of signification.[86] It remakes the symbol as a nearly illegible set of material facts.

It is central to what I want to argue in this chapter, however, that whatever redemptive materiality is on show in the flag sculptures, the works are also soaked through with an acknowledgment of the inevitability of abstraction. Their familiarity and heft are plainly quixotic—the tiniest of gestures in an America repurchasing a fleet of brand-new, nylon, mass-produced Stars and Stripes.[87] Even the specificity of Johns's versions, it turns out, is foiled by seriality. The one made in Sculp-Metal (fig. 2.38) was indeed built up by hand—Johns pasted in a postage stamp and a section of newsprint to make the blocky swatches at the lower right— but all the others were then simply cast with molds taken from this original.[88] If they resist the status of abstraction in America, these sculptural flags also admit the impossibility of any pure state of materiality.

Before concluding, we must address one more form of abstraction that Johns's practice, in its ambivalent way, was addressing. Three years before beginning his sculptures, Johns started to cast human body parts in plaster. He included in his first exhibition, for example, his 1955 work *Target with Four Faces* (see fig. 2.3), which matched a

collaged target with four indexical traces of a human face, materialized, as if objects on a shelf. The faces—actually cast from Johns's friend Fance Stevenson—are ambiguous about the most basic signifying categories of human identity, such as gender and race. In Johns's *Target with Plaster Casts* (fig. 2.39), also exhibited in that first show, the casts likewise seem to concretize their various body parts—including a penis—as discrete and purely material things. Jonathan D. Katz has argued that the plaster-cast paintings embody a queer subjectivity, presenting the body as a group of "unusable material resistances, unassimilable to any hegemonic discourse."[89] That is, these two works frame the human body as if it existed outside, or below, the signifying categories that normally govern our experience with it.

As we have seen, the sculptures, too, had a biological quality, if one that seemed petrified in fossil form. It has been noted further, by Roni Feinstein for instance, that this biological register is, in many of the sculptures, specifically phallic—a claim that invites us to view the sculptures not only as a grounding of consumer goods in the bodily, but also as imagined materializations of the male body itself.[90] I would add that the act of sculpting such concrete versions of genitalia, for a gay artist at the end of the 1950s, was tantamount to offering a dream of a purely material sexuality, a place for sex without its oppressive signifying categories. Johns's art, we might conclude, is not so much an expression of the elusiveness of subjectivity (as Fred Orton would have it) as it is an imagining of subjectivity remade, impossibly, as pure matter.

More broadly, the pressure of Johns's practice is to recast the world as a set of purely material phenomena. It is a resistance to—and later, a constantly rearticulated dialectic with—signification itself. Consider a work such as *Book*, in which a communicative thing is painted over, as if it could

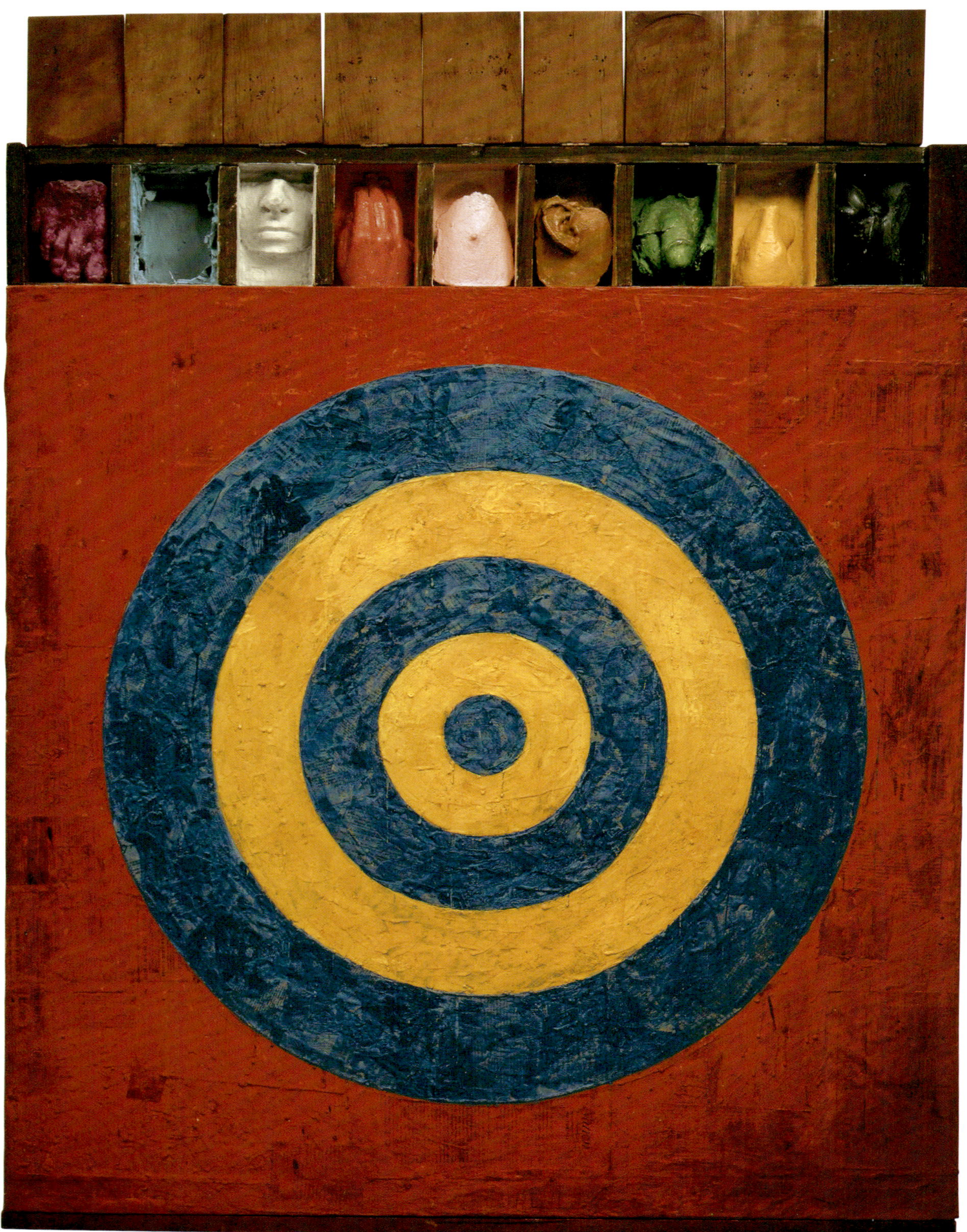

FIG. 2.39

**Jasper Johns**

*Target with Plaster Casts*, 1955

Encaustic and collage on canvas with plaster casts,

51 x 44 in. (129.5 x 111.8 cm)

Collection of David Geffen, Los Angeles

FIG. 2.40

**Jasper Johns**

*Book*, 1957

Encaustic on book and wood,

10 x 13 in. (25.4 x 33 cm)

Collection Martin Z. Margulies, Miami

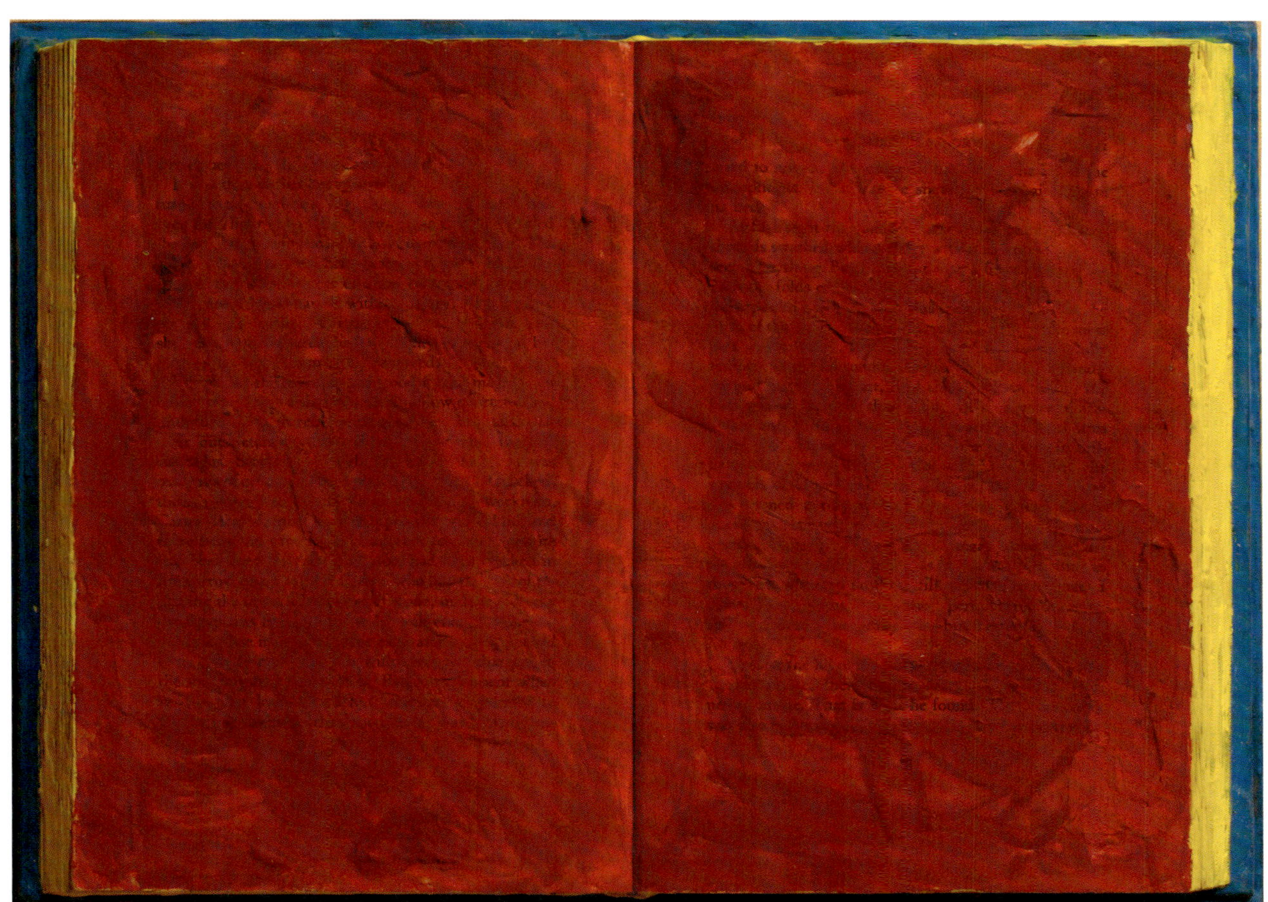

be claimed as a mere object (fig. 2.40). Even Johns's jokey sculptures, works such as the bricklike *The Critic Sees* (1961, fig. 2.41), are devoted entirely to a distrust of language. For its part, *Painted Bronze (Savarin)* (see fig. 2.28) serves as the bridge between the artist's sculptures and his paintings: with it, Johns offers an object that is far more present than meaningful, an obdurate little fact. But this sculpture only parenthetically addresses the world of common commodities, as if only to recall the other sculptures. Its true subject, however mutely handled, is the studio, the realm from which this unusually faithful imitation is drawn. The studio, Johns's can and brushes suggest, is the place of facts, of things.[91]

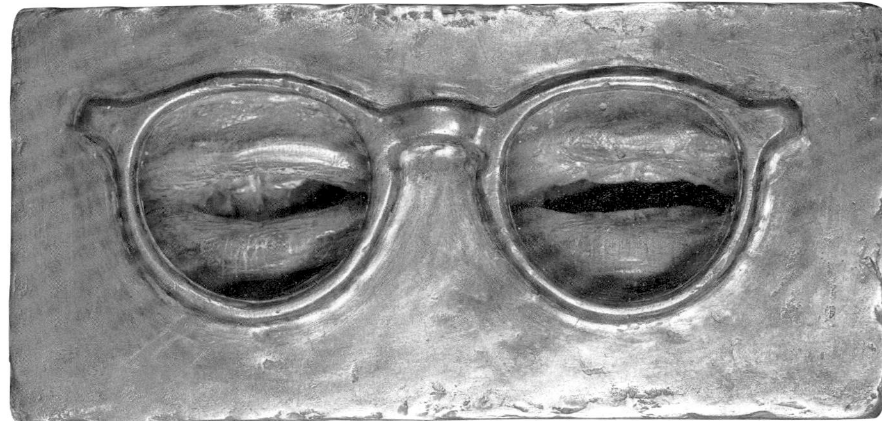



**FIG. 2.41**
**Jasper Johns**
*The Critic Sees*, 1961
Sculp-Metal on plaster with glass,
3 1/4 x 6 1/4 x 2 1/8 in. (8.3 x 15.9 x 5.1 cm)
Collection of Steven A. Cohen

**FIG. 2.42**
**Andy Warhol**
*Brillo Boxes*, 1969
Acrylic silk screen on wood, 100 boxes,
each 20 x 20 x 17 in. (50.8 x 50.8 x 43.2 cm)
Norton Simon Museum, Pasadena, Calif.,
Gift of the artist

Probably nothing in the art of the 1960s returns so closely to the concerns of Johns's ale cans as do Andy Warhol's *Brillo Boxes*, the first of which were made in 1964 (fig. 2.42). Here again we have a brilliant exploration of the role of signification in postmodern consumerism, with packages presented both as signs and as objects. In Warhol's case, however, the objects are unreservedly serialized and virtually indistinguishable; it takes the special efforts of a catalogue raisonné even to fathom how many were made. The boxes demonstrate, in their sculptural articulation of a painter's project, how much even objects are fundamentally signs: all surface, color, name. Their just-exaggerated heaviness and just-visible wood grain provide the barest of reminders of the material specificity of the world onto which the system of signs is projected.[92] *Painted Bronze (Ale Cans)* occupies a different position in the shifting, if forever unresolved, dialectic between the materiality of the new world of goods and the process of abstraction that drove it. It meets the capitalist dematerialization of objects negatively, muscling its way into as much material concretion and specificity as it can,

even while admitting the blindness of such an effort. It is this insistent materialization, nevertheless, that must have led Johns to exclaim, when interviewed by Gene R. Swenson for a 1963–64 *Artnews* series on Pop art, "I'm not a Pop artist!"[93]

It was not just Pop, among new art movements, that began to shun the materiality of modernist painting for the culture's ascendant language of signs. Starting quite early on, the first efforts of Conceptual art, too, imitated and even exaggerated the new abstraction of everyday life. Yves Klein—in a gesture at once mercenary and critically parodic—sold "zones of immaterial pictorial sensibility" in 1962 (fig. 2.43). Johns's work, spurred by the same developments, articulated a different path for art in the 1960s— one that would, by the end of the decade, seem less viable. Like the organic and particular works of Eva Hesse, like the "specific objects" extolled early on by Donald Judd, Johns's sculptures reworked the serial objects of the culture, imagining them outside the growing systematicity of abstraction.

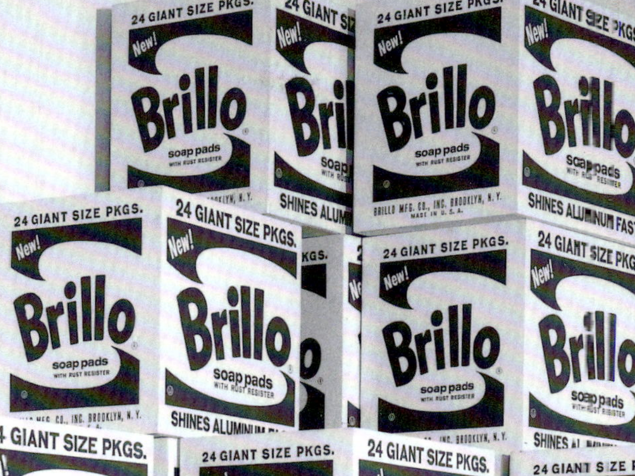
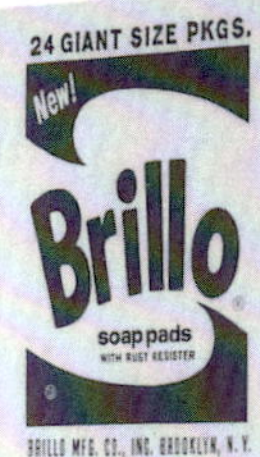
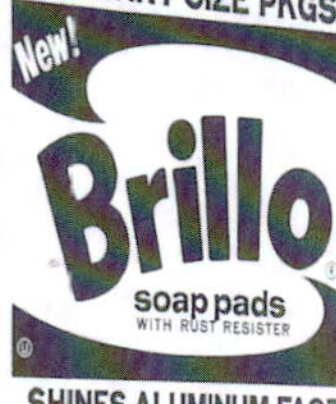
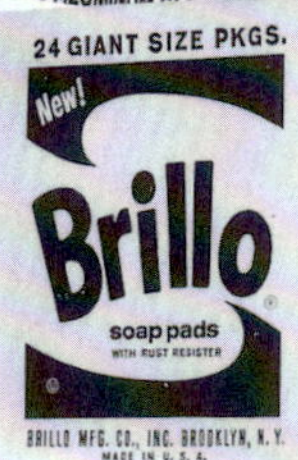
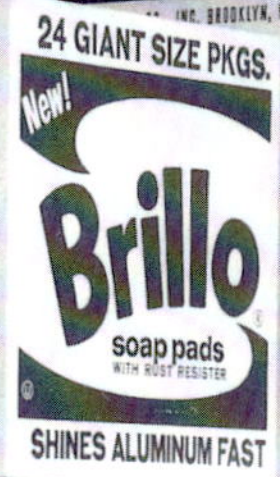
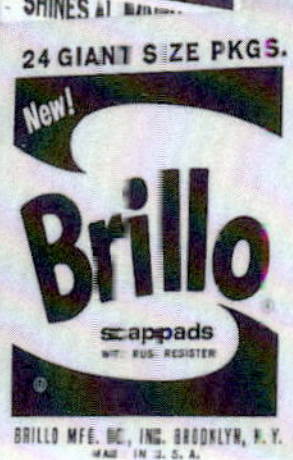
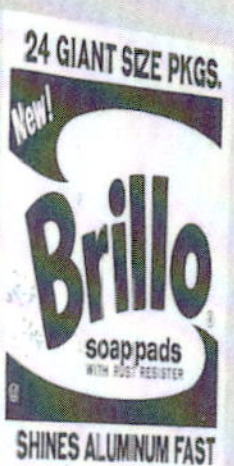
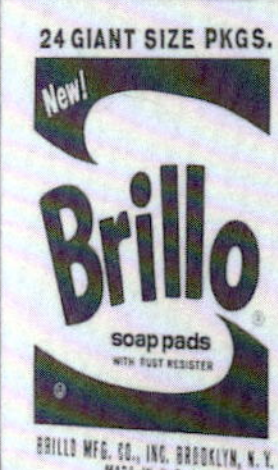
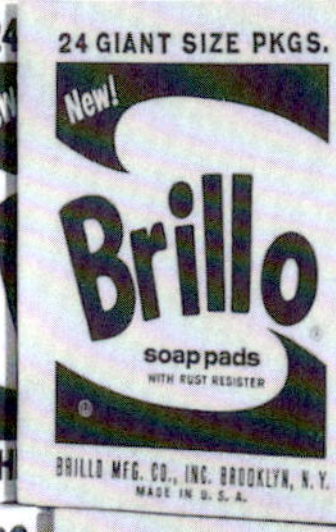
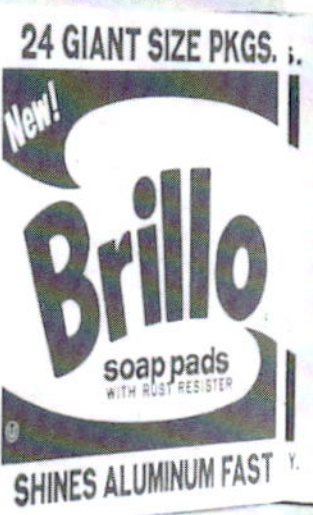
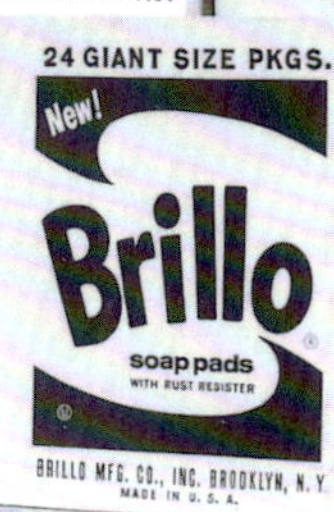
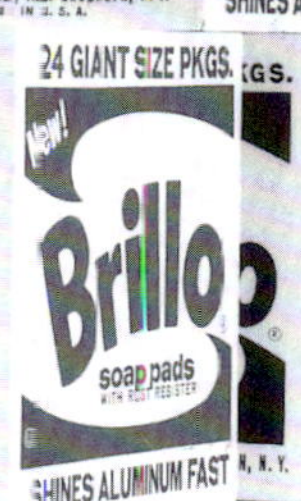
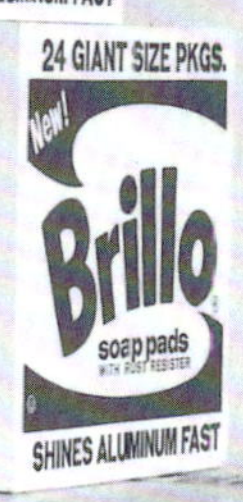
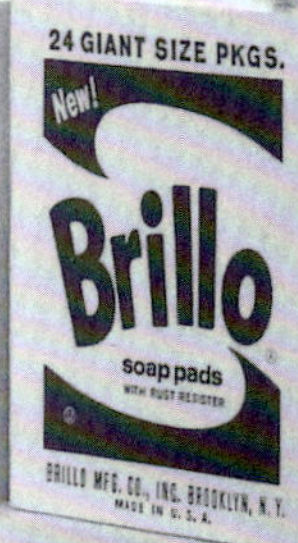
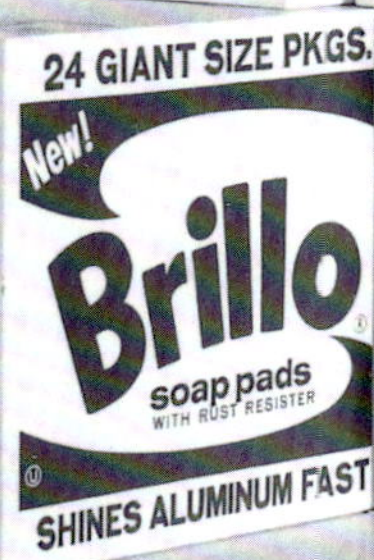
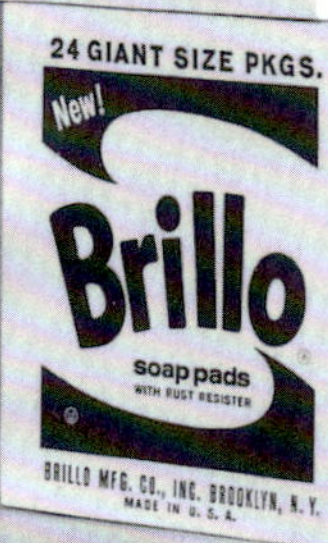
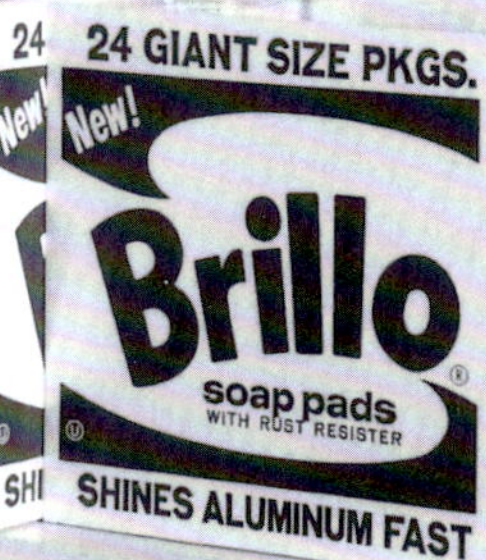
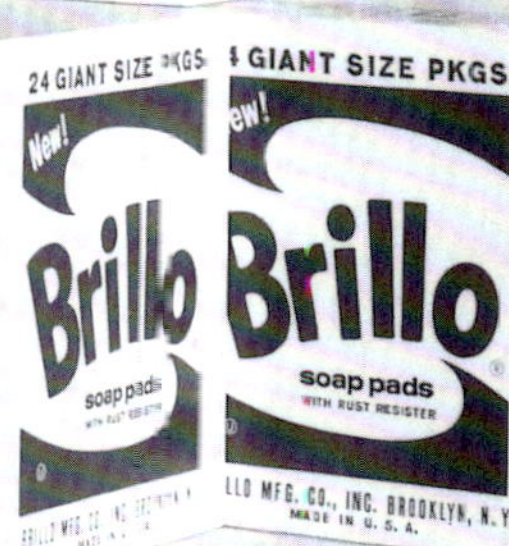
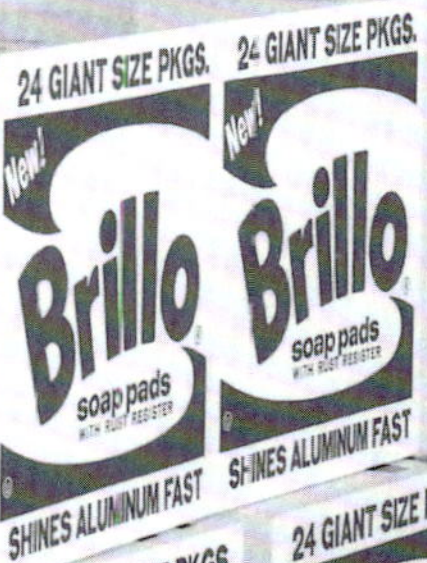
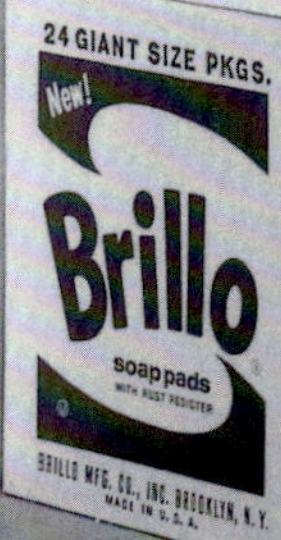
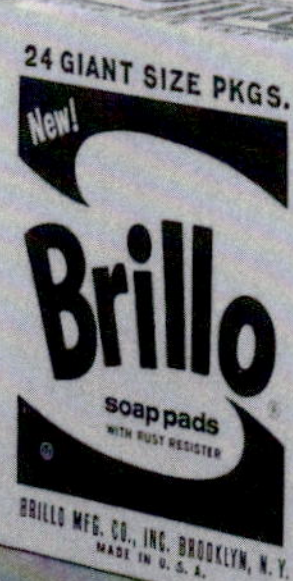
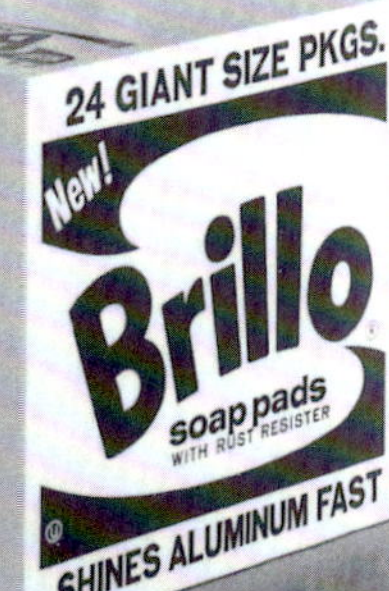
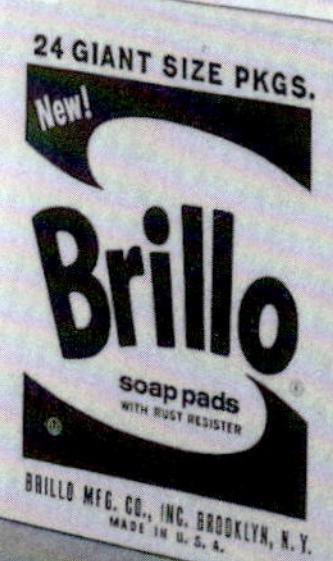
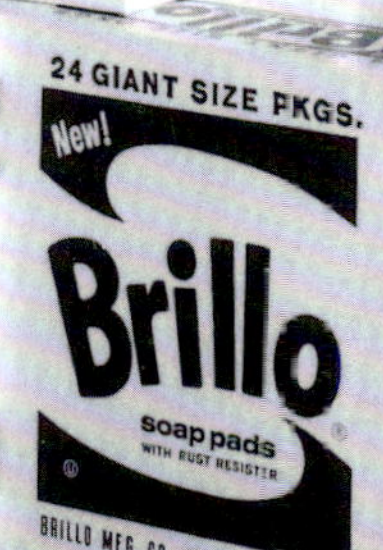
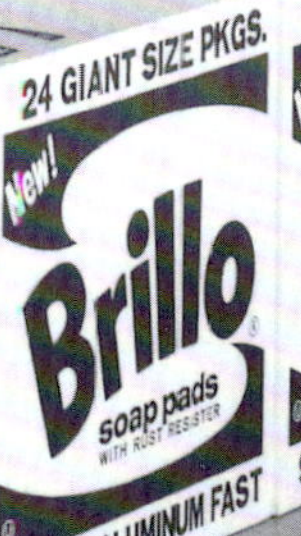
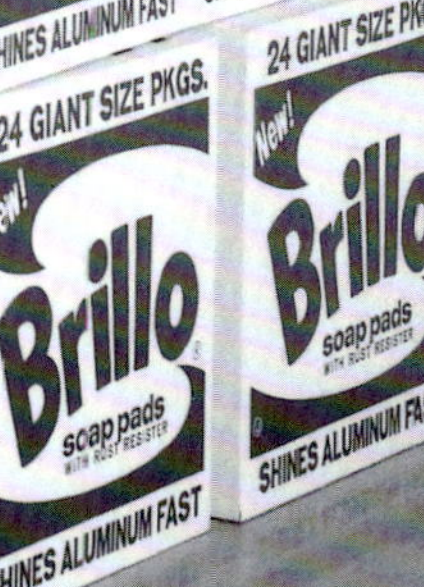

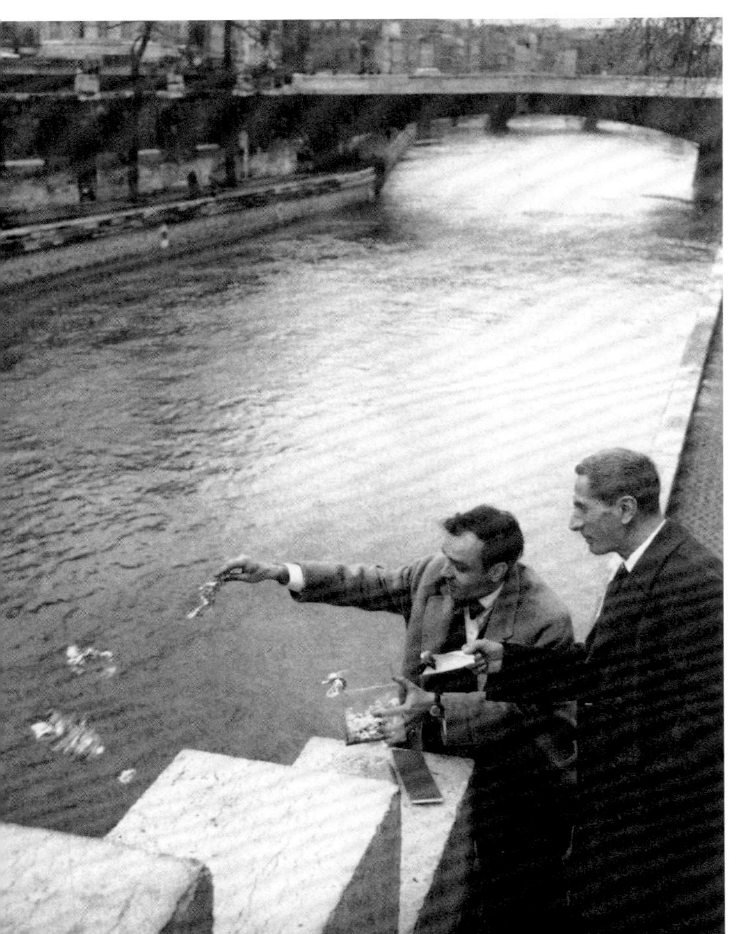

Writing seven years after Johns cast his ale cans, and on another continent, Guy Debord offered his era's fullest radical critique of the late capitalist abstraction of the everyday material world. He began it with a flat two-sentence statement of the new situation: "The whole life of those societies in which modern conditions of production prevail presents itself as an immense accumulation of *spectacles.* All that once was directly lived has become mere representation."[94] Debord's central concerns—that the new economy of images deepened alienation and mystified power—were not shared by Johns, painting and sculpting in New York. Johns's practice, however, provided its own negative meditation on the contemporary erosion of the material world. In his art around 1960, Johns articulated not only a connection between the growing abstraction of everyday experience and the modernist problem of signification in art, but also the connection of both of these developments with social abstraction more generally, with the painful inadequacy of language itself.

# 3 Black Market

RAUSCHENBERG

IN 1962, THE CRITIC GENE R. SWENSON was making periodic visits to an old building of industrial lofts at 809 Broadway. He was checking on the progress of a new assemblage of Robert Rauschenberg's, an untitled work that the artist was tinkering with most of that year, in his home and studio on the top floor. Swenson was working on an article for *Artnews*, one that—because of Rauschenberg's delays—would not appear until April of 1963.[1]

When Rauschenberg had finished adding and removing parts, and had settled on the title *Inside-Out*, the work had resolved as a three-foot box, backed by an outsize sheet of scored and torn pressboard (fig. 3.1). The finished assemblage was deemed by Swenson "a failure," an "unpleasant" work with parts that were "awkward" and "lacked grace." Although this assessment suggests that Swenson missed much of what was at stake in the making of *Inside-Out*, the work is indeed an inharmonious object, ruled by the artist's incongruous juxtapositions of discards. The front of the box, for instance, is dominated by scraps of decorative sheet metal and an old label at the right edge, which, incorrectly oriented, reads "C. T. & E. S. CO."[2] The door in the front face of the box—smudged with dirt on one side, heavily scratched on the other—is an odd one: too small to have shuttered a window, too thick and neatly coffered for an ordinary medicine chest.

Inside is a narrow chamber, backed with a Plexiglas mirror (fig. 3.2). A thoroughly rusted tin can hangs on this back wall, inside a niche that appears to have been cut for it, roughly, from the Plexiglas. Beside the can, another hole in the box permits the worn wheel of an abandoned baby carriage or golf cart to protrude to the outside. This wheel looks as if it ought to spin—powered by or powering some unseen mechanism—but it leans lamely instead against the edges of its untidy opening. The result is that the whole affair—eventually mounted on casters—looks like some improvised but long since failed industrial appliance of uncertain purpose.

The elaborate material junkiness of this work makes it seem odd that Swenson's article should have appeared under the title "Rauschenberg Paints a Picture." But *Inside-Out* is, at its heart, an Abstract Expressionist painting, and one that has literally been turned inside out: brushwork and color on the inside, banal material support facing out. The painting surface is never visible directly, but instead can be seen only through the door and reflected in the warped plastic mirror on the back wall. It is a patchwork of splotches, mostly in the neutral colors of antiquated junk: brown, black, yellow, and grayed-out white. There are also some areas in somewhat brighter oranges and reds.

This painting is not, however, simply a quotation of the artistic movement then just fading in New York. Note how different it is from the styles of the major Abstract Expressionists. In *Inside-Out*, the isolated swatches of paint provide nothing of the potential for illusionistic depth that animated the otherwise flat canvases of Hans Hofmann, say, or Jackson Pollock. The only depth here is literal: look at the thick pool of brown above the rag-encrusted transverse rod, or the palimpsesting of overlapped color patches throughout. Having been enclosed by its own material support, the paint indeed becomes just another element of the emphatic materiality of this "combine."[3] It is made equivalent with other elements of the material world cobbled together here, such as the cuff from a pair of khakis that the artist has applied to the painting surface.

If there is a denial here of illusion, a denial even of access to painting itself, then that gesture is underscored by the hidden, rear face of the work. An old fire bell, a wooden railing support, and a faded crate for 7-Up bottles are joined

FIG. 3.1
**Robert Rauschenberg**
*Inside-Out*, 1962
Combine: oil, paper, fabric, wood, embossed tin, metal, wire,
mirror, glass, bell, and wheel on wood structure mounted
on four casters, 40 x 50 x 16 in. (101.6 x 127 x 40.6 cm)
Kunstsammlung Nordrhein-Westfalen, Düsseldorf

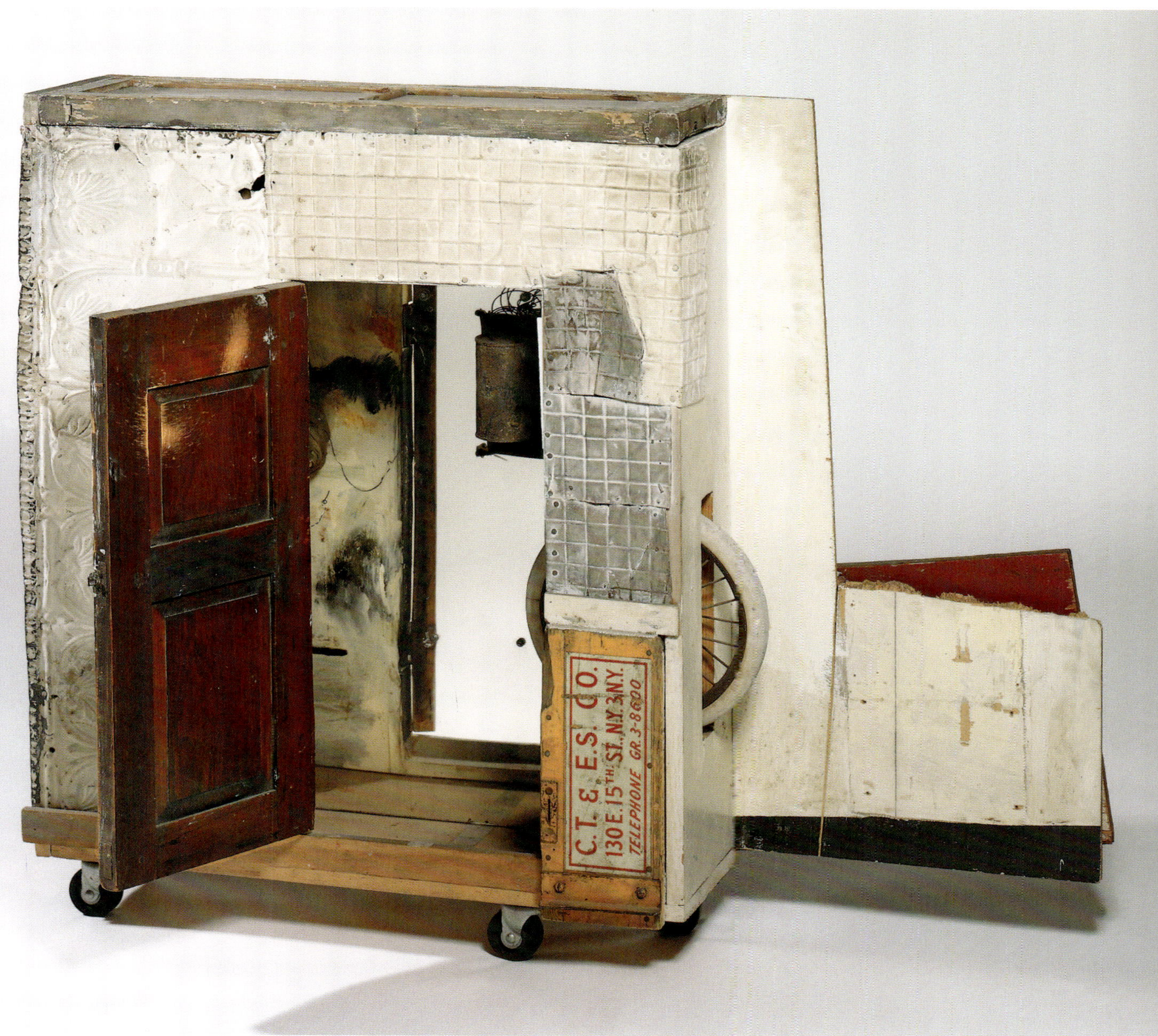
C.T. & E.S. CO.
130 E. 15TH ST. N.Y. 3 N.Y.
TELEPHONE GR. 3-8600

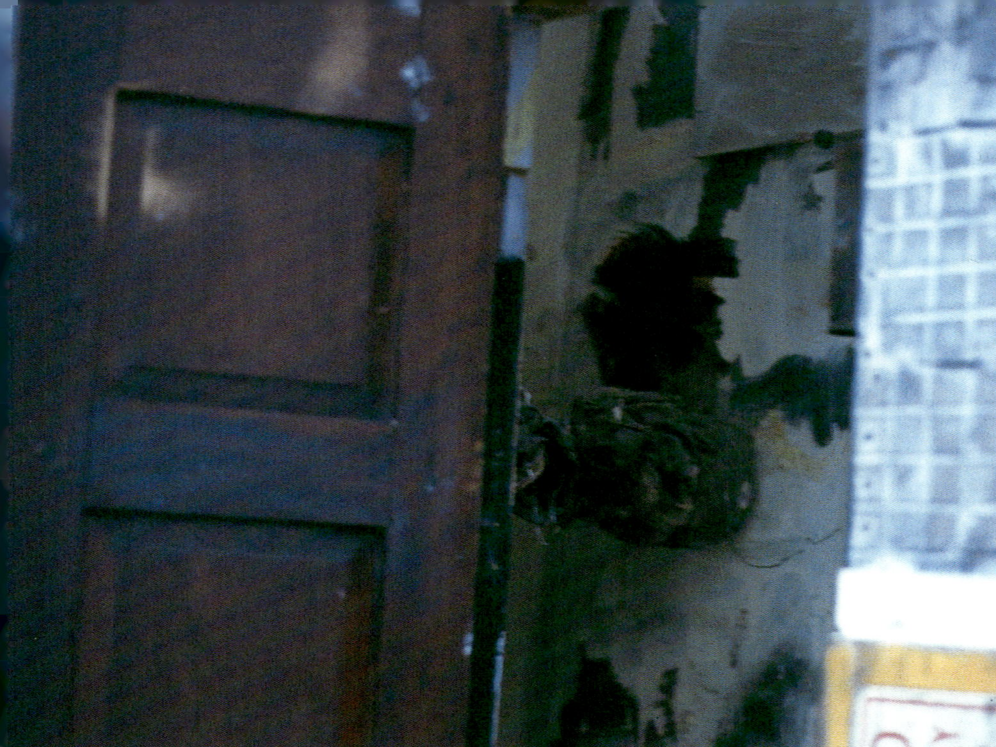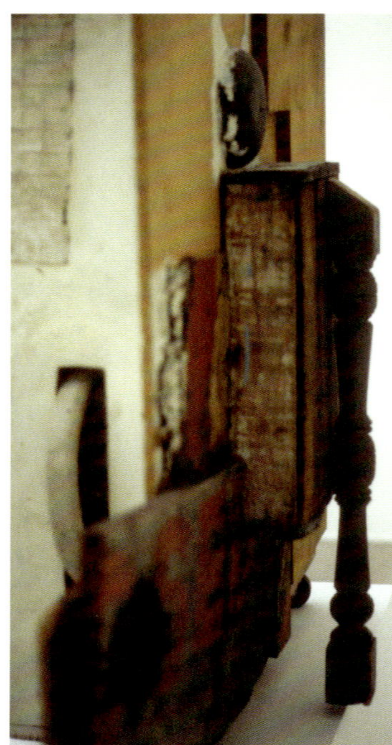



there by a large wooden sign marked with red capital letters (fig. 3.3). CLOSED, it must once have read, but now only the last four letters on the plank are visible, and even these are truncated and overpainted with a stain of black. This stunted expression seems to bespeak a central concern of the work: *Inside-Out* denies access to illusion, to painting, and—with its incongruous parts and unclear meanings—to interpretation. And there is a sense that, even as its gestures are repeated, Rauschenberg is trying to bring something about Abstract Expressionism to closure.

These impressions of *Inside-Out* will form the themes for our understanding of Robert Rauschenberg's practice at the start of the 1960s. The antiquated, the junky, the illegible—these are the terms that Rauschenberg put to work in the period. This chapter aims to understand what might have been at stake in these obsessions. It also seeks to determine why, in 1961 and 1962, the extreme flatness of Rauschenberg's painting was insistently paired with—

indeed, eventually subordinated to—the accretion of discarded objects.

These were particular years in Rauschenberg's career. From early in 1961 Rauschenberg began to focus intensively on junk and three-dimensional space; his new combines deployed broken traffic barricades, stamped tin, and rusted wheels where earlier works had used photographs, magazine clippings, and scraps of newspaper. (Compare *Inside-Out* with *Rebus* of 1955 [fig. 3.4], for example, or even with the transitional *Allegory* of 1960 [fig. 3.5].) This investment in material objects proved to be a short, but pivotal, one. By the fall of 1962, Rauschenberg had fully taken up the flat image-transfer practices that then dominated his work until his death. (See, for example, *Crocus* of 1962; fig. 3.6.) The artist's brief investment in junk sculpture, however, epitomizes what has been most interesting, in my view, about his work—namely its investigation of the possibilities for meaning in a disordered material world.

FIG. 3.4
**Robert Rauschenberg**
*Rebus*, 1955
Combine painting: oil, synthetic
polymer paint, pencil, crayon, pastel,
cut-and-pasted printed and painted
papers, and fabric on canvas mounted
and stapled to fabric, three panels,
96 x 131 in. (243.8 x 333 cm)
Museum of Modern Art, New York,
Partial and Promised Gift of Jo Carole
and Ronald S. Lauder, and Purchase

FIG. 3.5
**Robert Rauschenberg**
*Allegory*, 1960
Combine painting: oil, paper, fabric,
printed paper, wood, and umbrella
on three canvases, and metal,
sand, and glue on mirrored panel,
72 x 114 x 12 in.
(182.9 x 289.6 x 30.5 cm)
Museum Ludwig, Cologne

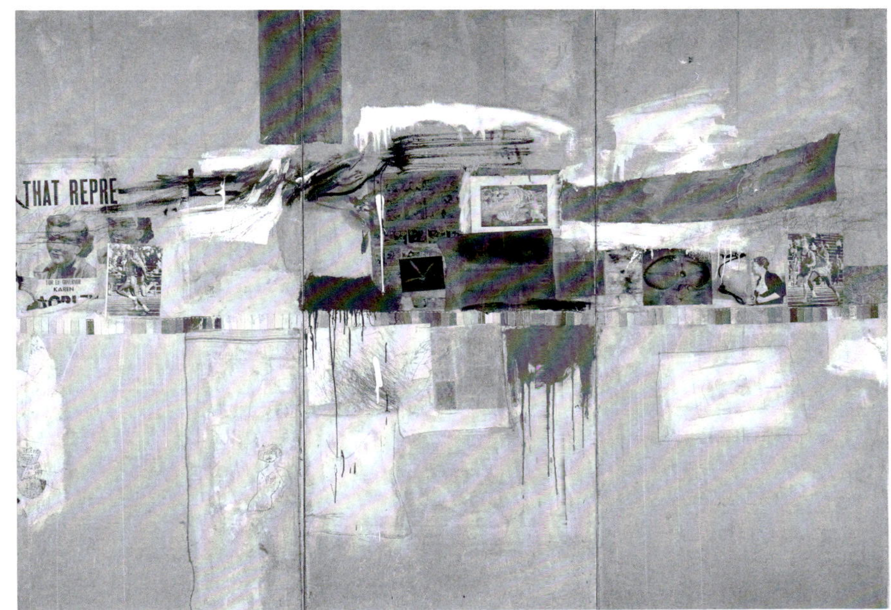
THAT REPRE
KARIN

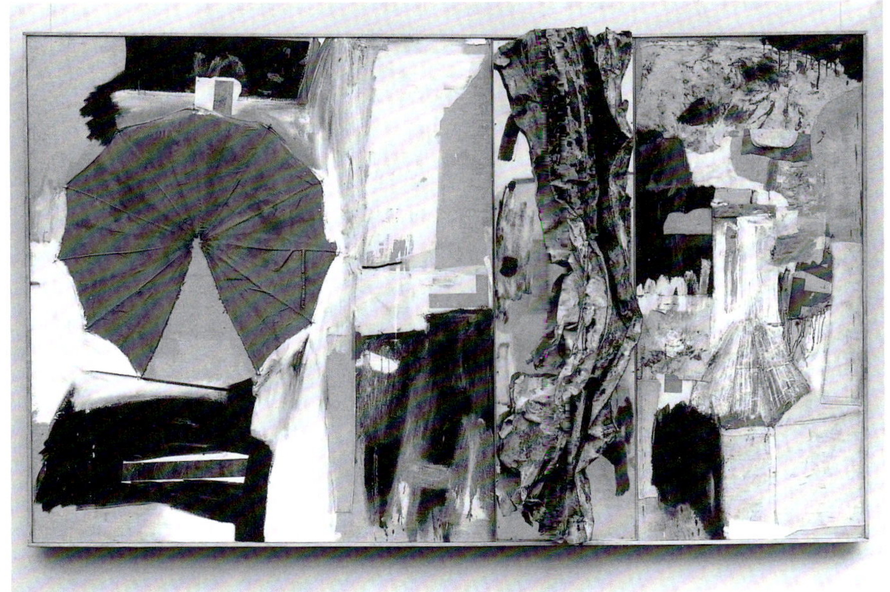

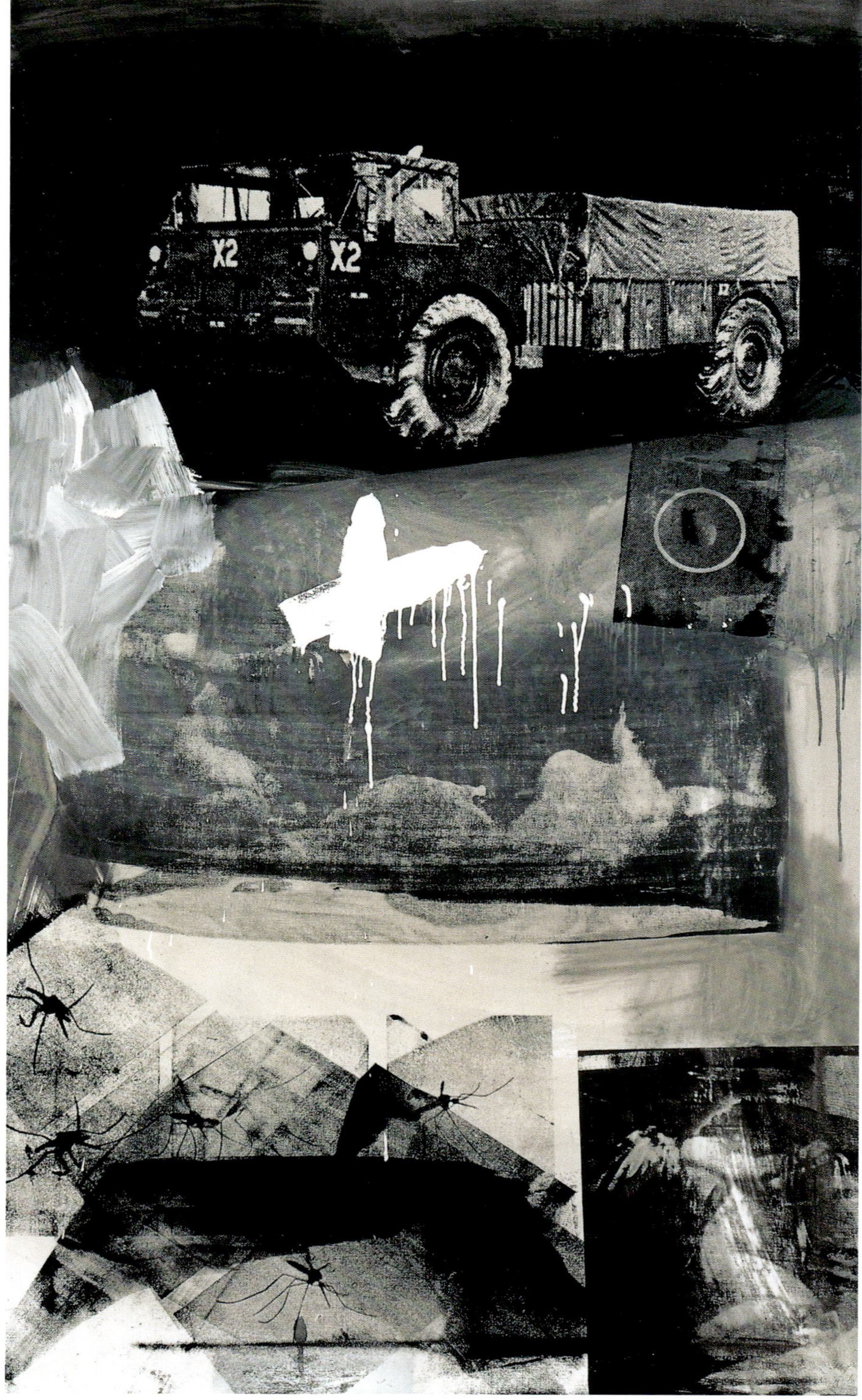



**FIG. 3.6**
**Robert Rauschenberg**
*Crocus*, 1962
Oil and silk-screen ink on canvas
60 x 36 in. (152.4 x 91.4 cm)
Collection of Linda and
Harry Macklowe, New York

The chapter that follows proceeds through five major sections. The first two discuss, respectively, the art-historical position of Rauschenberg's use of junk, and the resultant difficulties in legibility. (To date, these have been the focus of most of the advanced criticism on Rauschenberg's work.) The next two parts trace the histories and meanings of the particular kinds of junk that Rauschenberg marshaled in his works of 1961 and 1962, observing their origins in aging New York architecture and in consumer detritus. The final section argues, through a sustained discussion of the combine painting *Black Market,* that Rauschenberg's materialist work was a limited kind of negative response to the abstraction of the built environment around it. In articulating the historical specificity of Rauschenberg's famed investigations of meaning, that is, the chapter aims to discover what the combines have to teach us about contemporaneous efforts to render the local built environment (through a remaking of New York and its goods) newly abstract.

The years 1961 and 1962 were not only a pivotal time for the young Rauschenberg, but also an active one. In these years he traveled to the Netherlands, France, and Sweden; exhibited works at the Museum of Modern Art, the Guggenheim, and the Whitney; and helped plan his first solo museum exhibition.[4] He also broke up with his partner, Jasper Johns, and moved from a loft in the Financial District to his new home and studio on lower Broadway.[5] Critics, meanwhile (both generating and pursuing Rauschenberg's new stardom), were trying to come to terms with his new work.

## Rauschenberg the Formalist, and His Junk

Swenson's rejection of *Inside-Out,* as we have seen, is made on formalist grounds. His final assessment of the work (which, before becoming *Inside-Out,* had been called *Novice*) appears near the end of the article: "I first saw the finished piece at his gallery, Castelli, with its [original] title gone as well as its top and part of its side. It gave the over-all impression of a musical chord 'in which no note can really be heard'; visually it seemed too tightly organized and, like the final painting inside the box, overworked. Even the over-all impression was unpleasant; the wheels and the piece jutting out at the side were awkward. The box itself lacked grace." *Inside-Out's* failure, then, is that the composition does not cohere, that, in its raucous cobbling together of disparate objects, "no note can really be heard." This concern of Swenson's about the harmonious organization of pictorial elements—and his correlated lack of interest in the associative meanings of the objects used—is typical of Rauschenberg criticism at the time, even by those who favored his work. Although Irving Sandler, for example, notes that the artist's use of objects brings an "urban seaminess" into the combines, he stresses Rauschenberg's concern with "the way . . . large areas interact formally." "Rauschenberg is a consummate artist," Sandler writes, "with a sure sense of scale, feeling for color relationships and for the fluent transitions from one incongruous pictorial element to another."[6]

Reviewing Rauschenberg's 1963 retrospective at the Jewish Museum, the young Donald Judd offers an especially formalist gloss. Judd writes that the show as a whole was of an impressively "high quality," but he singles out the combine painting *First Landing Jump* (fig. 3.7) as an example of the very best of the artist's production. In his lengthy discussion of the piece, Judd expresses significant interest in Rauschenberg's use of objects, but chiefly for the shapes and colors they lend to the composition. He even compares the composition to a common structure of Giotto's. It is

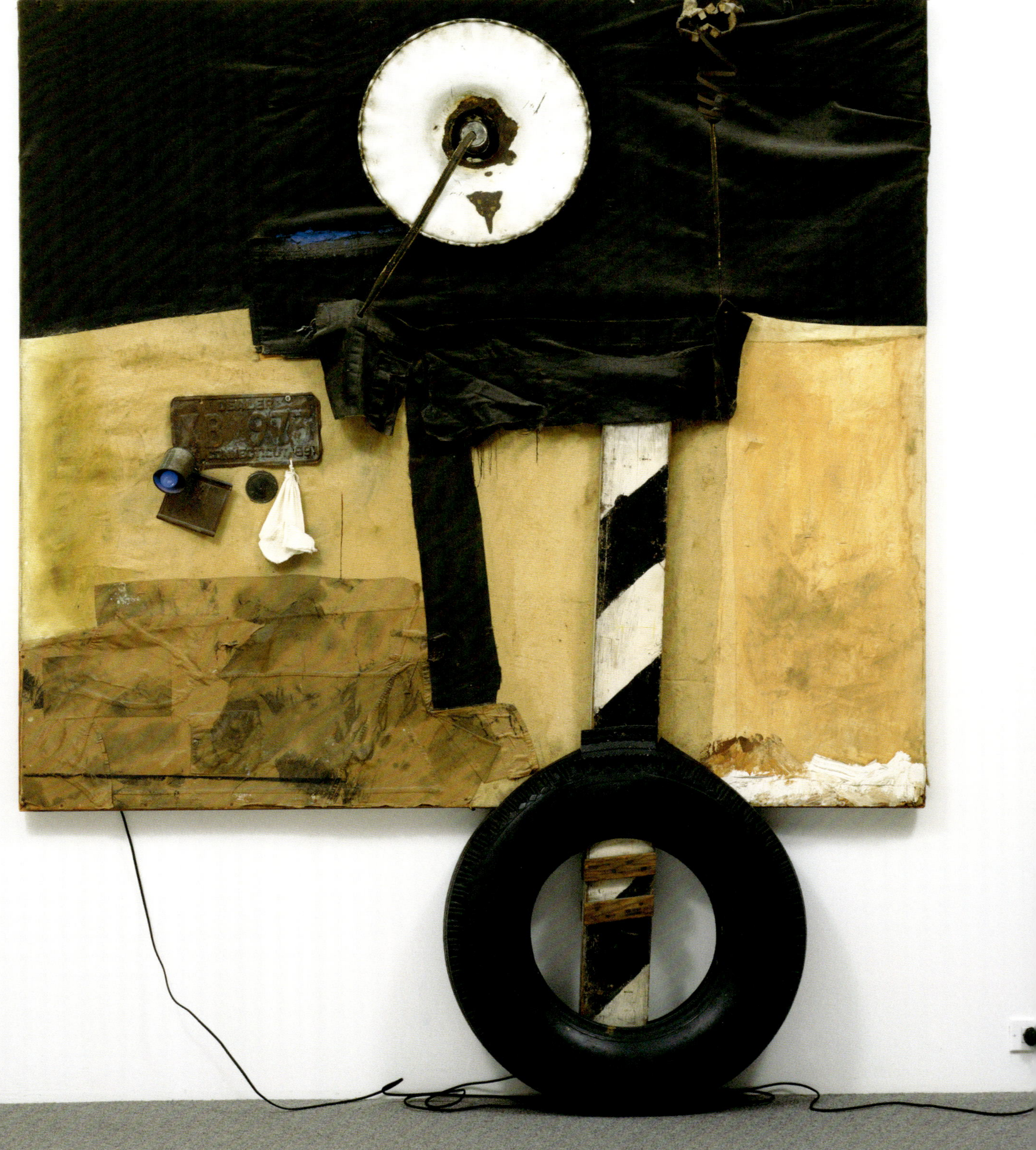

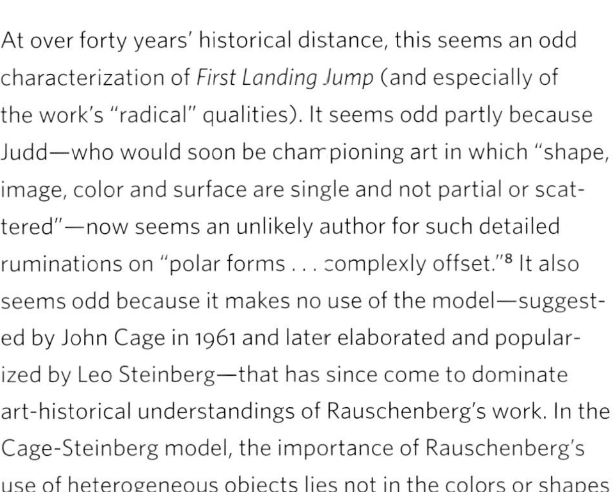

FIG. 3.7
**Robert Rauschenberg**
*First Landing Jump*, 1961
Combine painting: cloth, metal, leather, electric fixture, cable, and oil paint on composition board;
overall, including automobile tire and wooden plank on floor, 89 ⅛ x 72 x 8 ⅞ in. (226.4 x 182.9 x 22.5 cm)
Museum of Modern Art, New York, Gift of Philip Johnson

worth quoting the relevant passage in full, written as it is in Judd's clipped proto-Minimalist style:

> *First Landing Jump* has a tire sitting on the floor, slightly overlapping the canvas. A black and white striped barrier runs down the canvas and through the tire. The top half of the canvas is a black tarpaulin; the bottom is linen and an area of white parallel to the barrier. There is a white metal lampshade in the top half. A black strip, corresponding to the barrier, runs down from it across the linen. The tire is a relatively small but massive fulcrum for the broad canvas. The scheme is like Giotto's main one, e.g., the Arena Lazarus [fig. 3.8]. The lampshade and the tire are polar forms, in part simply opposite to one another and in part complexly offset, since each is offset from the axis given the other by its vertical. And so on down to the small parts, for instance, a blue light bulb in the linen and a matching blue crease in the black. The balanced mass and the polar and . . . offset arrangement are conspicuously traditional forms of composition. The color is black, tan and white—which is also old. There is little brushwork in this combine though. Despite all this, the tire is outside the canvas—which makes the primary shape of the composition a free silhouette—which is radical.[7]

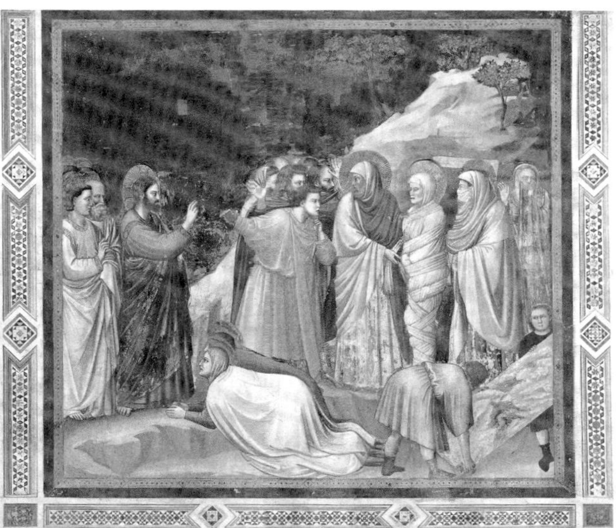

FIG. 3.8
**Giotto di Bondone**
*Resurrection of Lazarus*, c. 1305
Fresco, Scrovegni Chapel (Arena Chapel)
Padua, Italy

At over forty years' historical distance, this seems an odd characterization of *First Landing Jump* (and especially of the work's "radical" qualities). It seems odd partly because Judd—who would soon be championing art in which "shape, image, color and surface are single and not partial or scattered"—now seems an unlikely author for such detailed ruminations on "polar forms . . . complexly offset."[8] It also seems odd because it makes no use of the model—suggested by John Cage in 1961 and later elaborated and popularized by Leo Steinberg—that has since come to dominate art-historical understandings of Rauschenberg's work. In the Cage-Steinberg model, the importance of Rauschenberg's use of heterogeneous objects lies not in the colors or shapes they bring with them (and certainly not in any compositional *order* they might organize on the canvas) but rather in their accretion into a kind of epistemological diagram of a complicated world and our untidy experiences with it. Hence, Cage's vision of Rauschenberg's work as "'the imitation of nature in her manner of operation. Or a net,'" and Steinberg's understanding of it as "dump, reservoir, switching center . . . the outward symbol of the mind as a running transformer of the external world, constantly ingesting unprocessed data to be mapped in an overcharged field."[9]

Judd's concerns with composition (and Sandler's and Swenson's) were, however, endemic to a New York still under the sway of Abstract Expressionist painting.

Rauschenberg himself—constantly adding and removing parts for *Inside-Out*—was clearly quite deliberate about the formal effects of his work: it was he who had first expressed to Swenson his dislike of compositions "in which no note can really be heard." But Rauschenberg's intention in using these words was nearly opposite to that of Swenson's (and far closer, we could now say, to the interests of Cage and Steinberg). The artist was wary of too much visual coherence, not too little: he wanted to avoid, he had told Swenson, a work "in which no note can really be heard because the over-all vibrations are so unified." "I would like my pictures," he said, "to be able to be taken apart as easily as they're put together—so you can recognize an object when you're looking at it."[10]

Rauschenberg's continual efforts to perfect his composition, in other words, sought precisely to allow the specific identities of his gathered objects to come forward. Although Swenson was not alone in recoiling at this effect (another writer asserted that the "problem" in Rauschenberg's combines was that "some things resist transformation and remain themselves"), some critics, even at the moment, welcomed the strong identities of Rauschenberg's appropriated junk. In a very enthusiastic appraisal, for example, Henry Geldzahler noted that, in Rauschenberg's work, "Coke bottles are allowed to remain aggressively that." Even Donald Judd's odd review, for all its interest in the "scheme" of the combines, praised the "objectivity" of the works and declared that "the attached objects are first just things."[11]

This materialism, remember, was not without precedent. Allan Kaprow had written in 1958 that Pollock's legacy for contemporary art was his "[involvement] in the stuff of his art as a group of *concrete facts*." Pollock, Kaprow added, "left us at the point where we must become preoccupied with and even dazzled by the space and objects of our everyday life, either our bodies, clothes, rooms, or, if need be, the vastness of Forty-Second Street." Rauschenberg—who had helped to inspire Kaprow's thinking—echoed these notions a few months later: "A pair of socks is no less suitable to make a painting with than wood, nails, turpentine, oil and fabric."[12]

Whatever its precedents in literalist painting (or even in collage more generally), Rauschenberg intended his investment in objects to be polemical. His was an artistic practice of the ordinary world—famously meant to operate in "that gap" between art and life. It might, for example, "[begin] with a painting and then sort of [move] out into the room."[13] It was the literal use of ordinary material objects that led Cage to characterize Rauschenberg's works as "not ideas but facts," and that had led the artist himself to say of his objects, "What they mean is not as interesting as what they are."[14] But these last two statements press the most urgent question posed by Rauschenberg's appropriation of junk: if the works are "facts" (and not ideas or meanings), how, if at all, might we read them?

## Legibility

**Barbara Rose:** Looking at your paintings, the images aren't literal, they are allusive, like poetry.

**Robert Rauschenberg:** They're facts. They're all facts.
—INTERVIEW, C. 1987

I have an Etruscan hand that's just that. It's just so literal. It's a fact. A hand.
—ROBERT RAUSCHENBERG, 1958

Since the beginning of the 1960s, efforts to understand Rauschenberg's works have been dogged by this difficulty of

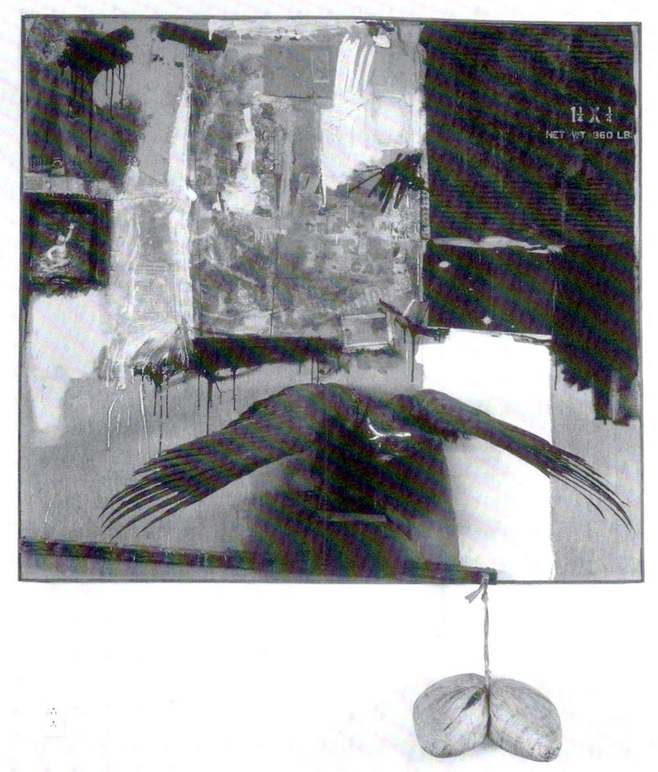

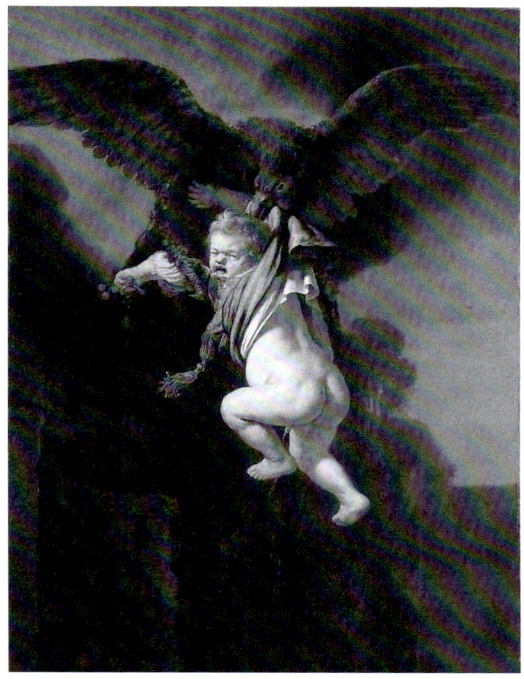

interpreting (or, equally, by the difficulty of *not* interpreting) material fact. There has been considerable disagreement about how much to understand the works as purely obdurate materiality, avidly resisting metaphor and narrative, and how much to see them as legible collections of meaningful objects. Predictably, some have favored the latter view so strongly as to publish comprehensive iconographic decodings. In 1982, for example, Kenneth Bendiner used his discovery of a Rembrandt allusion in *Canyon*—note the prominent eagle and the buttockslike pillow (figs. 3.9 and 3.10)—to argue that the whole work was a game of reference. He went so far as to suggest that the cacophonous paint and paper fragments at the center of the assemblage (elements endemic to nearly all Rauschenberg's work in 1959) expressed Ganymede's screams while being carried aloft, and that the title ("can-yonder," he rephrased it) referred to "the rising of Ganymede's buttocks into the sky."[15]

A more compelling set of iconographic arguments has been advanced recently by Jonathan D. Katz, Laura Auricchio, and Lisa Wainwright, who see in many of Rauschenberg's works covert references to American homosexuality in the 1950s. Indeed, Katz picks up on Bendiner's argument to stress the homosexual nature of Ganymede's abduction by Zeus (and therefore of Rauschenberg's allusion to it).[16] Katz and Auricchio persuasively suggest, too, that Rauschenberg's play with hidden meaning expresses the closeted subjectivity endemic to homosexual experience in the period. The deficit of this kind of account lies in its partiality: it does little to account for the overall effect of Rauschenberg's works—their unusual, junky materials and their half-organized compositions.

I am not the first to point out the inadequacies of the iconographic readings. Alan Solomon rejected such attempts as early as 1963, and Yve-Alain Bois has noted their

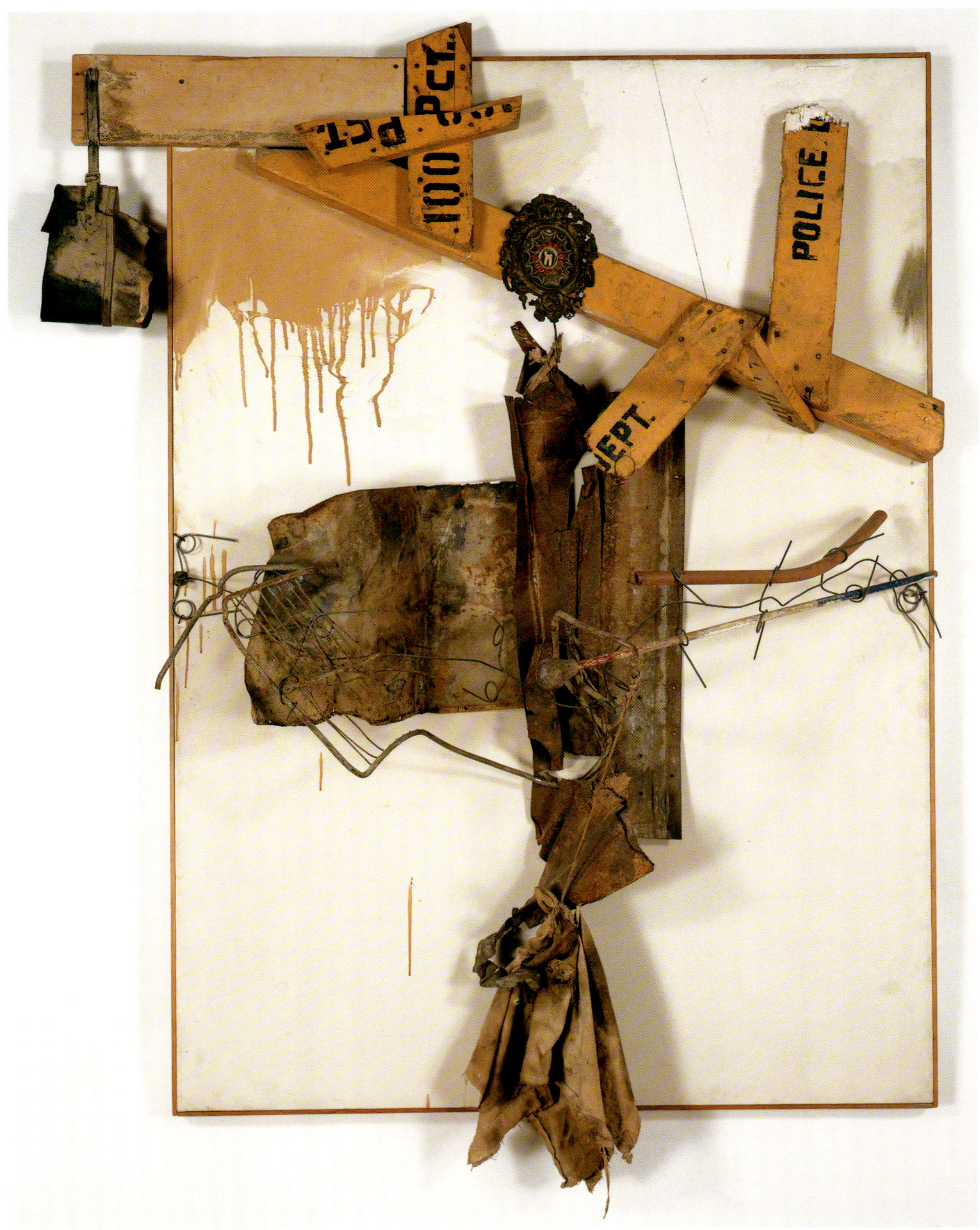
173d PCT.
1100
POLICE.
DEPT.

**Robert Rauschenberg**

*Co-Existence*, 1961

Combine painting: oil, fabric, metal, wood, wire,

rubber, and medallion with tooth on canvas,

66 3/4 x 49 7/8 x 14 1/4 in. (167.64 x 124.46 x 35.36 cm)

Virginia Museum of Fine Arts, Richmond, Gift of the Sydney and Francis Lewis Foundation

inherent partiality as recently as 2006.[17] Roger Cranshaw and Adrian Lewis offered some attempted decodings in 1981, only to remark, "We are faced with an abundance of competing semantic possibilities," and then to point out, "The works invite decodification, but frustrate its operation." Jonathan Fineberg, in a similar gloss, remarked that "the cross-tracking multiplicity of associations permits one to 'read' the individual images in any number of ways at the same time; thus, the 'decodings' by art historians attempting to rigidify the artist's associations into a systematically decipherable text have so far not yielded convincing results."[18]

In her 1997 essay "Perpetual Inventory," Rosalind Krauss offers an unusually rewarding discussion of the difficulty of reading Rauschenberg's work. She notes, for example, the artist's disappointment at emotive readings of his early black paintings, quoting him from a 1965 interview: "They couldn't see black as pigment. They moved immediately into association with 'burned-out,' 'tearing,' 'nihilism,' and 'destruction.' . . . I'm never sure what the impulse is psychologically. . . . If I see any superficial subconscious relationships that I'm familiar with—clichés of association— I change the picture."[19] Krauss notes also, however, that Rauschenberg's works cannot escape metaphor altogether, since associative meanings inevitably attach to all objects. She again cites the artist himself, this time speaking to David Sylvester in 1964: "We have ideas about bricks. A brick just isn't a physical mass of a certain dimension that one builds houses or chimneys with. The whole world of associations, all the information that we have—the fact that it's made of dirt, that it's been through a kiln, romantic ideas about little brick cottages, or the chimney which is so romantic, or labor—you have to deal with as many of the things as you know about."[20] Indeed, Krauss notes that Rauschenberg has

said that he titled one of his early silk-screen paintings *Crocus* (see fig. 3.6) "because the white X emerges from a gray area in a rather dark painting, like a new season." Krauss concludes that Rauschenberg's works tend to operate allegorically: references are always in play, but in a space that she characterizes, following Roland Barthes, as "a kind of echo chamber of unstable meanings." The works generate "multiple associational codes," or "anarchic and metastatic" chains of connotation. The result of all these uncontrollable and incoherent meanings is a "message of uncertainty, of slippage, of unreadability and fragmentation."[21]

Krauss's interest lies in the semantic form of Rauschenberg's practice (its deployment of allegory), and she declines to pursue any of the specific meanings being circulated and deferred. (Recently, Branden Joseph has picked up this understanding of the work as illegible, adding that it thereby offers a critical resistance.[22]) It seems to me, by contrast, that the objects and images in Rauschenberg's works are far from arbitrary, and that they reveal something of why the artist took such a sustained interest in frustrating representation. Let us see what it might mean to try to make sense of one of the 1961 combines.[23]

A section of bright yellow traffic barricade—not unlike a giant letter A—presides over the off-white canvas of *Co-Existence* (fig. 3.11). For all its vivid color, however, this fragmented barricade is splintered, worn, and sullied. Most of it is missing, and the parts that remain have been reaffixed to each other as if at random, with rusted nails. An earlier use of this object is legible from an indistinct NYPD branded into the wood, and from the black stenciled marks reading POLICE DEPT. 100 PCT. Onto this framework an antique metal medallion has been hammered, a bit callously, with shiny-headed nails. Its dark floral frame surrounds a partially rotten tooth, set behind glass and surrounded with red beads.[24]

Below the barricade, at the heart of the canvas, is a tangle of wires and metal sheeting. The thoroughly rusted, vertically oriented sheet of metal at center is ripped and brittle; a large shard peeled off at the bottom curves around a soiled rag. Another tiny scrap of cloth clings to the metal's upper edge. A second, more substantial sheet appears, like its frailer partner, to have been appropriated from a now unknowable industrial vehicle or machine. It is creased and dented, its surface rippled in places with a fine, fingerprint-like texture betraying some old strain. Its patina of rust and disappearing blue-black paint make it a palette of colors from bright orange to tan, brown, gray, and black.

The bramble of curving metal lines that screens these sheets of metal comprises two appropriated objects: a long string of thick wire brackets and a corroded grill. The wire curves messily in front of the canvas, attached only at the left and right edges. Any specific previous uses are unclear, but here it cradles a section of red rubber hose and a faded red-white-and-blue-painted stick, capped with a once-sparkly rubber ball. Intertwined with the wire and also curving around the wooden stick are the ripped-open remains of the grill, perhaps once used for cooking.

An attempt at wresting a coherent reading from *Co-Existence* might understand the stick—tangled as it is with ripped sheet metal, twisted grill, and shattered police barri-cade—as the gearshift lever at the center of some horrible car wreck. Such a reading might gather evidence, too, from the bloodlike dripping of paint at upper left and the memo-rializing effects of that rotten tooth. Another iconographic effort would have the medallion serve as a head and the rag as a loincloth to make the whole thing seem, in one critic's words, "a crazy golgotha cross."[25]

These readings, however, run into difficulty, and not only because they seem mutually exclusive or because of parts that can never quite be made to fit, such as the scrap of rubber boot hanging off the upper edge of the canvas. They run into difficulty primarily because we cannot for very long stave off the return of these objects' disparate identi-ties. In the place of a crucifix we see yellow wood; looking for a bloody car crash, we see dripping paint.

Indeed, it is the various formal effects of *Co-Existence* that provide the greatest obstacle to synthetic readings. With time, one feels that this work, like *Inside-Out*, is, above all, a painting (or at least a rumination about painting). The objects seem to have been selected and manipulated as if they were paint—the heavy cloth at the bottom stained to match the rusted metal sheets above it, and the whole as-semblage governed by subtly foiled symmetries and chains of formal correspondence (boot scrap, rag; medallion, rubber ball). We have also the painterly effects of the rust, and the network of wire looping in the style of an automatist drawing. Whatever its compositional logic, however, the detailed particularities of *Co-Existence* (and especially of its paint) lack any apparent representational purpose. Notice, for example, the bright, slightly pinkish white that irregu-larly blankets much of the upper half of the canvas, or the dirty-looking gray-brown area, near the upper right-hand corner, that looks like an accidental smudging. In particular, the richly specific details of the sandy yellow drips at upper left—zigging and zagging across the rigid lines of the coarse white brushwork below—stress the work's contingency on the material circumstances of its making. As such, the paint destabilizes our synthetic efforts, asserting (over the appeal of our interpretive leads) the unabstractable materiality of the things Rauschenberg has gathered.

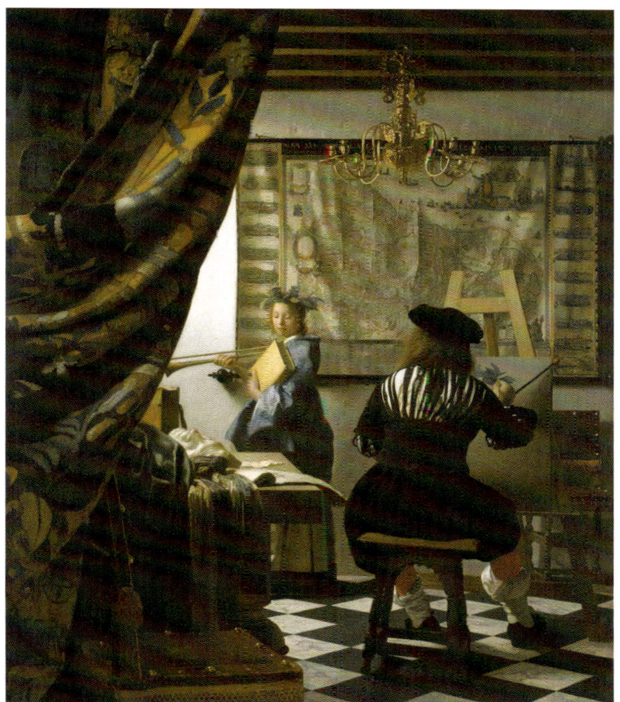

In *Co-Existence,* then, we do in fact have a work that enacts unstable meanings, or tensions between materiality and metaphor. We might, though, go further, and indulge the possibility of considering *Co-Existence,* more specifically and more traditionally, as a full-dress allegory of the art of painting. Such a reading would see the soiled cloth as a turpentine-stained brush rag, and the colored baton as a maulstick (and one positioned just as Vermeer positions the maulstick in his own *Allegory of the Art of Painting* [fig. 3.12]). The barricade, too, might be understood as an easel, appropriately broken, and—along with the other paraphernalia here—affixed to the canvas itself: rendered object rather than tool for the production of illusion. In the place, for example, of Vermeer's figuration and map, we would find in Rauschenberg's painting only real objects drawn from the urban landscape itself. The overall force of the allegory would be its performance of the Kaprow-Rauschenberg directive that art be made from the "objects of our everyday life," that it offer real, material things where illusion used to lurk.[26]

Such a reading seems just about tenable and also preposterous. For if there is a conclusion to be drawn here, it surely concerns the impossibility of interpretive conclusion, even along these lines. What is performed is precisely the unresolved nature of painting: its endless animation of a never-synthesized dialectic between possible readings on the one hand and a plenitude of incommensurable material fact on the other. The possibility of drawing any abstractions from the material world, we might say, is seen to be forever in doubt.[27] It is a central argument of this chapter, however, that the workings of combines such as *Co-Existence* are historically and geographically specific, and amount to far more than a philosophical observation about the nature of representation. We ought to ask why such frustrations of representation seemed to need such emphatic articulation in New York around 1960, and why Rauschenberg would have performed these articulations over the odd and very particular objects that he did. When Rauschenberg's combine paintings bring soiled rags or rusted metal into the space of the modernist canvas, that is, they do more than just intensify the tension—extended from earlier painting—between representation and materiality. They bring in particular kinds of signs, replete with their own specific (if forever insecure) associations.

In fact, as may already be clear, the objects Rauschenberg appropriated in making his most sculptural and heterogeneous combine paintings (the ones from 1961 and 1962) are drawn chiefly from two specific realms. First are objects from the architecture and streetscape of the city, such as the ceiling fragments of *Inside-Out*, the automobile tire and outdoor lampshade of *First Landing Jump*, and the traffic barricades crossing that work as well as *Co-Existence, Aen Floga* (fig. 3.13), and *Wall Street* (see fig. 3.29). Second are fragments of consumer detritus, including the rickety cart wheel of *Inside-Out,* the rubber boot scrap and old grill

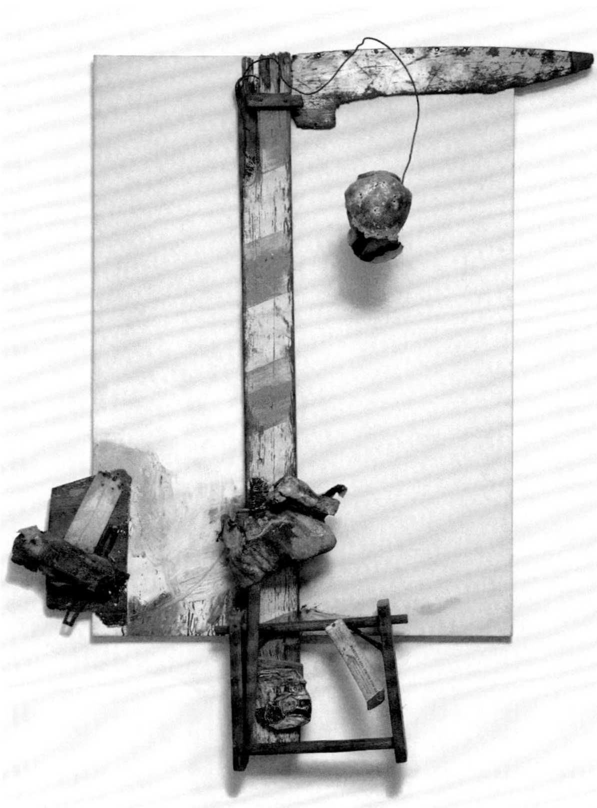



in *Co-Existence*, and the discarded tin cans that appear in no fewer than six of the combines from these two years.[28] The rest of this chapter is concerned with understanding why these are the kinds of objects that Rauschenberg picked up repeatedly when making his materialist combines of 1961 and 1962. What was it, we need to ask, about the city and about the discards of consumerism that made them the founts for Rauschenberg's explorations of the limits of legibility?

## The City

Although the claim has largely evaporated in the recent literature, there was an oft-repeated (if little-explored) notion in the 1960s and 1970s that something about Rauschenberg's work was fundamentally urban. In the 1963 retrospective catalogue, Alan Solomon had simply and briefly announced that the works after 1955 "reflect the urban environment completely." Nearly ten years later,

Steinberg published his pivotal essay, in which—on the way to making his argument about Rauschenberg's contemporary, "flatbed" epistemology—he explicitly mentioned the city: "I once heard Jasper Johns say that Rauschenberg was the man who in this century had invented the most since Picasso. What he invented above all was, I think, a pictorial surface that let the world in again. Not the world of the Renaissance man who looked for his weather clues out of the window; but the world of men who turn knobs to hear a taped message, 'precipitation probability ten percent tonight,' electronically transmitted from some windowless booth. Rauschenberg's picture plane is for the consciousness immersed in the brain of the city." Although his evocation of "the brain of the city" is suggestive, Steinberg's concerns lay in unveiling the overall morphology of the works as a plane for accumulated objects and processes, rather than in understanding what things appeared there or why.[29]

Lawrence Alloway—who, as we have seen, diagnosed in 1960 a "New York junk culture" movement in art—also wrote about the urbanity of Rauschenberg's work in particular. Comparing Rauschenberg's practice to Willem de Kooning's use of cotton in painting, for example, Alloway wrote in 1962, "Rauschenberg puts the cotton, or the box, into the art work, combining it with other objects from the waste or the stores of the city. The objects are not symbols (as some of Harnett's are, for example, of rest or vanity) programmed to spell out a theme, recognition of which brings unity to the conglomerate. The unity of the objects in an assembly [of Rauschenberg's] is in their source, the environment of the city."[30] Despite this prominent identification of the city as "the source" of Rauschenberg's objects, Alloway does not attempt to develop an understanding of Rauschenberg's urbanity; rather, he uses this characterization simply to further establish his point that Rauschenberg's art is involved with everyday life.[31]

In order to pursue an understanding along these lines, we might go back to one of the more revealing of the early critical mentions of the works' urbanity. Recall that Irving Sandler had written, "The Junk materials [Rauschenberg] uses introduce a rawness into his work, an urban seaminess." In another review, Sandler characterized the objects in Rauschenberg's work specifically as "urban debris," and in a third (in fact the earliest of the three) he wrote, "If Rauschenberg continues to make found objects precious, he treats them less in terms of private sentiments and associations, more in terms of the environment from which they come—the street. The rawness of the city asserts itself increasingly in his work."[32] Like the other early critics, Sandler did not attempt to understand what might have been at stake in Rauschenberg's address to the city, but his insistence on the words *rawness* and *seaminess* seems to me exactly right. Rauschenberg's version of urbanity *is* raw (the elements are unprocessed; they have not been made to merge), and it is, in every sense, seamy (the objects are the unwanted scraps from the underside of the city, and—taking Sandler's word at its literal meaning—everything is poorly, or at least evidently, stitched together).

Earlier, I characterized *Inside-Out* (see fig. 3.1) as an imaginative version of obsolete machinery. Pulled off the wall, it is an assemblage cut loose and made into a freestanding, useless apparatus. But there is another way to understand the autonomy of this structure—namely, to see it as a miniature building, as a metaphor for the city's architecture. Perhaps its most prominent feature, after all, is the (apparently) old and soiled wooden doorway at its center. This door gives way to an enclosed space built around coarse wooden floorboards and illuminated from above by a pair of dirty skylights. The dark metal fire bell on the back looks as if it has been sloppily painted over in a superintendent's rushed maintenance project. Indeed, Rauschenberg even covered the face of this piece with scraps of the countless stamped-metal ceilings of New York's turn-of-the-century building boom. These scraps are creased, punctured, and mismatched—the section at left appearing to have come from a formal Beaux-Arts space, the one at right seeming to belong to a far simpler decorative scheme.

These are not neutral architectural details. The old loft in which *Inside-Out* was made, at 809 Broadway, was itself a space of broad-planked floors, stamped-metal ceilings, and dirty skylights (fig. 3.14; fig. 3.15, location D).[33] Indeed, when he published photographs of it in a 1963 portfolio called "Random Order," Rauschenberg stressed that his studio belonged to a class of typical, antique New York buildings. In one shot we see a dark radiator below windowpanes, thick with dirt (fig. 3.16); the view is of the fire escapes and elaborate cornices of the similarly aging buildings across the street. Other photographs in the portfolio picture a confusion of rooftop water tanks and ventilation ducts, as well as the worn marble steps and mosaic floors typical of older New York buildings. One photograph, however—taken from a spot farther north along Rauschenberg's east wall—contrasts this old architecture with the vacant windows of the still-unfinished, smooth-faced white apartment tower going up across Broadway at 60 East Twelfth Street (fig. 3.17).[34]

There was a particular rhetorical force, I want to stress, to the architectural details brought on in *Inside-Out* and "Random Order." This was the architecture of an older New York—and one fast disappearing. This late in the book, I do not need to belabor the significance, in terms of urban form, of 809 Broadway's location at the northern edge of Greenwich Village. Living and working at this address placed Rauschenberg not only directly across from a construction

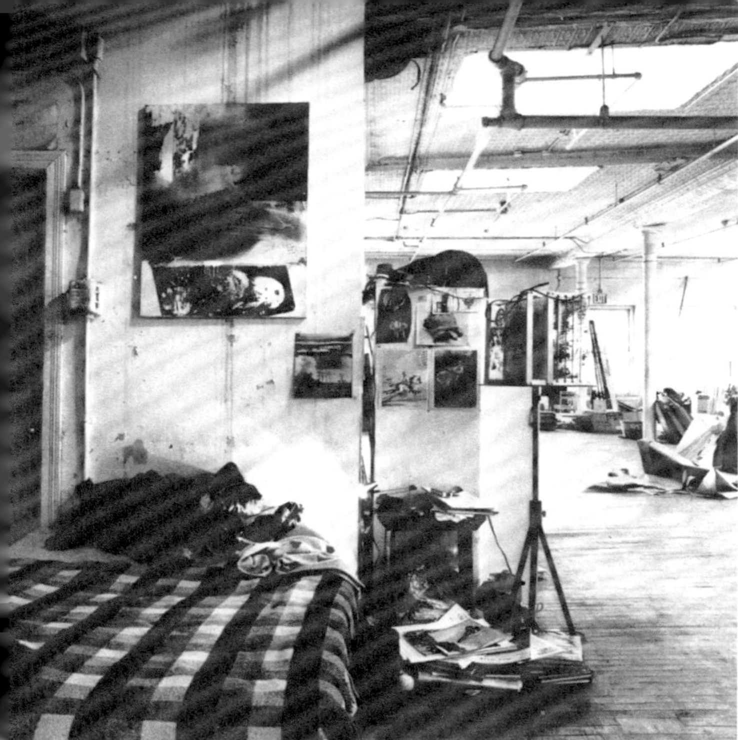

FIG. 3.14
Interior of Rauschenberg's home
at 809 Broadway

FIG. 3.15
Lower Manhattan, with marks added
by author to indicate locations of Robert
Rauschenberg's homes between 1953
and 1962, in chronological order:
(A) 61 Fulton Street,
(B) 278 Pearl Street,
(C) 128 Front Street,
(D) 809 Broadway.
From *Hagstrom's Map of Manhattan:
New York City House Number & Transit Guide*
(New York: Hagstrom, [1962])

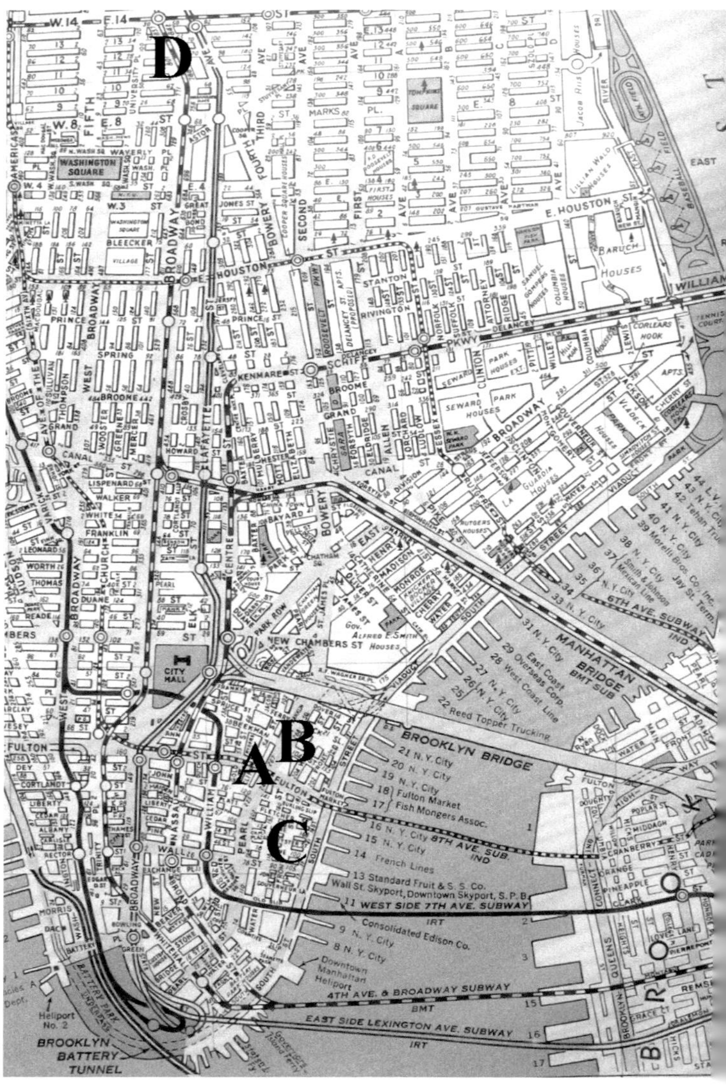

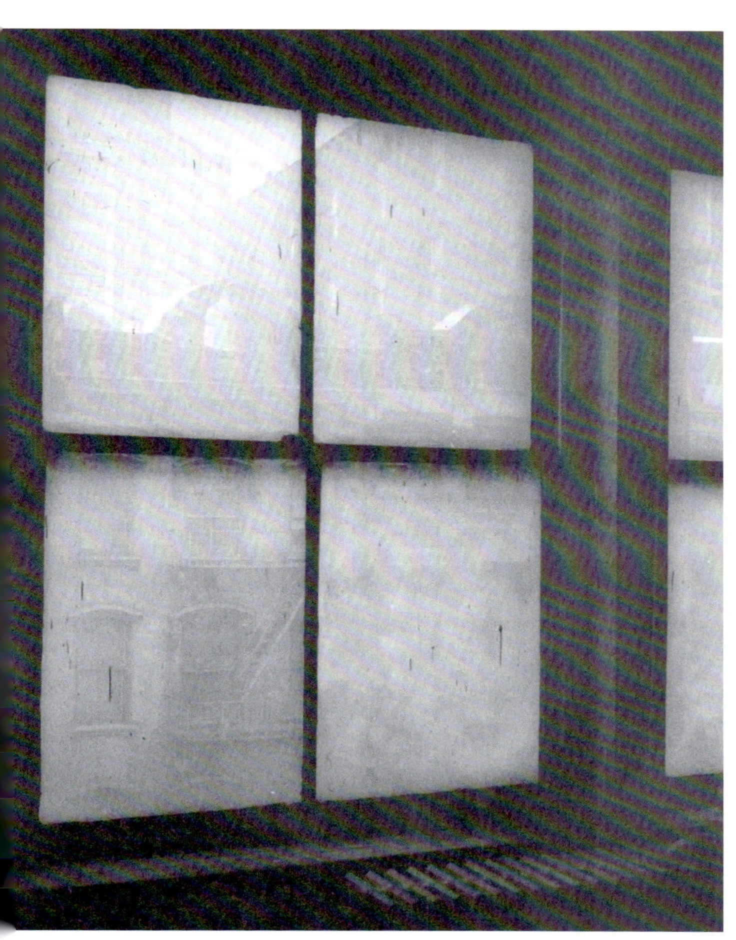

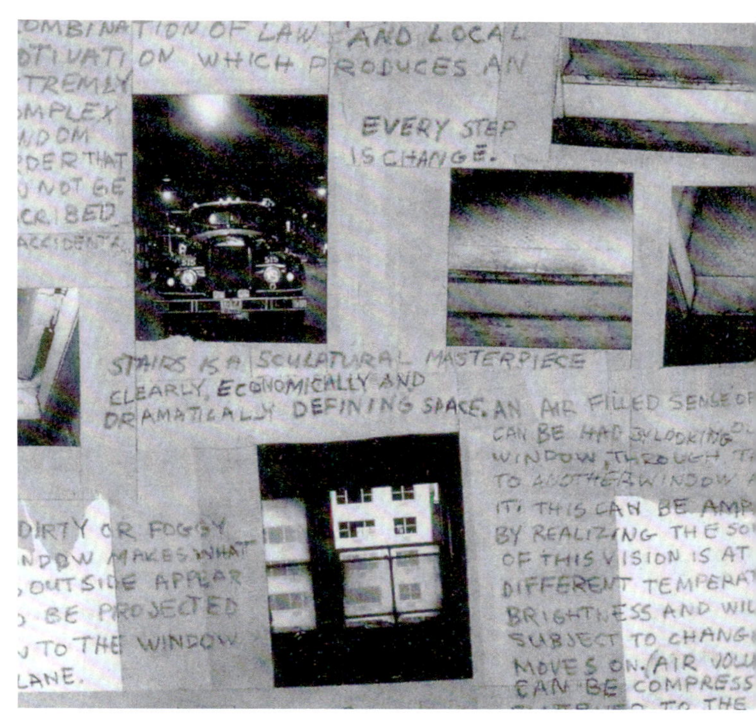



**FIGS. 3.16 and 3.17**
Views from 809 Broadway, from Robert Rauschenberg,
"Random Order," *Location*, Spring 1963, 31

site at which three older buildings were demolished to make way for a new thirteen-story apartment tower, but also at the edges of a giant districtwide wave of reconstruction.[35] Here, Rauschenberg was only eight blocks from Washington Square Village, six blocks from recently saved Washington Square Park, and two blocks from the Reuben Gallery and the whole-block modernist projects that faced it, at Cooper Union and at 70 East Tenth Street. Indeed, at his home, Rauschenberg was living within a five-minute walk of about a dozen new construction sites (see fig. 1.10). Jane Jacobs and the new Save the Village movement were active just down from his doorstep. This was the changing neighborhood that had inspired *New York Times* reporter Ira Henry Freeman to complain, "The mellow old landmarks of Greenwich Village are rapidly disappearing beneath modern glass monuments to . . . bourgeois respectability." In contrast to these new buildings, the sagging roof and exposed pipes of Rauschenberg's studio could have served—like Oldenburg's exhibition space at the nearby Reuben Gallery—to typify the "crooked studios" that Freeman claimed "used to huddle" in the area.[36] If *Inside-Out* is a building, it is certainly one of this kind—a piece of an older New York where architectural detail is worn and varied and where the translucence of glass is hampered by its role as a surface for the collection of dust.

We should not encounter any difficulty in reconciling *Inside-Out*'s metaphor of architecture with its metaphor of machinery. Rauschenberg's studio at 809 Broadway was an abandoned industrial loft. (Indeed, residential occupation was illegal when Rauschenberg lived there.[37]) Spaces such as this one—with their utilitarian cast-iron support columns, large windows, and skylights—had dotted lower Manhattan in the nineteenth century, forming a major part of the economic engine of the city. Since World War II, however,

the city's light industry had been steadily and heavily hemorrhaging to new factories in the suburbs and abroad. America's increasing reliance on large-scale mechanization, newly integrated freeways, and a globalizing economy meant that it was no longer viable in these years to undertake industrial production at the city center. Many lofts in Manhattan, such as those in the South Houston Industrial District (later to become simply SoHo, land of artists and galleries), were shuttered and dilapidated. In some cases, urban renewal efforts helped to push industry to the periphery; recall that the "slum" area cleared for the construction of Washington Square Village had actually been home to about one thousand small businesses, mostly hat manufacturers.[38]

Rauschenberg had not moved to Greenwich Village until sometime in 1961.[39] Since his 1953 return to New York from Europe, however, he had been living continuously in the shadows of the city's mid-century transformation. His first home in this period was at 61 Fulton Street, just south of the access ramp to the Brooklyn Bridge (see fig. 3.15, location A; figs. 3.18, 3.19). Also an abandoned industrial loft, this space was marked by thick wooden support beams and a pitched ceiling (fire-insurance maps from the period list the height of this building at 3 $\frac{1}{2}$ stories).[40] One photograph reveals an aging brick wall with its mortar deeply cracked; another shows walls made of cinder block and interrupted with a timber-supported shaft of indeterminate industrial purpose (fig. 3.20). When Rauschenberg moved in, this building faced a row of five similar buildings across the street. All of these were torn down at around the time Rauschenberg moved out, leaving a large vacant lot—stretching across most of the block—in their place.[41]

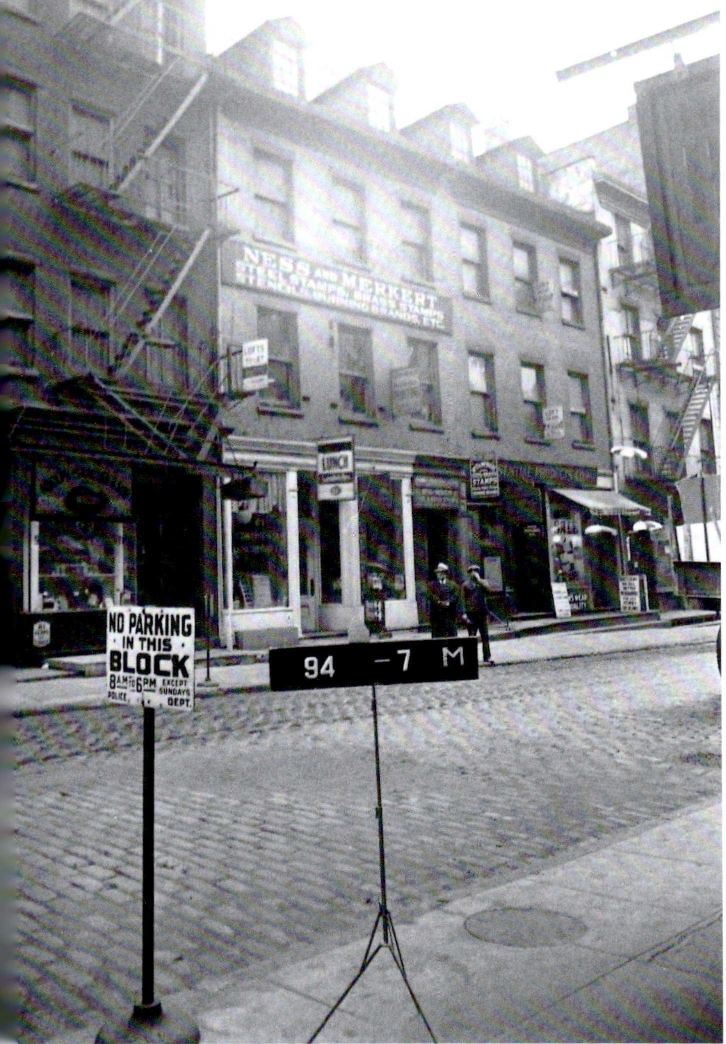

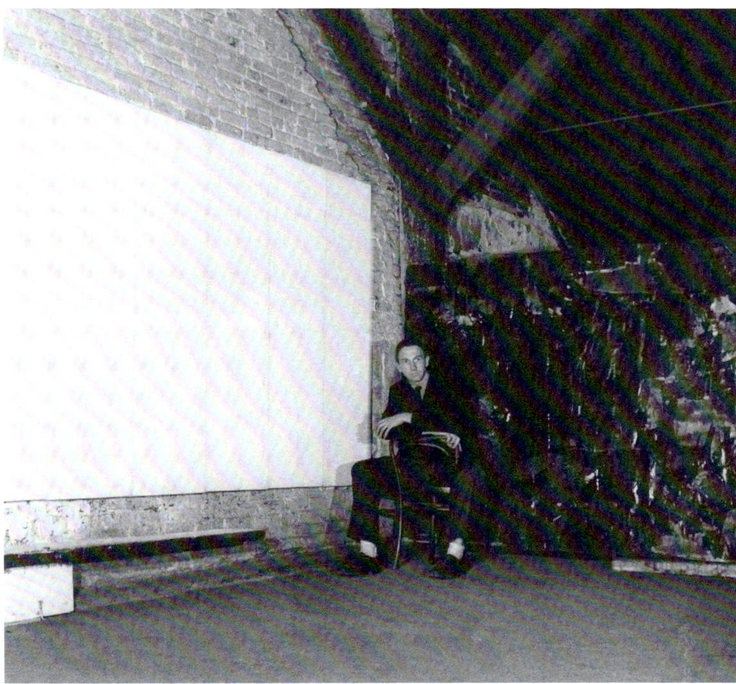

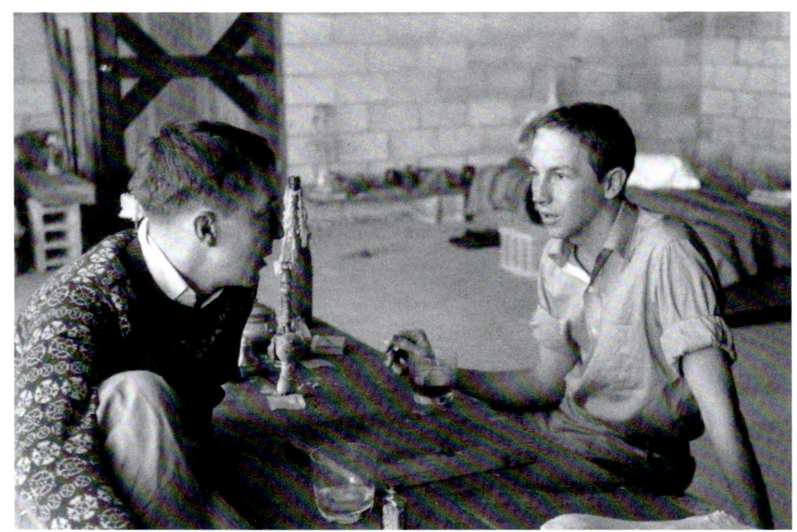

FIG. 3.18 (above)
61 Fulton Street (at center), c. 1940
NYC Municipal Archives

FIG. 3.19 (above right)
Robert Rauschenberg in his home at
61 Fulton Street, c. 1953

FIG. 3.20
Jasper Johns and Robert Rauschenberg in
Rauschenberg's home at 61 Fulton
Street, 1954

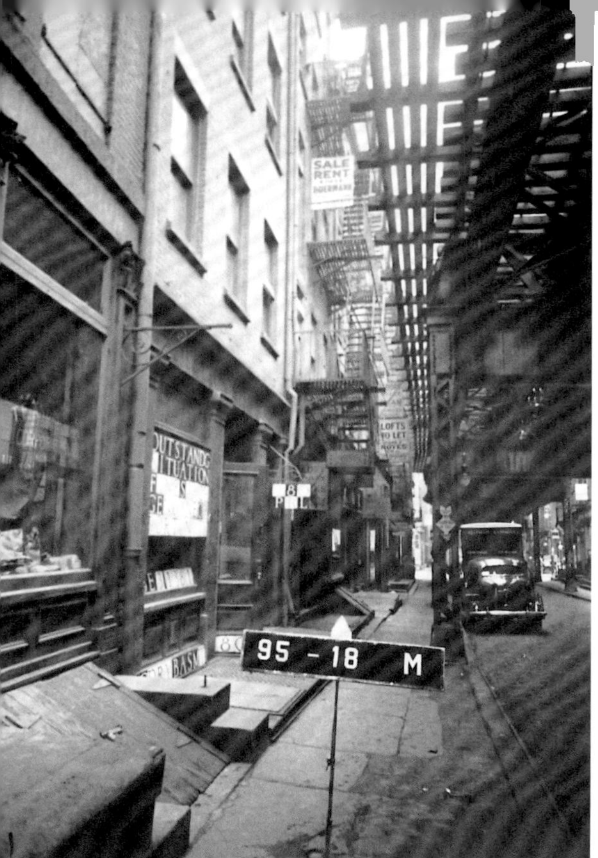

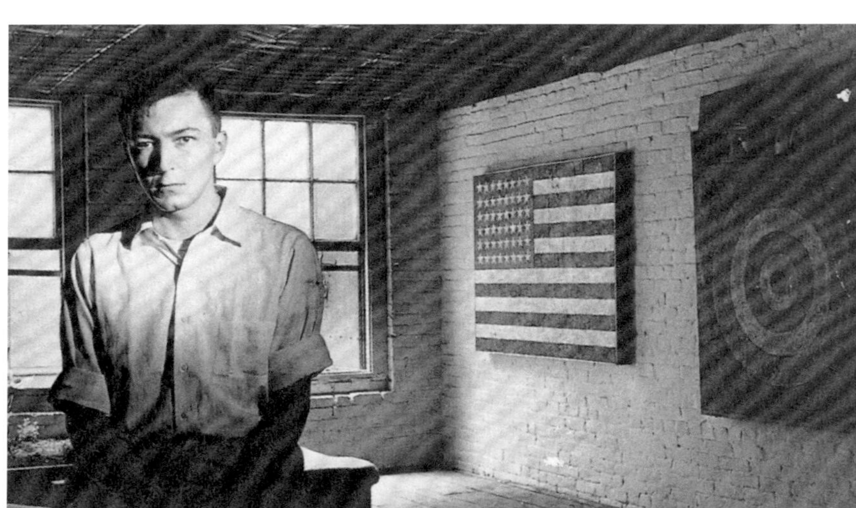



**FIG. 3.21** (left)
278 Pearl Street (with
fire escape), c. 1940
NYC Municipal Archives

**FIG. 3.22** (below)
Jasper Johns in his home
at 278 Pearl Street, 1955

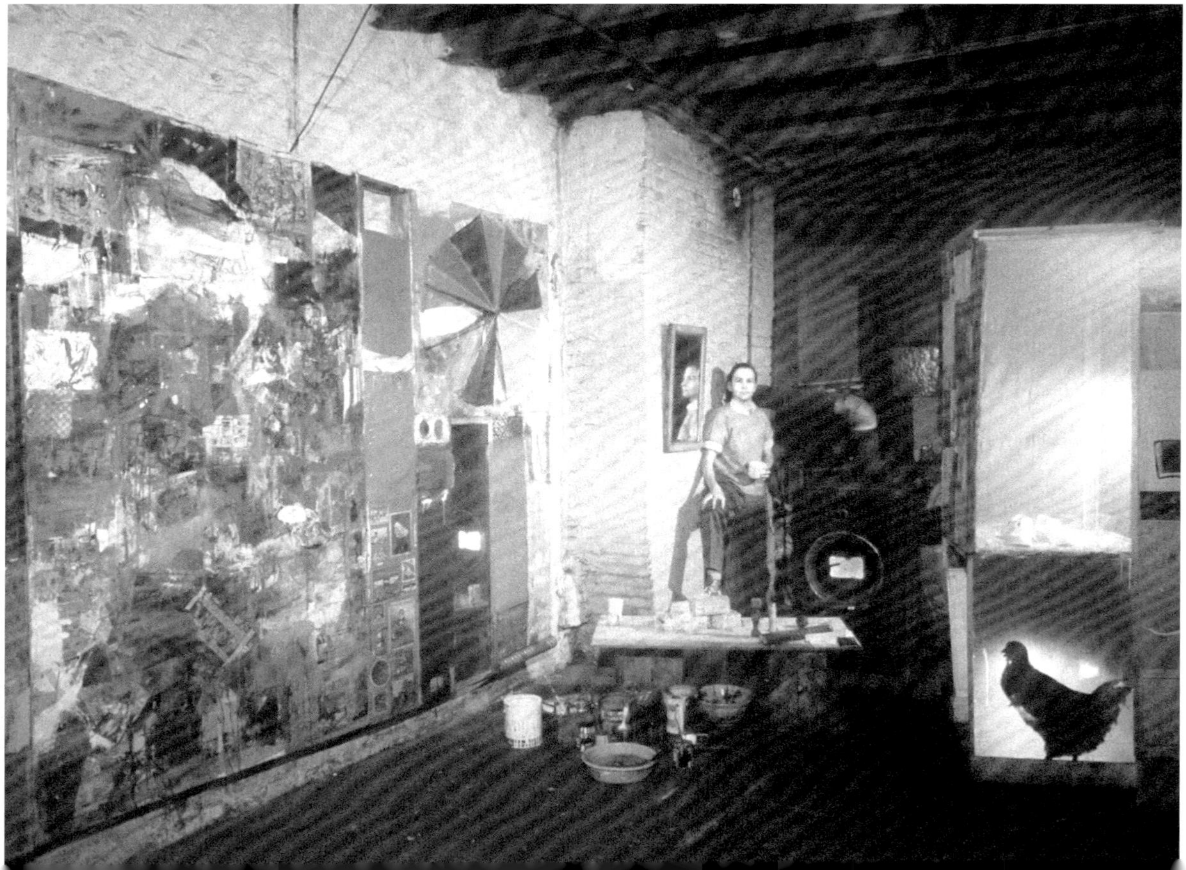

**FIG. 3.23** (bottom)
Robert Rauschenberg in his home
at 278 Pearl Street, c. February 1958

From the summer of 1954, Jasper Johns was living two blocks away, at 278 Pearl Street. He and Rauschenberg had met late in 1953 or early in 1954, and they became a couple gradually over the following months. In the summer of 1955, when their mutual friend Rachel Rosenthal moved out of the studio above Johns's, Rauschenberg, too, moved to Pearl Street (see fig. 3.15, location B; fig. 3.21).[42] Here, both artists lived in what Rosenthal described as "an incredible brick building": "It had been condemned by the city. It had only two lofts. . . . I had the top floor, Jap had one below. . . . There were four or maybe five floors, and a huge old pulley to pull stuff in and out of the printers on the second floor, and holes in the floors for the ropes to go through. The rent was something like $50 a month for mine. I spent some money and put in a tub and hot water." The building was quite narrow (at just over nineteen feet), and seems to have dated from the early nineteenth century, or perhaps even earlier.[43] The two lofts seem to have been designed for different uses. Johns's sparsely furnished space was defined by broad wooden floor planks, painted brick, and a low ceiling of stamped metal (fig. 3.22). The floor above, where Rauschenberg had moved, had the same white brick but a higher, beam-supported ceiling. In places, the walls seem to have been stained by the traces of industrial uses (as above Rauschenberg's head in fig. 3.23).

Rosenthal's indication that the building housed a printer's shop is fully in keeping with the other uses to which this district had been put. A map dating from the years before Johns and Rauschenberg moved in indicates that 278 Pearl Street had been surrounded by various kinds of small industry. One nearby building (at 272 Pearl) was marked "printers"; two others in the same block were labeled "chemicals." The block also housed a hospital, a bank, and buildings labeled "drugs & chemicals" and "burlap bags." In nearby blocks were buildings dedicated to similar concerns: "marine supplies," "waste paper," "lacquer spraying," "coffee roasting & packing"; one was simply labeled "ice mach."[44] The sounds and smells of the Fulton Fish Market, too, were nearby. The exodus of industry from lower Manhattan in just these years suggests that many of these light industrial businesses had left the area before Rauschenberg and Johns arrived—indeed, their cheap lofts must have been available for just this reason. Some of the stragglers (such as the printer's shop on the second floor at 278 Pearl) were no doubt disappearing even while these artists moved in.

When Johns and Rauschenberg moved to Pearl Street, the Third Avenue El rumbled by in front; it was in 1956, while they were both living there, that the tracks were torn down. Indeed, the whole area was in for a major reshaping. It has been observed that Johns and Rauschenberg were forced out of 278 Pearl Street in March 1958 because the building was slated for demolition.[45] The reason, which has not been noted, is that Pearl Street, now stripped of its elevated train, was to be broadened to accommodate more automobile traffic and to link it more smoothly with a broadened Water Street to the south (compare a 1957 map of the area with one from ten years later: figs. 3.24, 3.25). Indeed, after Johns and Rauschenberg's departure, their block was almost completely flattened to make more space available for pavement: of the nineteen buildings on the block, eighteen were destroyed. In their place was a new, narrow, triangular block filled mostly by a parking lot. Slightly less drastic demolition jobs were performed on the neighboring blocks to the north and northwest.

They did not move far. Rauschenberg and Johns again rented adjacent floors in their new home at 128 Front Street, six blocks to the south (see figs. 3.24 and 3.25, location C; figs. 3.26, 3.27). Lil Picard, who visited this building to

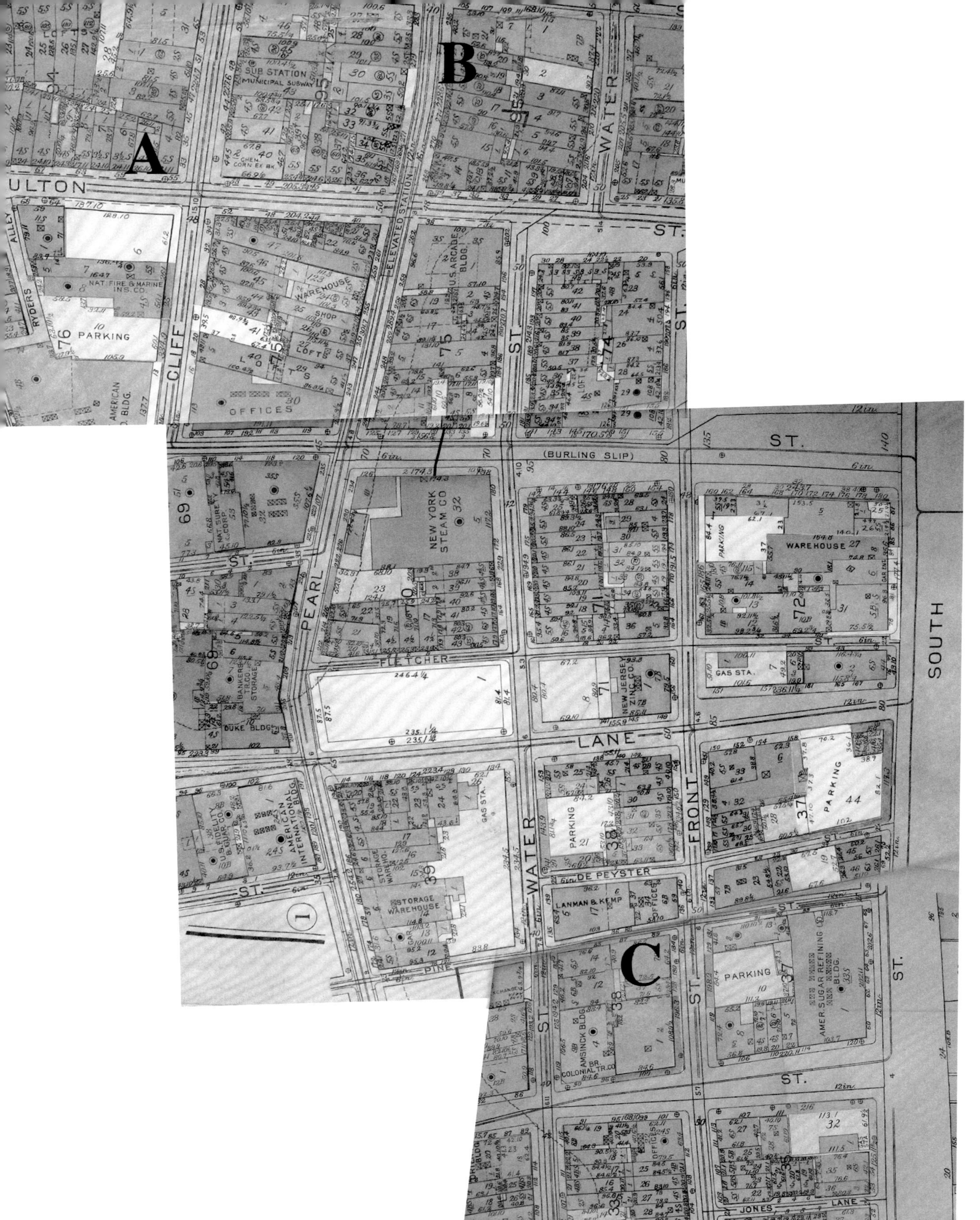
A
B
C
FULTON
CLIFF
RYDERS ALLEY
NAT. FIRE & MARINE INS. CO.
PARKING
AMERICAN BLDG.
OFFICES
SUB STATION
MUNICIPAL SUBWAY
CHEM. CORN EX BK
WAREHOUSE
SHOP
LOFTS
LOFT
WATER
ELEVATED STATION
U.S. ARCADE BLDG.
ST.
LOFT
PEARL
NAT. SURETY CORP.
ST.
BANKERS STORAGE
DUKE BLDG.
NEW YORK STEAM CO
FLETCHER
NEW JERSEY ZINC CO.
WAREHOUSE
PARKING
GAS STA.
SOUTH
FIDELITY & DEPOSIT CO.
U.S. SUGAR
AMERICAN INTERNATIONAL BLDG.
STORAGE WAREHO.
STORAGE WAREHOUSE
GAS STA.
LANE
WATER
FRONT
PARKING
GAS STA.
DE PEYSTER
LANMAN & KEMP
OFFICES
PARKING
ST.
PINE
BURLING SLIP
ST.
AMSINCK BLDG.
BR. COLONIAL TR. CO.
PARKING
AMER. SUGAR REFINING CO.
MAIN BLDG.
ST.
JONES LANE

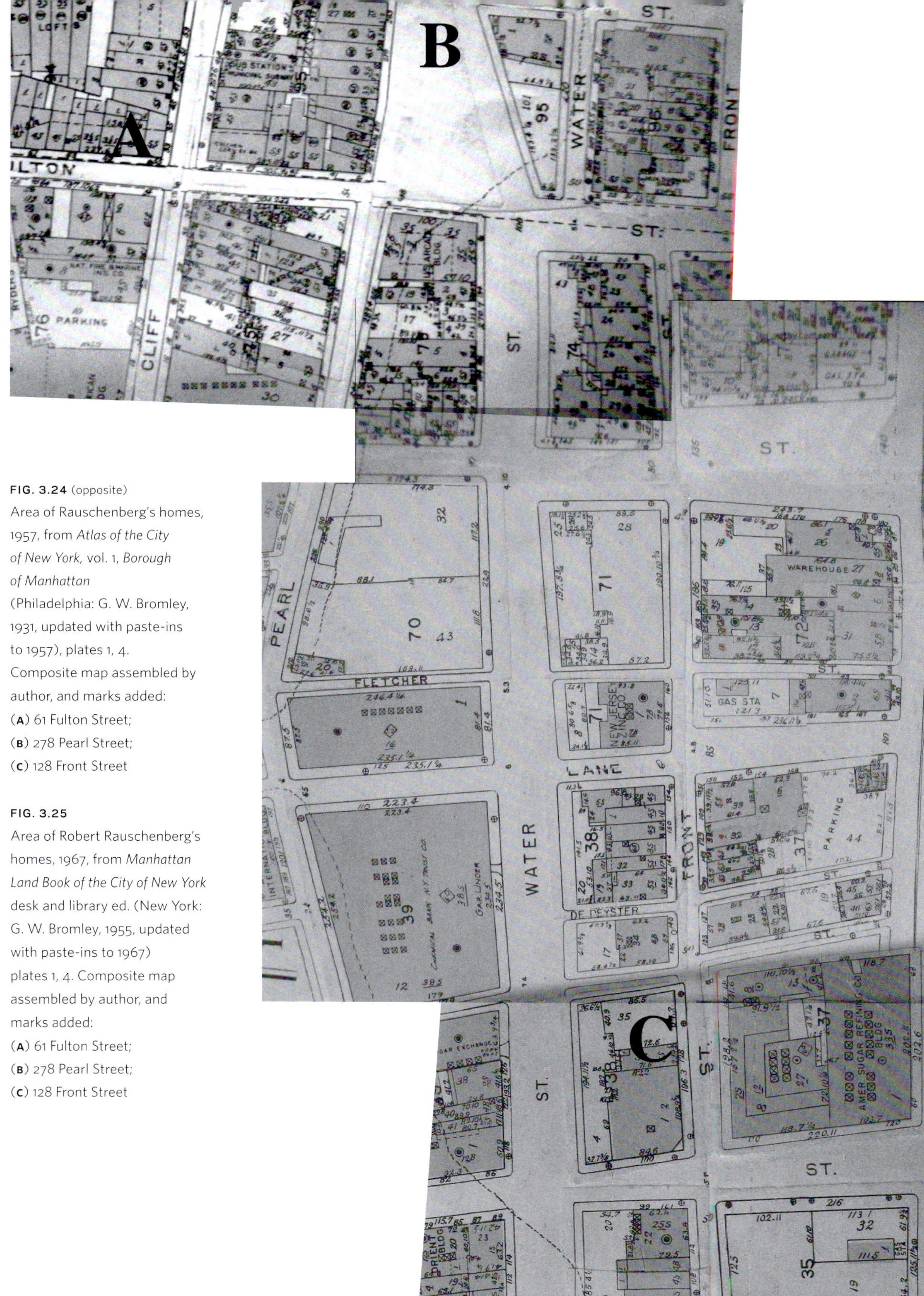



FIG. 3.24 (opposite)
Area of Rauschenberg's homes, 1957, from *Atlas of the City of New York,* vol. 1, *Borough of Manhattan* (Philadelphia: G. W. Bromley, 1931, updated with paste-ins to 1957), plates 1, 4. Composite map assembled by author, and marks added:
(A) 61 Fulton Street;
(B) 278 Pearl Street;
(C) 128 Front Street

FIG. 3.25
Area of Robert Rauschenberg's homes, 1967, from *Manhattan Land Book of the City of New York* desk and library ed. (New York: G. W. Bromley, 1955, updated with paste-ins to 1967) plates 1, 4. Composite map assembled by author, and marks added:
(A) 61 Fulton Street;
(B) 278 Pearl Street;
(C) 128 Front Street

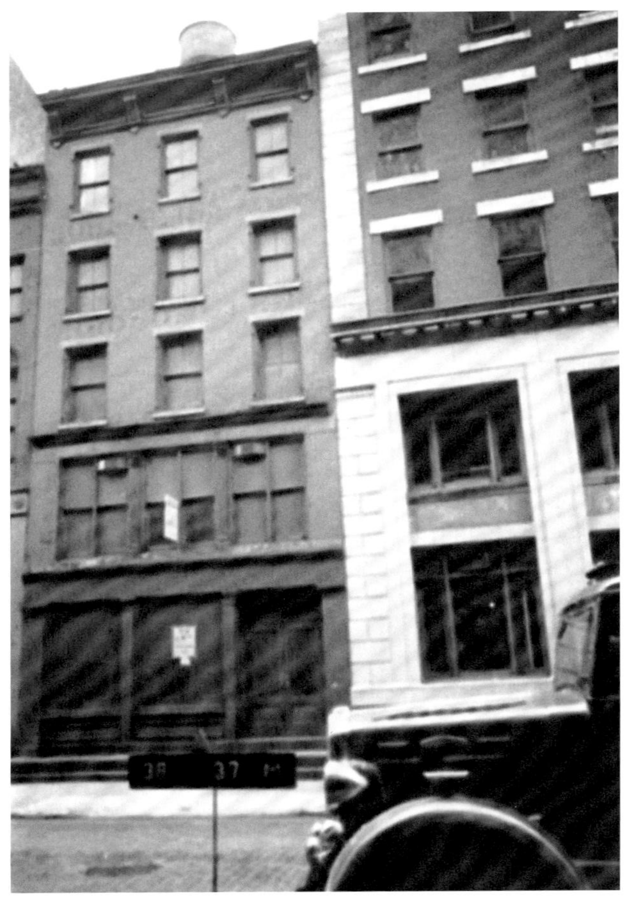

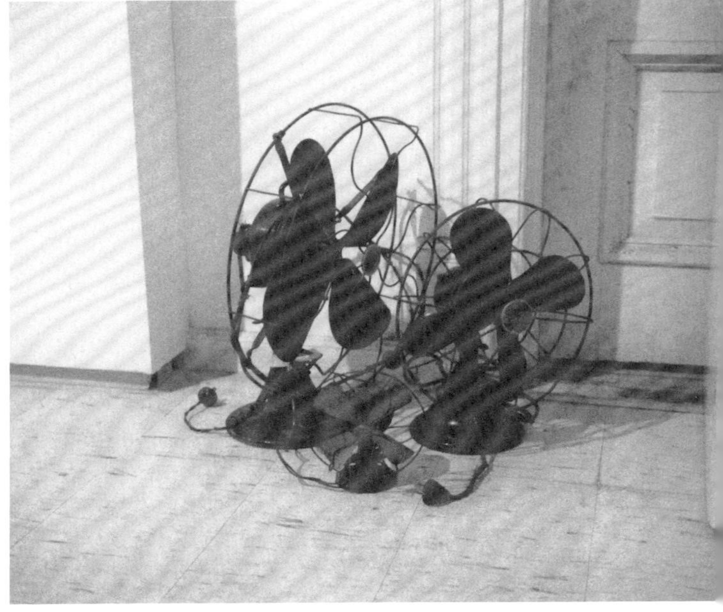

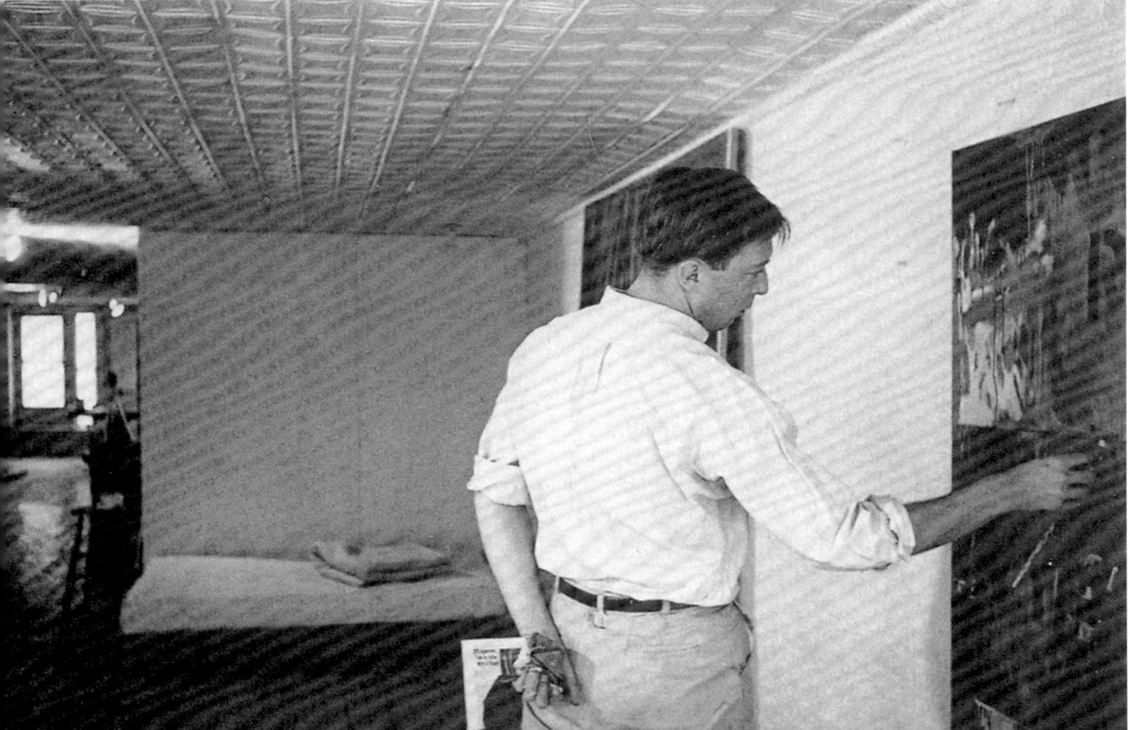

FIG. 3.26 (above left)
128 Front Street, c. 1940
NYC Municipal Archives

FIG. 3.27 (left)
Jasper Johns in his home
at 128 Front Street, 1963

FIG. 3.28 (above right)
Interior of Robert
Rauschenberg's home
at 128 Front Street, c. 1960,
with fans used in
*Pantomime,* 1961

research a story on Jasper Johns for the German magazine *Das Kunstwerk,* described the building in the following way: "Jasper Johns paints in a large studio with a relatively low ceiling. His paintings are never higher than the height of the room whose ceiling the painter, with outstretched arms, can just reach with his fingertips. The studio is located on the third floor of a three-story house. On the street floor is a coffeeshop, a specimen of this typical dreary New York institution, with counter, jukebox, cigarette slot machine, a few tables and chairs. It looks like a cafeteria in a railway station. One climbs a steep narrow staircase. On the second floor is the workroom of a Swedish collagist and constructivist, Öyvind Fahlström."[46] It is this other studio, occupied in Picard's 1963 account by Fahlström, where Rauschenberg lived and worked until 1961 (when he broke up with Johns and moved to Broadway). Johns's studio did indeed have a low ceiling—made of buckling stamped metal—and also walls of white-painted brick. Rauschenberg's, down a floor, must have been similar; a photograph of fans destined for the combine painting *Pantomime* (1961) reveals an old coffered door, moldings, and a linoleum-covered floor (fig. 3.28). It is almost certainly in his new studio here that Robert Rauschenberg made his 1961 combine painting *Wall Street,* named for the famous street at the corner, just a few paces away. This work is the product of one of Rauschenberg's most direct artistic engagements with the rapidly transforming urban landscape around him.

Like *First Landing Jump* and *Co-Existence, Wall Street* has a large piece of a wooden barricade prominently angled across its front (fig. 3.29). A section of an automobile tire caps one end of the barricade, and from it springs the worn fire hose (despite its frayed edges, labeled "YEATON TESTED 250 LB 1960") that coils neatly on the gallery floor.

A stamped-metal architectural bracket—ripped, paint-spattered, and rust-stained (fig. 3.30)—dominates the upper right-hand corner of the work. Carefully oriented along the vertical and positioned quite neatly in its corner, this antique building fragment seems almost to serve a proper architectural function. It is topped with a black-painted wooden box, which—together with the long horizontal band of black along the upper edge of the canvas—serves to offer the appearance of a supported ceiling beam. This beam looks not unlike those in Rauschenberg's old homes at Fulton and Pearl Streets. For its part, the barricade arm pushes uncomfortably at the curling, floral lower lip of the delicate bracket, which is bound in a dirty knotted stretch of string, as if against this very strain.[47] And its angle across the canvas allows the barricade to provoke a sense of closure and inaccessibility not unlike that which we observed in *Inside-Out.* The bracket, meanwhile, bears a remarkable resemblance to the decorative stone supports that studded the exterior wall of an old office block—the 1904 National Sugar Building (fig. 3.31)—that stood across the street from the Front Street studio in which *Wall Street* was made. Indeed, this architectural scrap might almost have been taken from the interior of that building, and it probably was in fact pulled from the ruins of another demolished building nearby.

In 1961, demolition sites were everywhere around the Front Street studio. Much of the destruction, in fact, was in service of the very same Water Street widening project that had forced Rauschenberg and Johns from their previous address on Pearl Street. The trafficway was to be widened by fifty feet, and this meant ripping down every building along the eastern edge of the roadway, from Coenties Slip to the Brooklyn Bridge (see figs. 3.24, 3.25). While Rauschenberg's old block, as we have seen, was almost completely demolished, his new block was hardly spared. While he was living

FIG. 3.29

**Robert Rauschenberg**

*Wall Street,* 1961

Combine painting: oil, paper, zinc sheet metal, fabric, and
string on canvas with wood plank, rubber, and fire hose,
62 $\frac{1}{8}$ x 72 x 9 $\frac{7}{8}$ in. (157.8 x 182.9 x 25.1 cm)

Museum Ludwig, Cologne

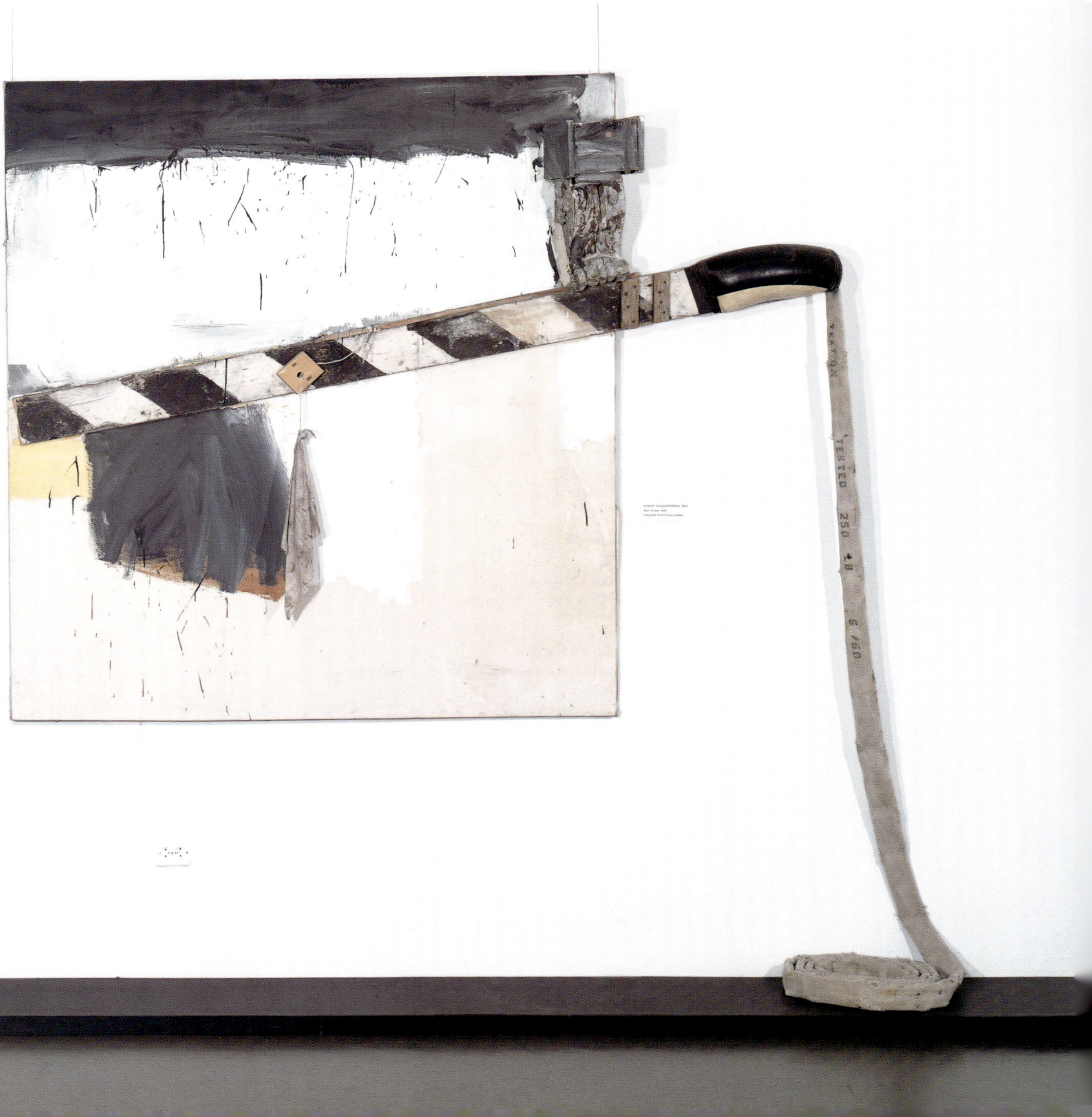

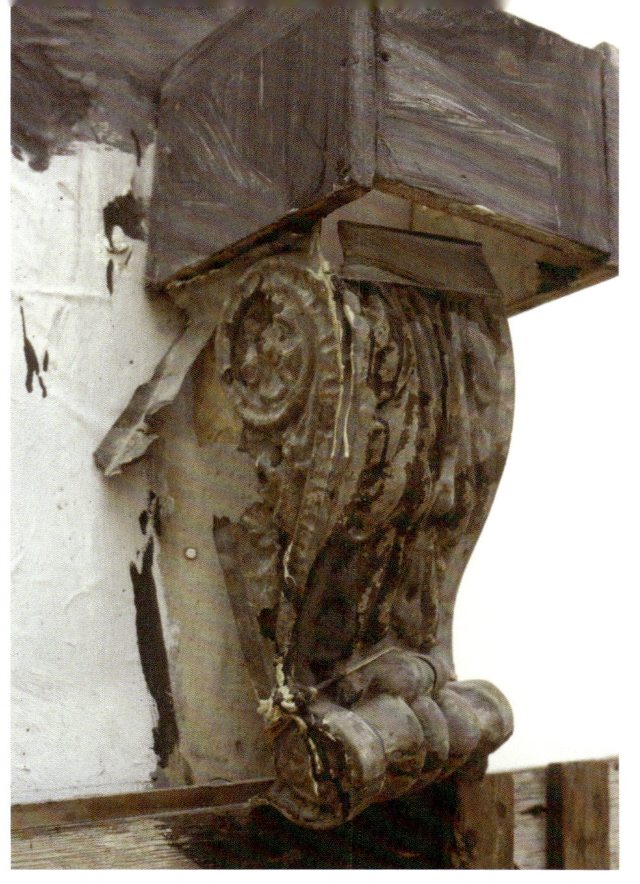

FIG. 3.30
Robert Rauschenberg
Wall Street (detail)

FIG. 3.31
National Sugar Building.
129 Front Street, 1904,
photographed 2003

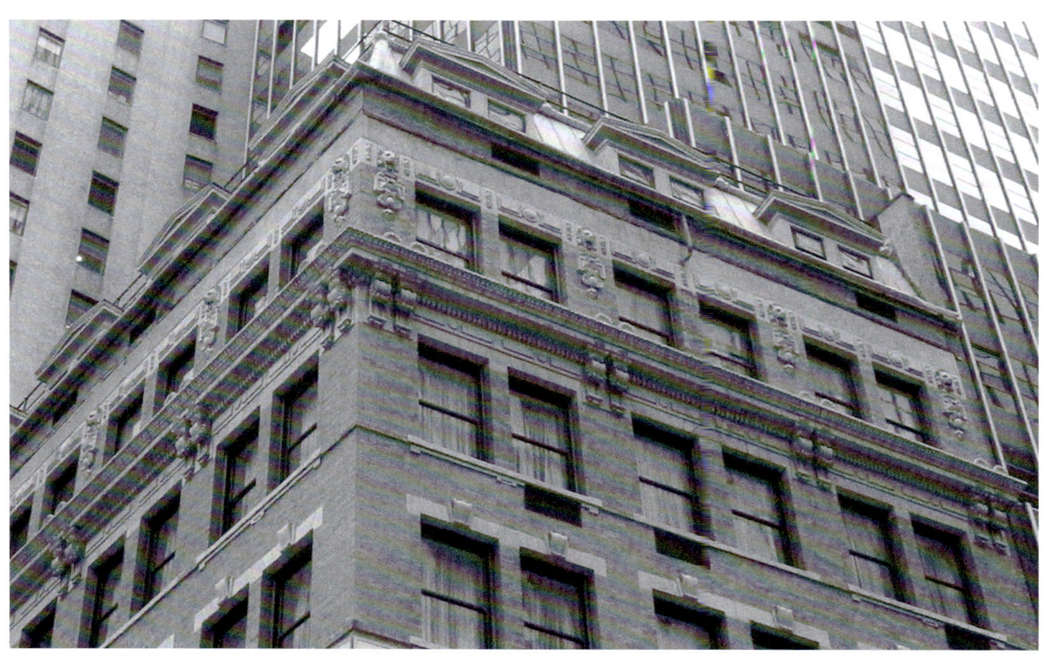

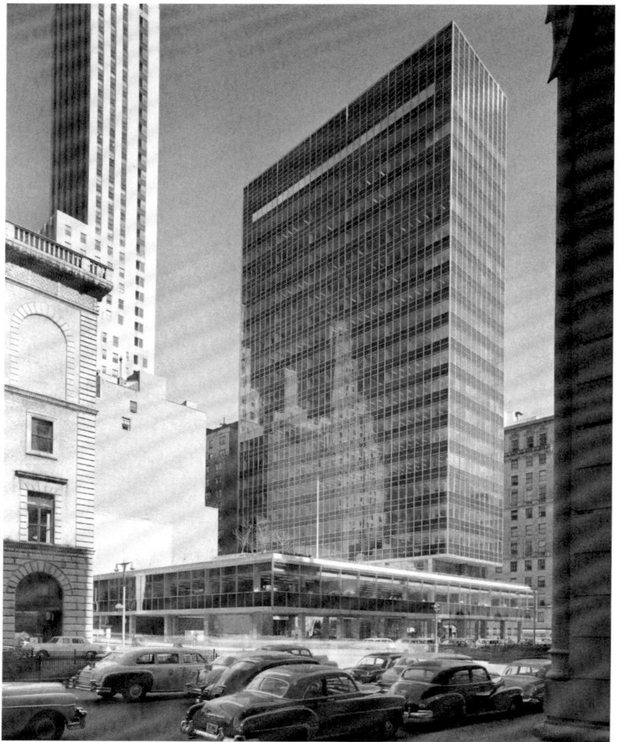

FIG. 3.32

Lever House, 390 Park Avenue,
Skidmore, Owings & Merrill, 1952

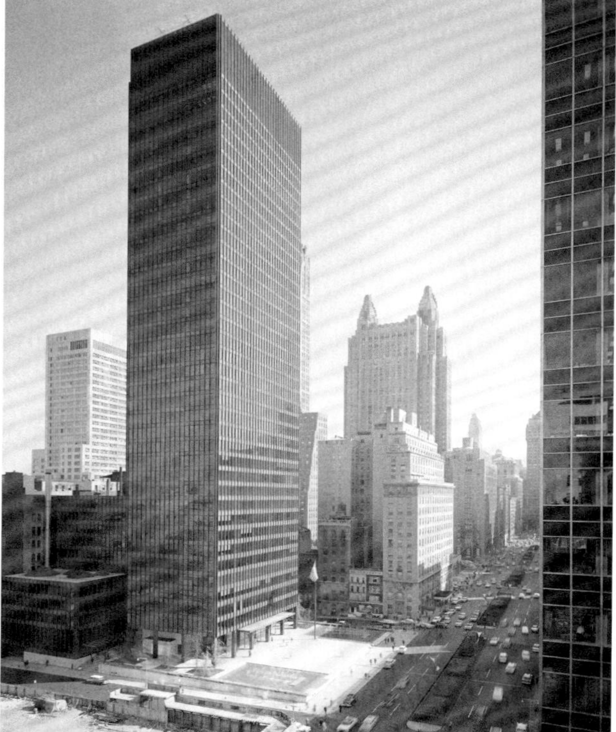

FIG. 3.33

Seagram Building, 375 Park Avenue, Ludwig
Mies van der Rohe, Philip Johnson, and
Kahn & Jacobs, 1958

there, the entire western half of his block on Front Street
was wrecked, leaving his building to back directly onto
a half-mile string of active demolition sites, some of
them destroying a group of Manhattan's last eighteenth-
century houses.[48]

It was not just the roadway project causing demolition
in the area in these years; indeed, the extent of the urban
destruction around Front Street in this period is difficult to
fathom. Of the eighty-seven buildings, for example, that
stood in Rauschenberg's block and the adjacent ones when
he moved in, forty-three—or nearly half—were demolished
within eight years. Only one of these blocks, the small
one to the northeast, experienced no major demolition or

reconstruction in the twelve years after 1955.[49] By the end of
this period, there were vacant lots in at least fifteen of the
blocks within a four-block radius of 128 Front Street, and at
least four blocks nearby had been entirely or almost entirely
flattened.

Most of the demolition around Rauschenberg was
undertaken not for the Water Street roadway project, but
rather in service of a wholesale rededication of the area to
support a new vision of American corporate capitalism.
The International Style had become—beginning with the
construction of Skidmore, Owings & Merrill's Lever House
in 1952 (fig. 3.32)—the definitive new language of corporate
architecture in Manhattan, its clean plates of glass and thin

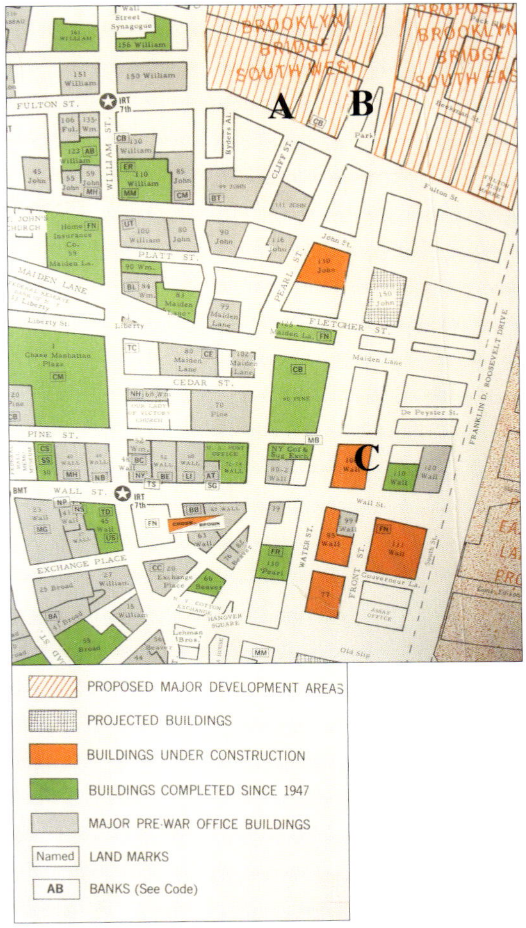



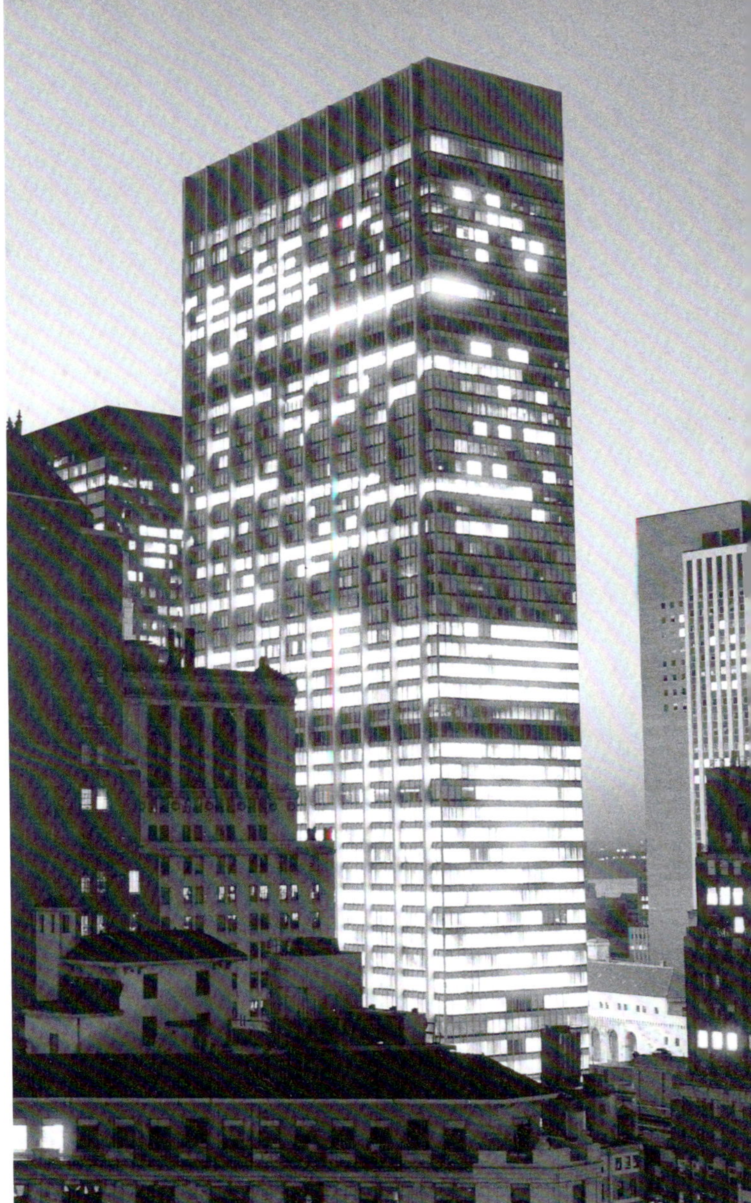

**FIG. 3.34** (left)

Lower Manhattan, 1968, from *Map of Lower Manhattan*, 2nd ed. (New York: Cross & Brown, 1968)

Marks added by author:

(**A**) 61 Fulton Street;

(**B**) 278 Pearl Street;

(**C**) 128 Front Street

**FIG. 3.35** (right)

Chase Manhattan Bank, One Chase Manhattan Plaza Skidmore, Owings & Merrill, 1960

strips of steel communicating a homogeneity and simplicity that appealed to firm after firm. In addition to Mies's famous Seagram Building of 1958 (fig. 3.33) and Skidmore, Owings & Merrill's Union Carbide Building of 1960 (see fig. 4.40), a nearly countless number of the new towers went up around midtown during the 1950s, and then, as the decade turned, in lower Manhattan as well.

In the summer of 1960 the largest and most conspicuous of the new downtown buildings, Chase Manhattan Bank, opened just three blocks west of Rauschenberg's studio (figs. 3.34, 3.35; see also fig. 2.20, which shows the clearing of the Mutual Benefit Life Building for this site). Rising sixty stories and comprising 1.7 million square feet

Chemical Bank, 110 Maiden
Lane, 1960, photographed
2003

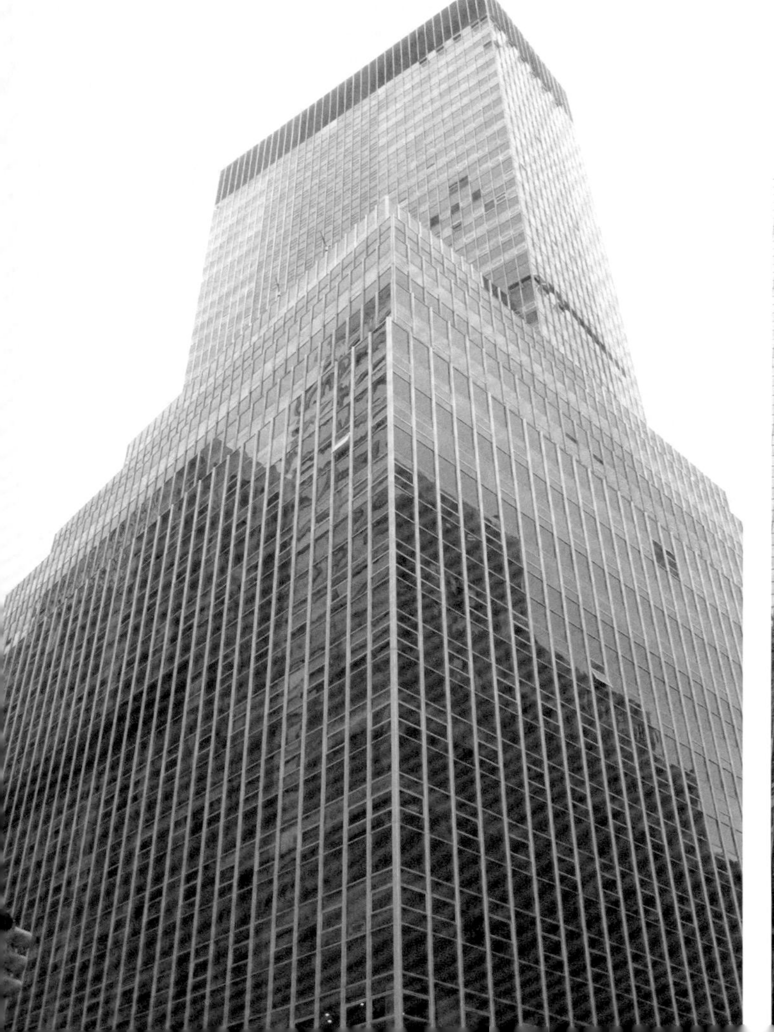


110 Wall Street, 1964,
photographed 2003

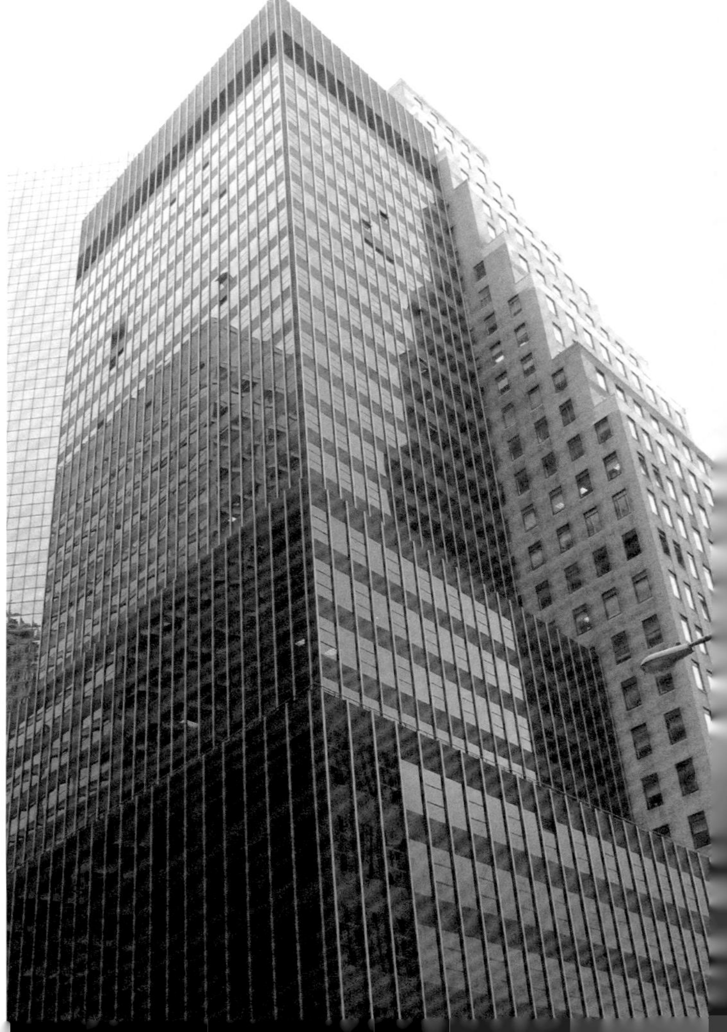

of office space, the tower was so large that two blocks were combined, swallowing a city street, to accommodate the necessary footprint. The new superblock (like Washington Square Village) denied any connection to the street grid below, and the address of the tower was rendered as One Chase Manhattan Plaza.[50] Also in 1960, Chemical Bank finished a thirty-eight-story building occupying the entire block immediately to the northwest of Rauschenberg's own (fig. 3.36). Meanwhile, others, just as close, were under construction. A twenty-four-story tower was completed on Hanover Square in 1961, and another fourteen-story bank building went up on Water Street in 1962. Even the 1922 office block that had faced Rauschenberg's home when he moved in—together with three narrow buildings that must have been very much like the artist's own—was destroyed in these years to make room for a three-tiered, twenty-seven-story International Style tower that was completed in 1964 at 110 Wall Street (fig. 3.37).[51]

All this new corporate construction was hastened by the rezoning of lower Manhattan. A land use map published in 1956 by the City Planning Commission shows that the part of the island below the Brooklyn Bridge was at that time still devoted to a diversity of purposes. The blocks where Rauschenberg had lived on Fulton and Pearl Streets, for example, while containing some office space, were dedicated chiefly to light manufacturing. Even the 100 block of Front Street showed a mix of light industry, office space, and parking.[52] The long-awaited rezoning of 1961, however, aimed to force a major shift for lower Manhattan. Although "high-performance" manufacturing was still allowed on the piers, and low-performance manufacturing was permitted on a single block west of Water Street, 168 of the 169 blocks south of the Brooklyn Bridge were now to be dedicated to commercial space.[53]

The nature of commercial space, too, was changing, and in a way that the new architecture was intended to express. Earlier in the century, the office buildings downtown had served collectively as the seat of America's industrial capitalism, and this meant buildings dedicated not only to banks but also to the commodity-specific conglomerates that those banks served. Maps from the period reveal, for example, the British Colonial Trading Company, the Di Giorgio Fruit Corporation (along Pier 12), and Lanman Kemp Barclay & Co. Druggists Supplies.[54] Even around the time that he moved there, Rauschenberg's immediate Front Street neighborhood seems to have included—in addition to the National Sugar Building—Hard and Rand's Coffee Importers, the Colonial Trust Company, and another sugar conglomerate called the American Sugar Refining Company.[55] Starting in the late 1950s, however, the diversity of lower Manhattan was buckling under the growing hegemony of the banks. And the International Style offered these banks the perfect visual vocabulary in which to express their interlocked homogeneity, their ability to efficiently administer the abstract flow of money. *Architectural Forum* enthusiastically appraised the unity and abstraction in the new Chase building as if the efficiency it was meant to express were a fait accompli: "It works, and looks, like a big, handsomely designed business machine, its complex anatomy of systems multiplies the efforts of its users . . . ; art has not been spooned on for appearances, but carefully integrated into every detail down to the paperweights on the desks." Like their simple new logos—Chase adopted theirs (fig. 3.38) in the same year they built Chase Manhattan Plaza—the new corporate towers were marked by a unified abstraction befitting their role in the new meta-industrial economy of late capitalism.[56] Lower Manhattan—not long before characterized by *Fortune* magazine as a place of

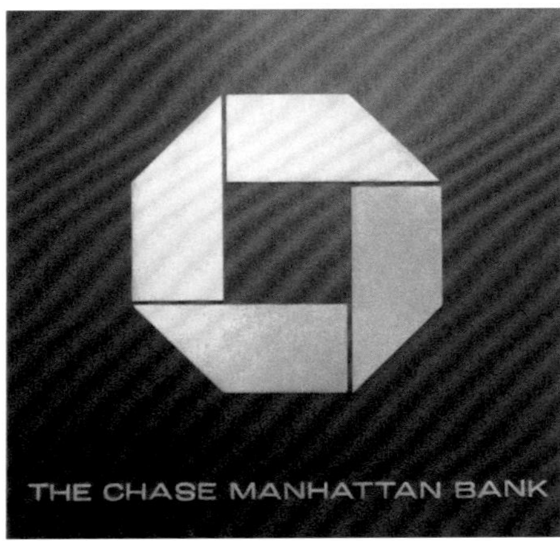


FIG. 3.38
Chase Manhattan logo, designed by Thomas Geismar, 1960

"cacographic towers," "peeling lunch joints," and "hardware shops glutted with sleazy pliers"—was being retooled to express the new hegemony of finance and to accommodate the traffic flow deemed necessary to support it.[57]

Robert Rauschenberg, it seems, was leaping into the demolition sites all around him, pulling out rusting ventilation ducts, worn bits of industrial machinery, and neoclassical architectural details made of sheet zinc.[58] *Wall Street*, we might therefore say, is about the old, disappearing architectural particularity of its namesake neighborhood, put together just as the area was being remade in a sleek, new, uniform image (fig. 3.29). The barricade might have been taken from the edges of the new roadway, or else from the face of an active construction site. In either case, the pressure it puts on the old bracket would seem the most straightforward of metaphors.

Some readers may now object that, however historically and geographically specific it might be, I am advancing an iconographic reading after all: Rauschenberg's works are nostalgic allegories of a disappearing New York of dirty tenements, quirky architectural detail, and small businesses. Partly this is what I mean to suggest. But we are certain to miss the import of Rauschenberg's weighing in on these changes if we ever lose sight of the fact that his address to them is forever in sputtering, incoherent messes, in assemblages that don't make sense. If we have a comment on the transformation of the city in these works, we also have particular objects, whose very service as "comment" is undermined by their untranslatable materiality. Remember that *Wall Street* is mostly a large expanse of blank canvas and flat paint. Even an iconographic reading would lead us back to the facts of painting: the soiled rag at the heart of the combine might be said to come from a demolition heap, but it looks at least as likely to have been soiled by the turpentine of freshly cleaned brushes.

Indeed, *Wall Street*—with its relatively few objects—is as much a painting as are any of Rauschenberg's assemblages from the period: long black drips speckle the canvas from top to bottom, and large blocks of coarsely applied color lie edge-to-edge on the surface. Characteristically, this paint delivers the flattest of effects, and the uncolored portion in the lower half only underscores the viewer's awareness of the material presence of the canvas. The large field of white above the barricade has bits of gray and black mixed into its broad brushstrokes, which serve to darken and materialize it. Wrinkles, such as the one just to the left of the black wooden box (see fig. 3.30), betray the fact that Rauschenberg used elements of collage to complicate the texture of the painting's surface. Even the bracket serves, in part, as just another surface for color, marked as it is with

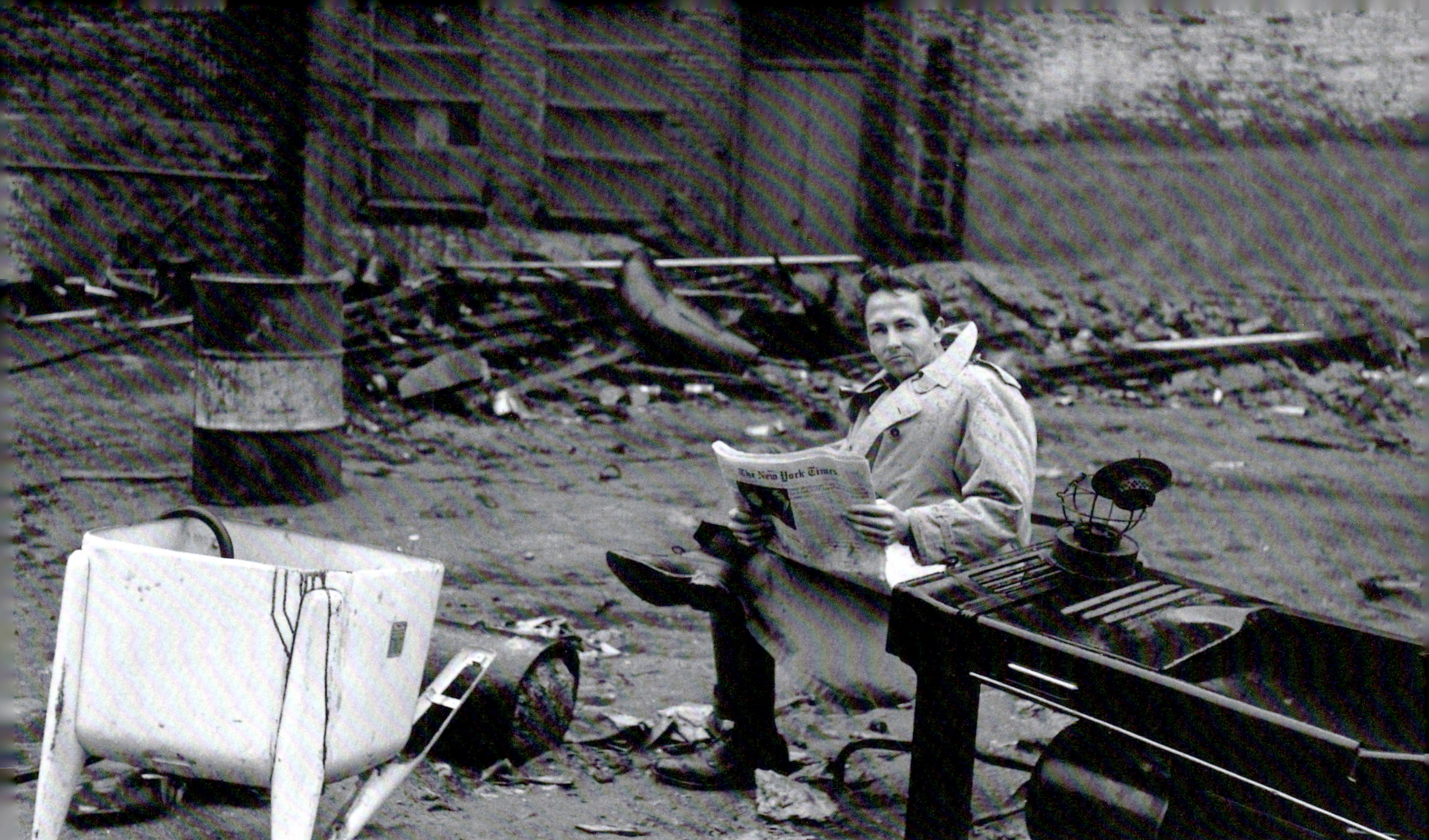



**FIG. 3.39**
Robert Rauschenberg in a Water Street lot, c. 1960

dripping lines of white, brown, gray, and black. Its spots of red-brown rust look almost as if they, too, were applied with a brush.

Rauschenberg, dubbed by *Time* magazine art's "most happy fella," was not in any case a radical critic of urban policy. His was a fascination with the constant incongruencies (the "rawness," in Sandler's formulation) of the city: "I was busy trying to find ways where the imagery and the material and the meanings of the painting would not be an illustration of my will but more like an unbiased documentation of my observations, and by observations I mean that literally— of my excitement about the way in the city you have on one lot a forty-story building and right next to it you have a little wooden shack. One is a parking lot and one is this maze of offices and closets and windows where everything is so crowded. . . . It was this constant, irrational juxtaposition of things that I think one only finds in the city."[59]

It was these incongruencies of the city—precisely the places where the city seemed not to belong to a unifying, abstract (and instrumentalist) schema—that Rauschenberg was so intent on representing and reasserting time and again. His was a literalist observation of the particularities of the city, of the places where it resisted synthesis. If planners were imagining a clean, deindustrialized, uniform city of the future, Rauschenberg was busy showing that this picture was not (at least not yet) a reality. Rauschenberg's New York was still illegible, still particular, still material and impossible to summarize. When he had himself photographed (fig. 3.39) in a vacant lot on Water Street (it could have been any of several dozen), he posed, complete with

*New York Times,* like a banker waiting for his office to rise from the ruins of an older New York. His smug smile, however, bespeaks nothing if not his real delight at the fact that, in the meantime, he could enjoy being surrounded by a chaos of misshapen metal hardware and piled-up bricks.

About the meaning of all this, we will need to say more, but first—if we are to see what is really at stake in these particularized assemblages of 1961 and 1962—we need to turn to that other (and deeply related) arena from which Rauschenberg pulled the objects for these works: the castoffs of New York's postwar consumerism.

**Consumer Goods**

A section of sheet metal—rolled to look like an apartment-building ventilation duct—stands vigilant at one end of *Trophy IV (For John Cage)* (fig. 3.40). A dark and gauzy inner lining pokes out irregularly from its top. At its side stands a naked umbrella spine, stripped of even its last scraps of fabric. These two miniature towers have been fitted onto *Trophy IV*'s stagelike platform of floorboards, which is worn at this end of its dark paint, as if by heavy foot traffic around a large piece of industrial-loft machinery. A cloth-wrapped flashlight lies chained at the foot of the air duct, rust stains seeping through the fabric like blood soaking a bandage.[60]

At the opposite end of the work stands another pair of twinned verticals—crudely decorated dowels joined by a horizontal bar. Together, these three rods look like a fragment of cheaply made Victorian furniture, from which layers of antique paint have rubbed away unevenly. An unlaced, discolored boot hangs motionless within this odd structure, as if from a gallows, and beside it a lancelike dowel points toward the center of the work. In a cursory nod to the absence of canvas, a rusted tube of paint is fixed to the edge of the deck here, held down with an old bolt and wing nut.

At the middle of the six-foot-ten-inch platform, a twisted piece of unpainted sheet metal rises from the floor. It just straddles a thin section of rubber tire, encroaching on a sheet of blue-painted metal that seems to mark a boundary between the two ends of the work. The raised end of the crumpled sheet, through this vague sense of territorialization, seems almost in martial confrontation with the lame boot and its supporting lance. Even though we cannot sustain this drama of conflict for long—again our reading seems too tenuous, the material particularities too many—we are left with a sense that the parts here should be moving, a feeling that *Trophy IV* is some kind of contraption that was only recently at work. Just as the little wheel in *Inside-Out* seemed as if it should spin productively, the flashlight here, we imagine, ought to pull at its chain, the boot ought to swing.

Instead, our theater is dead. And the players are not only the now-familiar scraps of a disappearing industrial Manhattan (such as the implied ventilation duct, the twisted metal, and the worn floorboards) but also discarded scraps of old consumer objects: the worn-out boot, the broken umbrella, and the rusted flashlight. These are goods whose uselessness—if partly redeemed by their inclusion in this assemblage—is dramatized at length by their abiding inaction. These bits of consumer trash are the material remainders of once useful products. What they signify here is their own physical presence, abiding wiltingly in the world beyond the period of their utility.

Rauschenberg's early critics did not miss his interest in worn-out objects. Alan Solomon noted in the 1963 catalogue that the "real objects" in Rauschenberg's combines were "almost invariably 'found' materials of great variety and in a relative state of decay." Brian O'Doherty, in his review of this same show, wrote, "The collage materials are lovingly

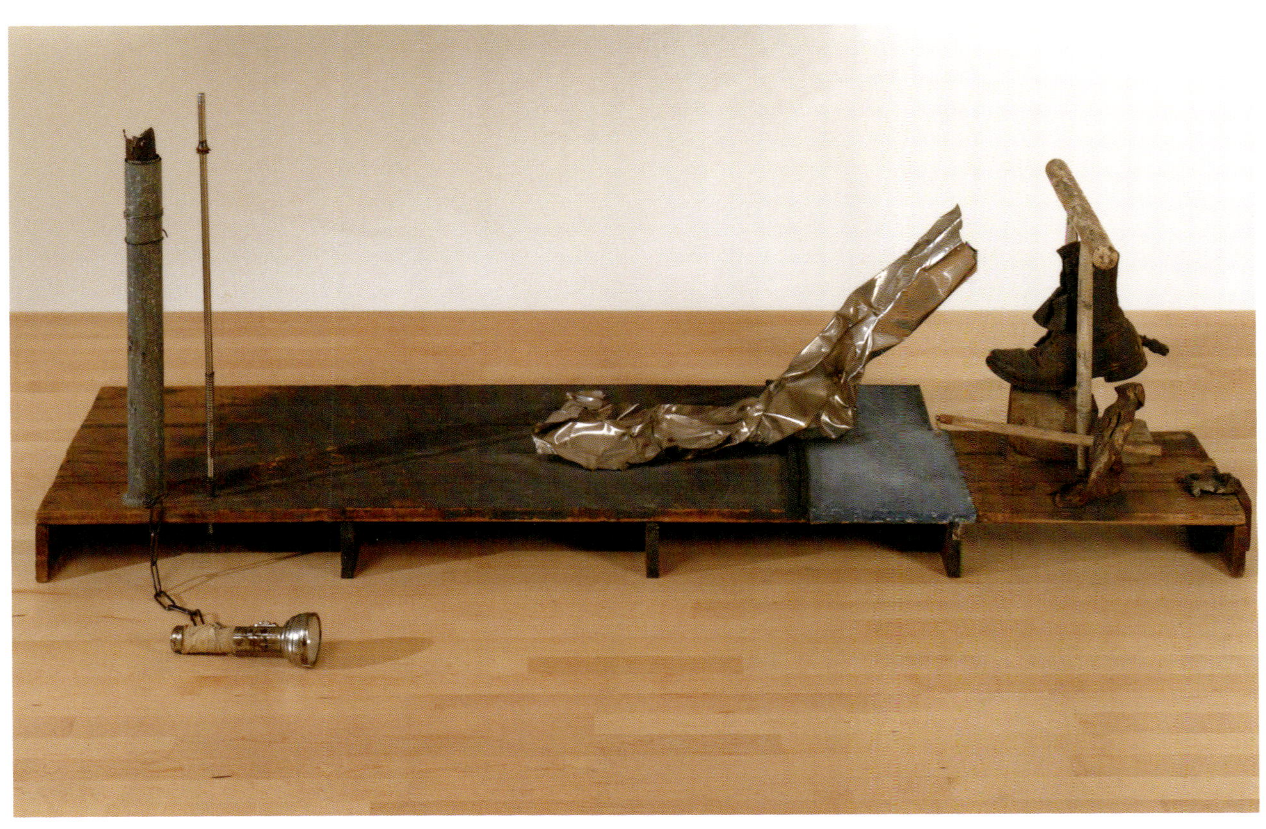

FIG. 3.40
Robert Rauschenberg
*Trophy IV (For John Cage)*, 1961
Combine: metal, fabric, boot, wood,
tire tread, paint tube, chain, and flashlight,
33 x 82 x 21 in. (83.8 x 208.3 x 53.3 cm)
San Francisco Museum of Modern Art,
Purchased through a gift of Phyllis Wattis

gathered from the encounters of real life—he has a fondness for such rejects as old tires, old newsprint, old clothes. As if in tribute to the Unknown Bum, this flotsam is battered by time and the anonymous hands that have touched it, used it, thrown it away." O'Doherty's piling-on of imagery is a bit heady, but his force is clear: Rauschenberg is drawn specifically to old objects, ones worn through use and discarded.[61]

Of course, objects of this kind held a special place in the American imagination around 1960; Rauschenberg's environment was precisely the one in which Johns was working. As we have seen, this was a moment not only of great volatility in the appearance of everyday objects, but also of growing concern about the waste generated by their consumption. While Johns sculpted as if to drop objects below the abstract expedience of the material world, Rauschenberg appropriated trash as if to reengage the leftovers of that expedience.

Consider again Vance Packard's *Waste Makers.* The opening chapter expressed a vivid fantasy of a future dystopia called Cornucopia City:

> One fourth of the factories of Cornucopia City will be located on the edge of a cliff, and the ends of their assembly lines can be swung to the front or rear doors depending on the public demand for the product being produced. When the demand is slack, the end of the assembly line will be swung to the rear door and the output of refrigerators or other products will drop out of sight and go directly to their graveyard without first overwhelming the consumer market. . . .

> Wednesday will be Navy Day. The Navy will send a surplus warship to the city dock. It will be filled with the surplus playsuits, cake mix, vacuum cleaners, and the trampolines that have been stockpiled at the local United States Department of Commerce complex of warehouses for surplus products. The ship will go

thirty miles out to sea, where the crew will sink it from a safe distance.[62]

Packard's worries, as we have seen, were motivated by a utilitarian impulse. This passage points out, however, that one of the aspects of this worry was an anxiety specifically over the material remainders that an overproductive economy manufactured. Packard's dark fantasy of countless material objects needing to be hidden below cliffs or under the sea is a fear of objects detached from any second-order values, whether use or some other meaning. It is an anxiety about a material world populated with objects failing to signify.

Such fears of a material world severed from its meanings were only exacerbated by the proliferation of the soft sell, which also loosened the connections between material objects and their meanings. Recall Packard's observation that image-building was the creation of "distinctive . . . 'personalities'" among "products that were essentially undistinctive." Or consider Daniel Boorstin's observation that image advertising required consumers to "plainly confess a distinction between what we see and what is really there."[63] Underlying the cultural discourse over waste was a growing concern that the legibility of objects (or, at least, their materially motivated legibility) was threatened.

One of the effects of *Trophy IV (For John Cage)* is a redemption of objects from just such a threat. The stripped umbrella and laceless boot—hyperbolically useless discards—are now made useful again, turned into the building blocks of avant-garde art. At the same time, however, this usefulness is of the most tenuous kind, dissolving again into the deathly inaction so conspicuously on show. Any redemptive meanings promised to these objects by their admission to the gallery—ordinarily a realm of semiotic rewards—are frustrated by their plainly abiding status as material shells, from which meaning, as much as use, has been plucked.

The artist offered a different kind of visual rumination on the utility of the human-made environment in the announcement poster mailed out for his 1961 show at the Castelli Gallery. It is no surprise that his announcement engaged these concerns: this exhibition was the first public showing of his new sculptural combines (the ones this chapter aims to understand). *Trophy IV, Wall Street, Co-Existence,* and *First Landing Jump,* for example, were all included.[64] The poster—a blurry black-and-white foldout printed from a photograph of Rauschenberg's—depicts a collection of detritus, slightly more organized than a real garbage pile (fig. 3.41). A bent wheel hub occupies the center of the image. Just above it lies a rag—like those in many of the combines of the period, but cleaner—together with a tidy sheet of white paper. On the paper, the word RAUSCHENBERG appears, in small capital letters and slightly out of focus. A flattened bucket dominates the left side of the image, its curving handle echoing the form of the broken wheel hub, and a small scrap of paper has been placed just here, with the word CASTELLI neatly printed on it. A third circle appears at lower left, in the form of an open paint can, apparently of white, with a broad stick or matted brush inside. The paint appears ready to be coarsely pasted over the assembled objects, as if to transform them, in situ, into a typical Rauschenberg assemblage.

More circles appear in the coiled bits of wire at upper right and lower center, as well as in the rocks at center right. These small stones are gathered in a box with bits of hardware—having lost any former uses and awaiting poten-

tial future ones—in a drawer reminiscent of some of the artist's first assemblages (such as *Soles* of 1953). The box has a manicured quality; it seems a *collection* of discards, not just a happenstance of trash. One of the ovoid forms within it might even be an egg rather than a rock.

Other signs of deliberate artistic intention include both the stick at upper right, corresponding formally with the paintbrush, and the flattened tube of paint (not unlike the one at the edge of *Trophy IV*) just underneath the centrally placed photograph. This photograph of a neat suburban or small-town street—telephone poles, cars, and plenty of open macadam in the foreground, small houses and trees at rear—is the great foil to everything else in this pile. Stencil-painted to indicate the date of the exhibition (2ND WEEK NOVEMBER), it is strikingly clean and white. It appears, unfolded and unstained, to be gingerly balanced on something underneath it. Its vision of functional suburban order seems, along one continuum at least, the opposite of the dirty, broken-down scraps assembled in this pile. That the rag and paint seem poised to tidy the heap with a gloss of cleanliness suggests that art-making is figured here as a potentially redemptive, intentional act—a process that might just wrest meaning from material chaos. At the same time, the abidingly dirty and sandy mass of junk suggests that such a move would indeed be superficial, and it suggests itself as the inevitable by-product of any vision of ordered civilization. Tidy houses, cars, and streets may be built, but they forever contain and require the accretion of meaningless junk.

In the Castelli announcement, Rauschenberg pictures trash as if in a state of nature, and in doing so, he suggests that his own works also court such a state. However deliberate, he seems to say, his combines are indeed very much like junk: they are things, first and foremost, and any

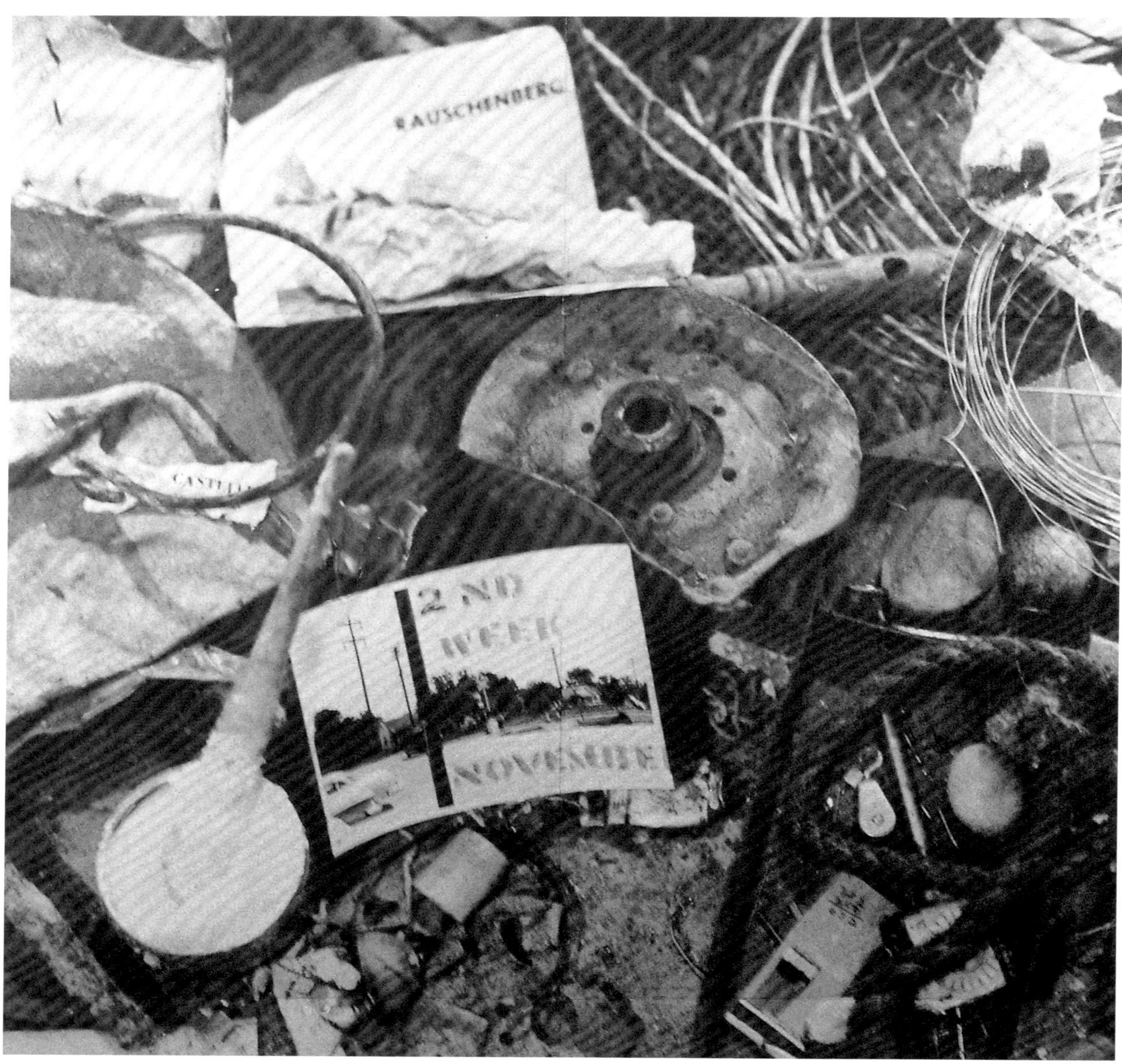

FIG. 3.41
Robert Rauschenberg,
announcement for exhibition
at the Castelli Gallery, 1961

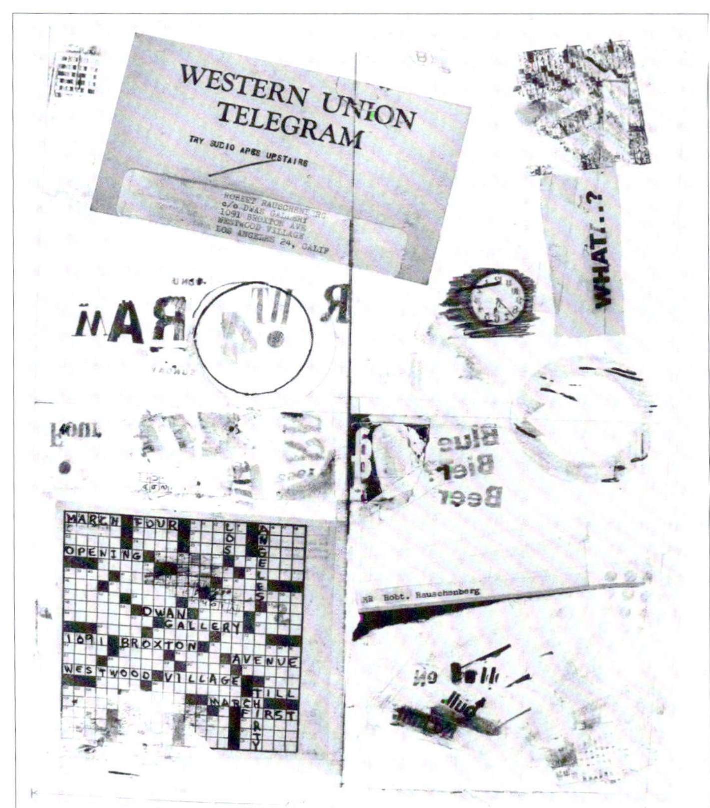




effort at bending them to intention—however superficial or grand—will not prevent the perpetual return of their materiality, the reassertion of their very lack of coherence.

For his next major exhibition of this group of 1961 combines, Rauschenberg made an announcement emphasizing a different side of his concern with meaning. The show was at the Dwan Gallery in Los Angeles, and its announcement was again an image of eclectic scraps, from which the exhibition information was barely legible (fig. 3.42).[65] In this case, however, the emphasis is not on the materiality of the scraps but rather on the r (thwarted) participation in systems of communication. Although the announcement conveys the name of the artist (once in full, once as "Robt. Rauschenberg," and once just as "RR"), the name and address of the gallery (twice), and the dates of the exhibition, it does so amid a sea of other, apparently nonsensical, bits of information. A clock reading 6:23 appears backward and partly crossed out, and groups of reversed letters—where they are legible as words at all—spell out *Blue, Beer,* and *Bier,* the last word possibly in German, possibly in English.[66] The block-letter question WHAT . . . ? expresses something of the overload of information here, the mysterious, misfiring units of communication. Indeed, two crossword puzzles, partly smudged out of legibility, epitomize this collection of seemingly unrelated bits of language. For its part, the telegram that dominates the image seems to stand for both the difficulty of communication (TRY SUDIO APCS UPSTAIRS) and also its potential successes (the artist, we know, eventually received his message). If the Castelli poster emphasized Rauschenberg's interest in material excess, the Dwan announcement expressed his interest in a different kind of detritus (and one, as we shall see, deeply related): the castoffs of language, the scraps of communication that might, or might not, be rehabilitated for meaning.

## Black Market

Do people buy Rauschenberg to share in his quiet protest against what they think is a cellophane-wrapped sort of world?
—TIME, 1960

It has been implicit in our discussion so far that there is something held in common between Rauschenberg's investments in the city and in consumer goods. Recall that this was also a presumption of some of his early critics. Lawrence Alloway had identified Rauschenberg as a leader in a movement whose very name implied a tight correlation of these two concerns: "New York junk culture." Discarded objects and the city were so tightly associated in Alloway's conception of the genre that he indicated that "the source of junk culture is obsolescence, the throwaway material of cities, as it collects in drawers, closets, attics, garbage cans, gutters, waste lots, and city dumps." Irving Sandler, too, had associated Rauschenberg's "urban seaminess" with his use of "junk materials."[67]

The close association of these two concerns was no doubt propelled in part by Rauschenberg's inclusion of consumer detritus and architectural fragments side by side, as in *Trophy IV* and *Inside-Out*. But the ceiling fragments, old doors and other elements of the streetscape were any-way trash in their own right (the city that most interested Rauschenberg was an obsolete one, one now being junked), so their affinity with the consumer discards in the assemblages was natural. This is the point emphasized by the artist's surroundings in Fred McDarrah's Water Street photograph. Streetscape and trash were also fused in the single element of the flattened trash can in *Cartoon* (fig. 3.43), a gesture repeated in the 1965 work *N.Y. Bird Calls for Öyvind Fahlström* (fig. 3.44). If Rauschenberg's work of this period expressed a commonality between New York's urban forms and consumerist trash, it is because it found in

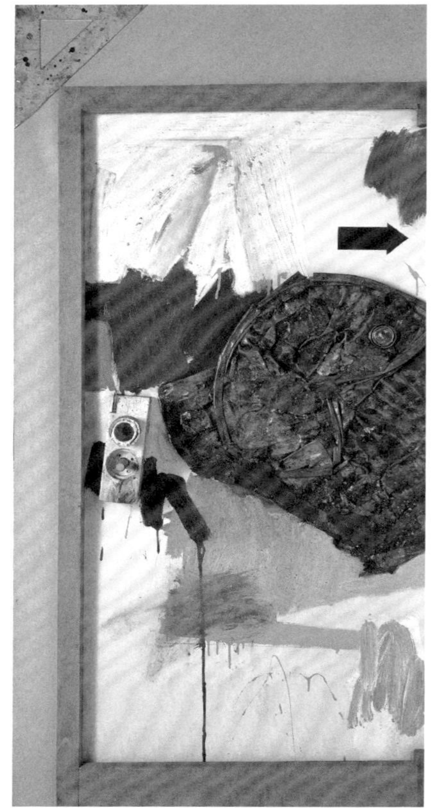

them a common difficulty regarding the nature of the material environment more generally, a set of questions about its order, systematicity, and legibility—its ability to be abstracted. None of Rauschenberg's works was so deeply invested in these questions as the elaborate *Black Market* of 1961.

Made in the spring for an exhibition at the Stedelijk Museum in Amsterdam, *Black Market* is the most complicated of the 1961 combine paintings (fig. 3.45).[68] The work is first of all a large painting—over four feet across—spattered in places and coated thickly in others with paint from the Rauschenberg palette: blacks, grays, and muddied whites. These tones—evocative of photography before color and of garbage before plastic—are balanced in this case by a lone, if prominent, patch of turquoise. An uneven wash of smudgy gray pervades the canvas, looking especially filthy in the patches that are otherwise uncovered, such as at lower left and upper right. Bright bits of red and blue appear among the collaged and

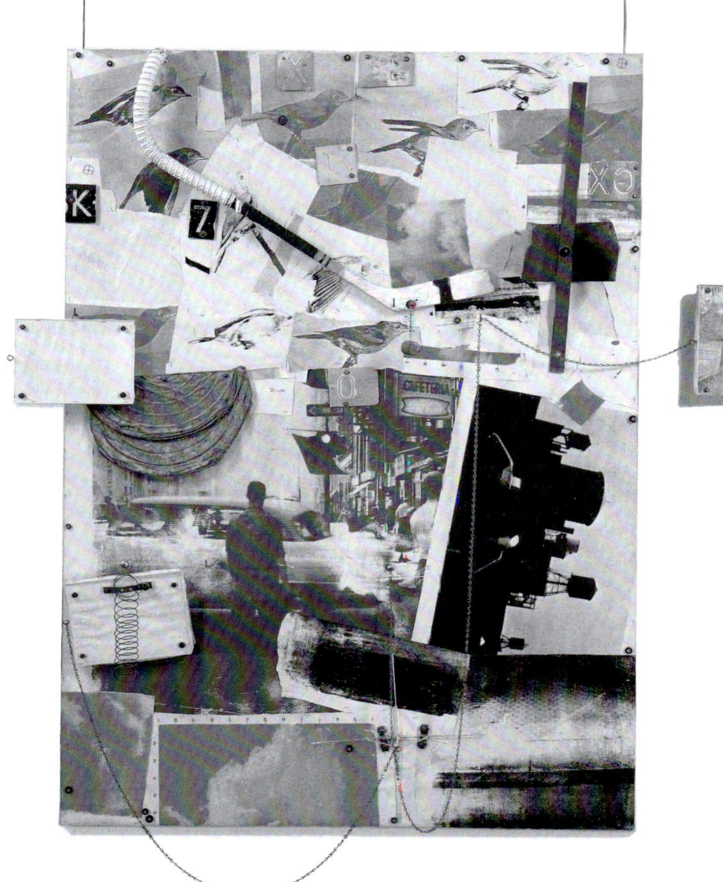

crumbly poster fragments on the lower half of the canvas, but this section of the work, too—a chaos of occasionally legible block capitals—is predominantly gray and black.

A black horizontal line painted prominently across the center of the lower half is balanced in the upper half of the canvas by a dented metal panel, covered in patches of glossy paint and rust. Although supported at three corners by small rubber feet, the panel is nailed at its center to the support behind. In the opposite corner of the canvas, Rauschenberg used three screws to attach a just-outdated Ohio license plate. This license plate, which matches in color the red-and-white poster scraps, has been claimed for the combine by careful overpainting in gray wash, finger-applied impasto, and bits of bright white, thinly applied (fig. 3.46). Some of its stamp-pressed lettering is only just obscured. A magazine illustration showing the U.S. Capitol, through a scaffold probably built for the Kennedy inaugura-

tion, presides over the lower-right corner of the canvas, importing faint associations of Americanness, of construction, and of the very recent past.[69]

If we have anything in *Black Market,* it may now seem, we have a version of Steinberg's flatbed picture plane. Here are discarded scraps from the material-visual experience of everyday life—license plate, news photograph, rusted panel, billboard posters—accumulated, as if at random, on this surface. Paint, too, lies flat (or else sits up) on the opaque and smudgy canvas, its emphatic materiality and relative meaninglessness underscoring the same qualities in the attached objects. The objects reciprocate, making the paint just another substance. All of this reminds us that the flatbed picture plane—despite Steinberg's appropriate insistence that its recognition required "other criteria" than those already in use—owed much to Abstract Expressionism. The incorporation of

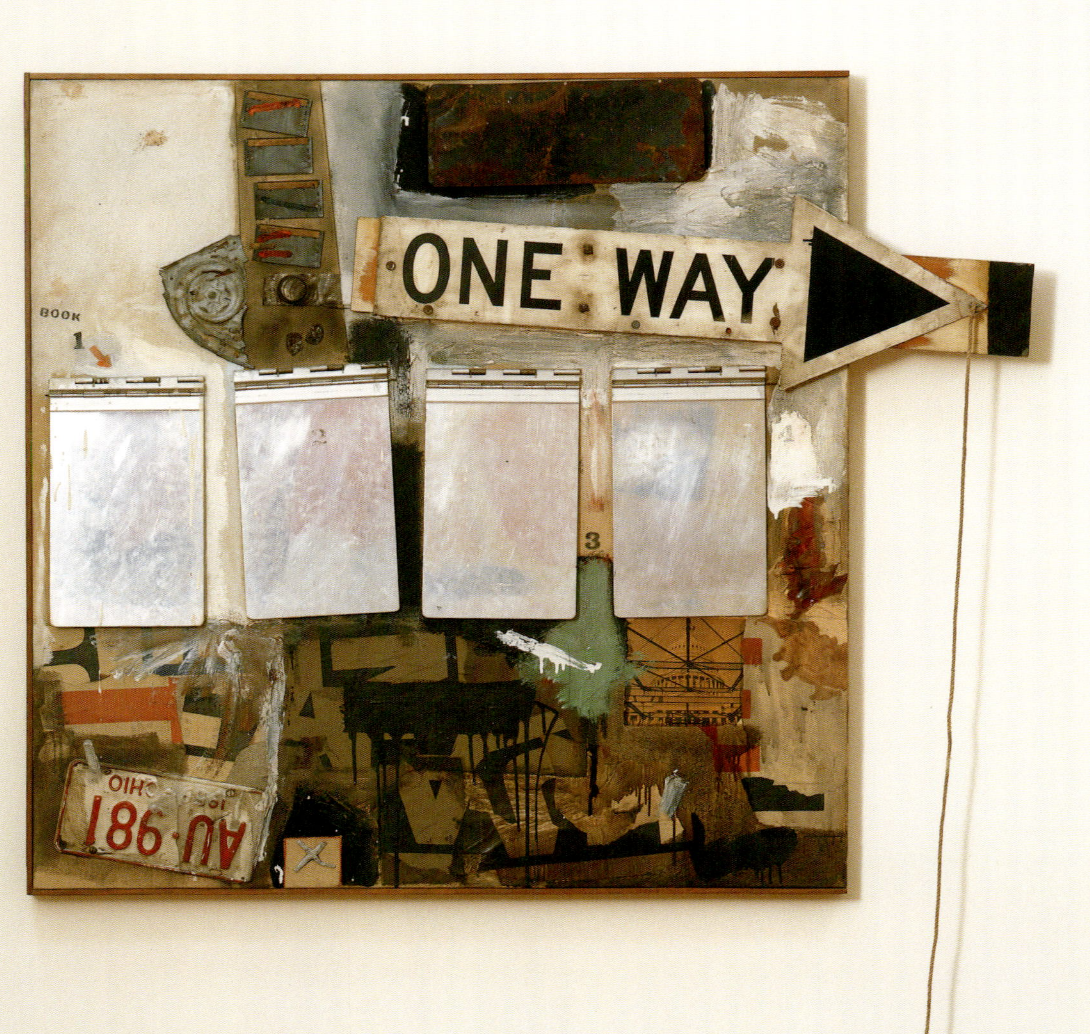

BOOK
1
ONE WAY
3
OHIO
AU·981

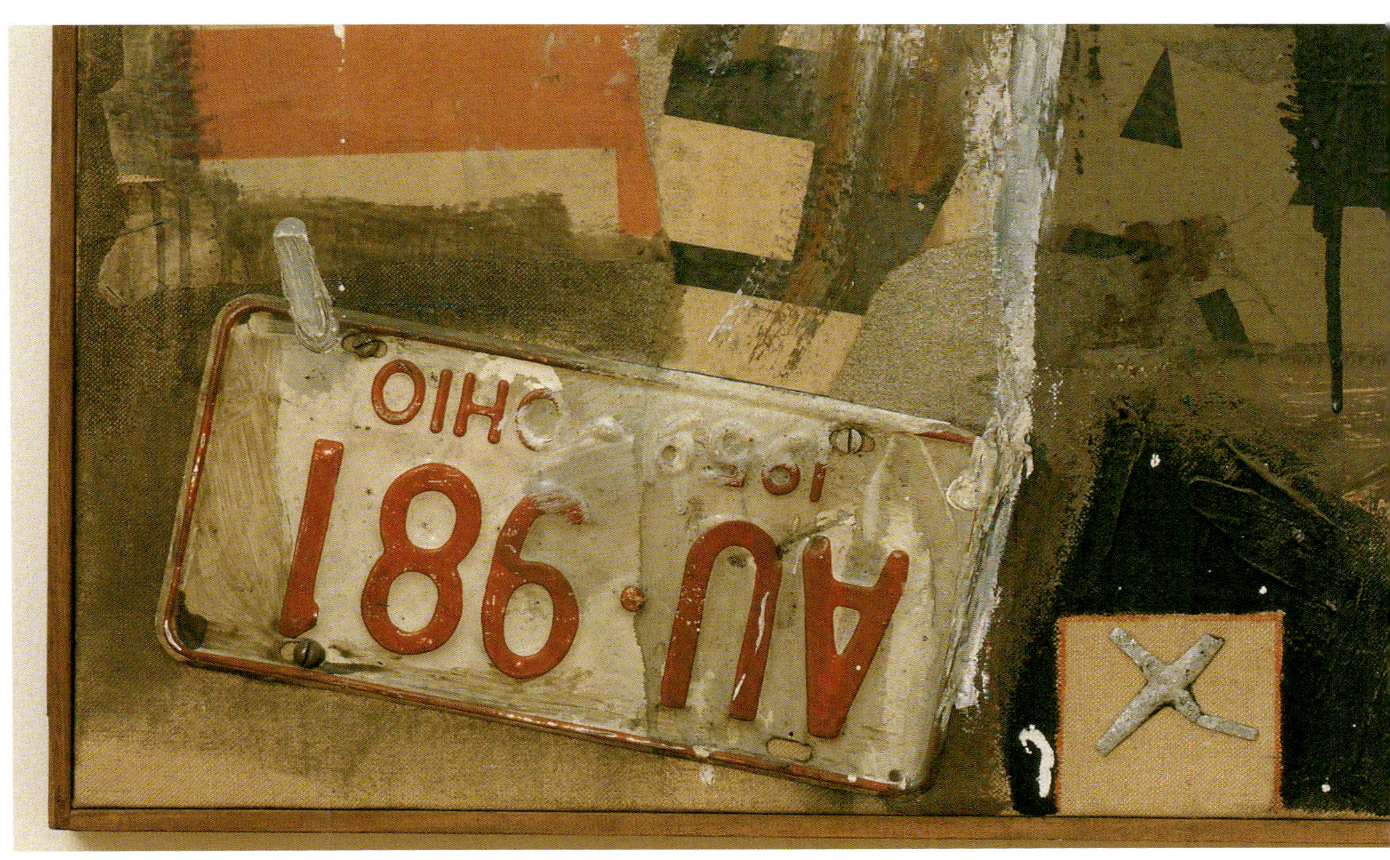

FIG. 3.45

**Robert Rauschenberg**

*Black Market*, 1961

Combine painting: oil, watercolor, pencil, paper, fabric,
newspaper, printed paper, printed reproductions,
wood, metal, tin, and four metal clipboards on
canvas with rope, rubber stamp, ink pad, and
wood valise; canvas, 49 x 59 in. (124.5 x 150 cm);
valise, 6 $\frac{1}{2}$ x 24 $\frac{1}{4}$ x 16 $\frac{3}{8}$ in. (16.5 x 61.6 x 41.6 cm)
Museum Ludwig, Cologne

FIG. 3.46

**Robert Rauschenberg**

*Black Market* (detail)

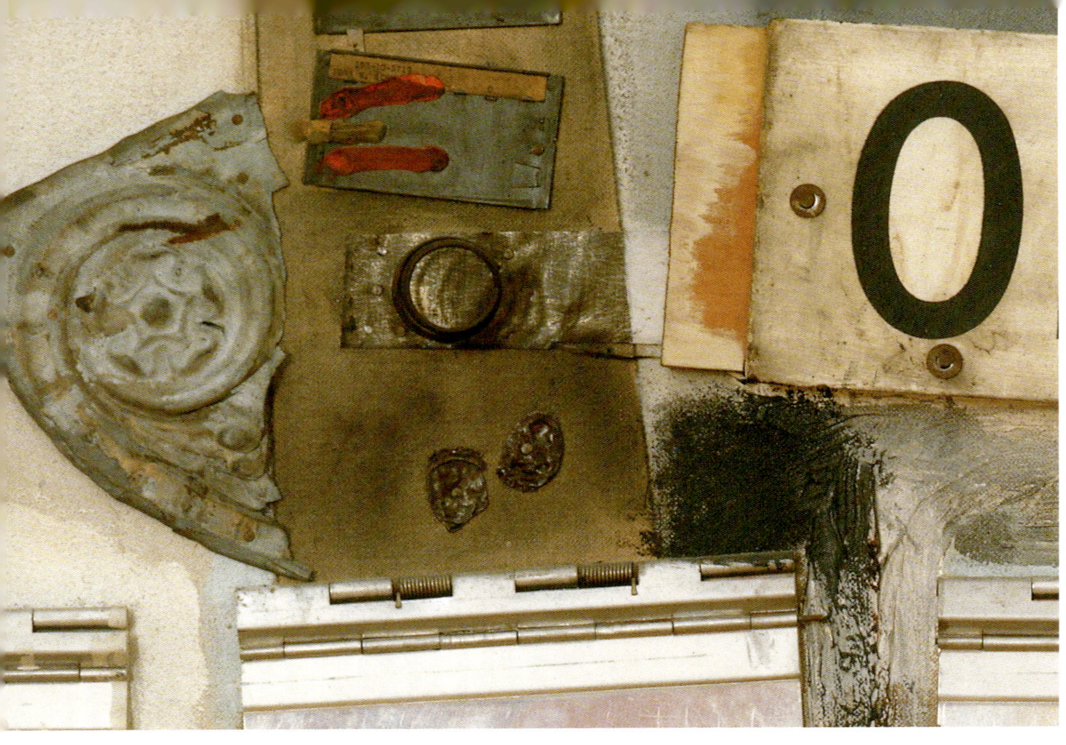

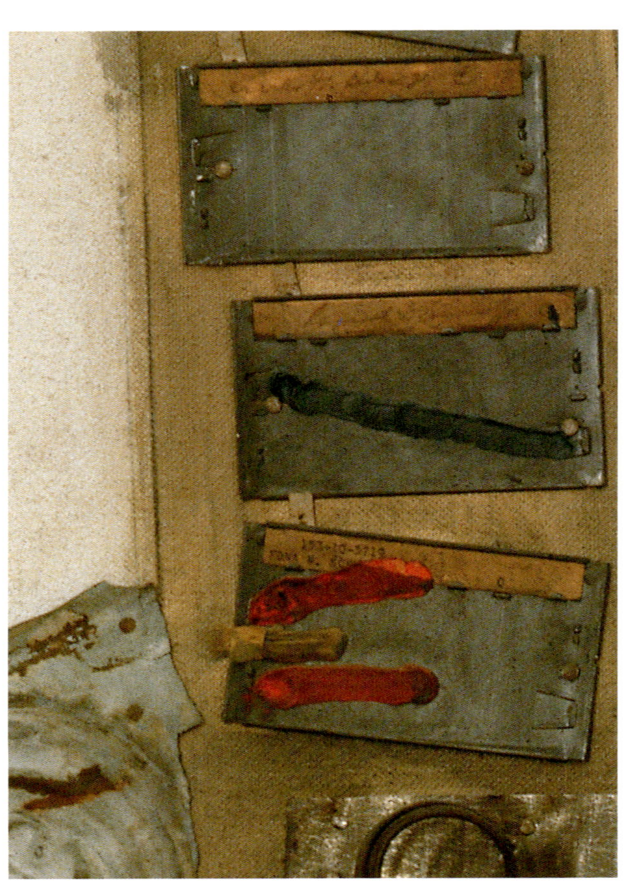

FIGS. 3.47 and 3.48
**Robert Rauschenberg**
*Black Market* (details)

useless objects on the canvas was an extension of a late-modernist investigation of the tension between the materiality of paint and its capacity for i lusionism. The thick silver X applied over the clean square of canvas at *Black Market*'s lower left corner (see fig. 3.46) might be seen even as an object lesson in Greenbergian dialectics: it is at once just *paint* and also the most rudimentary of *paintings,* a vague figure or object, appearing on a ground.[70]

A similar tension is at work in a complicated passage near the upper left-hand corner of the painting, where Rauschenberg gathered a group of five round forms (fig. 3.47). On the one hand, these shapes constitute a compositional rhyme, a legible expression of directive artistic will. On the other hand, however, they register as the unrelated things they are: a scrap of stamped-metal ceiling, a printed letter O on a one-way sign, a spring, and two crushed bottle caps. If, however, this passage presents a game in which viewers are made (impossibly) to decide between recognizing a legible expression of intention and seeing a meaningless accretion of useless objects, then it is a game played with a very particular set of pieces. These are, after all, familiar Rauschenbergian objects. The bottle caps typify the material leftovers of consumerism; the ceiling fragment is sliced from the ruins of an older New York. The spring, nested in a tin plate, might belong to either realm, a shard of a discarded appliance or, more broadly, of the disappearing Manhattan of industry. The oscillation between the legible and the purely material is staged here as a dilemma inherent to mass-produced objects and to the fabric of the city.

In at least one passage, this problem in legibility is explicitly correlated with a problem in administrative order. Just above the five circles, and in a field of dirty gray neatly edged by two straight lines, lies a row of what appear to have been metal file dividers for index cards (fig. 3.48). On browned labels, these slats are marked—some in penciled cursive, some in typed cap tals—with people's names and social security numbers. Note, for example, "Edna W. Sch . . . ": 153-10-5719. These material fragments of administration are further materialized by their covering in darkened lines of yellow orange, and blue paint.[71] Whatever function they had in categorizing bits of information and making them accessible, it is mostly ceded now in their new equivalence with the other objects gathered here. The trappings of systematicity are maintained, but only as particularized scraps.

A small suitcase—appropriately identified by one source with the antiquated word *valise*—sits on the floor below the canvas (fig. 3.49).[72] Worn and made mostly of finely jointed wood, the suitcase has had its lid replaced with a sheet of nailed-on, stamped-metal ceiling. Marks reveal where labels, long stripped away, bore addresses to which the case was sent. See, for example, the hand-lettered remains of one just-illegible label hanging on at the left of the handle (fig. 3.50). It was in this case that *Black Market*'s most elaborate involvements with the meanings of objects played out. When the work was first exhibited, viewers were invited to exchange objects they had brought with them for ones in the valise on the floor. They were also asked to sketch their contributions on one of the attached, shiny-lidded clipboards (fig. 3.51).[73] In this system, the suitcase contained four objects at any given time, one pertaining to each clipboard. We have almost no record of any specific objects that circulated through *Black Market,* but in 1969 Rauschenberg made his own submission of objects: a small plastic flashlight, a photograph of himself on a New York City rooftop, an old lightbulb with barnacles grown over it, and a plain plaid-printed handkerchief (fig. 3.52).[74]

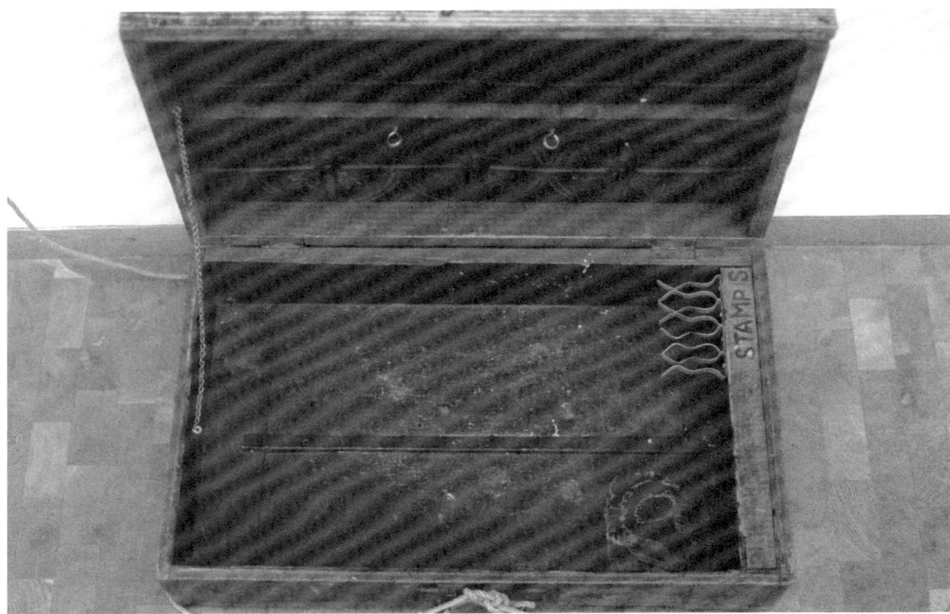



FIGS. 3.49 and 3.50
**Robert Rauschenberg**
*Black Market* (details)

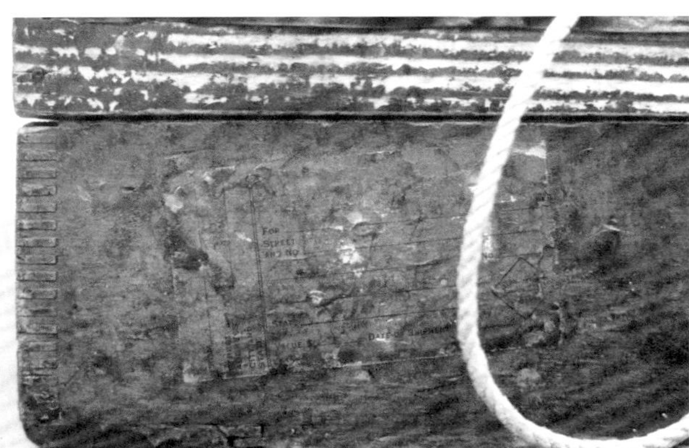

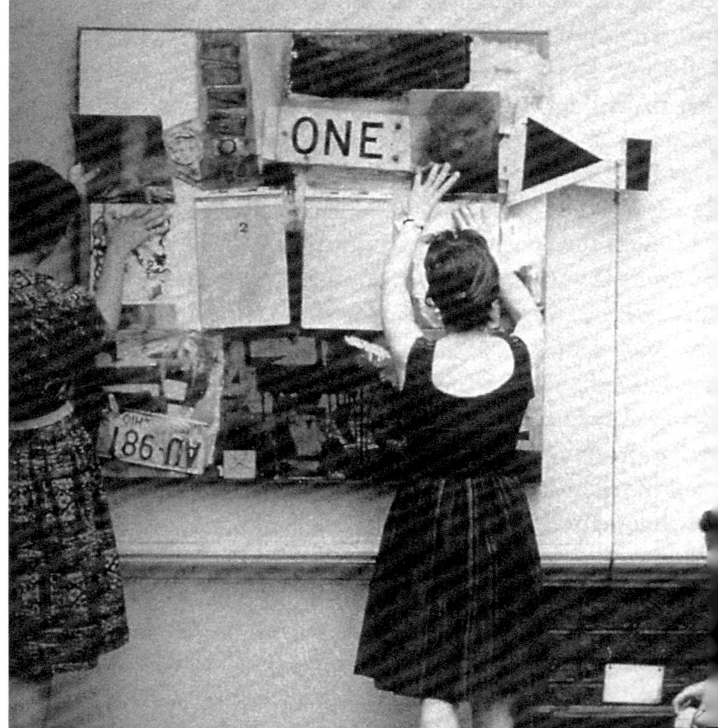



FIG. 3.51
Viewers with *Black Market*, at Oberlin College,
Ohio, 1962

**Robert Rauschenberg**

Drawings contributed to *Black Market*,
11 February 1969

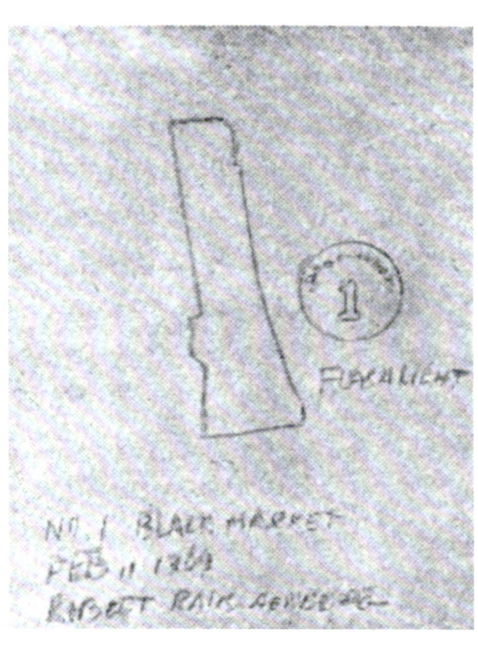


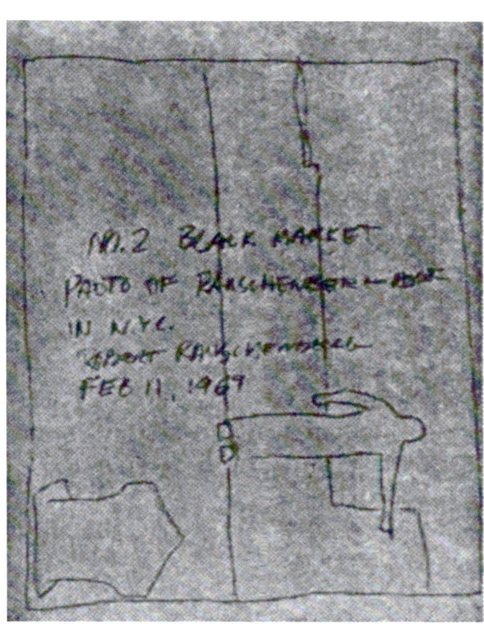


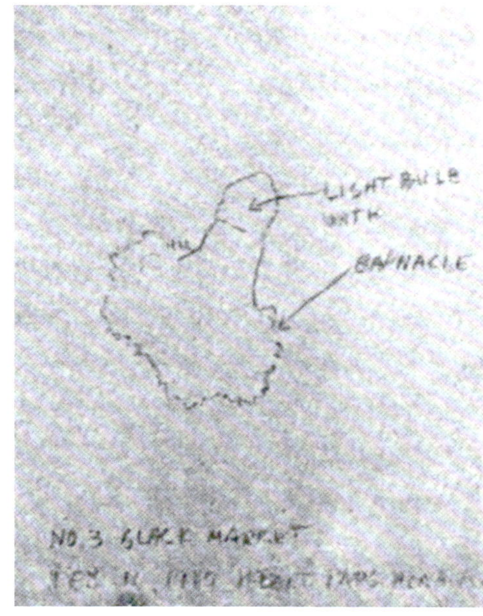


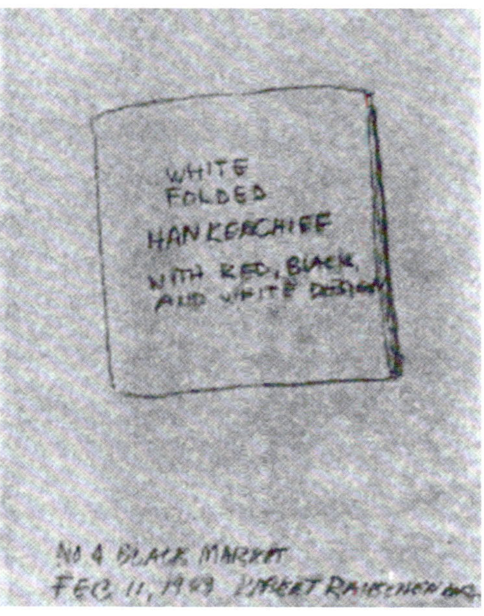

By allowing viewers to unload their own unwanted items in exchange for a choice of others, this work aimed to give function to junk, to make meaningless objects meaningful. *Black Market* had the potential to perform this rehabilitation both by connecting objects to new people who wanted them, and—since viewers were instructed to mark their contribution with one of four special stamps—by literally stamping them with their participation in an avant-garde artwork.[75] Whatever the success of this transformation of matter, however, *Black Market*'s intricate system of viewer involvement was deeply hopeless as well. Each useless object given new meaning by the work spoke to millions more rusting, devoid of purpose, in closets, empty lots, and landfills. Even the objects that did participate in the work's circuit of exchange enjoyed only a shallow redemption: once they were removed from the gallery, their new meaning would have seemed external to them, residing only in the special mark inked on their surfaces.

The objects of *Black Market*—both those that are permanent and those that pass through the valise—are at once filled with meaning and shown to be drained of it. They seem both special and ordinary, both particular and arbitrary. They are part of a painting, but a painting that dissolves into a mere collection of junk. By running discarded objects through a context that both gives them meaning and shows them to be without it, Rauschenberg emphasizes the broader cultural relevance of his deployment of philosophical tensions between the pictorial and the literal, between meaning and sheer materiality. The industrially produced objects of consumer society are seen to be very much like the very specialized matter of paint used in painting: they do have meanings related to their forms, but these meanings are perpetually at risk of changing or of simply dropping off. Just as paint can be made to give way

to meaning only in limited and flawed ways, so, too, the manufactured commodity objects of America's postwar abundance oscillate between sustaining the functions and meanings claimed for them by advertising and returning to mere obdurate stuff.

*Black Market*'s most direct engagement with the streetscape is of course in the large one-way sign that dominates the upper portion of the canvas. It is from this object that the canvas is connected (by a narrow rope) to the valise below. Early in 1961, the one-way sign would hardly have seemed a neutral object in New York: a front-page controversy had erupted in 1959 and 1960 over a plan to convert four of Manhattan's avenues to one-way traffic flow. Several avenues on the West Side had been converted in the late 1950s, and on New Year's Day 1959 the *New York Times* reported that Mayor Wagner had enthusiastically endorsed a plan to make Third, Lexington, Madison, and Fifth Avenues into one-way thoroughfares as well.[76] One-way avenues streamlined the flow of cars not only by eliminating the holdups caused by left turns across opposing traffic, but also by allowing the timing of lights for nonstop travel. Opposition in 1959 prevented the Board of Estimate from voting on the plan, but Traffic Commissioner T. T. Wiley nevertheless announced in February 1960 that the mayor had ordered him to go ahead with the conversion, beginning with Third and Lexington Avenues.[77] Although the board refused to decide the issue, on 17 July the signs were posted, and Manhattan's number of one-way avenues grew to ten (fig. 3.53). Commissioner Wiley called the transition "smooth and efficient." The *Times* agreed and pulled a phrase directly from the vocabulary of modernist planning in citing the "steady flow of traffic." Where signal-timing problems had been worked out, the paper reported "a traffic dream."[78]

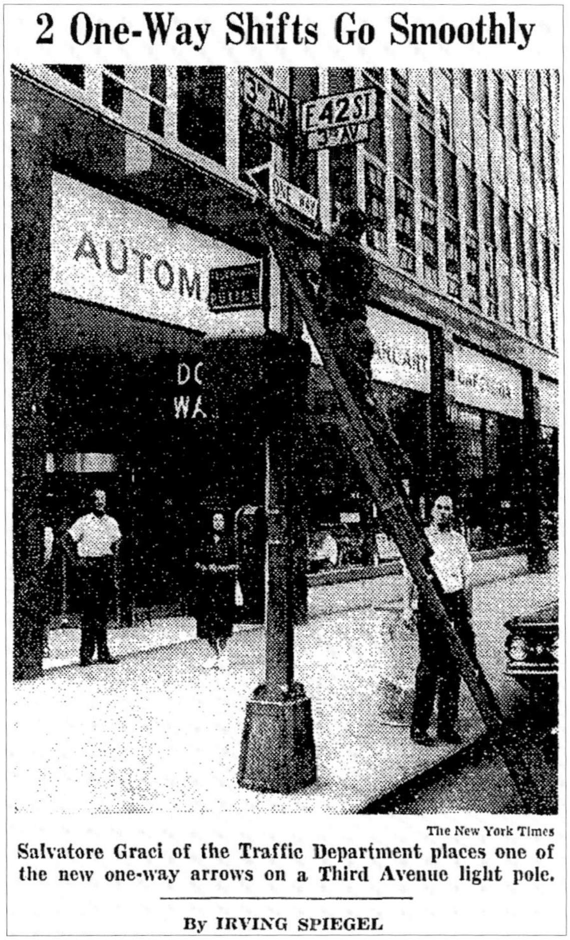

## 2 One-Way Shifts Go Smoothly

The New York Times

**Salvatore Graci of the Traffic Department places one of the new one-way arrows on a Third Avenue light pole.**

**By IRVING SPIEGEL**

FIG. 3.53

Installation of one-way sign on
Third Avenue, 17 July 1960,
*New York Times*, 18 July 1960

In order to accommodate the new timing of signal lights, which were keyed to a twenty-two-mile-per-hour flow, three seconds were shaved from the time pedestrians were given to cross the avenues. This change, which both presented a threat to pedestrians and also symbolized an apparent shift in the values of the city, was a major cause for opposition to the new scheme. One citizen, writing to the *New York Times,* objected particularly to the new situation on Third Avenue: "Third is a wide avenue and obviously any pedestrian crossing it must be not only ready to start the instant the light favors him but must have one foot in the air, his first step half taken, if he expects to get over on the green light. . . . The Traffic Commission seems to concentrate its attention only on vehicles with four or six wheels rather than on human beings with one, one-and-a-half or two legs."[79] Three City Council members vowed to fight the change, with minority leader Stanley M. Isaacs writing in a letter to the *New York Times* that 'there is a tremendous difference between the threat of an overwhelming parade of cars, all in motion, and the situation when autos must start from scratch before they can run you down." Despite this brief opposition, claims for the increased safety of the one-way plan were eventually vindicated, at least by the Traffic Commission's own statistics; and Manhattan's avenues continue overwhelmingly as one-way thoroughfares today.[80] In 1961, however, the one-way scheme seemed to place the passage of traffic paramount over particular, local needs. It was another instance of the desire to remake the city as a newly systematized place of negotiability, order, and flow.

Rauschenberg's appropriation of the one-way sign as the centerpiece of *Black Market* has some similar meanings. The work, after all, does offer its own versions of the period's abstracting impulses, its desires to wrest meaning

FIG. 3.56
**Robert Rauschenberg**
Installation at *Dylaby*, 30 August–30 September 1962
Stedelijk Museum, Amsterdam

and order from the material environment, to make that environment negotiable and systematic. Objects are exchanged in *Black Market,* fresh meanings are generated, records are kept. The one-way sign expresses the flow of objects through the case, the redemptive possibilities of exchange.[81] But the sign—big at this level, and dirty—is not transparently semiotic, not an uncomplicated herald of unchecked flow. Very much an object, it is bent and dirty, bearing holes, nicks, and even an excessive drip of black paint that looks original to the factory. Smudges are especially heavy around the thick bolts that must have once connected it to its signpost (fig. 3.54). Mounted off-kilter and nailed to an unevenly painted, apparently meaningless wooden board, the sign—even as it suggests the work's circuitry of exchange—is tethered by a coarse rope to the local, material resistance of the old suitcase and its junky contents (fig. 3.55).

*Black Market,* then, is the site of a forever unresolved alternation between blockage and flow. On the one hand, it is illegible, chaotic, and particular. On the other, it is the site of real exchange, and of the generation of new meanings for

junk. The work is, as its title suggests, a black market—not because its exchange is illegal, but rather because it is counter to the exchange of public fantasy. The exchange here is awkward, frustrated, even doomed. (It has been reported that Rauschenberg, in extending the invitation for viewers to pick up and leave objects, knew that the arrangement would fail.) The market enacted by this combine is an alternative to the glass-clad machine of exchange value rising around it; in the place of the homogenized and abstracted nature of financial-services capitalism, *Black Market* tenuously imagines a world of material particularity and specificity.[82] This work, like the other combines of 1961 and 1962, suggests that, while values can flow from commodity purchases and traffic can flow through New York, these operations are inevitably limited by the tethering of meaning to things.

In 1961 and 1962, Manhattan was in the throes of economic postmodernization, and Rauschenberg was cobbling together the most sculptural of his combines. The result of Rauschenberg's work is a representation of the texture of that transformation. Looking at the works closely now, we

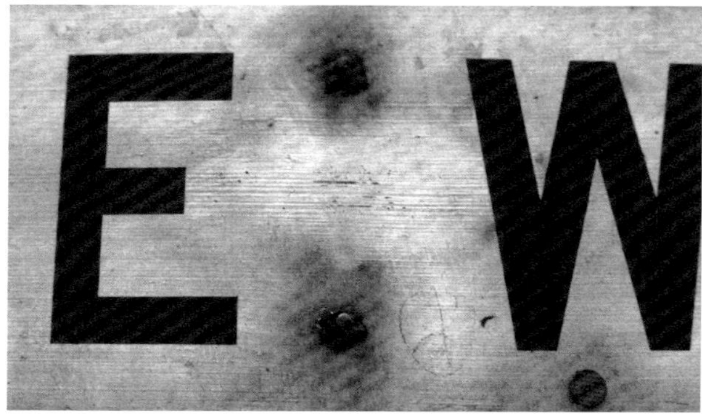

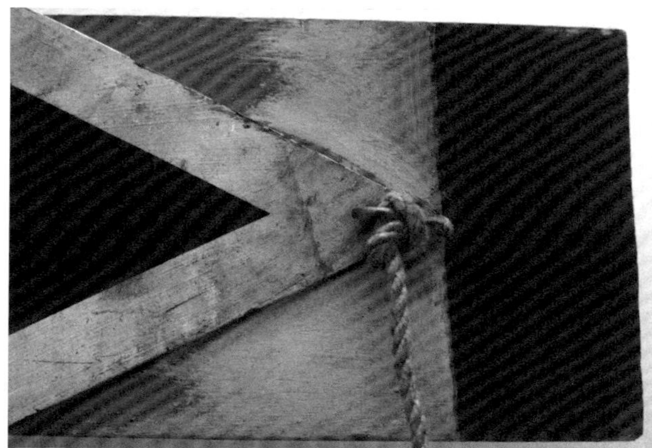

FIGS. 3.54 and 3.55
**Robert Rauschenberg**
*Black Market* (details)

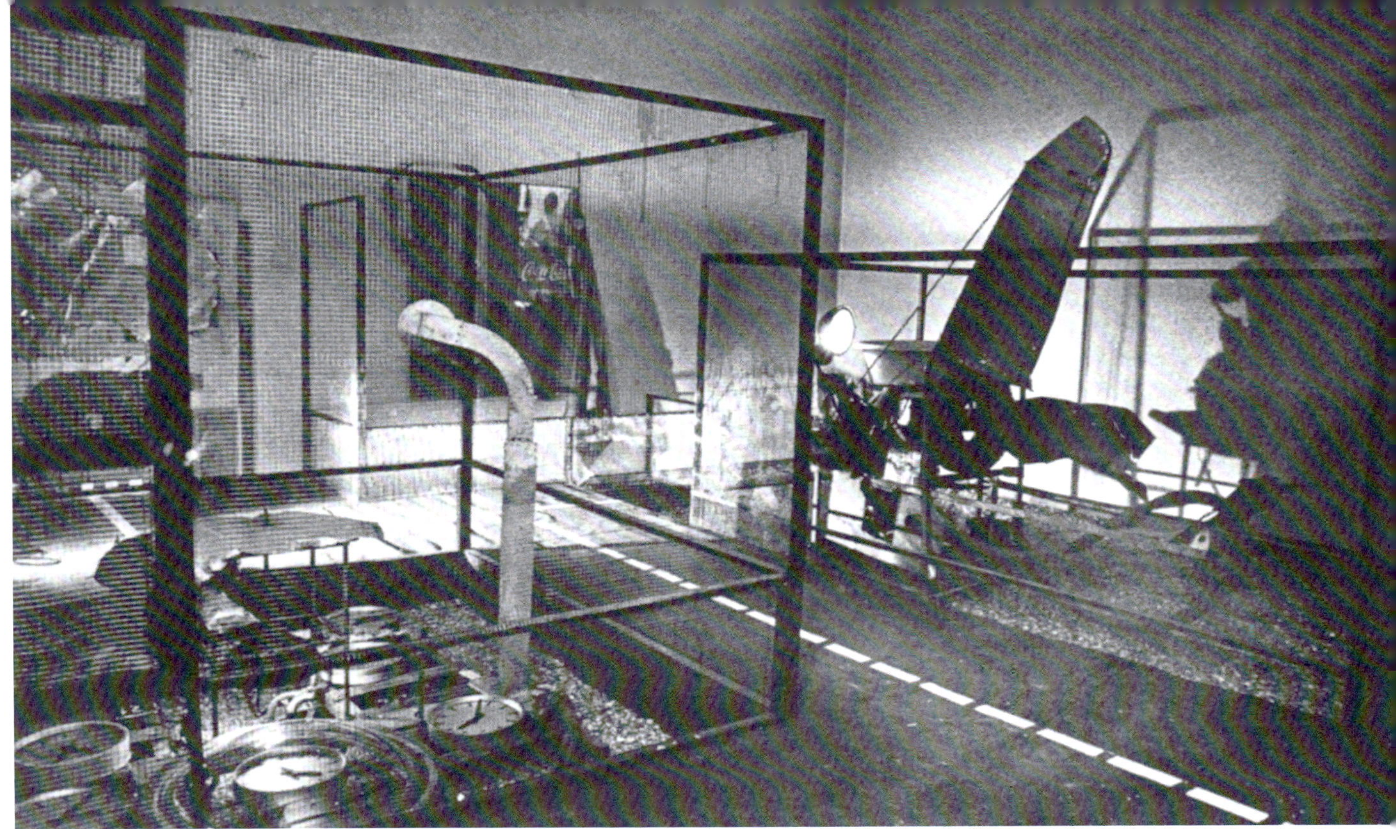

see not only what we have long known about New York in this period (that it was a time of much rebuilding, for example, and visible waste), and but also much that we have not. That is, Rauschenberg's combines—wallowing in the space between the dead-end street and the expressway, between the printer's loft and conglomerate's monolith, between the scrap heap and the consumer's fantasy of fulfillment— allow us to see that this transition in the history of capitalism had a specific set of effects on those living at its center. The combines show us that New York City in this moment— encouraging its residents to relate more abstractly to their streets, their buildings, and their consumer objects—was effectively relinquishing its long-standing relationship to the materiality of industrial modernity. Although their emphasis is materialist (as early as 1958, the artist had said simply, "I want fragments"), the combines are seduced, too, by the ever-increasing levels of systematicity around them.[83] Their force, then, is in their rich representational power rather than in any clean critique. The combines of 1961 and 1962

figure a grappling with the new economic and architectural conditions of their city, an uncertainty about how much a city dweller might embrace the new economy (of saved labor, saved time, even saved lives) and how much she might resist its evaporation of material situatedness.

Rauschenberg went to Amsterdam in the summer of 1962 to participate in a special show—with Martial Raysse, Niki de Saint Phalle, Daniel Socerri, Jean Tinguely, and Per Olof Ultvedt—at the Stedelijk Museum. For the exhibition, called *Dylaby* (short for *Dynamisch Labyrint*), each artist converted one or two of the museum's rooms into an environment through which visitors would walk.[34] Rauschenberg's room was given over to an explicitly urban environment: he converted the floor into a simple plan of streets, complete with dashed white lines running down the center. Four main constructions, each enclosed in an architectural cage of mesh, formed the buildings of this little city (fig. 3.56). All four were like loose, especially sculptural versions of the

FIG. 3.57

**Robert Rauschenberg**

*Barge*, 1962–63

Oil and silk-screen ink on canvas, 80 ¼ x 386 in. (203.88 x 980.44 cm)

Guggenheim Bilbao Museoa and Solomon R. Guggenheim Museum, New York,

with additional funds contributed by Thomas H. Lee and Ann Tenebaum,

the International Director's Council, and Executive Committee Members

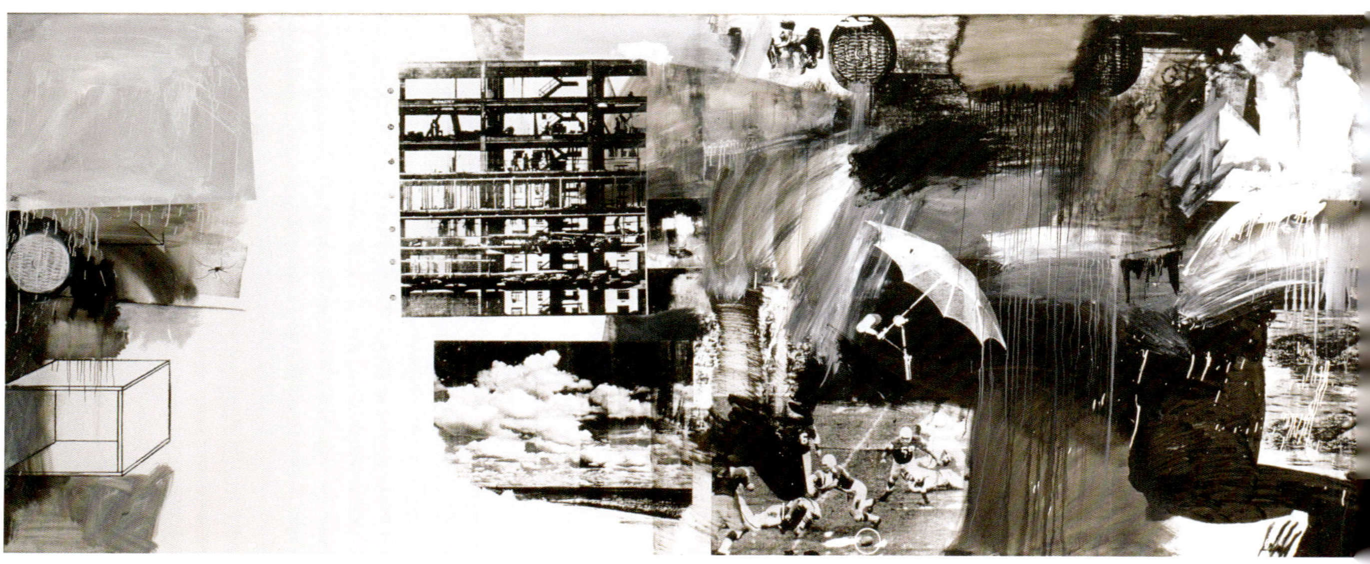

1961 and 1962 combines, constituted from a vocabulary of large-scale industrial and consumer trash, including wooden warehouse palettes, an inverted bicycle frame, a scattering of numberless clocks, and the usual sections of sheet metal. The audibly humming clocks were set to run at different speeds, and a pump uselessly bubbled air through a tub of water, helping to render an urban environment of fruitless process and of order gone haywire.[85]

*Dylaby* was the final literalization of the 1961 and 1962 combines. It diagrammatically enacted the conflation of system and chaos that had driven the smaller works made in New York. And it did so in a setting that was explicitly urban. When Rauschenberg was done with *Dylaby*, however, he was also finished working in this mode. As he later put it, "I was really sick of sculpture. Nothing appealed to me more when I got back than the gentility of a beautifully stretched piece of canvas." Indeed, when the artist returned to New York, he picked up silk screens, which formed the center of his practice for the rest of his life.[86] His next works, such as *Crocus* (see fig. 3.6), and, soon, the enormous *Barge* (fig. 3.57), worked in the fluid, two-dimensional register of reproducible photographic images. Having indulged a quixotically materialist vision of New York for two years, Rauschenberg all but abandoned the palpable object in favor of a nearly endless number of flat canvases, thinly marked with images of public figures, highways, and satellite dishes.[87]

A word, then, about the relationship of the works of 1961 and 1962 to the earlier combines. Not all of Rauschenberg's quasi-sculptural work was centrally concerned with the city and its consumer objects; the

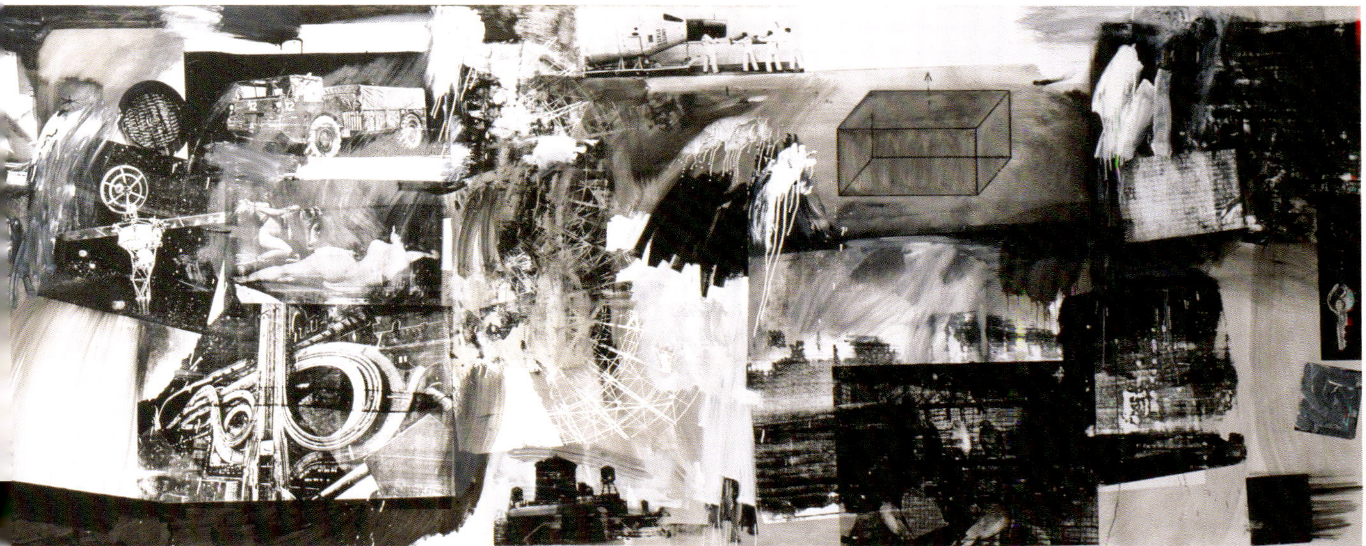

materials and references of the combines from the mid-1950s, in particular, are widely varied, ranging from art history and government to taxidermy and his own personal relationships (recall *Rebus,* fig. 3.4). Clearly, in making those earlier works, Rauschenberg had no particular sense that his artistic concerns intersected those of the city and its goods. I find it no coincidence, however, that in the last and most sculptural of his combines, Rauschenberg did come to lay special emphasis on the urban environment. The early combines had worked to extend Pollock's painterly materialism into the everyday environment, resisting instrumental or synthetic understandings of the detritus of ordinary life. Eventually Rauschenberg seems to have recognized that the desire to make this extension stemmed from the fact that materiality was especially problematic in New York in this period. While Rauschenberg ruminated on the obduracy of loft architecture and rusted flashlights, Robert Moses proposed a city in which these specific things all but disappeared.

Rauschenberg never returned to a full-dress investigation of the materiality of the built environment.[88] In turning to silk screens and to the images of global communications, however, Rauschenberg did bring with him the one-way sign. And although its appearance is photographic rather than material, this sign appears, doubled, in a screen the artist used several times in the following years, as, for example in *Estate* (fig. 3.53).[89] Both one-way signs in the photograph are bent, so that they point almost directly opposite each other, and they are joined by a third sign with an arrow pointing in yet another direction. A stop sign

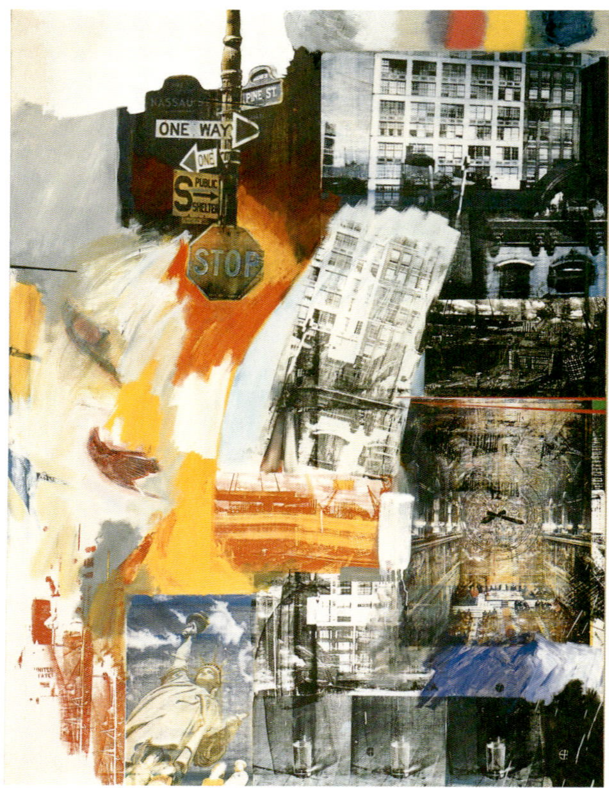


**FIG. 3.58**

**Robert Rauschenberg**

*Estate*, 1963

Oil and silk-screen ink on canvas,

96 x 70 in. (243.8 x 177.2 cm)

Philadelphia Museum of Art, Gift of

the Friends of the Philadephia Museum of Art

and two antiquated street signs, identifying this as the downtown intersection of Nassau and Pine—site of the Chase Manhattan development— complete the image. This halting constellation, although now laid flat into a fluid sea of images, faintly registers the abiding incoherence and specificity of things.

# 4 A Loft Without Labor

JUDD

THE OPENING OF DONALD JUDD'S solo exhibition at the Whitney Museum of American Art in 1968 sealed his reputation as a central figure in contemporary art. William C. Agee, the curator, had packed Judd's sheet-metal sculptures fairly tightly into what at least one critic described as a warehouselike installation, and the tidy right angles and repetitive modularity of the works made a neat match to the stone tiles and concrete ceiling coffers of the museum's two-year-old Marcel Breuer building (fig. 4.1).[1] Sitting brightly in the middle of the space, *Untitled (DSS 128)* (fig. 4.2) exemplified the overall appearance of the exhibition: a shiny rectangle of amber Plexiglas with a thin and hollow stainless-steel core. Critics considering the works were undecided about their meanings, and their importance. Some dismissed the show as empty novelty ("He is about as minimal as can be. . . . Do you suppose that next year, with the skirts, art will go midi?"), while others lauded it as newly canonical ("The most important event of the month . . . a tremendous success").[2]

Although the responses plainly lacked any certainty over the critical terms in play (*Artnews* titled their review "Judd the Obscure"), a cluster of related phrases appeared again and again. James R. Mellow, writing for the *New York Times,* saw Judd's sculptures as "a matter of brilliant factuality," while Jane Harrison Cone emphasized the sculptures' "inescapable factuality," and Grace Glueck called the works "actual, specific facts in themselves."[3] Indeed, critics had already been tripping over the factual quality of Judd's work for a couple of years. In 1965, Barbara Rose had claimed "concreteness and substantial presence" as the "prime quality" of Judd's sculpture. In 1966, Lucy Lippard had added that "[Judd's] metal and plastic boxes are among the most factual and radically assertive works today," while Mellow had written of an untitled floor box (now known by its

catalogue raisonné designation *Untitled [DSS 79]* [fig. 4.3]), "As an object, the box was very much there . . . Its whole purpose seemed to be the declaration of some blunt quiddity and nothing more."[4] In the years since, Judd's works have likewise appeared "blunt, unambiguous," "completely present," "just existing," and "simply 'there.'"[5] Each sculpture has asserted itself as "simply another thing in the world of things."[6] In the 1967 essay "Art and Objecthood," which remains the single most influential account of Minimalism, Michael Fried characterized Judd's work (together with that of Robert Morris and others) as a "literalist art" that insisted on its own occupation of ordinary space and time.[7] By the time of the Whitney exhibition, literalist characterizations of Judd's work predominated, with one clause becoming paradigmatic. Glueck's review appeared under the title "A Box Is a Box Is a Box," while the anonymous critic at *Time* wrote, "For Judd, a box is a box is a box, and nothing more." A year later, Rose concluded, "[The] principal statement [of Judd's early Minimalist works] appeared to be the tautology that a box is a box is a box."[8]

If we find echoes here of Stuart Preston's declaration, in a review of Jasper Johns, that "a flashlight is a flashlight is a flashlight," then we should hear an assonance, too, between Mellow's understanding of Judd's floor box and John Ashbery's view of *White Flag*: "It has tremendous—though silent—impact. It is *there,* though for what purpose it would be hard to say."[9] Despite these critical parallels, the most cursory glance at Judd's work makes it clear that his brand of literalism, especially after the Minimalist turn of 1964–65, is quite different from those of the other artists treated in this book. Judd's Minimalist sculpture has none of Johns's heft or palpability, none of Rauschenberg's discordance, none of Oldenburg's mad mark-making. Instead, it is thin, serial, often shiny; the artist directly declared that he "didn't

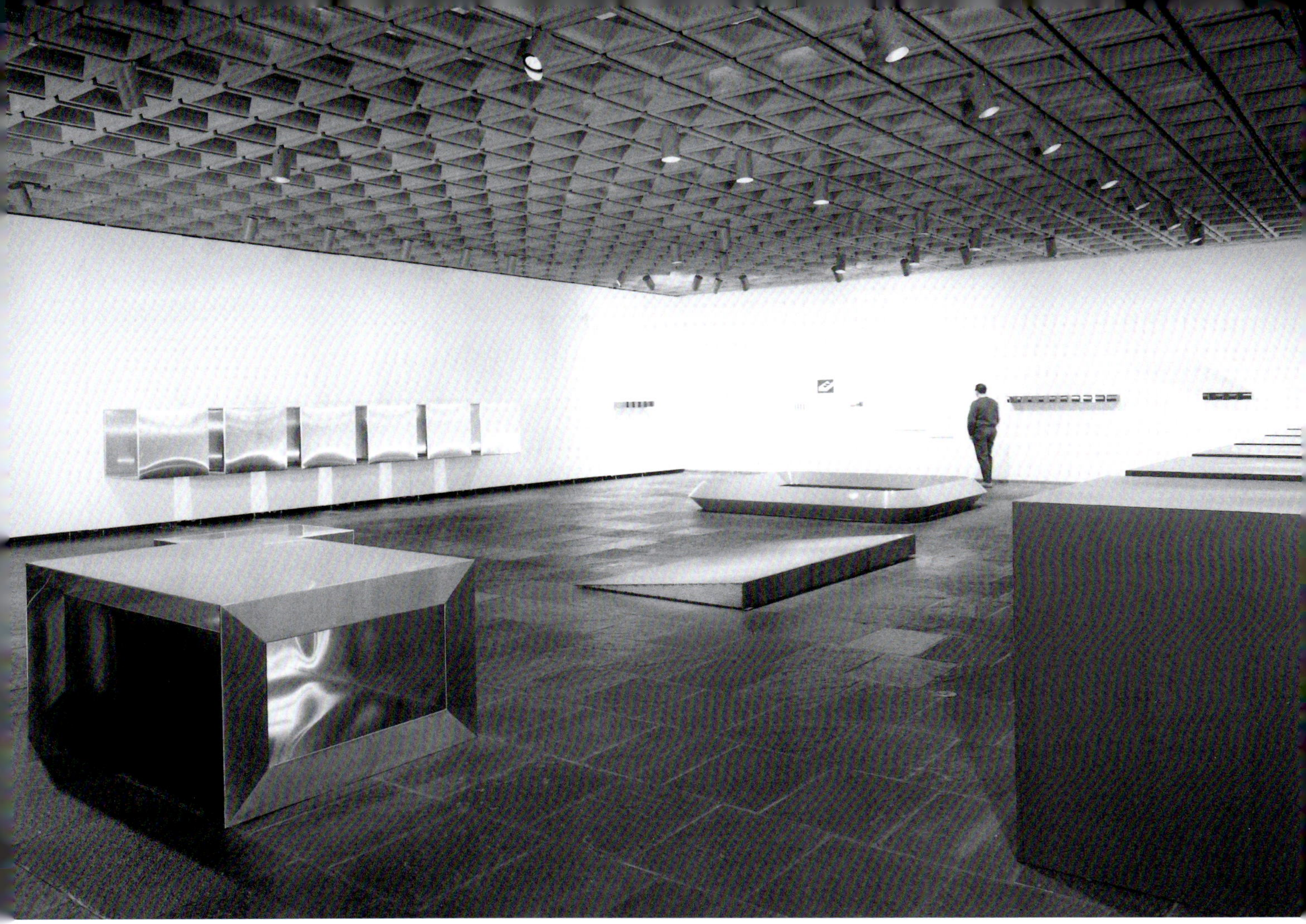

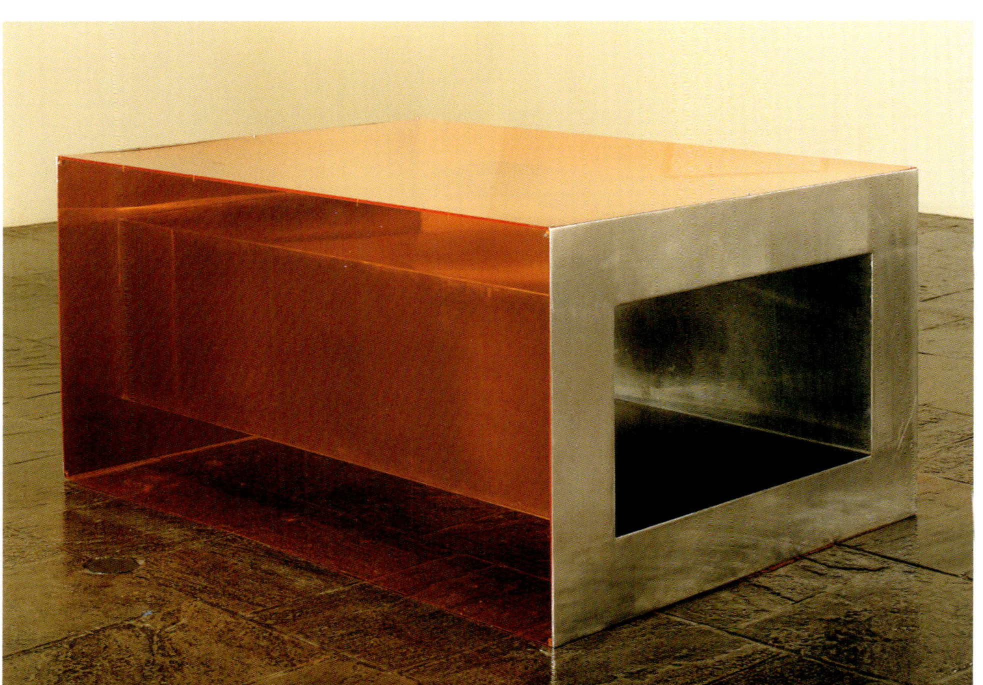


FIG. 4.2
Donald Judd

*Untitled (DSS 128)*, 1968
Stainless steel
and Plexiglas,
overall 33 x 68 x 48 in.
(83.8 x 172.7 x 121.9 cm)
Whitney Museum of
American Art, New York,
Purchase, with funds
from the Howard and
Jean Lipman Foundation, Inc.

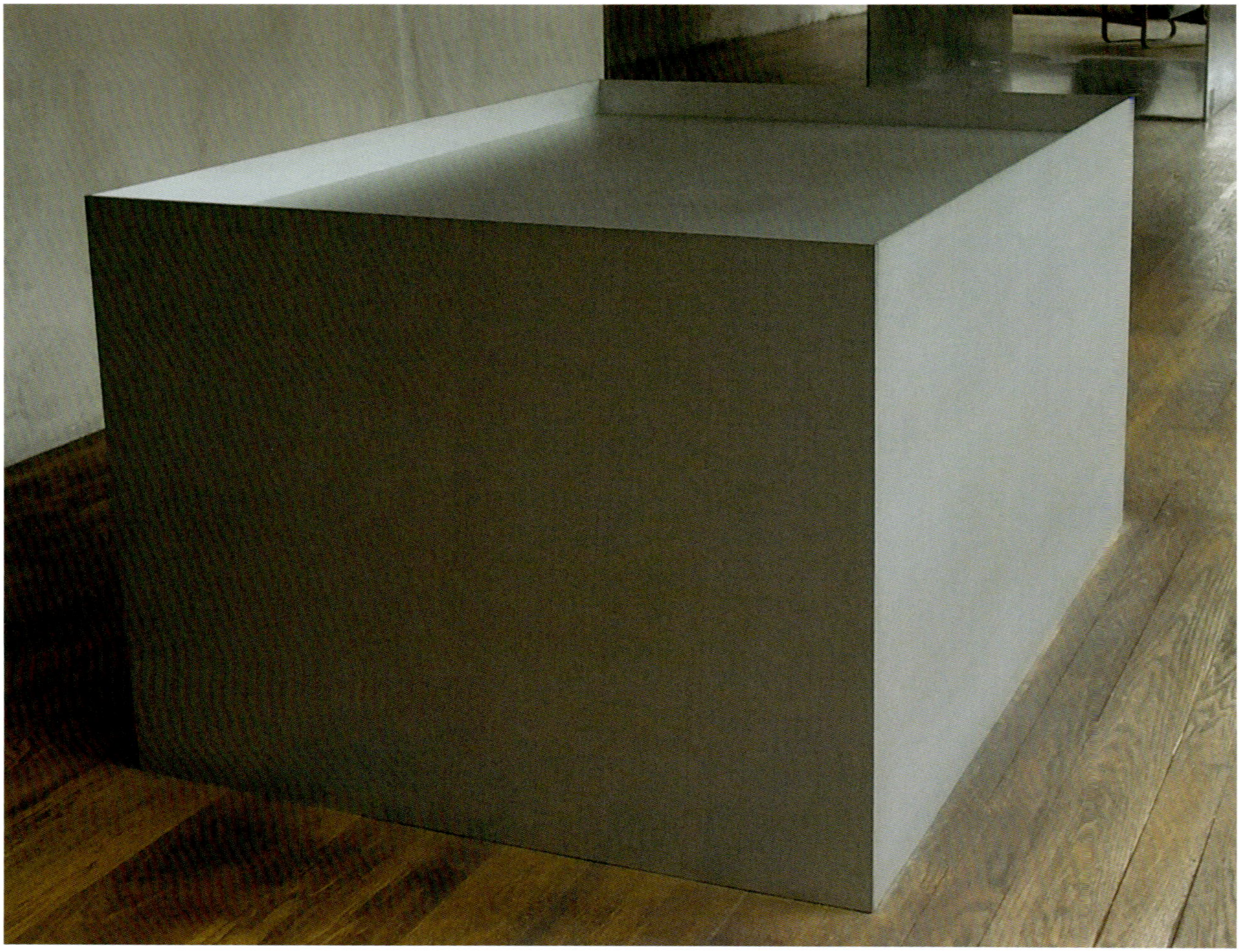

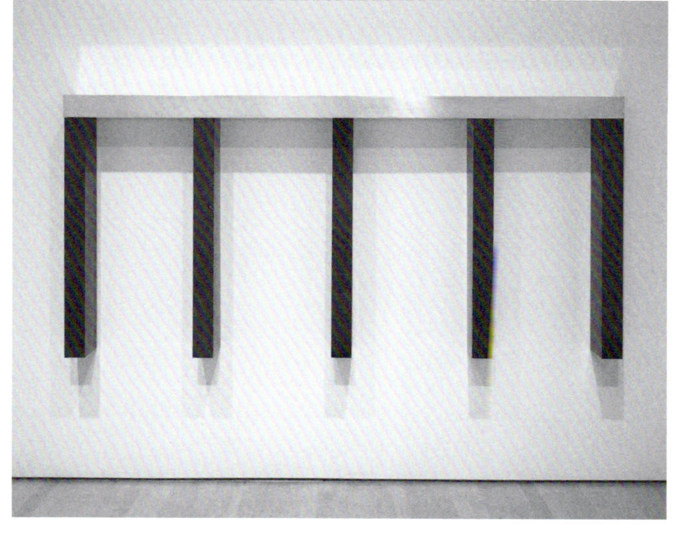

FIG. 4.3
**Donald Judd**
*Untitled (DSS 79)*, 1966
Aluminum, 40 x 72 x 51 in. (101.6 x 182.9 x 129.5 cm)
Collection of Judd Foundation

FIG. 4.4
**Donald Judd**
*Untitled (DSS 55)*, 1964
Brass and galvanized iron with blue lacquer,
40 ¹⁄₂ x 84 x 6 ³⁄₄ in. (102.9 x 213.4 x 17.2 cm)
National Gallery of Canada, Ottawa, Purchased 1974

want to make just lumps."[10] If we wish to unpack what the critics might have meant in diagnosing a *factuality* in Judd's sculpture, we will have to consider the specifics of the case.

For one thing, the literalist reception of Judd's work was complicated from the beginning by another, competing strain in the criticism. Take for example Harold Rosenberg's 1967 claim that many Minimalist sculptures, even while "affirm[ing] the independent existence of the art object as meaningful in itself," also aimed to "disguise themselves as ordinary objects[,] . . . to pass as machine or building parts, as those of two or three years earlier passed as billboards or comic strips."[11] In Rosenberg's view, Minimalism eschewed reference and quoted the built environment at the same time. Other critics betrayed a similar ambivalence. Despite its claim that "for Judd a box is a box is a box," *Time* proposed that viewers might ask, "What is a box . . . if not a coffin, a house, a treasure chest?"[12]

Rosalind Krauss pursued architectural references in a 1966 essay titled "Allusion and Illusion in Donald Judd," seeing similarities between *Untitled (DSS 55)* (fig. 4.4) and "the colonnades of classical architecture or . . . the supporting members of any modular structure." The next year, Clement Greenberg, attacking Minimalism, suggested that the movement had been infiltrated by the "good design" of recent home and office furniture.[13] Although the art-historical mainstream now largely treats Judd's sculpture as intractably literalist about its own space and materials, several recent essays, too, have found references to the everyday built environment, "echoes of Plexiglas jukebox windows, car parts, cutlery, and shiny metal turnstiles."[14]

It seems to me that this Janus-faced quality of Judd's sculptures—their being at once literalist and bound up, as one writer has put it, in "the spaces and surfaces of the modern city"—is a strange quality, one needing

explanation.[15] It also seems to me a quality that allows the sculptures to speak with a unique fullness to the changes facing New York at the time, and especially (far more than the other artists we have considered) to the rapid transformation of the city's economy—its shift away from manufacturing and toward the provision of financial services.

To be sure, Judd's own statements underscored his antipathy toward representation. Art historians have leaned especially heavily on Judd's essay "Specific Objects" ("Three dimensions are real space. That gets rid of the problem of illusionism[,] . . . one of the salient and most objectionable relics of European art") and on his radio interview with Bruce Glaser and Lucy Lippard ("I'm using actual space").[16] As early as 1963, Judd had emphasized the importance of "actual materials, actual color, and actual space," and he told a New York symposium audience in 1966, "I'd like work that didn't allude to other things and was a specific thing in itself."[17]

For Judd, the primary problem with pictorial representation was that it inevitably imposed a fallacious human order on things, rather than simply delivering fact. "Earlier painting," Judd said to Glaser and Lippard, "was saying that there's more order in the scheme of things than we admit now, like Poussin saying order underlies nature." That is, pictorial representation (especially "illusionism") was "linked up with" ways of thinking that Judd characterized variously as "rationalism," "humanism," "anthropomorphism," or "the philosophy of a man-centered universe." These views of the world, replete with implicit organization, were "pretty much discredited now" or "wrong and not credible."[18]

It seems that Judd, trained as a painter, had finally concluded that none of the modernist efforts to perfect representation could save it from its fundamental fraudulence, its inevitable organization, systematization, or abstraction of the world. On the occasion of the Whitney exhibition, Judd spoke to Lippard about his early frustration with drawing from life. His remarks make clear that his eventual rejection of optical representation was also a denial of idealist notions of the material world:

> You know, you can't sit and draw something out there as if somehow you're putting it down on paper. Which was a very live, hard problem one time. And I used to go down and try to draw things off the dock at 27th Street; drawing, say, the limb of a tree on a piece of paper as if there's something in the tree that you're putting down on the piece of paper. And it became pretty obvious after a while that the thing was only a tree and that the gap between the tree and what I had on the paper was just a lot of baloney. . . . It was really pretty horrible. I mean I was very bothered by it. But, see, once you quit believing that you can see something in a tree and get it down, that it's really in the tree, then that's it.[19]

Even after rejecting the "baloney" of representation (and of its faith in capturing essences), Judd, like his critics, clearly recognized that his sculpture did make reference to its world. In 1962 he wrote, "All good art has a certain amount of social content."[20] Judd claimed for his own work a particular relationship to the contemporary built environment. Talking with Bruce Hooten in 1965, he compared his own work to Edward Hopper's, which he said had been influenced by the look of the United States in the 1930s: "I think some of the things I deal with, Hopper probably has dealt with also, since it's somewhat the same environment and I have pretty strong reactions to what this country looks like. It looks pretty dull and spare, and you like this and dislike it and it's very complicated. . . . I don't much like the idea of representing the United States in my work. It's just that

you live here and you are involved in your sense of what's around you."[21]

Seeing Judd's work fully requires that we manage to keep always in view both its literalism and its engagement with the built environment. What might it have meant for Judd to refuse representation even as he worked with the architectural vocabulary of his city? These two claims made for Judd's sculpture, both by his critics and by the artist himself, may not be mutually reconcilable. Listening to their awkward jostling, side by side, however, might allow us to see what was at issue in Judd's resolutely spartan project as an artist. Specifically, such a view may allow us to recognize that Judd's work identified an ascendant idealism in its city, and that it responded with an oddly qualified, materialist alternative. To learn what we can from Judd's art, let us now turn to the two pivotal moments of his early career: the years 1962–63, in which the artist picked up wood and hardware to make his first sculptural constructions, and the years 1964–66, in which he turned to sheet metal, helping to develop the style that would come to be known as Minimalism.

## Useless Objects: 1962–63

Donald Judd had been painting in New York since 1949. When he did make his first sculptural construction, in 1962, it was a decidedly strange thing.[22] *Untitled (DSS 32)* (fig. 4.5) stands not quite four feet tall, an open assemblage made from the scraps of a discarded warehouse pallet, a section of asphalt pipe, and a bowed sheet of Masonite pressboard. Properly speaking, the construction has neither front nor back, although its outside, painted in light cadmium red, contrasts sharply with its deep black interior. Its heavy wooden planks, riddled with nail holes and broken staples, bear prominent notches and scuff marks. Judd did not true

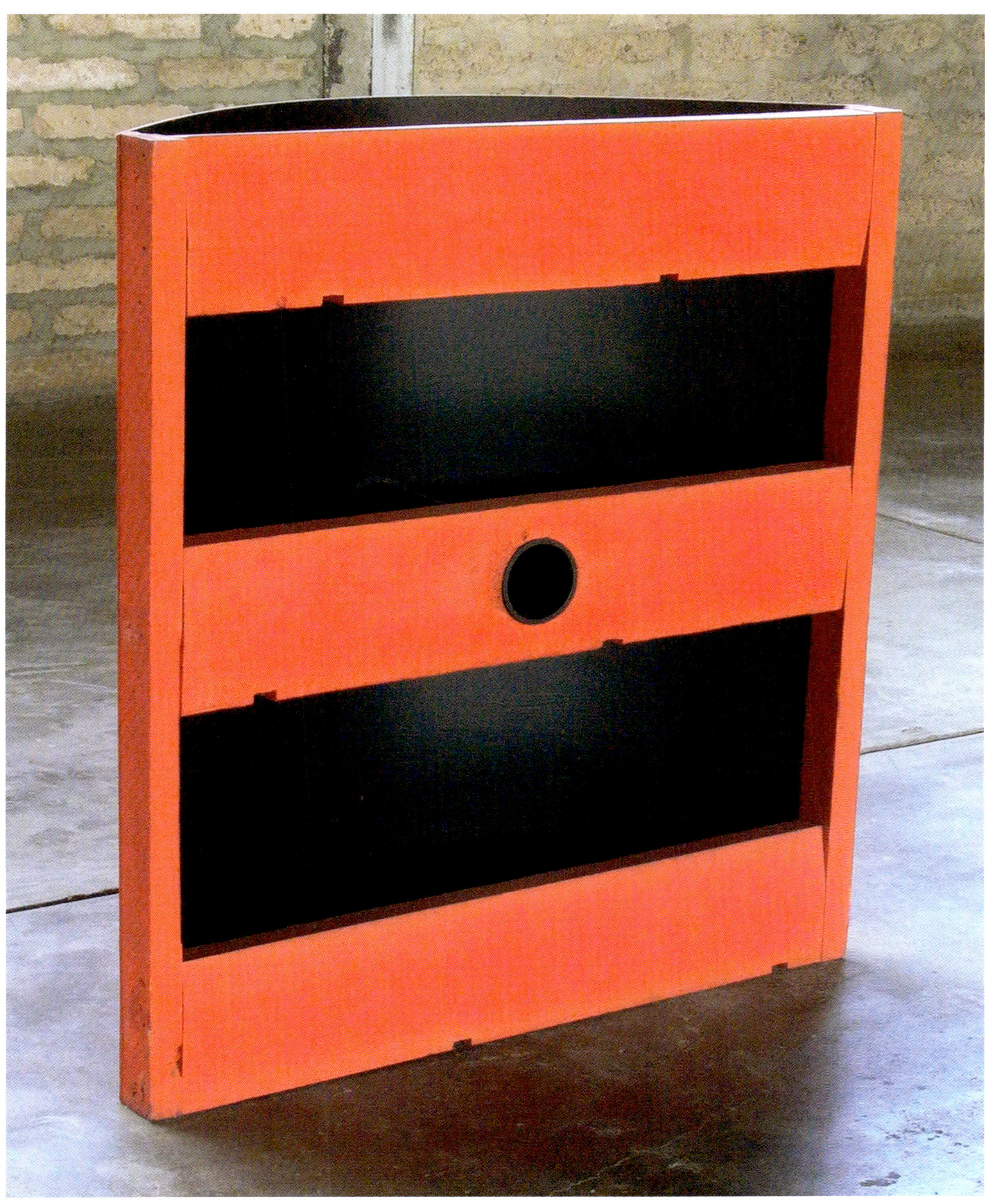

the boards to their frame, so they contribute, together with the texture of the asphalt pipe, to a feeling of casual roughness. Although suggestive of cheap industrial infrastructure, this useless object persistently refuses any familiar identity or purpose. It speaks vaguely and pointlessly in the language of small-scale manufacturing, where forklifts and large packages meet the labor of hand tools and bent backs.

Many of Judd's early constructions similarly drew materials from an ad hoc realm of industry and construction. The artist included a lath for wall plastering in *Untitled (DSS 36)* (fig. 4.6), a metal pipe and wooden planks in *Untitled (DSS 33)* (fig. 4.7), and a wire-reinforced window in *Untitled (DSS 14)* (fig. 4.8).[23] The paintinglike construction now called *Untitled (DSS 34)* (fig. 4.9) works only slightly more obliquely. Above and below this work's central surface—a plywood board, mechanically striated and painted red—Judd attached an odd concave frame of galvanized sheet iron. If we have any doubts about this frame's relationship to the sheet-metal cornices of New York's nineteenth-century manufacturing buildings, a period drawing dispels them (fig. 4.10). The artist could even have copied the frames sketched at lower right from the roof of his own future home, the 1870 industrial loft building at 101 Spring Street (fig. 4.11).

When Judd showed some of his early constructions at the Green Gallery in the winter of 1963–64, several critics, as if unconsciously struck by an industrial quality, dwelled on their conspicuous lack of utility. Brian O'Doherty, writing for the *New York Times,* described the works as "red wooden-shelved constructions with occasional grills, washboards with curved aluminum-covered ends, pipes running hither and thither." Barbara Rose, reviewing the show for *Art International*, commented, "At first, Donald Judd's simple wood constructions look more like useless objects than like sculpture," and Sidney Tillim, in his review for *Arts,* concluded

that Judd's works "resemble storage units of an unidentifiable kind."[24]

The planks Judd used in *DSS 32* (see fig. 4.5) were, as the artist well knew, of a rather specific origin. Roberta Smith noted in 1975 that these were "materials found on the street," and we can see indentations in the wood suggesting they were once baled with metal straps.[25] (In assembling the boards for the work, Judd turned the bottom one around, so that the notches, lined up in the top two boards, appear off-register there.) While discussing the rough look of the piece in a 1971 interview, Judd explained that it was "made out of printing material skids, salvaged wood."[26]

It would have been easy, in 1962, for Judd to pick up the leftover industrial pallet on his own block. He was living at 53 East Nineteenth Street, in a modest nineteenth-century brick loft building with a corner doorway and a single cast-iron column (fig. 4.12). Judd seems to have had the top floor, for $100 a month; the lease stipulated that it was to be used only as a studio.[27] Across Nineteenth Street stood a grander structure, the American Lithographic Building, which in 1962 listed no fewer than fifty-seven commercial occupants, mostly in printing, typography, lithography, direct mail, label finishing, and binding.[28] Judd's own building had been the home of small apparel firms; in 1955, Hughes and Thomas Clothing, Mrs. E. Fatta (a manufacturer or merchant of trousers), and Vincent Remini (a tailor) all had quarters there. Other buildings nearby had recently housed the Loyal Shirt Company, Hudson Clothes, and A. S. Greenberg & Son Woolens and Worsteds.[29]

By 1962, however, manufacturing of all kinds in Manhattan was in rapid decline. In 1947, it seems, 90 percent of the area's manufacturing had taken place in Manhattan; fifteen years later, this proportion had dropped to no more than 70 or 75 percent.[30] In just the six years after 1958,

FIG. 4.6 (below)

**Donald Judd**

*Untitled (DSS 36),* 1963, reconstructed 1975
Light cadmium red oil on wood with metal lath,
72 x 104 x 49 in. (182.9 x 264.2 x 124.5 cm)
National Gallery of Canada, Ottawa

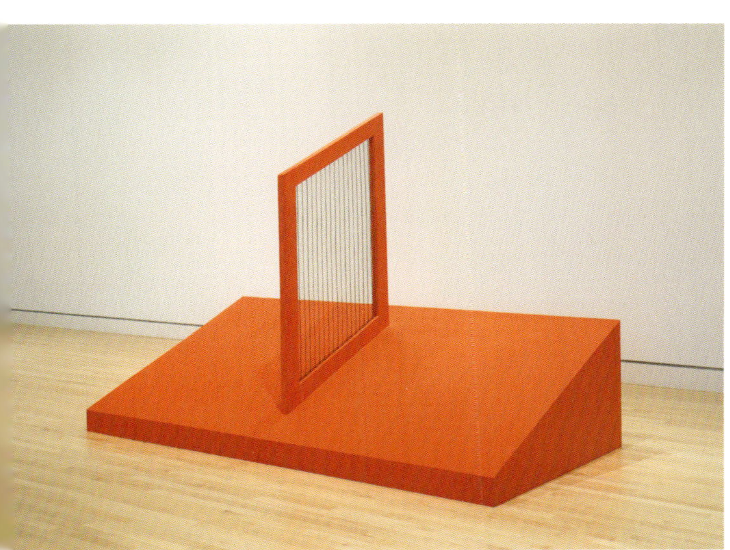

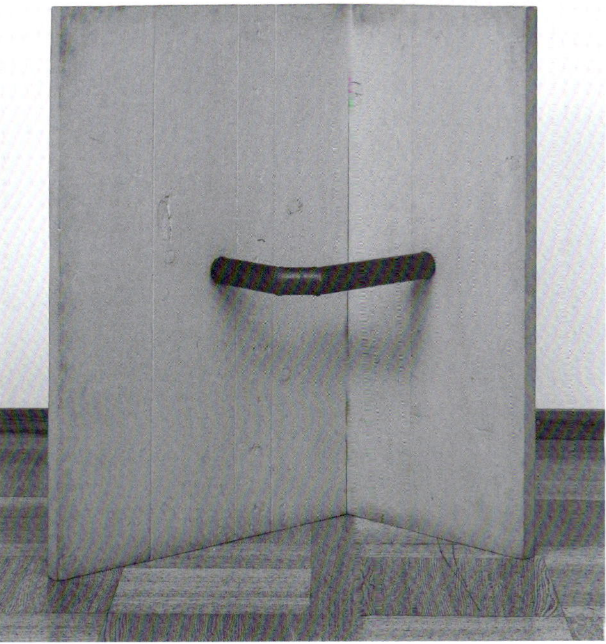

FIG. 4.7 (above right)

**Donald Judd**

*Untitled (DSS 33),* 1962
Light cadmium red oil
on wood with black
enameled metal pipe,
48 x 33 1/8 x 21 3/4 in.
(121.9 x 84.1 x 55.2 cm)
Kunstmuseum Basel

FIG. 4.8

**Donald Judd**

*Untitled (DSS 14),* 1961
Maroon enamel on recto and
light cadmium red oil on verso of
wire-reinforced glass,
18 x 31 in. (45.7 x 78.7 cm)
Collection of Judd Foundation

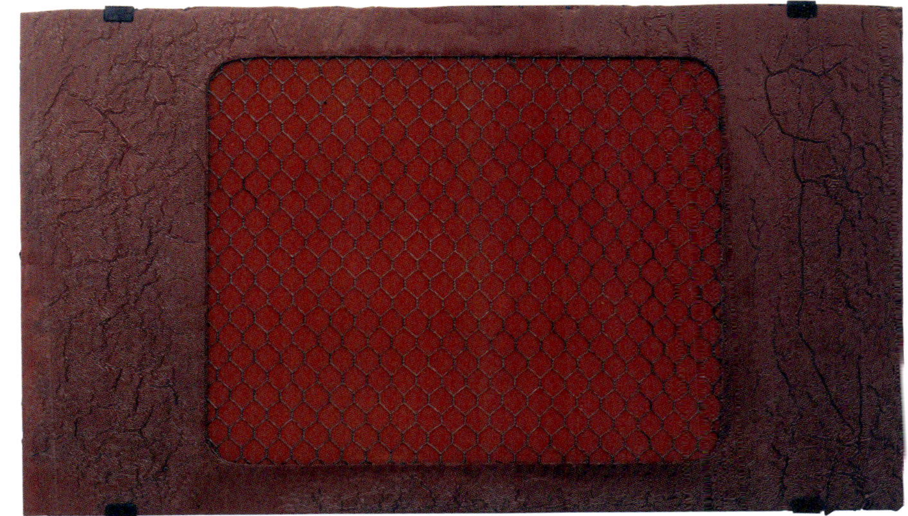

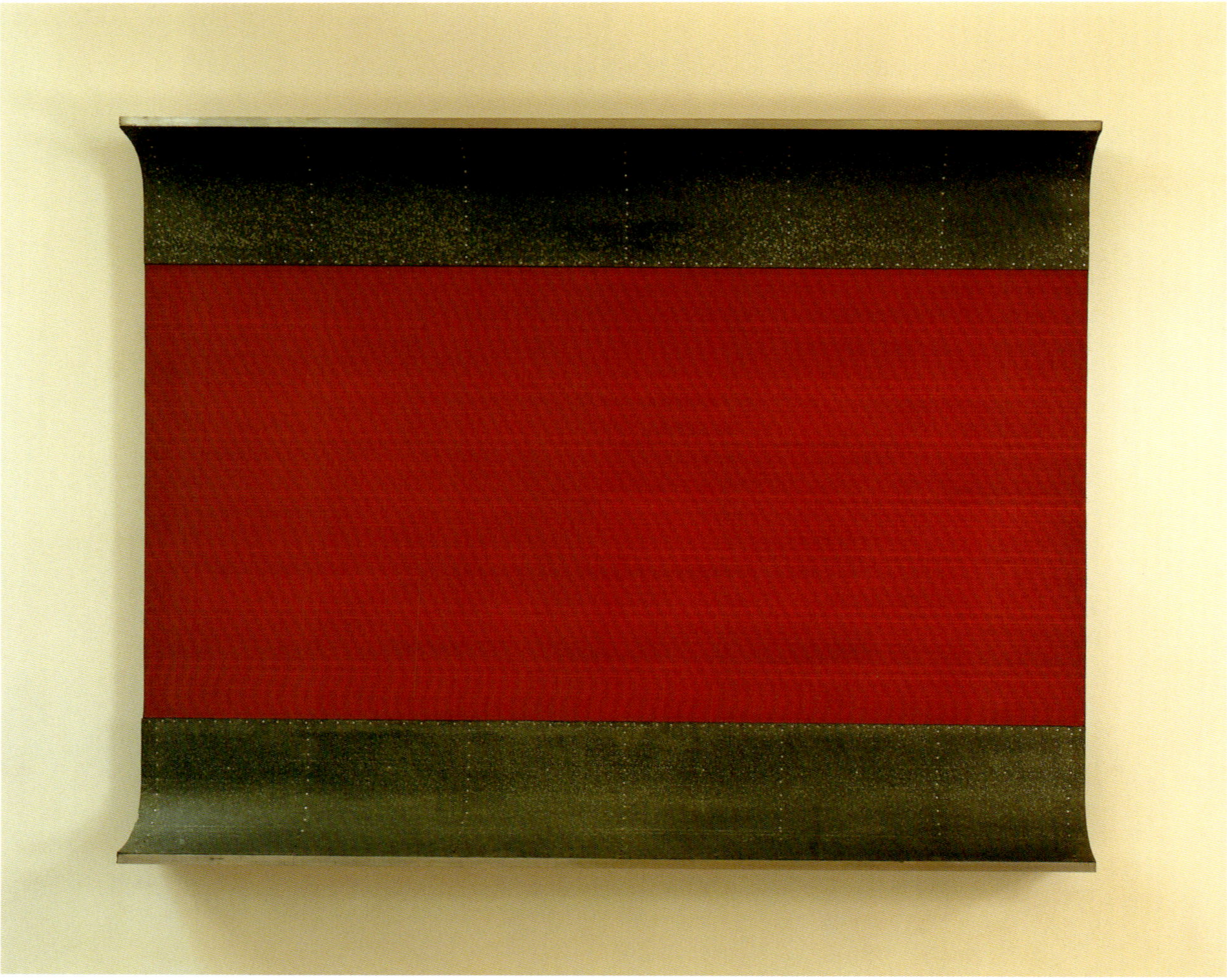

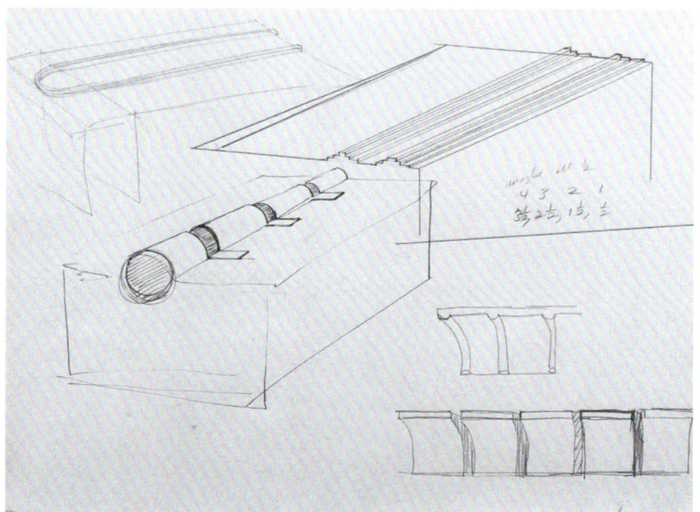



FIG. 4.9 (above)
**Donald Judd**
*Untitled (DSS 34),* 1962
Light cadmium red oil on
striated plywood, black oil
on wood with galvanized
iron and aluminum,
76 x 96 ¼ x 12 in.
(193 x 244.5 x 30 cm)
Kunstmuseum Basel

FIG. 4.10 (left)
**Donald Judd**
sketch, book 1, no. 38, 1963
Pencil and ink on paper,
11 x 14 in. (27.9 x 35.6 cm)
Collection of Judd Foundation

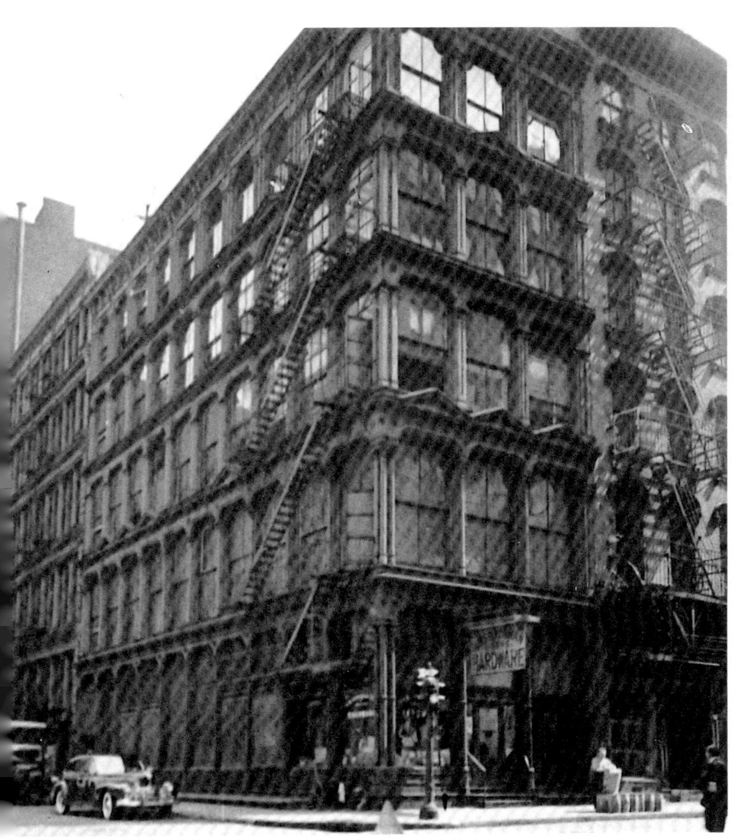



**FIG. 4.11**

Judd's home after 1969: 101 Spring Street
Nicholas Whyte, architect, 1870
Photograph c. 1940. NYC Municipal Archives

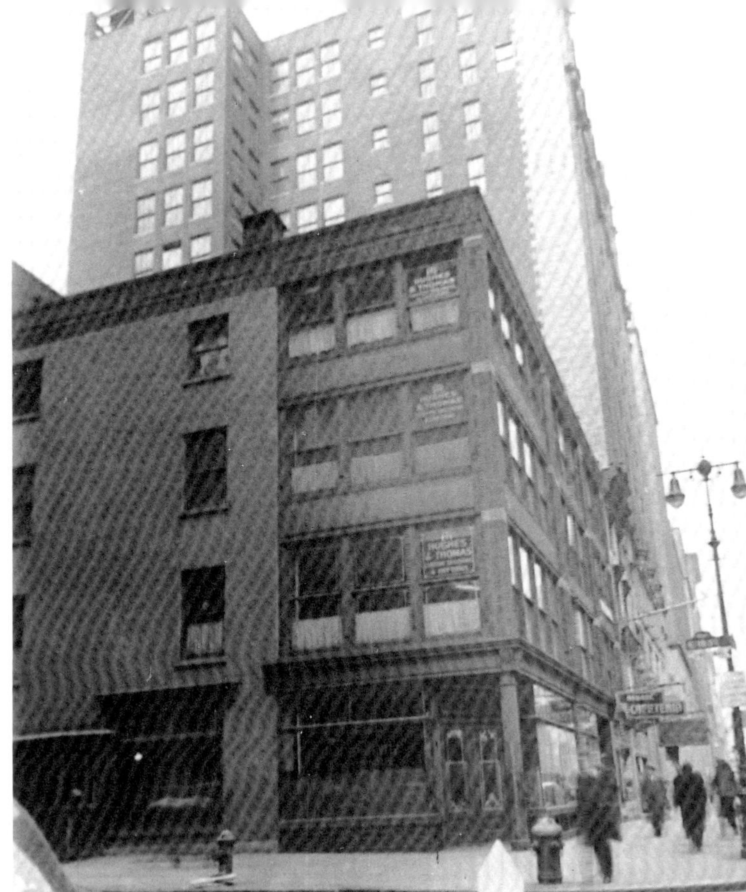

**FIG. 4.12**

Judd's home from 1959 or 1960 to 1969:
53 East Nineteenth Street
Photograph c. 1940. NYC Municipal Archives

Manhattan lost 66,000 manufacturing jobs, 12.25 percent of its total. (The years around 1960 dramatically represented a longer trend. The 1,122,000 manufacturing jobs in all of New York City in 1947 had by 1976 dwindled to 543,000.) Fully six hundred Manhattan loft buildings were demolished in the years 1959–62, representing nine million square feet of manufacturing space, or 5 percent of the borough's total.[31] The need for larger continuous floor spaces to accommodate higher scales of automation, together with the incentive of easy access to new highways and ports, was driving manufacturers to the suburbs. In an account of SoHo—where Judd would move in 1969—Charles R.

Simpson characterized the change along the following terms, which one could extrapolate to characterize the situation in Manhattan as a whole:

Large, low plants that could take full advantage of mechanical material-handling required tracts of land available only on the outer rings of metropolitan regions. The most competitive plants were very large, one-story buildings that could incorporate the new continuous material flow systems. Mechanization, the key to the competitive advantage, had raised the average floor area per employee from 1,140 square feet in 1922 to 4,550 square feet in 1945. The buildings in the South Houston District had become too small. Their material flow lines were strangled at elevator points and by the complete absence of off-street truck docks. While suburban plants were accommodating block-long continuous-bake ovens and huge rotary presses, firms in the South Houston District were finding that even forklift trucks were too large for use in thirty-foot-wide structures and eight-by-eight elevators. The district came to depend upon low-profit firms, which could survive with labor-intensive procedures.[32]

Even as this decline of urban industry was ravaging the city, Manhattan was already transforming itself to serve the so-called FIRE industries—finance, insurance, and real estate. In each year between 1956 and 1965, developers completed over three million square feet of new office space in the city's central borough.[33]

On East Nineteenth Street, these changes were taking their effect. Although the printing building across from Judd's still claimed fifty-seven tenants when he lived there,

it had housed seventy-one firms just seven years earlier. Of the three clothing firms in Judd's own building in 1955, only Hughes & Thomas, by then listed as a supplier of uniforms, survived to the time of *DSS 32*.[34] (The number of apparel jobs in metropolitan New York, having climbed to 228,900 in 1950, dropped by one-fifth over the next decade, to 180,400.[35]) It was this deindustrialization that had made Judd's loft available to an artist on the cheap.

Upstairs, in that loft, the artist's proto-Minimalist works appeared to sit just on the edge of this dying world of industry. In July 1964, Judd was stacking parts of several of his works—including those since given the DSS numbers 36, 38, 42, 43, and 50—alongside open cardboard cartons, discarded paper, and scrap wood (fig. 4.13). He had just taken delivery of a new sculpture from a neighborhood metalworking shop: *Untitled (DSS 50)*, an eight-foot loop of sheet iron. Presaging a major shift in Judd's oeuvre to which

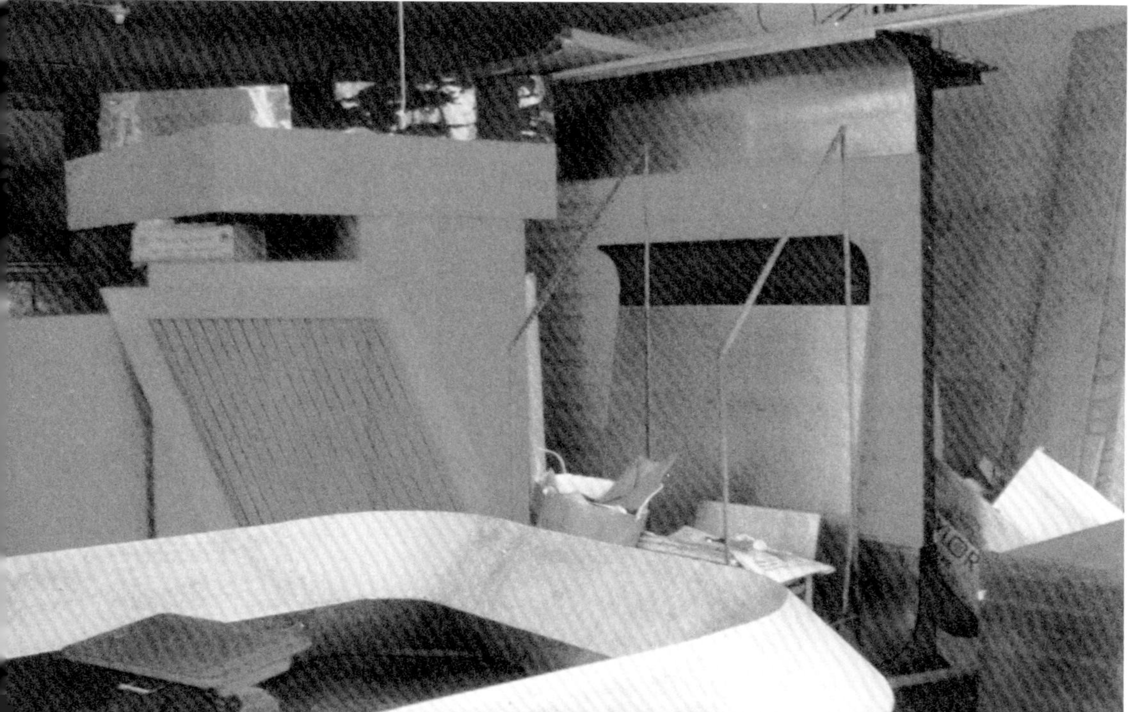

FIG. 4.13

Judd's studio at
53 East Nineteenth Street,
July 1964

we shall return, the work looked radically out of place: all thin, bright regularity in a world of piled-up planks. Judd had cleared a little space so he could paint the new piece, but he had not had room to relocate an outmoded machine—perhaps a foot-operated printing press—that he left encircled by the loop. In our photograph of the scene, taken by the critic Ellen H. Johnson, we can just make out its heavy iron workings and stained wooden top.

*Untitled (DSS 29)* (fig. 4.14) had been Judd's first work to take the shape of a box. It was central enough to the artist's thinking about his own practice that he kept it all his life, installing it over his bed at 101 Spring Street, where it still hangs. Despite the robust claim to object status made by its centrally placed asphalt pipe and its double-wide frame of two-by-fours, the work is fundamentally a painting. The main vertical surface is a canvas, crudely stapled to a sheet of wood and covered in a now-cracking surface of wax, sand, and oil paint. Its texture is varied and thick, aggregating slightly in a loose pattern that, when looked at from a slight distance, just marks out a rather inexact grid. In assembling the box, Judd neatly fitted the scuffed pipe in front of a rough vertical plank, orienting it so that a tidy line of glossy tape would provide a rhyming horizontal line near the construction's upper edge. The sides of the frame, too, he painted black, contrasting them sharply with the bright red canvas.[36]

The resulting object pushes and pulls between its own awkward particularity and something of a systematic order. The thick planks appear graceless while functioning as an organizing edge; the pipe registers as a soiled street object even while providing a tidy focus for the composition. Judd's two-mindedness about the work appears especially evident in his unusual appropriation of the modernist grid. The artist

probably built up its slightly soiled speckles of wax and sand by irregularly pinching his thumb to his forefinger in the wet surface. In sections, as at lower left, he worked with near-total disregard to pattern, while in other places, as at the top, he arranged the marks carefully into lines and rows.

Earlier in his oeuvre, too, Judd had animated these tensions between gummy surface and organizing pattern. In another work that he kept all his life, *Untitled (DSS 21)* (fig. 4.15), the artist marked out a neat set of stripes that he never finished painting; it seems he wished to stop short of cleanly systematizing it. *Untitled (DSS 27)* (fig. 4.16), while finished, likewise proffers an inexact skein of gobs, against which a pattern of shallow stripes reads as counterpoint. At first, it is difficult to tell, even when examining this work in person, how its stripes were made: their edges are just deep enough to make them appear neither superficially applied to the work nor fully consubstantial with it. Markers of logic or administration, the stripes are laid over this surface as rails over a landscape, but the degree of their domination is insecure.

Obdurate materiality and integrated pattern were competing orientations in the city, too. A variety of old loft buildings—short, heavy, and relatively thick with architectural detail—was falling victim to abandonment and destruction. A fresh class of uniform office towers—their smooth facades lined with delicate grids—sprang up meanwhile, seeming almost to float above the city's streets. As both aspects of this architectural transition proceeded, printing pallets, iron pipes, and sheet-metal cornices cropped up as loose things, the rejects of an ever-more-ethereal urban environment. It was in this uncertain terrain that Judd's sculpture operated, picking up these objects and half-integrating them into incomplete patterns.

**Donald Judd**

*Untitled (DSS 29)*, 1962
Light cadmium red oil, wax, and sand on canvas and
wood, black enamel on wood with asphalt pipe,
50 ½ x 45 x 9 ⅝ in. (128.3 x 114.3 x 24.4 cm)
Collection of Judd Foundation

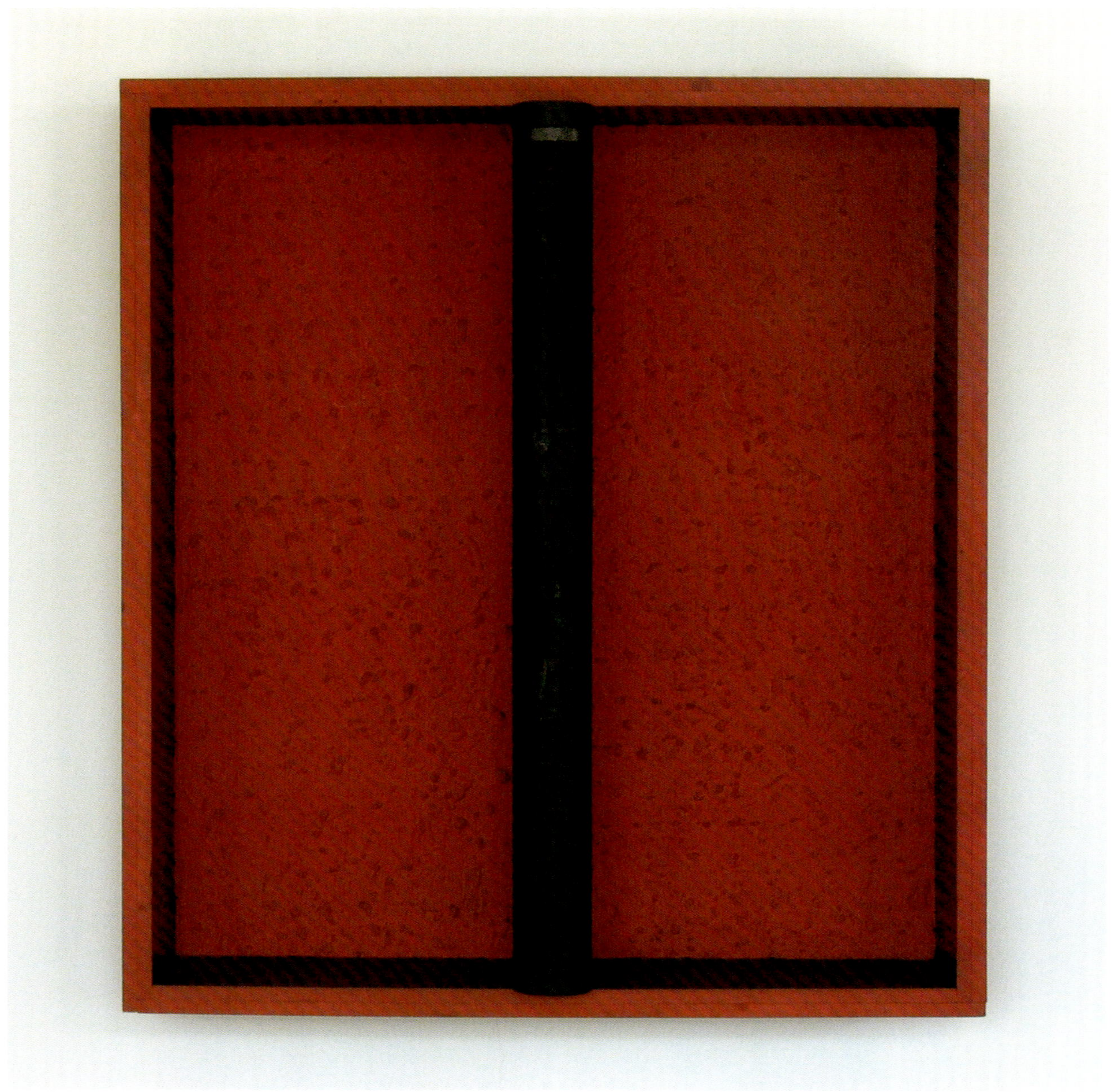

FIG. **4.15** (top)
**Donald Judd**
*Untitled (DSS 21)*, 1961
Oil and sand on canvas,
46 $\frac{1}{8}$ x 50 in. (117.1 x 127 cm)
Collection of Judd Foundation

FIG. **4.16** (bottom)
**Donald Judd**
*Untitled (DSS 27)*, 1962
Oil and wax on canvas,
69 x 101 $\frac{3}{4}$ (175.3 x 258.4 cm)
Collection of Judd Foundation

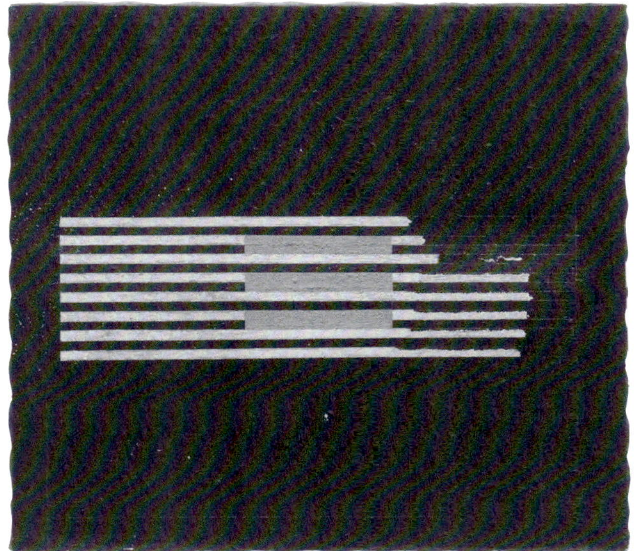

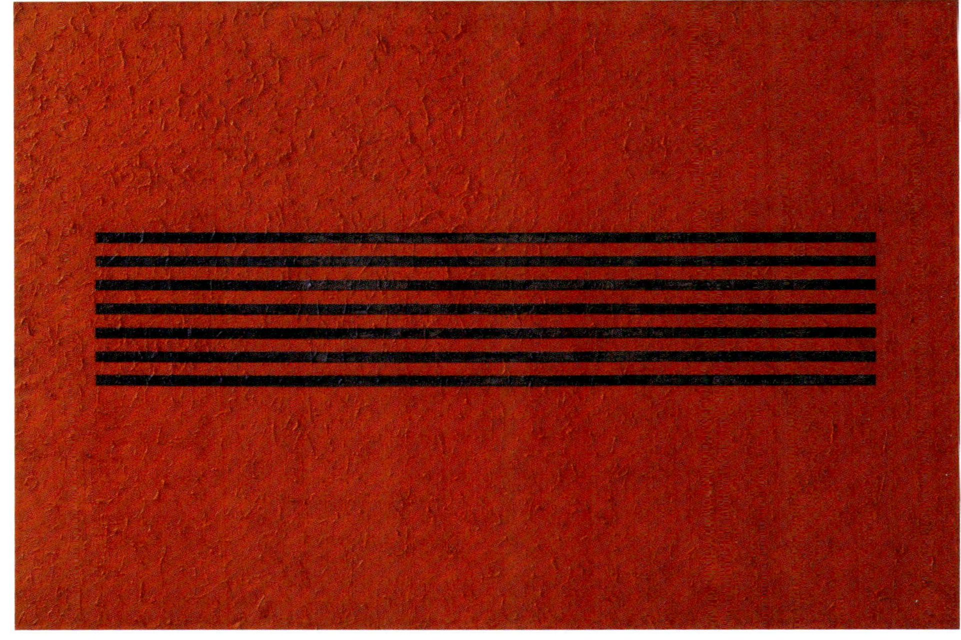

The citywide rezoning of 1961 further hastened New York's transformation, explicitly organizing and aggregating the uses of the city. Adopted 15 December 1960, to go into effect a year later, the new law replaced the famous zoning law of 1916—the nation's first—which had since become subject to thousands of picayune amendments. The sweeping new regulation had three chief goals: to bring more light into architectural planning, to spur the development of more parking (at least outside the densest parts of the city), and to increase separation of uses—clearly designating different areas for residential, commercial, and manufacturing purposes.

Architecturally, the law's chief impact was to allow tall buildings with no setbacks, a provision that amounted to a semiofficial endorsement of the International Style tower. Just before the ordinance went into effect, the *New York Times* ran a pair of articles comparing the architectural styles (both residential and commercial) encouraged by the old and new codes (fig. 4.17). In one, a journalist offered this assessment, now comical for its understatement: "The design of the new building indicates the shape that may well become predominant among new Manhattan office buildings."[37]

The new code identified some areas of the city for intensive redevelopment, and Judd's building at Nineteenth Street and Fourth Avenue lay squarely in a zone earmarked for dramatic upgrading. Back in the spring of 1959, the city had renamed the section of Fourth Avenue between Seventeenth and Thirty-second Streets, officially dubbing it Park Avenue South. The change was intended to express a costlier character for the neighborhood as its industry declined. Office rentals in fact picked up there even before the 1961 rezoning, while plans were laid to prohibit certain kinds of storefronts and overhanging signs.[38] When it came,



the new planning designation reshaped this whole stretch of the avenue, from an area primarily of light manufacturing to one exclusively for commercial use.[39] In the following year, as the artist assembled *DSS 27, 29*, and *32*, the upgrading continued: it was in 1962 that Park Avenue South was torn up beneath Judd's windows, to make room for its planted median (fig. 4.18).[40]

As the city was systematizing unruly parts of lower Manhattan, Judd himself was deploying a language of stripes and grids, gingerly half-organizing the rough surfaces of his works. In his paintings of 1961 and 1962, the artist constantly rearticulated this tense dialectic between random surface particularities and abstract linear order. As he began to work in sculptural reliefs, Judd brought these tensions to bear on the forms of the city, focusing for a time

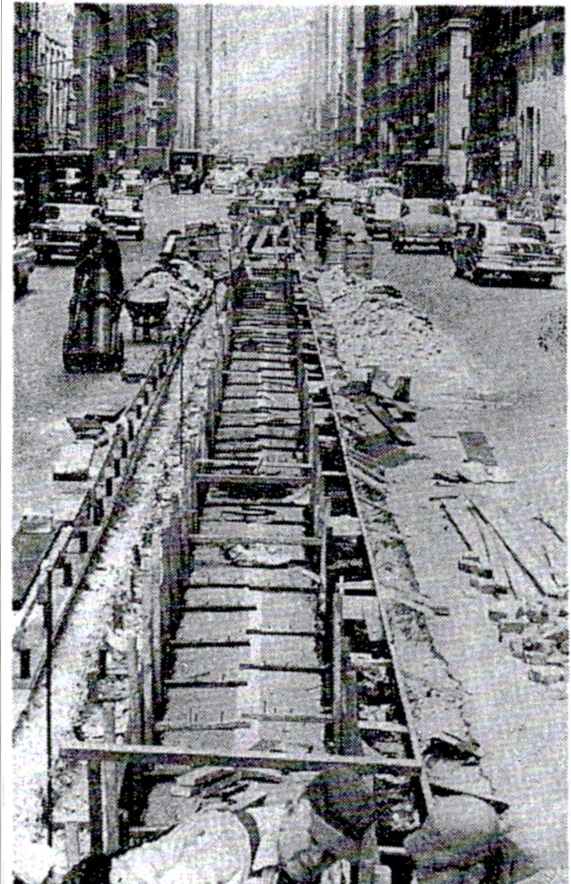



Workmen at Eighteenth Street dig foundations for a center mall that will run the length of Park Avenue South.

on the fading materiality of the urban environment, the ungainliness of iron, asphalt, and discarded two-by-fours.

In that first box, *DSS 29*, Judd seems to have wanted to make an object that would hang free, if just barely, from integration into a productive system. Extrapolating from his earlier interests as a painter, the assemblage is awkwardly cobbled together, built coarsely around blotches of sticky sand, wood grain, and the granules of an asphalt pipe. The crudeness of its materials suggests both a fading period in urban history (one of wood and asphalt, rather than glass and steel) and also the hidden materiality of city infrastruc-ture, the subterranean work of improvised fix-it jobs. All of this untidiness in the work hangs just beneath the imagined supremacy of a system of pipes and the governance of a universal and infinitely expandable grid. Speaking the terms of organized expedience, *DSS 29* is just ungainly enough to distinguish itself—to favor, in the end, the haphazardness of human bodily encounter. The work wishfully reimagines the independence, declared from within a network, of the unique and palpable thing.[41]

In this respect, *DSS 29* begs comparison to a slightly earlier Jasper Johns sculpture with which it has a kind of formal assonance: *Untitled* of 1960–61 (see fig. 2.36). Both works juxtapose fragments of hardware with grids—grids that, in both cases, are slightly clotted and irregular. Each bit of hardware appears discrete and thinglike: Judd's pipe is removed from the city sewer, Johns's lightbulb has been cut free from its network of wires. The two works, it seems to me, present cases of what Judd would come to call "specific objects": each has taken a piece of a system, isolated it, and delivered it back to us in a state of anti-instrumental objecthood.

As the old city disappeared around him, however, Judd's materializations became increasingly riven with contradiction, displaying an ascendant abstract organization. In *Untitled (DSS 31)* (fig. 4.19), for example, Judd redeployed his thick surface of sand and paint on Masonite, but this time he centered the splotches around a tidy copper disk and had them snap obediently to the columns and rows of their grid.[42] Slightly later, he abandoned painterliness altogether, drilling holes at the vertices of a grid he had marked out on *Untitled (DSS 43)* (fig. 4.20); the resulting sculpture looks almost like a plater for a system of telecommunications wires. The labor imagined by this work is not the manual tinkering actually undertaken to make it, but

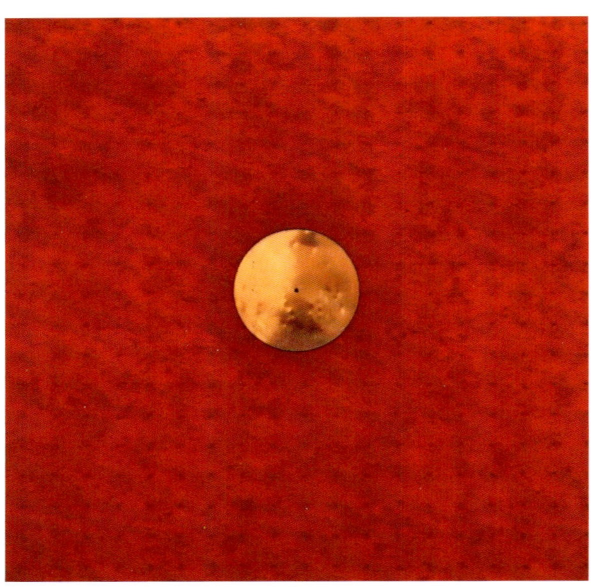

rather that of disembodied mass production. Judd told an interviewer that, while he had to drill "thousands of holes all over" the sheet of galvanized iron at the center of *DSS 43*, he would have preferred to have it stamped out systematically, "[all] at once."[43]

Judd's earliest sculptures, perched on the edge between his neighborhood's obsolescent manufacturing and the city's new systematicity, embodied a tension between materiality and abstraction, between manual labor and modular production. Assembled by an artist who also wrote against depiction and order in art, they willed a materiality into the productive forms of New York, as if that materiality might be made to predominate. Any such predominance, however, was always tentative, the gritty surface only just refusing its ordering stripe or grid. Soon, it seems, Judd felt that it was no longer adequate to dwell on his city's out-moded forms, and by 1965 he had developed a new kind of sculpture—one that would articulate a rather different and more complicated understanding of his changing world.

## Flash Gordon Bank Vaults

A drawing dated 1963–64 (fig. 4.21) demonstrates that Judd, around the time of his Green Gallery show, was already reconceiving the possible forms of his art. Although the sculpture imagined here was never executed, it clearly marks out a new direction: the pointless, vaguely industrial contraptions of his last couple of years were to be followed by simple boxes.[44] While the sketch still evokes a feeling of

**Donald Judd**
Study for a wood sculpture, 1963–64
Pencil, 11 x 14 in. (27.9 x 35.6 cm)

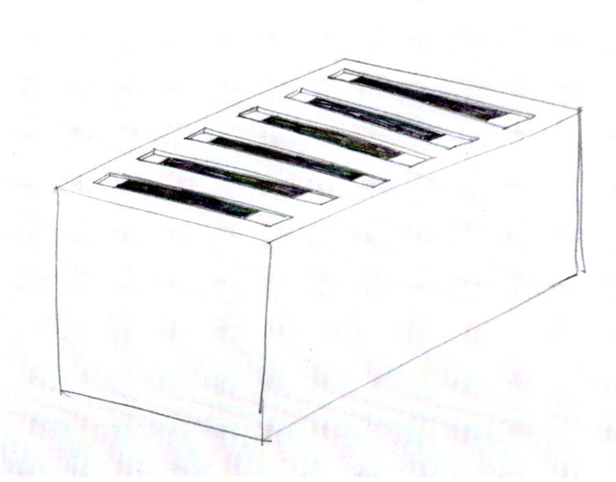

frustrated utility—what moving parts, we wonder, are meant to emerge from and recede into those slots, and to what end?—the vocabulary has shifted. Unlike the earlier works, this object does not appear to have been plucked from a tangled infrastructure of pipes and forklifts; instead, sitting neat and square, this box emphasizes simultaneously both its own crisp autonomy and its potential for seamless integration into an imagined system of matching modular units.

The definitive turn came in 1965. It was in the spring of that year that Judd ordered the fabrication of *Untitled (DSS 64)* (fig. 4.22), his first totally rectangular wall box.[45] Made from three sheets of galvanized iron, the work—although now a clear herald of the artist's Minimalist style—was an incongruous object, at once the plainest and the oddest of things. Even today it seems strangely blank and isolated, an empty horizontal object in the place of painting's semiotic functions. (Hung horizontally at eye level, its dimensions are about those of a half-length portrait.) Its matte finish—

especially as compared with later works in shiny materials such as stainless steel, copper, and brass—calls attention to the materiality of the work itself. Galvanized iron, after all, is the stuff of furnace ducts, not of gleaming corporate lobbies; it is a substance of utility, not semiosis.[46]

In fact the surface of *DSS 64* is rather particular, irregular enough to invite close looking. Broad splotches of zinc, the result of its protective galvanization bath, spatter the iron. These flecks create a slightly mottled look, even while appearing just uniform enough to make a neat, if hardly showy, finish. Indeed, the zinc marks create a visual tension between order and randomness that recalls the loosely organized sand gobs in some of Judd's early paintings. This dynamic is deepened by an interplay between the splotches and a faint black pinstriping—barely visible in photographs—created in the laying of the iron. The flecks of zinc on *DSS 64* largely obscure these stripes, but Judd and his fabricators must have been conscious of them: they run precisely parallel to the sculpture's seams.[47]

*DSS 64* has a bifurcated character, too, on the basic level of its fabrication. Like Judd's other Minimalist sculptures, the box looks as if it had been mass-produced on an assembly line, evoking, as one critic put it, "the slow, determined beat of a stamping machine."[48] In fact, like all of Judd's early Minimalist work, the sculpture was made by hand, at a piecework shop called Bernstein Brothers Sheet Metal Specialties, Inc. The process, adapted from the shaping of ventilation ducts and industrial sinks, involved measuring and cutting the sheet iron, notching it with hand shears, and folding it in a brake die. Whoever undertook the work—possibly José Otero, soon Judd's favorite technician—finished the sculpture by truing its angles with a rubber mallet and, finally, reaching inside the back to solder its three pieces carefully together.[49]

FIG. 4.22
**Donald Judd**
*Untitled (DSS 64),*
4 examples 1965, 6 examples 1970 (illustrated example 1965)
Galvanized iron, 6 x 27 x 24 in. (15.2 x 68.6 x 61 cm)

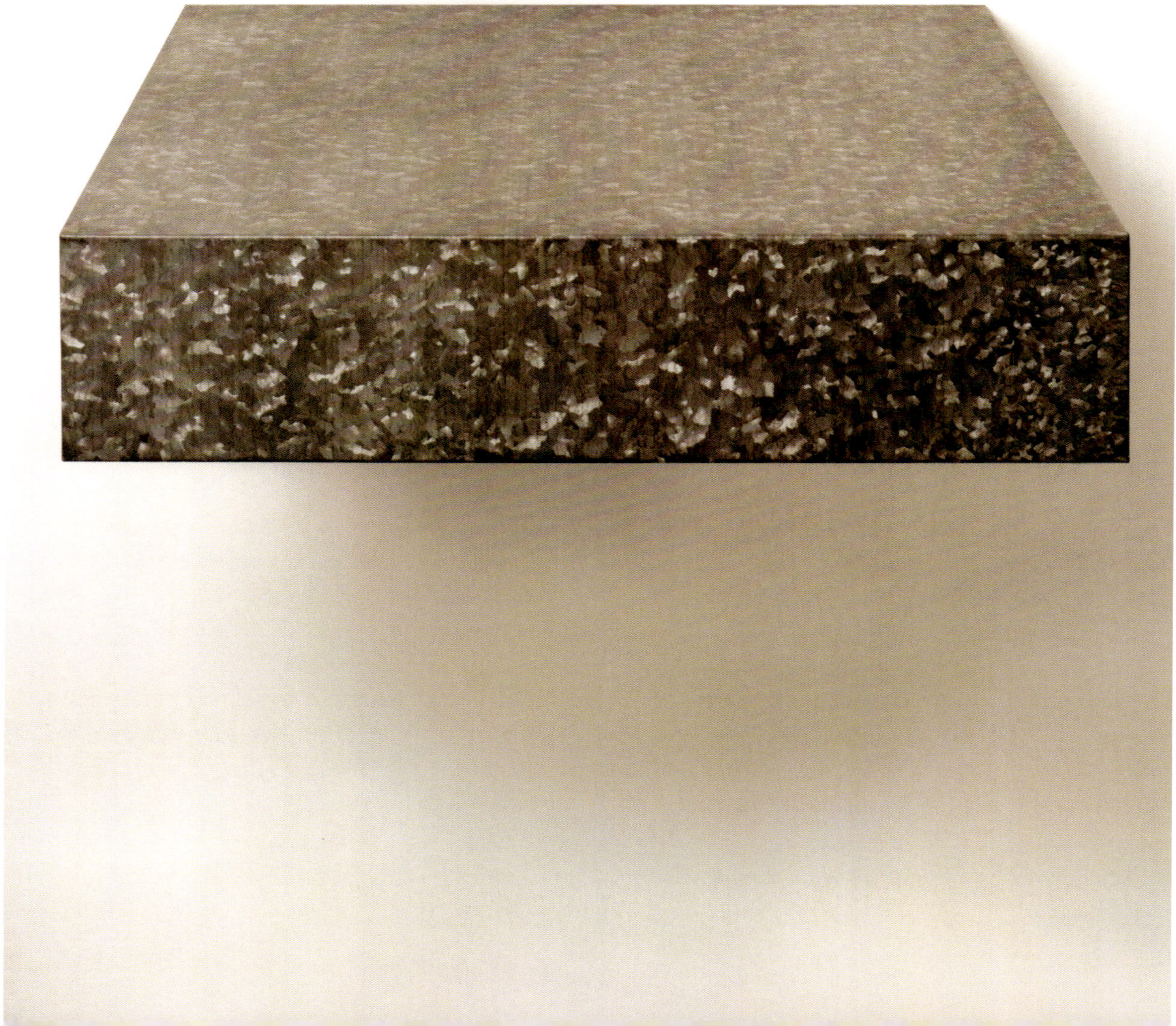

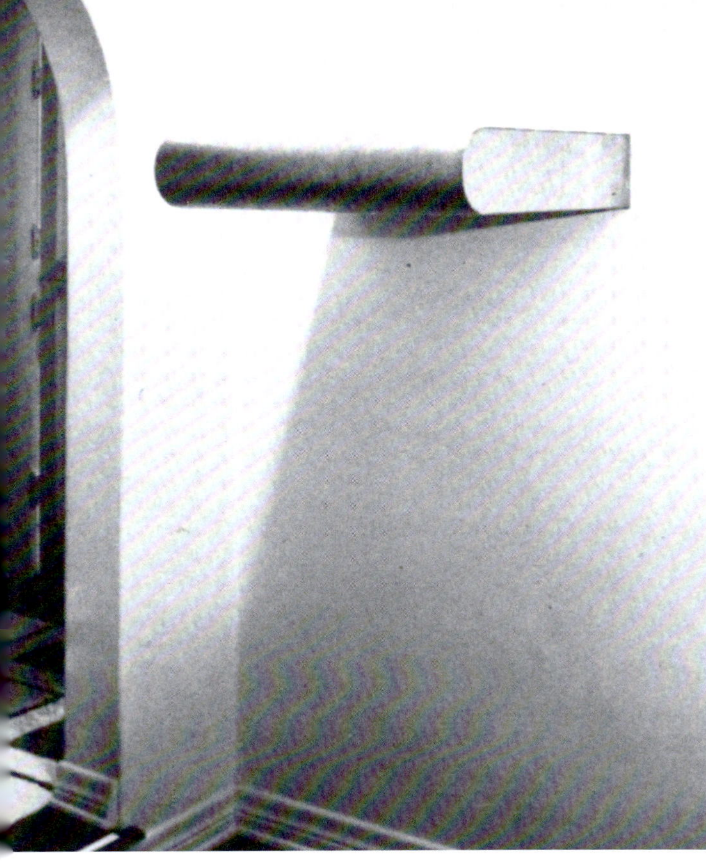

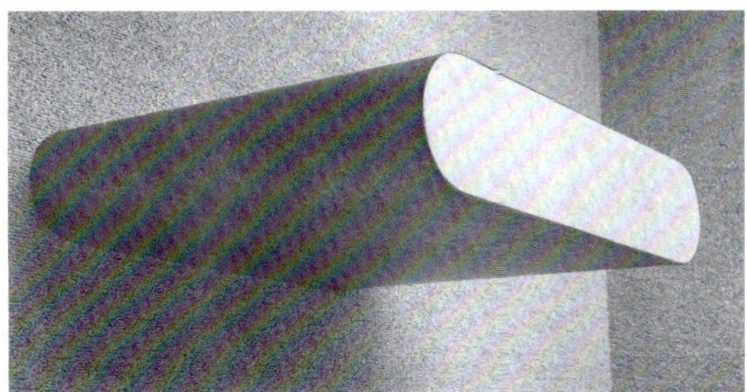

FIG. 4.23 (left)
**Donald Judd**
*Untitled (DSS 66)*, 1965
Galvanized iron,
6 x 27 x 26 in. (15.2 x 68.6 x 66 cm)
Private collection

F G. 4 24 (above)
**Donald Judd**
*Untitled (DSS 63)*, 1965
Ga vanized iron,
6 x 29 x 24 in. (15.2 x 73.7 x 61 cm)
Private collection

As part of the same order, Bernstein Brothers made two other works quite like *DSS 64*. The three works, built at the same scale and in the same material, formed a kind of suite. One, *Untitled (DSS 66)* (fig. 4.23), took the shape of a box capped with a bullnose front; the other, *Untitled (DSS 63)* (fig. 4.24), projected a flat, ovoid front from curved sides. It may have seemed to Judd at the time that the three sculptures offered a panoply of essential geometric shapes, but ultimately it was *DSS 64*, the perfectly rectilinear one, that would prove uniquely generative. In fact, this sculpture seemed to replicate itself from the very beginning: Judd asked Bernstein for two instances (or examples, as the cataloguers call them) of *DSS 64* in that first job, and, by the end of the year, he had ordered two more, as well as four examples of an identical form in stainless steel (fig. 4.25). Even as the original trio of sculptures was being made,

Judd had already ordered his first wall stack: a sculpture that adopted the form and material of *DSS 64*, at a slightly larger scale, in a column of seven iterat ons (fig. 4.26). Soon the artist was ordering similar boxes with Plexiglas tops and bottoms, in a variety of colors.[53]

At the source of Judd's new direction lies the fact that just about everything about *DSS 64* —its form, the details of its surface, the look and means of its fabrication—seems to teeter uncertainly between the specific and the general. On the one hand, the work seems almost a purely indepen- dent object: a unique thing to be encour tered in space. On the other, it suggests a total generic fungibi ity. As we shall see, it is this perpetually indeterminate identity, poised between objecthood and abstraction, that allows *DSS 64* to represent so fully the oddness of its own historic and geographic context.

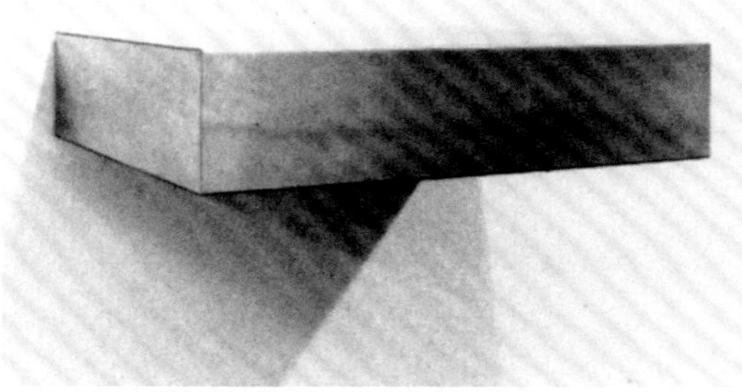

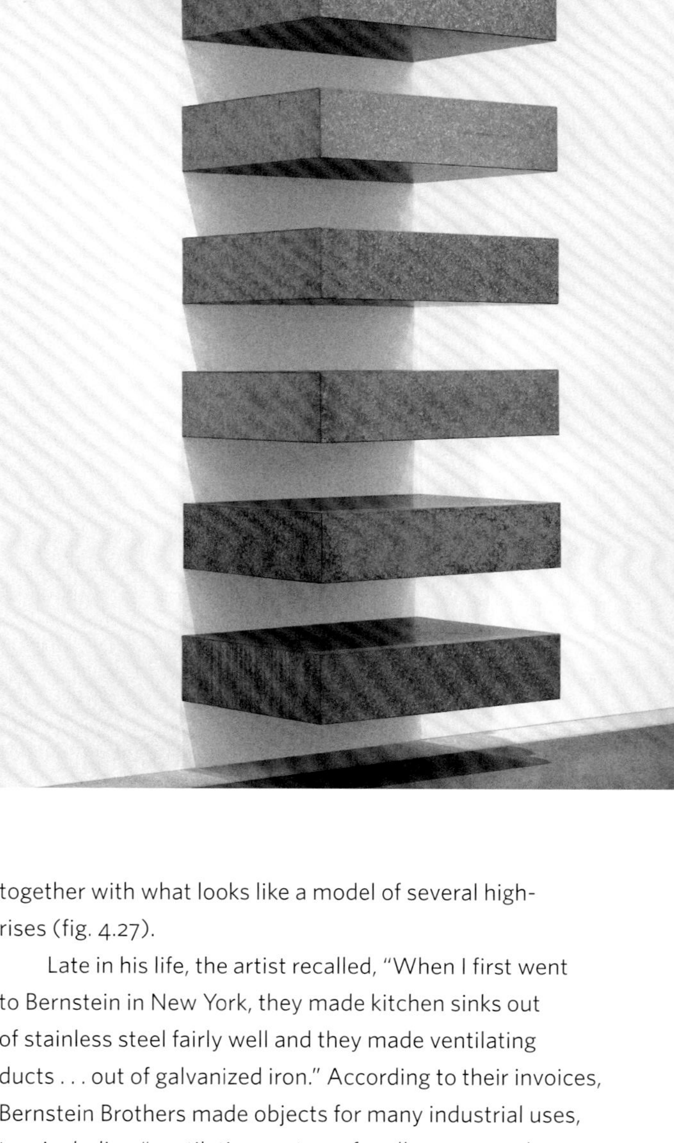

**FIG. 4.25**
**Donald Judd**
*Untitled (DSS 72),*
3 examples, 1965, 1 example 1966
Galvanized iron,
6 x 27 x 24 in.
(15.2 x 68.6 x 61 cm)

**FIG. 4.26**
**Donald Judd**
*Untitled (DSS 65),* 1965
Galvanized iron, 7 units,
each 9 x 40 x 30 in.
(23 x 101.6 x 76.2 cm),
with 9 in. (23 cm)
intervals
Moderna Museet, Stockholm

In seeking a firm to fabricate his work, Judd may have decided on Bernstein Brothers for the simple reason of proximity—their shop lay just three blocks from his Nineteenth Street loft. But the artist certainly had other options. Sheet-metal shops dotted much of lower Manhattan in the period, and Judd had lived immediately adjacent to three of them for most of the 1950s. (A & A Sheet Metal Works, Eagle Sheet Metal Works, and Emil Vanderleenden Sheet Metal had been clustered right by his home on the 300 block of East Twenty-seventh Street.[51]) When the artist, making a sketch toward his first metal progression piece, hit on the idea of having a sculpture fabricated in such a shop, he jotted down the names of no fewer than five possibilities,

together with what looks like a model of several high-rises (fig. 4.27).

Late in his life, the artist recalled, "When I first went to Bernstein in New York, they made kitchen sinks out of stainless steel fairly well and they made ventilating ducts . . . out of galvanized iron." According to their invoices, Bernstein Brothers made objects for many industrial uses, too, including "ventilation systems for all purposes, dust collectors, spray booths, photo engravers, . . . drainboards, shelves, . . . smoke stacks, boiler breeching, general roofing, [and] skylights."[52] Established in 1916 under a different name, the firm was gradually taken over by its employees Arnold and Sandor Bernstein, immigrants from Hungary.

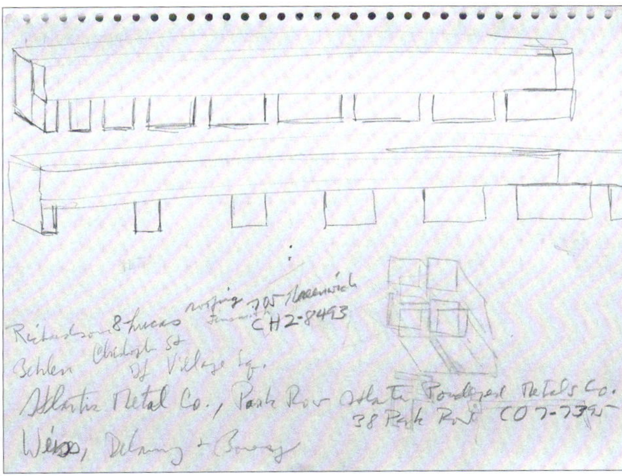

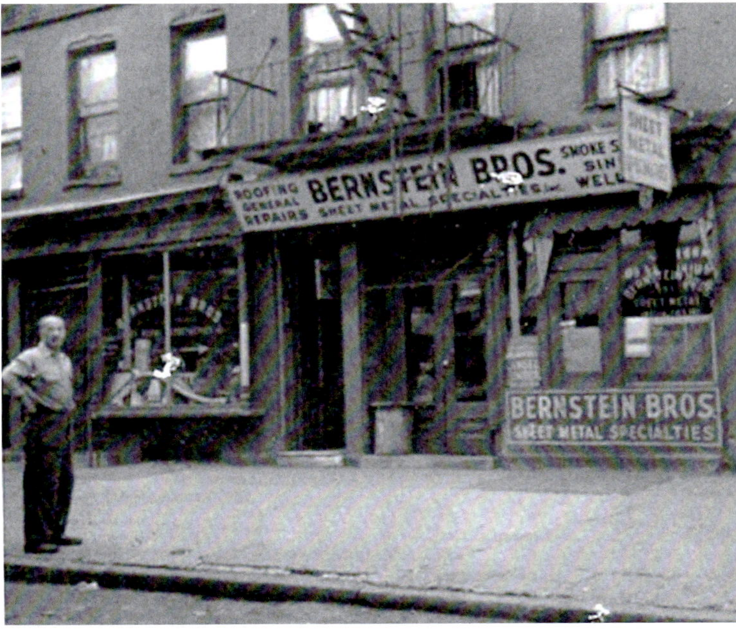

By the time of Judd's arrival, the shop had been passed down to Edward Bernstein, who oversaw the jobs, and his brother in-law Martin Kornbluth, who kept the books. The shop occupied a nineteen-foot brick walk-up at 191 Third Avenue and, eventually, the one next door at 193 as well.[53]

In an early Polaroid Sandor Bernstein stands, half-proud, above the avenue's paving stones and in front of the building's fire escape and simple decorative stonework (fig. 4.28). The shop appears crowded inside and out, its entrance framed by no fewer than six business signs and a trash can with an ill-fitting lid.

Manhattan's loss of small industry in these years did not spare the borough's sheet-metal shops: between 1950 and 1961 the number of such businesses fell by more than 20 percent.[54] For Bernstein Brothers, a move became inevitable. Their stretch of Third Avenue had been undergoing rapid redevelopment since the demolition of its elevated train in 1956, and new high-rent apartment towers were replacing many of the storefront row houses in the area.

The 1961 zoning change accelerated this process, and according to an article that year in the *New York Times*, ten new luxury apartment buildings had just been built in the immediate neighborhood, while twenty-six others—ranging in height from six to twenty stories—were under construction or planned for completion by 1963.[55] The resulting contrast in grain and scale was dramatic; by 1964, Bernstein's little three-story brick houses shared an intersection with two of the smooth new towers (figs. 4.29, 4.30).

Bernstein Brothers finally succumbed in the fall of 1964, barely six months after Judd had taken his first job there.[56] The firm was paid handsomely for its storefronts, which were soon demolished to make way for a new high-rise.[57] Like many other light-industrial concerns, the shop relocated to Long Island City, just across the East River, in Queens. Judd stuck with them through the move, and it was in fact in Queens that *DSS 64* was made. Here Bernstein enjoyed a much larger floor, in a low-slung eight-year-old brick building on Twenty-fourth Street.[58]

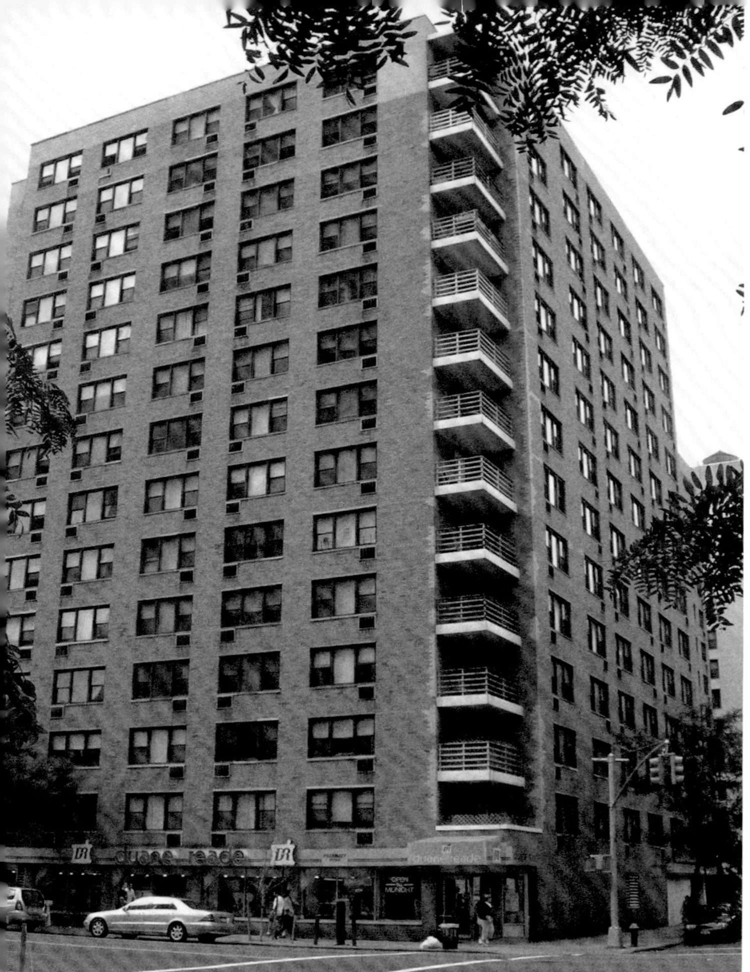



**FIG. 4.29**

150 East Eighteenth Street (southwest
corner of Third Avenue), 1960,
photographed 2007

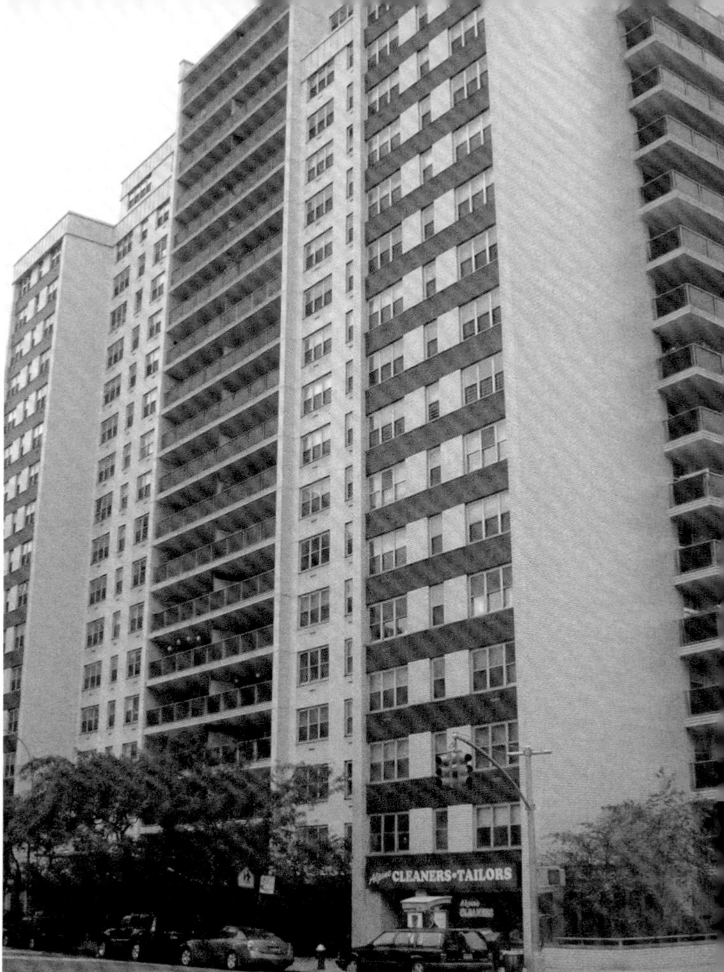

**FIG. 4.30**

205 Third Avenue (northeast corner
of East Eighteenth Street), 1964,
photographed 2007

Even after the move, Bernstein hardly operated a pristine assembly line. Jobs were piecework, executed by hand. We do not have a photograph of the making of *DSS 64,* but an image taken during the fabrication of one of the later Minimalist works (fig. 4.31) shows Judd and a Bernstein employee working together to close a joint.[59] Exposed belts, hanging wires, and dented buckets fill the space, and someone, perhaps Ed Bernstein, stands at the back, working by hand to pry an object free of his machinery. The sculpture, all hard-edged and gleaming, looks out of place among the shop's surplus scraps. Indeed, this object—

like all of Judd's sculpture since *DSS 64*—appears to belong less to the manual labor of the Bernstein shop floor than to the uniform modularity of Third Avenue's new towers.

Judd sometimes emphasized the antiquity of his fabrication methods, remarking, for example, to John Coplans, "I use an old-fashioned technique—basically a nineteenth-century metal-working technique."[60] Although the artist also referred to Bernstein Brothers in 1965 with the outmoded word *tinsmith* (a term that Robert Smithson echoed in his own essay about Judd's work), he came over time to prefer the word *factory*.[61] It is a term suggesting a scale of

Donald Judd, right, at Bernstein Brothers,
Long Island City, probably, 1966

production at which Bernstein never operated, but which the sculptures forever propose. Riding this uncertainty, Judd eventually declared, "I like the quality of mass production," he said, "but I want them to do one or two."[62]

Announcing the new direction of Donald Judd's work, *DSS 64* refers ambivalently to both the small-scale urban piecework shop and the fully automated assembly line. As it took form in New York in the summer of 1965, the work typified its city's divided character, oscillating between outmoded particularity and systematized abstraction. Unlike the wooden constructions Judd made only a year or two earlier, however, *DSS 64* seems not to privilege the old palpability. Rather, the work seems to have picked up the ascendancy of the abstract side of the dialectic, embodying above all the metallic rectilinearity of the new city. It is the aim of the rest of this chapter to understand what this work's delicate identity can reveal about the historically pivotal moment of its creation.

The early postmodernization of New York had a visual style. It was difficult to recognize as such, because it labored to demonstrate its own neutrality, efficiency, even naturalness, but it was a style nevertheless—one founded on the modular metal box. It was this vocabulary that came to dominate new architecture, new modes of manufacturing, and new technologies of administration and exchange. And it was this style, too, that came to characterize Judd's art. Even as we recognize that the work pointedly resisted direct quotation as such, we must briefly consider the several currents by which Judd's Minimalist sculpture rhymed with the new visual forms of his city.

Consider first the architectural forms of manufacturing itself. Manhattan's nineteenth-century lofts had been stitched into the urban landscape, adopting inexpensive

versions of the ornate stone and wrought-iron neoclassical styles that then dominated New York City as a whole (see figs. 4.11, 4.12). The much larger new plants and warehouses at the edge of the city, by contrast, stood just one story tall, perfectly rectangular and unadorned. They were often white and perforated by rows of identical, square loading docks; the work inside them was done not by hand so much as with whole fleets of integrated equipment (figs. 4.32, 4.33). Whereas urban factories had teamed with the oiled springs, hand trucks, and levers of iron machinery, the new floors encased stainless-steel assembly systems with a minimum of protruding parts for manual manipulation.[63]

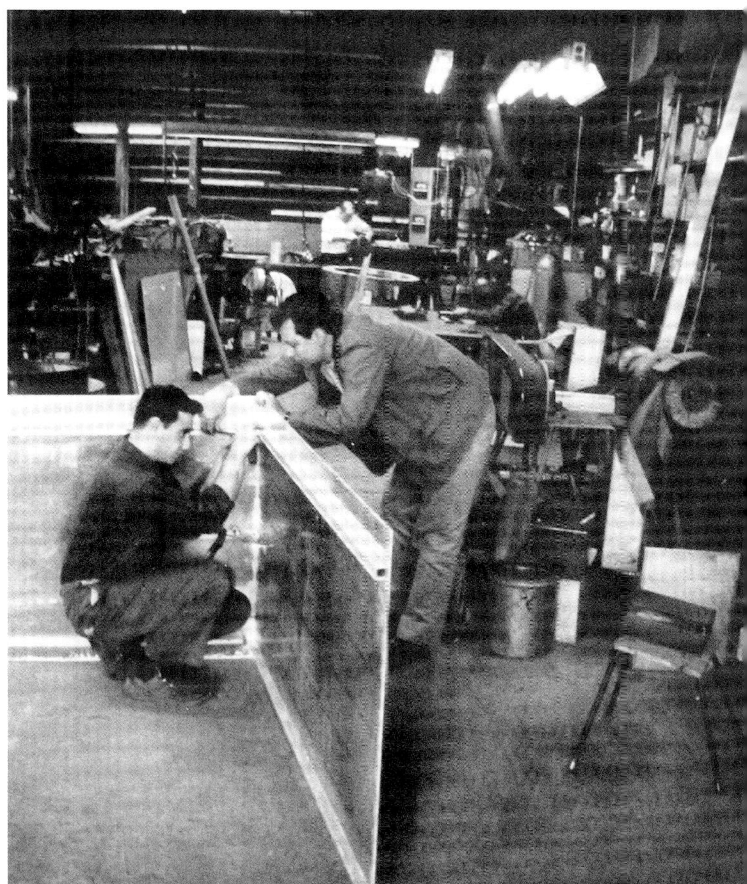

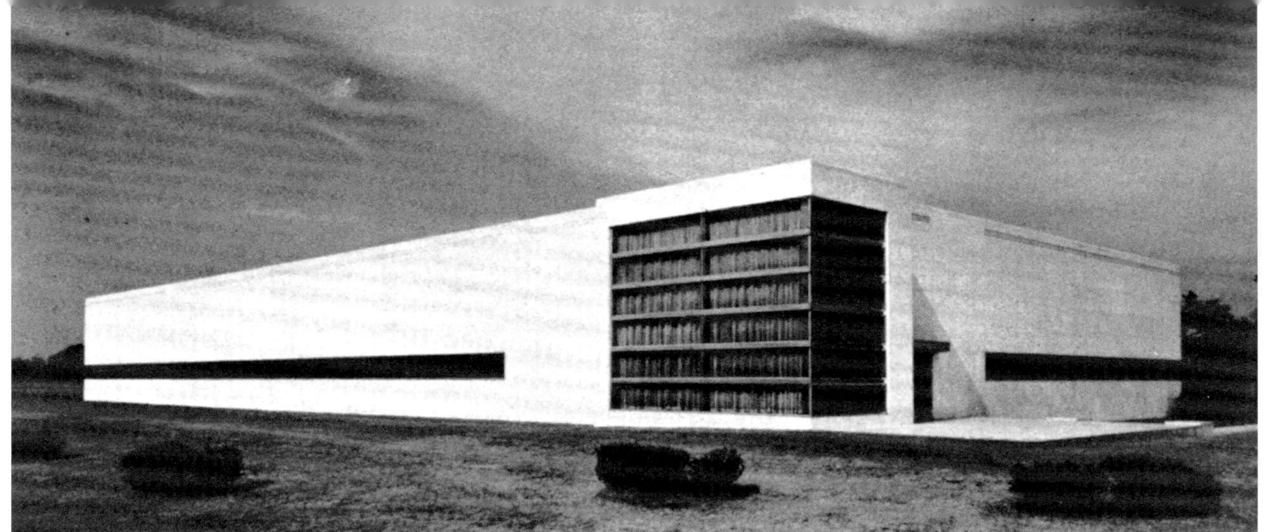

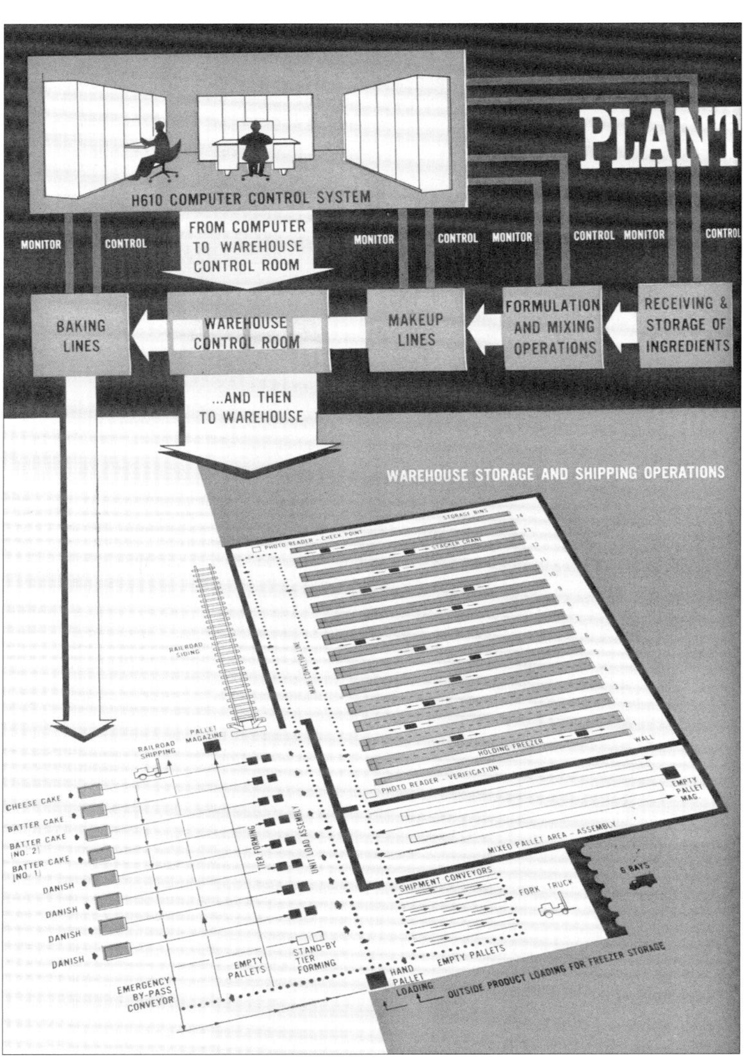


**FIG. 4.32**
From "An Enlightened Look at a Factory," *Buildings for Industry, Architectural Record* Books (New York: F. W. Dodge, 1957), 14

**FIG. 4.33**
From "Plant of 1970 Is Here in '64," *Factory,* February 1964, 62–65

**FIG. 4.34** (opposite)
Photograph from Farnsworth Fowle, "Container Port Marks Fifth Year," *New York Times,* 20 August 1967. General Research Division, The New York Public Library, Astor, Lenox and Tilden Foundations

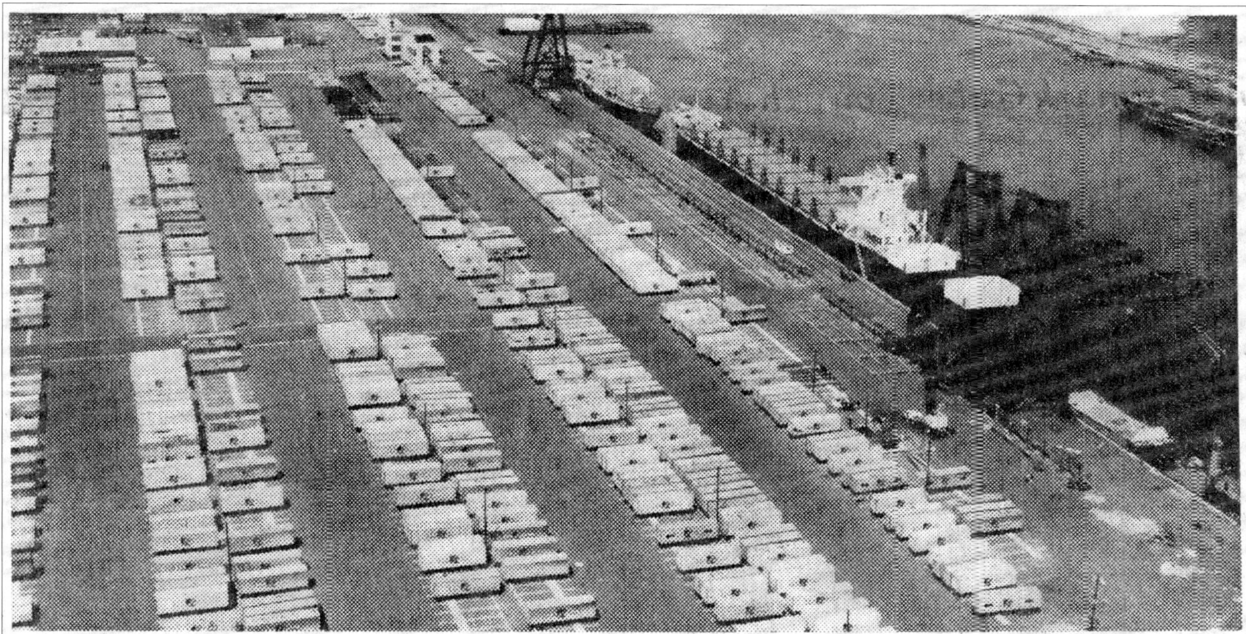



Meanwhile, the standardized shipping container was thoroughly transforming, and further enabling, the transportation of the goods produced in new factories. For centuries, freight had been handled by the break-bulk method, by which longshoremen used picks and dollies to move individual crates, barrels, and sacks. Manhattan's economy had depended on the proximity of the port and on the fringe businesses supporting its slow labor.[64] All this changed with containerization, which began in earnest in 1956 at Elizabeth Seaport in New Jersey, just across the Hudson River. The new technology aggregated cargo into identical, corrugated steel boxes that could travel unopened all the way from manufacturer to retailer. Containers—eventually standardized the world over to a size of eight feet tall, eight feet wide, and either twenty or forty feet long—could be moved straight from ship to truck or train. Ships, fitted with steel supporting grids called spar decks, could carry hundreds and, before long, thousands of containers at a time. Even in the early years, containerization could cut a ship's standard port time of eighty-four hours down to thirteen and could shrink the necessary force of longshoremen from 126 per

vessel to just 42. All in all, loading and unloading a container ship cost anywhere from 39 to 74 percent less than break-bulk work.[65]

It was Malcom McLean, owner of a trucking company, who conceived and initiated containerization, carefully selecting Elizabeth as his hub. At the fringe of America's largest city, the port enjoyed ample room for storing containers as well as direct access to the New Jersey Turnpike, which had opened five years earlier. In 1960, McLean Trucking adopted the name Sea-Land Service, Inc.; by 1962, it was serving ports in Miami, Tampa, San Juan, and Oakland, all from New Jersey.[66] The area's port authority, meanwhile, converted all the piers at Elizabeth, making it a designated container port.[67] The metropolitan docklands, more heavily containerized than any other port in the world, adopted a new advertising slogan, "The Port of New York—America's Container Capital," and by 1966 the two-state harbor was moving 13 percent of its cargo in containers.[68] An article in 1967 noted that Elizabeth Seaport which once had 25 acres of uplands, had come to boast 158 acres of the "shiny steel boxes," with 185 more under construction (fig. 4.34).[69]

The shipping industry in Manhattan was decimated. In 1964, the Port of New York Authority joined the City Planning Commission in directing all port expansion to the outer boroughs and New Jersey. The Authority's executive director, Austin J. Tobin, declared, "Manhattan Island is no place for cargo piers. . . . [It has been] obvious for ten years that Manhattan could not keep pace with new trends in cargo handling."[70] Without direct freeway access or adequate space for storage, the central city could not compete; along a stretch of piers on the West Side, employment fell 14.5 percent between 1965 and 1966 alone, while one Manhattan local reported a decline in membership of over 70 percent in ten years. An economic historian has argued that this shift significantly fueled the exodus of the city's manufacturing, too, which competed to remain close to the freight network.[71] This suburbanization of labor was accompanied by a change in the character of the labor itself. While the break-bulk method had been defined by manual work, containers were literally impossible to move by hand. The new longshoreman did not bend his back to lift objects but rather learned to guide the hooks and press the buttons that in turn transferred the goods, 1,280 enclosed cubic feet at a time.

Manhattan's piers, once teeming with the eclectic look of break-bulk bales, spools, and crates, were now rusting and awaiting cleanup. They had yielded to a new and gargantuan scene across the river: thousands of identical steel boxes, moving mechanically from stack to stack. Although Donald Judd rarely made sculptures that directly resembled shipping containers, he must have been aware, on some level, of the visual assonance. When Paul Katz came to photograph the artist at Spring Street in 1970, one of them had the idea for Judd to stand outside, in front of the crumbling facades of the South Houston Industrial District.

The architectural backdrop there contrasted nicely with the glossy finish and parallel lines of a shipping container, fortuitously parked on a flatbed out front (fig. 4.35). We almost forget that this apt image, used as the frontispiece for Judd's catalogue raisonné, does not in fact picture the artist with one of his sculptures. Indeed, a picture of Judd and his work taken the same year at the Whitechapel Gallery (fig. 4.36) similarly positions him—confident, in the midground—as a casual claimant on the metal rectangles beside him.[72]

As industry and shipping took on the look of metal rectangles in this period, so did the increasingly predominant work of administration. As we have seen in previous chapters, the new boom in office building had a uniform style of boxy glass-and-steel grids, while new housing projects were only slightly less simple and homogeneous. Judd worked in a similar visual vocabulary. Some early sketches (for example, figs. 4.37, 4.38) indicate that he was considering modernist architecture, both inside and out. The executed sculptures, too, share salient traits with the International Style: flat and highly departicularized surfaces, regular rectangularity, and a formal limitation to the metallic and translucent. Over the years following *DSS 64,* Judd's work came to look more and more like the buildings redefining the look of New York. One can tease out a specific assonance, for example, between *Untitled (DSS 204)* (fig. 4.39) and the exterior of the Union Carbide Building (fig. 4.40), or, more directly, between the connected units of *Untitled (DSS 85)* (fig. 4.41) and that building's modular interior (fig. 4.42).[73]

Within these offices, the computer was making an increasingly prominent appearance. Especially visible was the IBM System/360, the 1964 launch of which was described by *Fortune* magazine as "the most crucial and portentous— as well as perhaps the riskiest—business judgment of recent

FIG. **4.35** (below)
Judd at 101 Spring Street, 1970

FIG. **4.36** (below right)
Donald Judd with *Untitled (DSS 119)*, 1968,
at the Whitechapel Gallery, London, 1970
Courtesy Whitechapel Gallery,
Whitechapel Archives

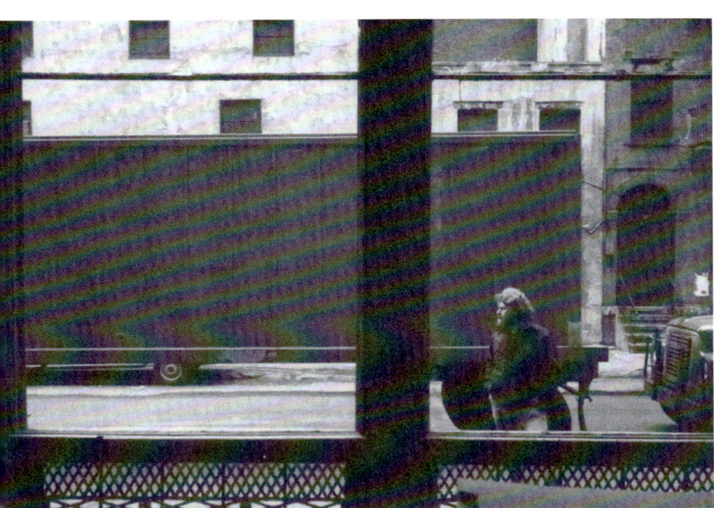

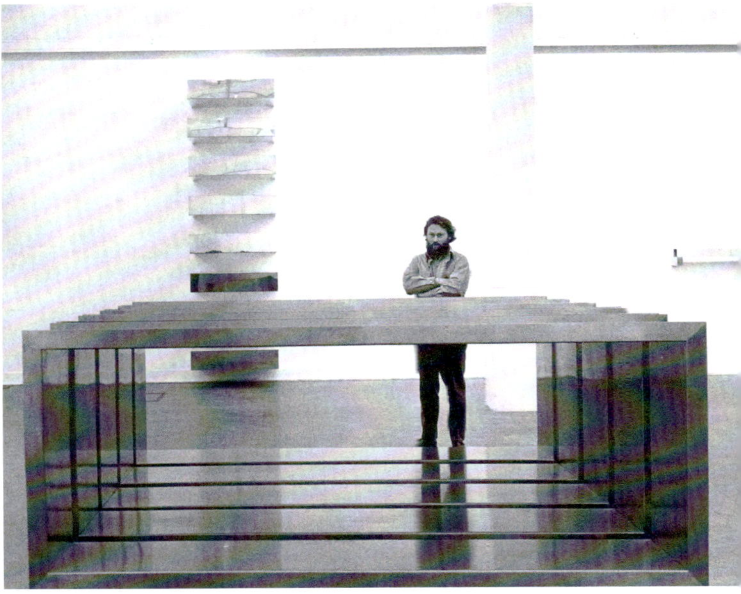

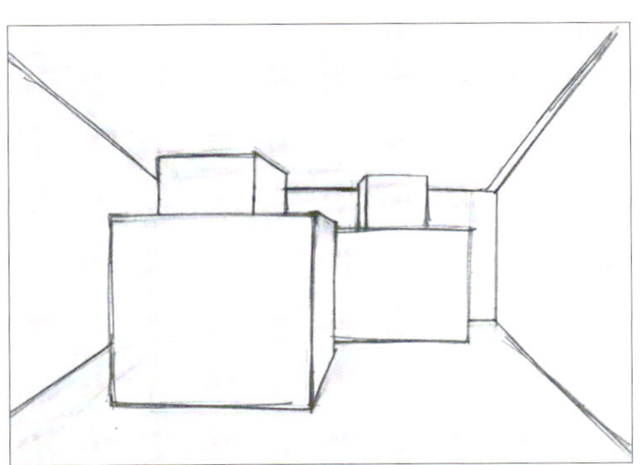

FIG. **4.37** (above)
**Donald Judd**
Architectural study: cubic rooms within
a large room with skylights, 1964
Pencil on paper, 11 x 14 in. (27.9 x 35.6 cm)

FIG. **4.38** (right)
**Donald Judd**
Architectural study: skylights
above four rooms, 1964
Pencil on paper,
11 x 14 in. (27.9 x 35.6 cm)

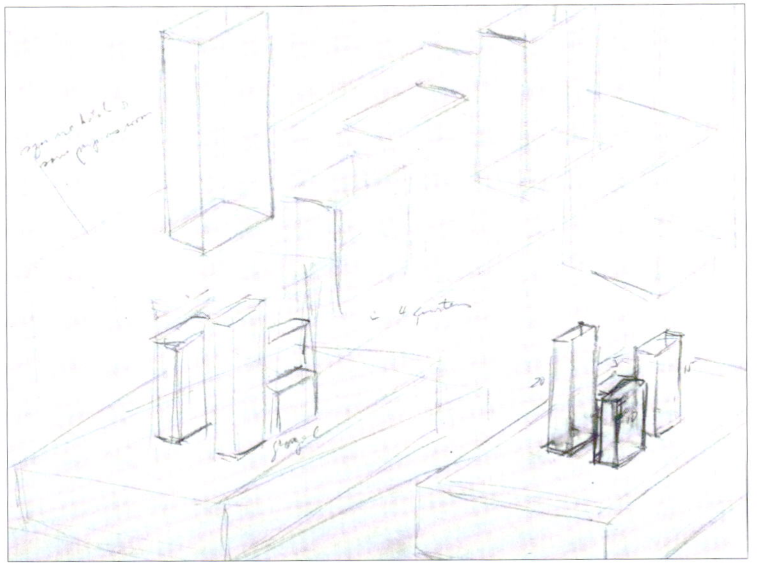

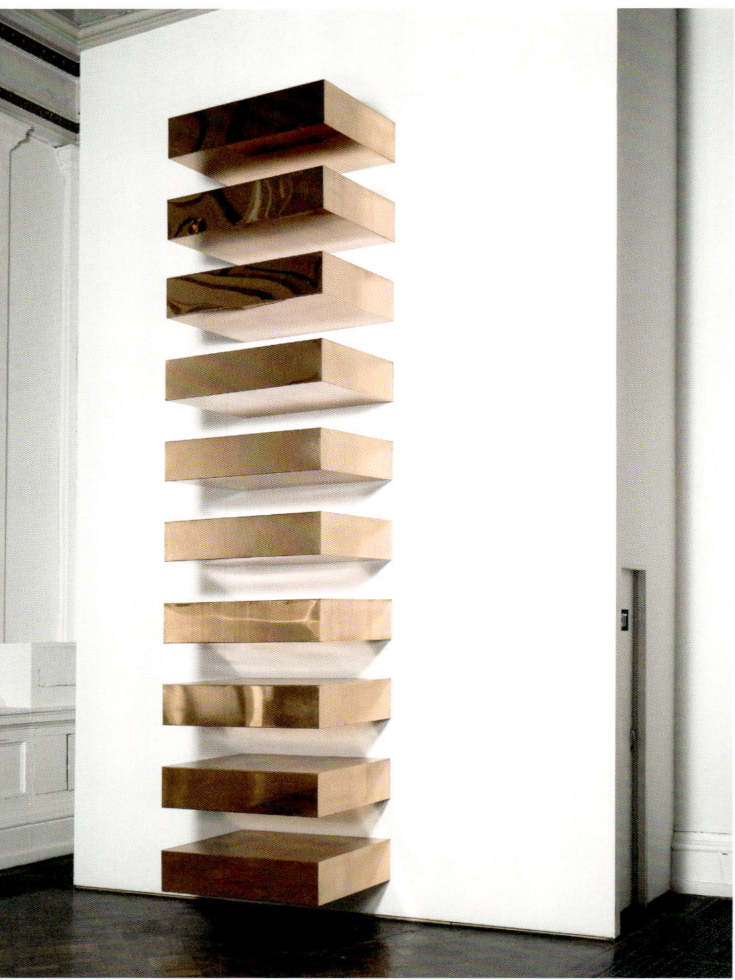

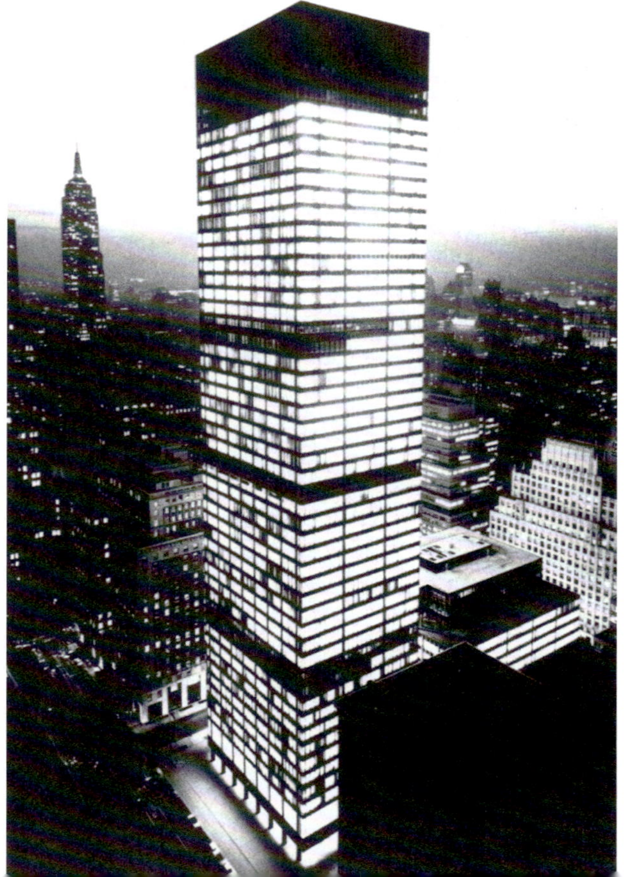

**FIG. 4.39**
**Donald Judd**
*Untitled (DSS 204),* 1969
Copper, 10 units each 9 x 40 x 31 in.
(23 x 101.6 x 78.7 cm),
with 9 in. (23 cm) intervals
Solomon R. Guggenheim Museum,
New York, Panza Collection

**FIG. 4.40**
Union Carbide Building, 270 Park Avenue,
Skidmore, Owings & Merrill, 1955–60
NYC Municipal Archives

FIG. **4.41** (below)

**Donald Judd**

*Untitled (DSS 85)*, 1966
Blue lacquer on aluminum,
galvanized iron, 40 x 190 x 40 in.
(101.6 x 482.6 x 101.6 cm)
Norton Simon Museum,
Pasadena, Calif., Gift of Mr. and
Mrs. Robert A. Rowan

FIG. **4.42** (right)
Interior, Union Carbide Building,
270 Park Avenue, 1955–60

FIG. **4.43** (bottom)
IBM System/360, model 85
(introduced January 1968;
earlier System/360s
introduced 1964)

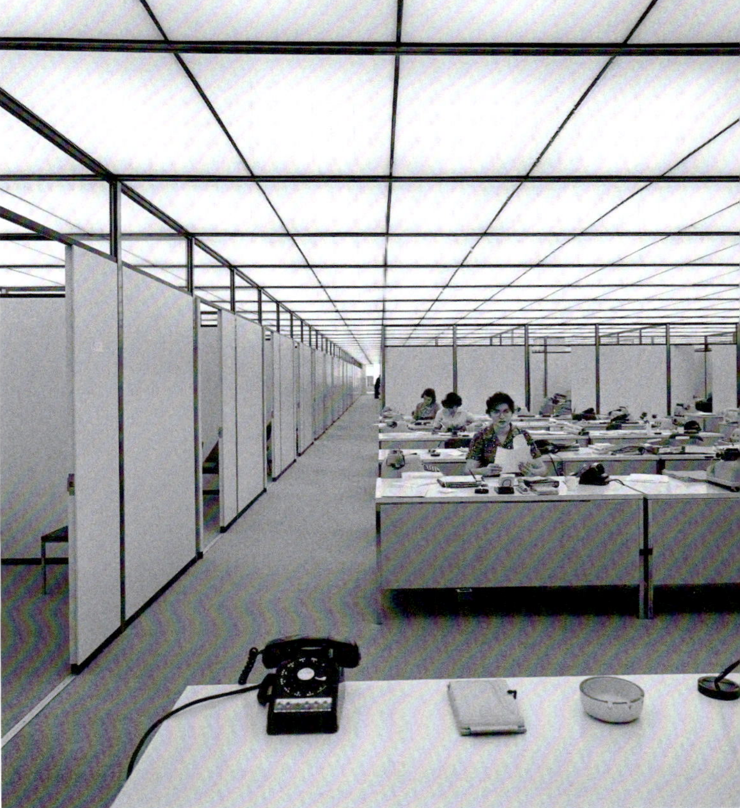

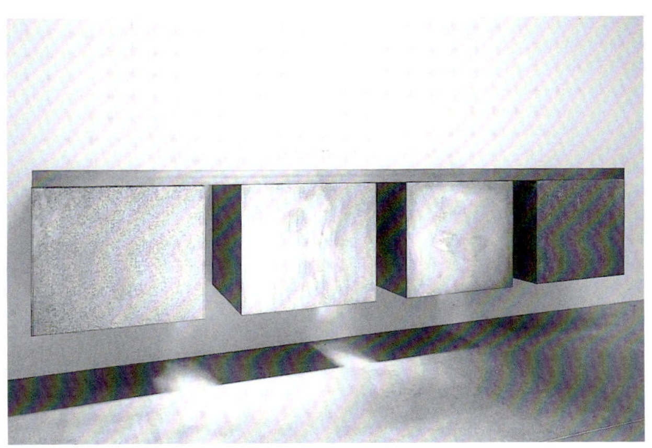

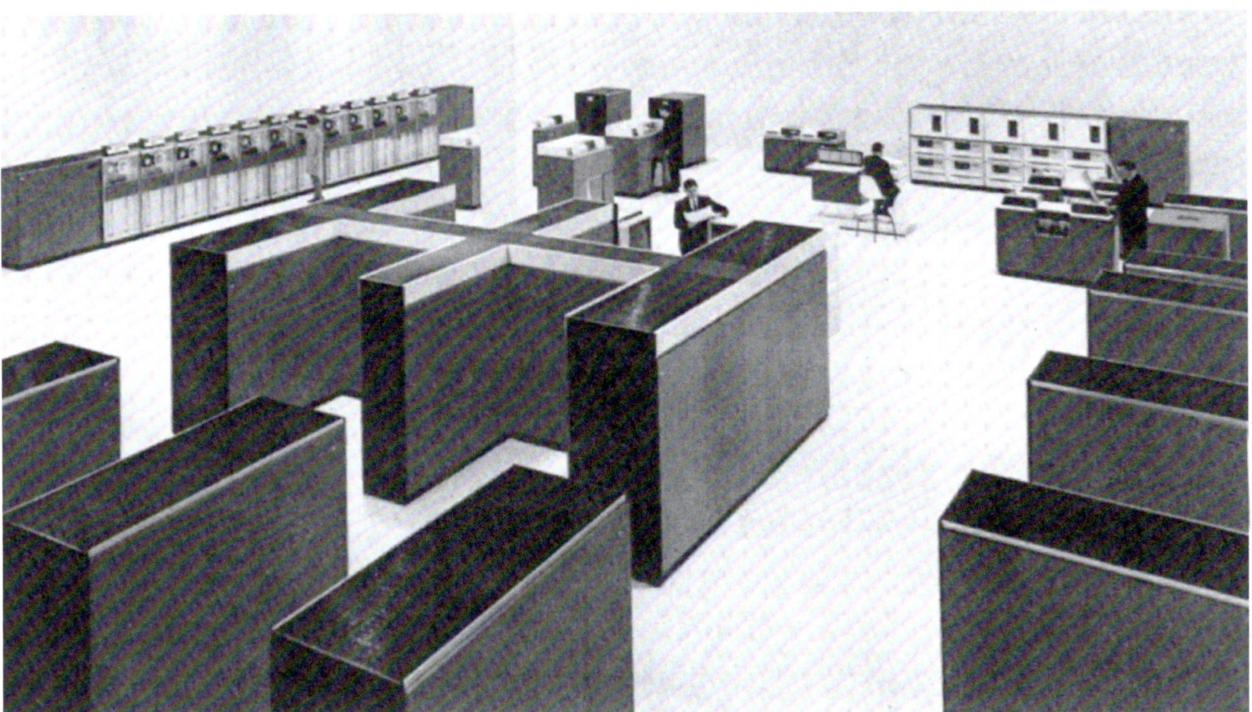

times." Predicated on the promise of modular compatibility, the System/360 allowed users to make custom configurations of interchangeable units, each of which was encased in a rectangle of thin sheet metal, sometimes punctured by a plane of translucent Plexiglas (fig. 4.43). (It has since been claimed that the invention of this product was the single biggest revolution in the history of the computer industry; by 1970 IBM had installed 35,000 of the systems.) If Judd had little occasion to operate a System/360, he might well have seen one. The New York World's Fair of 1964–65 was open just as the artist was making the transition to using boxes of sheet metal and Plexiglas in his sculpture; with its own pavilion at the fair, IBM would have been touting its new product. Other corporations with pavilions—companies such as American Interiors, Bell, duPont, Formica, Simmons, and Westinghouse—were boasting new modular designs of their own.[74]

Computers resembled the new buildings that housed them, inside and out. But their repetitive modularity also expressed the digital nature of their work, which processed information in binary strings of 1s and 0s. Thus both the form and the logic of computers echoed a trend already in popular evidence. William H. Whyte's 1956 book *The Organization Man* had portrayed the postwar employee as a victim of the quantitative analyses of an increasingly abstract power structure.[75]

Critics of Judd's work after *DSS 64* emphasized, if obliquely, his work's relationship to the modular forms of the new economy. John Perreault, writing for the *Village Voice* in 1967, saw "IBM numerology" in Judd's sculptures. A year later, reviewing the Whitney exhibition (see fig. 4.1), he added, "The entire floor looks like a science-fiction warehouse, dramatically lit to emphasize the gleaming hardware

lined up across the floor or attached to the walls." A *Time* magazine article appearing at the same time likened Judd's art to "an assembly line or bank vault," while characterizing the broader sculptural movement as "a cool school of binary esthetics which would delight an IBM research mathematician."[76] Computers, assembly lines, bank vaults, futuristic warehouses—these were the paradigmatic forms of a new, postmodern capitalism, then displacing the iron hardware of New York's modern manual labor. But the critics had little to say about the content of Judd's quotations. It remains to us here to ask *how* Judd's work represented its moment in history, and to what effect.

Certainly these Minimalist sculptures, in quoting the forms of New York's new economy, engage in a representational project far richer and more complicated than aesthetic mirroring. First of all, they peel the style of the new city away from its functions, rendering it properly visible as style. At the same time, these sculptures also exaggerate the uniformity and departicularization of the new city—*Untitled (DSS 119)* (see fig. 4.36), for example, is even more uniformly planar, even more devoid of detail than the shipping container with which Judd's portrait-photographers subtly compared it. Approaching their world in this fashion, the sculptures manage to represent not only the *forms* of the new stage in capitalism but also the logic that those forms endeavored to naturalize or hide.[77]

One of the rhetorical claims of new design in this period was that it derived naturally from utility. In some cases, per Louis Sullivan's dictum, form really did follow function: modular assembly lines produced goods more efficiently, and containerization got those goods to market in less time. In other cases, however, function was more emphatically represented than embodied. As we have seen, critics could praise a new International Style skyscraper as a "superbly efficient instrument for work," even while many such towers proved downright anti-utilitarian: inefficient to heat and cool because of their glass walls, and uncomfortable because of their rigid furnishings.[78]

Much of the appeal of the functionalist style lay in its claim to timeless and natural efficiency. For centuries, neoclassical styles had served structures of power by associating them with idealized historic civilizations. Critiquing just this mystification, functionalist design had developed in the early twentieth century as a spur toward a more democratic society, one adhering to reason and the laws of science. Functionalism was for decades a phenomenon of the avantgarde, at least in the West; only in postwar New York, with the rising dematerialization of the city's economy, did the plain metallic box finally become the house style of corporate capitalism.[79] Using this form, economic power in the period aimed to express its own inevitability, its adherence to the immutable law of the invisible hand. The economy's many rectangular, modular parts—from assembly plant and container to office block and computer—were to appear united in a single grid of maximum, reasonable productivity.

Judd's Minimalist sculpture, like and unlike New York's other new boxes, can help us now to see this ascendant ideology of the 1960s. But it was not the artist's chief aim to represent the conditions of the city in his work. Judd hoped instead that the shiny, translucent box could be used to realize his own late-modernist utopia—one in which truth might supplant rationality, in which things, rather than being instrumentalized, might simply be laid bare. At the same time, however, Judd also signaled that such a project might eventually amount to a kind of representation: "The experience of another time and society," he later claimed, "can . . . almost uniquely be gained through art."[80] At not yet fifty years' distance, Judd's Minimalist work is indeed

revealing, showing us with unusual clarity the essence of postmodernity in its early days.

I have already mentioned John Perreault's 1967 association of Judd's work with computers. In making the suggestion, Perreault intertwined it with a related evocation of the future of banking. His remark, both offhand and startlingly specific, was that the "'mystery'" of Judd's work lay in "the implied IBM numerology and the icy, science-fiction surfaces of Flash Gordon bank vaults."[81] If any particular work suggested this formulation to Perreault, it was probably *Untitled (DSS 79)* (see fig. 4.3), recently on view at the center of Judd's solo exhibition at the Leo Castelli Gallery. A little over three feet tall and exactly six feet long, the box is totally regular except for its upper horizontal surface, dropped a few inches from the top to emphasize the thin edge of the semi-matte aluminum.[82] The sculpture does seem implacable enough to suggest a bank vault, although one oddly lacking thick walls, heavy lock wheel, or any visible aperture. If it were to be opened, we imagine, it would be through the ethereal technology of a computer password, or by a hand waved through an infrared beam.

Despite Perreault's allusion, Judd's sculptures did not much resemble the future represented in the *Flash Gordon* television series of the 1950s, populated as that had been by levers, decorative orbs, and heavy iron machinery finished in Art Deco detail. Perreault may have been thinking instead of a more real and immediate future, then appearing in New York. In 1954, in response to its president's argument that weighty, fortresslike architecture was no longer appropriate for banks, Manufacturers Trust had opened a Skidmore, Owings & Merrill–designed branch on Fifth Avenue (fig. 4.44). The look of the building's four-story box of glass and aluminum elicited the response, from one critic, that "it is a design, not of substance, but of color, light and motion." The

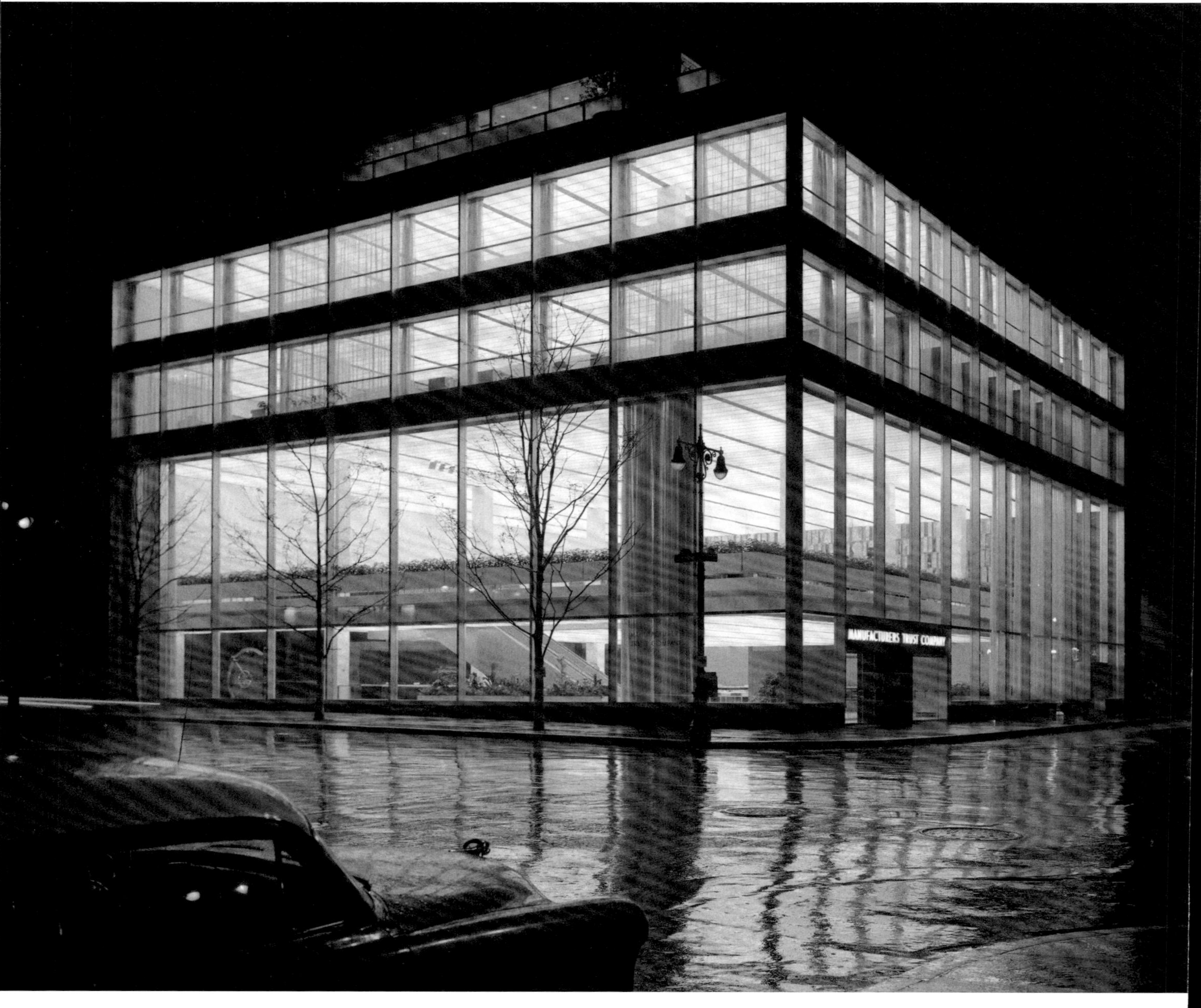


**FIG. 4.44**

Manufacturers Trust Company, 510 Fifth Avenue,
Skidmore, Owings & Merrill, 1954

very hallmark of this shimmering new bank was its sleek, unornamented vault, confidently exposed behind a sheer wall of glass.[83]

With his formulation, Perreault, perhaps more than any of Judd's other critics, seems to have understood the stakes of Judd's Minimalist sculpture. The world this art imagines *is* the future—a future characterized by the metal modules of a postindustrial economy. The work imagines a society in which the most impenetrable things, retreating from touch, can afford to be fragile.

Over the course of the 1960s, Judd's sculptures, increasingly produced in series, became gradually less attached to the dark, matte forms of New York's industrial past. The artist tended increasingly to brighter, glossier, and more uniform surfaces, eventually using aluminum, stainless steel, and Plexiglas far more often than galvanized iron. Even by 1965, he had already rejected the heavy hand-tooled double crimp—the "Pittsburgh lock"—used to close his first metal sculptures, in favor of subtler seams.[84]

Donald Judd appropriated the style of New York's postmodernization, hyperbolizing its look of rectilinear systematicity. In doing so, he quoted the economic transformation of his day—the decline of blue-collar labor and the modularization of all remaining kinds of work. The break-bulk longshoreman, the piecework seamstress, the individual printer or metalworker, all these were rapidly being displaced by an increasingly abstract economy. Representing itself with a metal box, New York capitalism in this period turned definitively toward administration and away from the manual manipulation of objects.

Judd's appropriation of this new style was, to a degree, a materialization of it—an effort to return some fixity to the ever-more-fungible world around him. On one level, that is, these sculptures imagined a contemporary world that refused sheer expedience. In the event, however, the works had remarkably unstable effects: any anti-instrumental uniqueness in them always strained against their infatuation with abstract modular systems. With the making of *Untitled (DSS 64)*, Judd's articulation of this tension hit upon what would become its settled form. It is significant that in Judd's sculpture—unlike most of the rest of the art considered in this book—this form was one in which abstraction dominated and particularity was reduced to the faintest trace. At the time, New York City's modern industrial heyday was itself giving way to an economy of abstraction, and to a newly integrated language of architecture and urban design planned to support it. Judd's work—conceived on East Nineteenth Street and built in a piecework shop—distilled the new rhetoric of its society, making visible as nowhere else the character, means, and reach of that society's aspiration to frictionless systematicity.

## An Abstract City

The version of industry at work in the sculptures of Mark DiSuvero is a greased and swinging one of cranes, winches, cables, and bolts (fig. 4.45).[85] Often his sculptures imagine a slightly antiquated dock or construction site, run by a pleasant version of manual labor and directed to expressive rather than instrumental ends. Judd developed his own sculpture, just after DiSuvero's, in the same urban environment: New York City undergoing economic postmodernization. From within this context, Judd's version of industry occupies the opposite pole; his is the suburbanized container port, the automated factory floor the computer of centralized command. Rather than softening and antiquating the forms of industry, Judd presents them in all their resolute alienation from the human hand. His sculpture differs from the forms it quotes, however, in its willful specificity, its

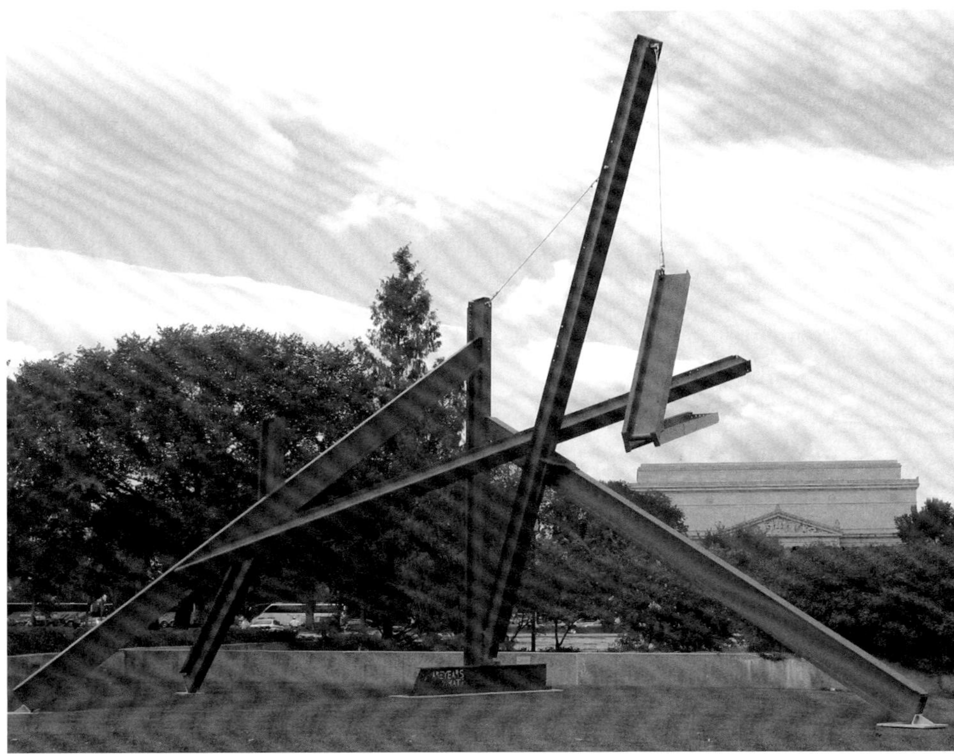



**FIG. 4.45**
**Mark DiSuvero**
*Are Years What? (For
Marianne Moore)*, 1967
Painted steel and cable
Hirshhorn Museum
and Sculpture Garden,
Washington, D.C.

**FIG. 4.46** (opposite)
**Anthony Caro**
*Prospect*, 1964
Museum Ludwig, Cologne

presentation of them as discrete and independent. Judd, that is, imagines a world in which the forms of an integrated global economy sit free and stable, disconnected from the system. He stressed again and again that his work rejected the ordering inherent to representation ("I can't even begin to think about reflecting 'universal order' as the Europeans did. The work is—well, just like lining up eight boxes"). At the same time, Judd's work tentatively rejected another kind of order, too: that of the abstract and fully integrated economy. His boxes are not fungible units, but rather "specific objects," "actual" things made "real" and "credible."[86] If a pernicious ordering had for years afflicted painting, Judd's practice suggests, a similar force was reshaping the contemporary city.

Judd's effort to counter that force, however, is saturated with futility and ambivalence. His version of the new box is detached from utility, but it also derives its aesthetic animation from the coursing power, just deferred, of the military-industrial complex. The distinct clean rectangle of

*DSS 64* offers a rare particularization of the look of the new economy, but it meanwhile madly courts the highest levels of abstraction. Judd himself conceded to one reviewer, "Nothing made is completely objective, purely practical, or merely present."[87]

It seems to me futile to try to hierarchize these opposing vectors in Judd's work. Although art historians have been joining a tug-of-war over its political implications for decades, Judd's sculpture—both emphatically particular and all but totally abstract—cannot be made to sit neatly as safe critique or simple complicity, whatever the terms.[88] Rather, the promise of Judd's sheet-metal boxes lies precisely in their power as representation, their exaggerated but unstable embodiment of the directions of their society. Judd's Minimalist sculpture isolated and hyperbolized the new city. In doing so, the new work shows us that the apparently disparate (and sometimes barely recognized) changes affecting New York in the 1960s—deindustrialization, containerization, computerization, increasing automation, and the construction of glass towers—together in fact formed a major historical transition, one that left the relationship of human beings to the things around them forever more general.

The representational power of this ambiguity in Judd's art does not derive solely from its forms. The mode of labor by which the sculptures were produced itself closely tracked the ascendancy of administration in New York. His work entailed not chiseling, modeling, or casting, but rather the conspicuously abstract act of preparing schematics. In one of the 1968 reviews, James R. Mellow expressed the artist's role this way: "In preparing for the Whitney show, Judd found that the problems of his art had become managerial— specifying materials, scheduling their shipment to the metal shop, overseeing the production of the works themselves." Asked late in his life about his working methods, Judd thought back to the loft on East Nineteenth Street, former home of Hughes & Thomas's garment factory: "I had a lot of cactus in it and I mostly sat around making sketches. . . . [M]ostly, my work is done by me carrying a bunch of papers around and sitting around and thinking." At his next house on Spring Street—as recently as 1962 the noisy home of a machinist, an offset printer, an envelope company, and four other light-industrial firms—Judd even more commodiously appropriated seven lofts for the activities of living, sketching, and viewing art.[89] His doing so was itself a richly ambiguous representation of his rapidly changing world. In the context of the removal of manual labor from Manhattan and the retooling of his city for the look of naturalized administration, Donald Judd occupied the leftover spaces of industrial modernity in order to think.

In closing, I would like to return briefly to the discourse that has animated most of the sophisticated discussion of Minimalism over the past forty years. Michael Fried's 1967 essay "Art and Objecthood" envisioned a terminal antipathy pitting Minimalist sculpture such as Judd's against modernist sculpture such as Anthony Caro's (fig. 4.46). The former was "literalist" and "theatrical"—locked perniciously into the viewer's everyday time and space—while the latter offered an experience of suspended aesthetic timelessness, an experience Fried explicitly characterized as "grace." This opposition, which Fried called a "war," has come to dominate the subsequent literature on Minimalism.[90] With some distance, however, the severity of this opposition registers as a fact needing historical explanation. Why did it appear that these two kinds of sculpture, both using industrial metals, were engaged in such a bitter disagreement?

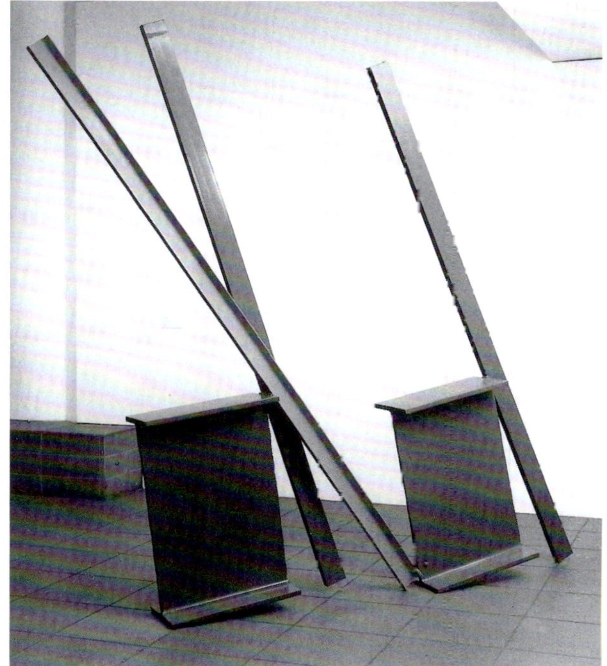

It now seems clear to me that this debate, just follow-ing the canonization of Clement Greenberg's criticism, was animated in part by a larger cultural dialectic forever just under the surface.[91] That is, the oppositions between literal-ism and grace, between flatness and pictoriality, were more than coincidentally parallel with the transition, everywhere working itself out in New York City, from materiality to ab-straction. The debates over what character or essence was desirable for art, that is, were also debates about whether it was correct (or desirable) to see the world as having a transcendent order.

Putting it differently, we might say that New York art in the twenty years after World War II was obsessed with materiality—with the physicality of Pollock's paint, the self-evident nonreferentiality of Judd's boxes. At the same time, it was obsessed with abstraction—with concept, with pictoriality, with the graceful transcendence of the everyday world. One could shade this division as a displaced reli-gious dispute—I'm not the first to note Fried's use of sacred language—over the degree to which god or some human-ist correlate subtends the material world. But in New York in this period, the abstract order in question was not only quasi-religious. The ancient materialist-idealist debate was intensified and modulated in this period by a salient transi-tion in the history of capitalism. Extending the ambivalence of Pollock's painting into the environment of the new city, Judd's early sculptures staged tensions—then especially ap-parent in New York—between cast-iron loft and glass-clad tower, between hand truck and container port, between the manufacture of things and the administration of capital.

I do not mean to reduce pictoriality to a transparent sign for late capitalism, still less to suggest that Fried and Greenberg were simply complicitous in the effort to rebuild lower Manhattan to serve abstract corporate functions

rather than bodily industrial ones. I mean rather to argue that the formalist dialectics of modernism, despite their supposed hermeticism, were in fact a means of thinking about a changing world. It seems to me no coincidence that materiality and abstraction, awkwardly contested in every-day life throughout the twentieth century, became central obsessions of modernist art. In the years around 1960, however, in lower Manhattan, the terms of modernism and of capitalist history became especially intertwined. For Judd—as for us now again in our own moment— the ascendancy of abstraction was for a time especially visible and unresolved.

# Into Air: The Late 1960s and After

Money talks quietly, like me. It's all zeros. Duels now are fought with zeros. The best tables are bought with zeros. The best seats are bought with zeros. Money whispers. Bills no longer crackle in the hands of a headwaiter or a cop. Power used to be noisy. Not now. Now typewriters are silent. Now carpets are thick. Now acoustical tile (simulating travertine) soaks up sound everywhere. And, even in the general offices, vinyl has replaced asphalt; it's quieter, easier on the feet of clerks who wear sponge-rubber soles so thick one hardly hears them take their coffee breaks. For them, the day is all soft, silent foods, a mush of doughnuts and danish and coffee, mid-morning and mid-afternoon. At lunch, they have hamburgers and ice cream, while I chew glass.

—B. H. FRIEDMAN, 1972

[There was a time when] all the paintings were black and people still talked about the texture. No one nowadays talks about texture anymore. Paintings are neat and slick, all the galleries look like clinics, paintings are white, colors are fluorescent and the more color the better.

—MARTIAL RAYSSE, 1967

This book has been an effort to see the work of New York's avant-garde around 1960 as a uniquely revealing representation of the city's first stages of postmodernization. Specifically, the art examined here has revealed that the many changes in New York in the period—including urban renewal, the ascendancy of the commodity-sign, deindustrialization, and computerization—amounted together to an abstraction of the city, a shift toward systematicity and away from particular, palpable objects. I have argued that Oldenburg's *Street* provided an obdurate but ambivalent resistance to this increasingly ordered and legible New York, and that Johns's sculptures wished impossibly to materialize both the American consumer landscape and language itself. I have also urged an understanding of Rauschenberg's combines as representations of a city divided between

the systematic and the particular, and a view of Donald Judd's sculptures as an attempt to preserve the specificity of things, even from within the logic of the new economy. Together with their peers, these artists mounted a last modernist engagement with the materiality of their city— an engagement they ultimately abandoned. Although material particularity of course persisted (indeed more so in New York than in many places), New Yorkers around 1960 experienced a rapid change in the texture of everyday life. Much of the best art of this period lingered on a particular moment within this shift—a moment at which the new architecture and the new economy noisily confronted, in the back alleys of lower Manhattan, the unincorporable materiality of things.

It is important to underscore that these transformations (and the questioning around them) did not constitute an unprecedented break with the past. Karl Marx and Friedrich Engels long ago understood the rise of capitalism itself as a turn away from the materiality of labor and toward the abstraction of capital: it was the destabilizing effects of such a transition that made for the state of alienation in which "all that is solid melts into air."[1] Nor has the process stopped. In the years since 1966, continued globalization of corporations and consumption, along with the ongoing growth of the freeway landscape, containerized shipping, jet travel, television, and the Internet, have made our places and objects seem forever less unique and forever more fluidly interconnected. Nevertheless, the abstraction of the built environment experienced a period of particular visibility in New York around 1960. At that moment, consumer goods appeared to be losing solidity, architecture appeared to be becoming more ethereal and uniform, and manual labor seemed in decline. Trained in the dialectics of Abstract Expressionist painting, several New York artists recognized these changes as a decline in the materiality of everyday life. Theirs was an art that directly addressed, if always in a qualified voice, the forces of dematerialization then remaking New York.

In recent years, art history has taken an intensive theoretical interest in structures of representation, and especially in those structures that seem to resist or refuse meaning. One of the results has been an increasingly sophisticated understanding of twentieth-century art, including the works of Claes Oldenburg, Jasper Johns, Robert Rauschenberg, and Donald Judd. This interest in modes of meaning, however, has not developed into a full-dress inquiry into *which* meanings were deferred or why. In this book, I have aimed to focus not only on problems of interpretation, but also on the specific objects and references over which those problems were played. It is my hope that doing so has revealed that the materialism and illegibility of New York art around 1960 was not just philosophical in nature but also a representation of city being made less material and more legible all the time.

In the later 1960s New York art followed a different path, pursuing the immateriality of its society. Many artists relinquished the intensive palpability of their practice for interests in images, networks, and concepts. However, even much of this later art in fact shared the central preoccupations of the previous decade, exploiting—if from a new position—the failings, even the illogic of systems.

Take first the case of Andy Warhol, whose evolving practice exemplifies the change in the direction. *TV $199* (fig. 5.1), a 1960 oil painting based on a newspaper advertisement, is very much like the early, materialist works of the other artists treated in this book. In the painting, Warhol takes up the subject of the increasingly fluid and immaterial

image world, addressing both television (the very epitome of the dematerialized image) and also advertising, in its thinnest and most ephemeral form. Like much of Johns's art, *TV $199* is materialist in rendering, resisting legibility while emphasizing paint, canvas, and hand-facture. Drips of brown on and around the television set violate the painting's pictorial illusion and call attention to its flat support. Dry fields of grayed-out color appear to block out the advertisement's simple text, and even the ellipse in which the titular price appears, while still just legible, is obscured by a broad and cloudy overpainting. What little text the artist has preserved is limited to a broken message: "2 . . . 1 Inch TV . . . NSO . . . 230." Here Warhol has appropriated a fragment of America's growing image culture only to render it isolated, materialized, and incommunicative.

As soon as four years later, Warhol painted *16 Jackies* (fig. 5.2). By comparison, this painting seems preoccupied, even enthralled, with the disembodied images of television and other popular media. Its subject is the representation in the news of John F. Kennedy's assassination, and it presents us with four images, each repeated four times, that circulated in newspapers, in magazines, and on television in November 1963. Warhol's silk-screen technique imitates the trademarks of these media—the duotone format of cheap magazine printing, the blue flicker of period broadcasts The repetition of these photographs—two from before Kennedy's death, two from after—emphasizes the hegemony of the image, its mobile and disembodied character. The silk screens therefore seem severed from the events they represent: Jackie here is more image than person, an abstraction propped up by photography. At the core of the work of course is the missing and very real material fact of the murder—a fact that neither the painting itself nor the increasingly ubiquitous trade in photographs can adequately

FIG. 5.1
**Andy Warhol**
*TV $199*, 1960
Casein, oil paint, and wax crayon on cotton
68 ⅛ x 52 ⅜ in. (173 x 133 cm)
Andy Warhol Foundation for the Visual Arts

FIG. 5.2
**Andy Warhol**
*16 Jackies*, 1964
Synthetic polymer paint and
silk-screen ink on canvas
16 panels, each 20 x 16 in. (50.8 x 40.6 cm);
overall 80 x 64 in. (203.2 x 162.6 cm)
Andy Warhol Foundation for the Visual Arts

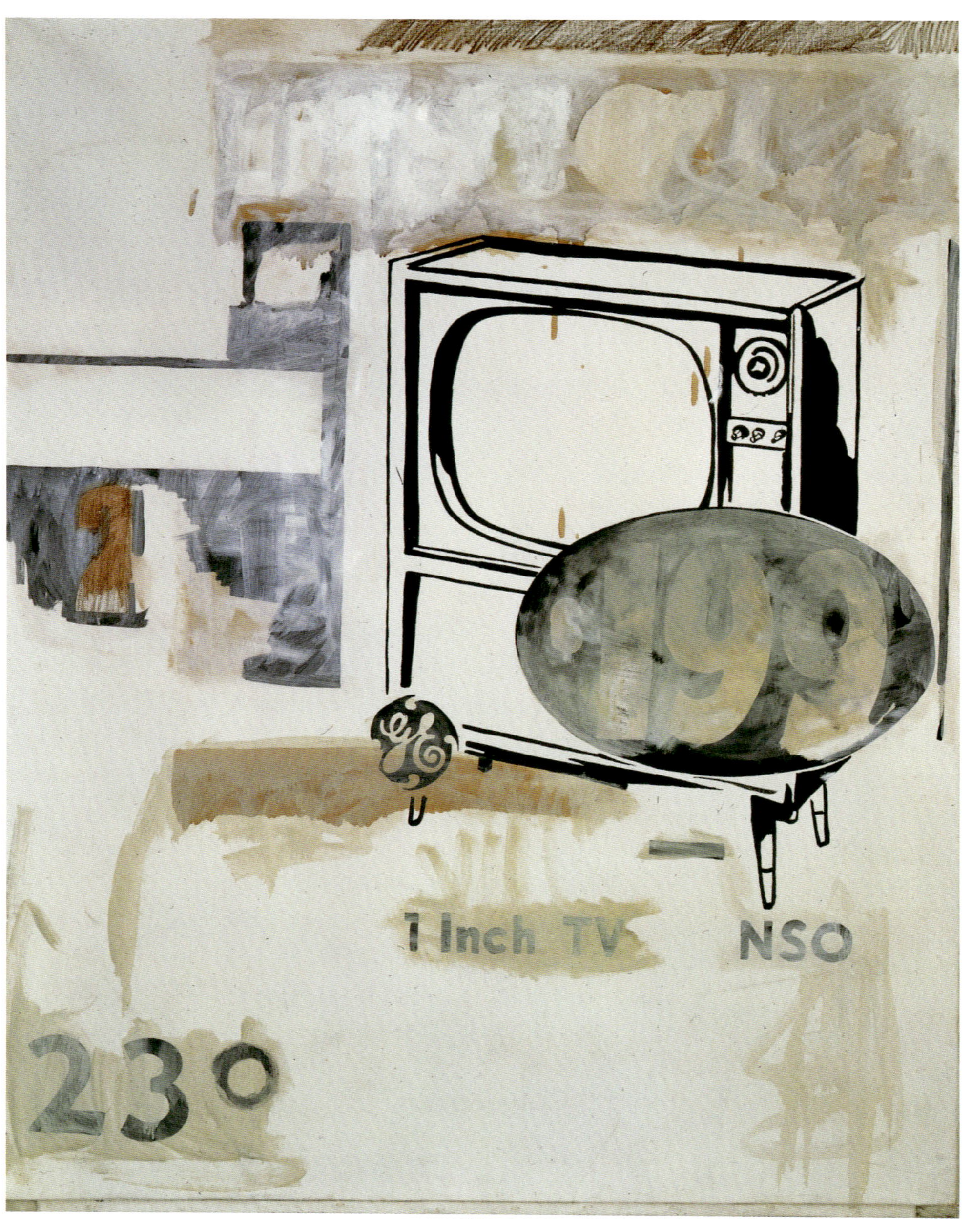
1 Inch TV    NSO
230

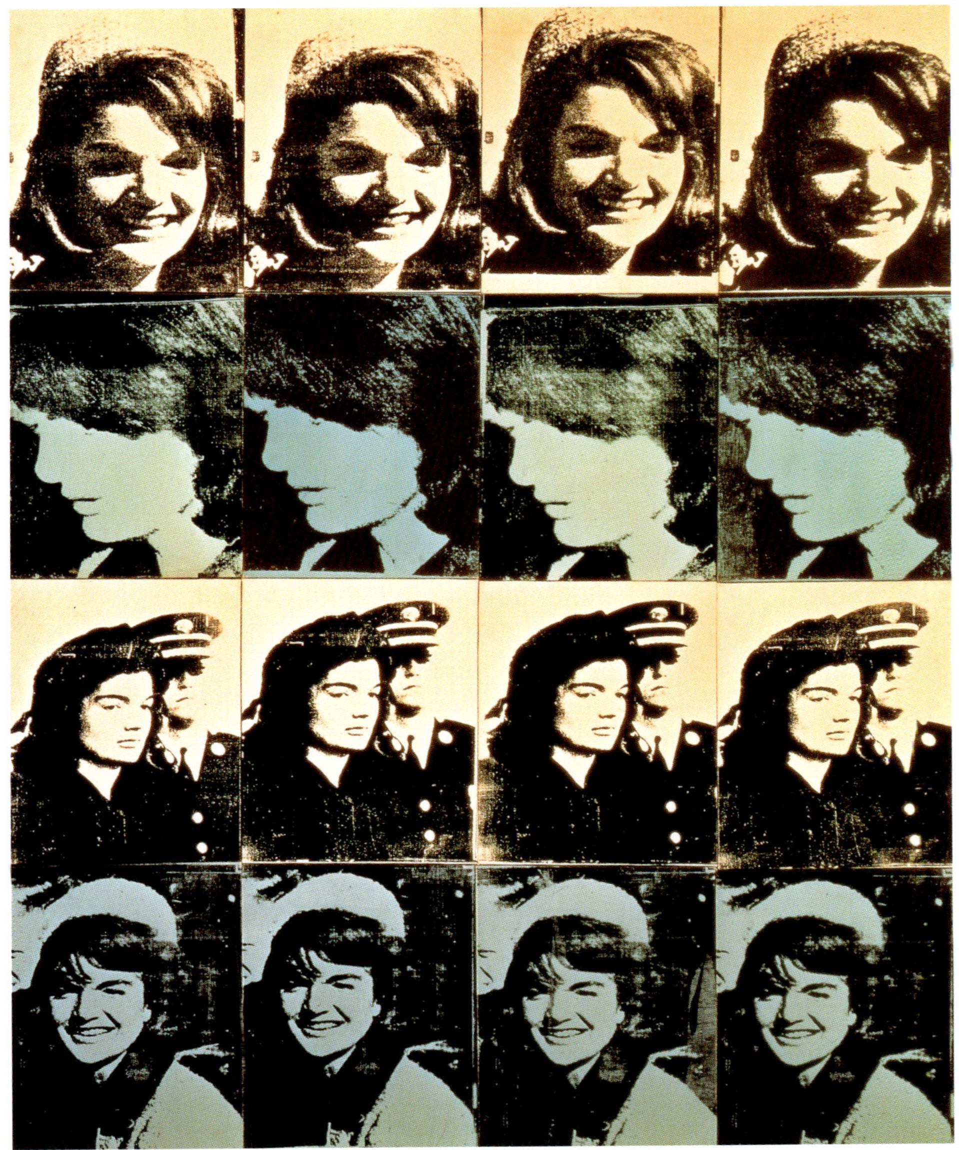

deliver. *16 Jackies*, while continuing an old modernist inquiry into the failures of representation, presents those failures to us as especially endemic to a newly abstract world.[2]

Looking slightly longer, however, we recognize that *16 Jackies*—even while indulging the ubiquity and immateriality of contemporary images—also quietly insists on the abiding materiality of representation. We see the effects of a grainy photographic emulsion, for example, in the top register of images, and we note an uneven saturation of color— perhaps the effect of a poorly inked squeegee—throughout. The many portraits are also imprecisely aligned, returning the faintest quality of specificity to each.

Warhol's case is paradigmatic, both in its infatuation with the immateriality of its society and in its emphasis on the persistence of a material reality still unsystematized. Conceptual art, despite its apparent extremism, continually animated similar tensions.[3]

Take the case of Lawrence Weiner's project *Staples, Stakes, Twine, Turf,* which the artist made at Windham College in Vermont in the spring of 1968 (fig. 5.3). The work involved the installation of a crisp grid of twine onto an oddly shaped, unevenly worn lawn. It is a gesture that vividly highlights the absurd disjunction between the procedures of measurement or cartography and the particular facts of a muddy patch of New England grass.[4] In 1969, Robert Barry undertook the Inert Gas Series, a group of artworks in which he journeyed from New York to release transparent gases in the western desert (fig. 5.4). We might see Barry's series as an allegory, the ultimate representation of a society undergoing dematerialization. However, the odd energy of these works, as the photographs ironically emphasize, depends entirely on the slightest shred of matter—that fleeting, invisible gas—remaining in the work of art.

In the later 1960s, artists in New York and elsewhere pursued the ascendant abstraction of their surroundings. Today, one strain of artistic practice continues to explore the growing generalization of our global landscape and economy. But much of this work, like the New York art of 1960, insists on the fecundity of palpable remainders, on the value of lingering among the isolated fragments still loosely populating the everyday world.

**FIG. 5.3**
**Lawrence Weiner**
*Staples, Stakes, Twine, Turf,* 1968
Temporary installation of twine
and hardware on lawn
Windham College, Putney, Vermont

**FIG. 5.4**
**Robert Barry**
*Inert Gas Series: Helium,* 1969
Gas released into the atmosphere with
photographic documentation

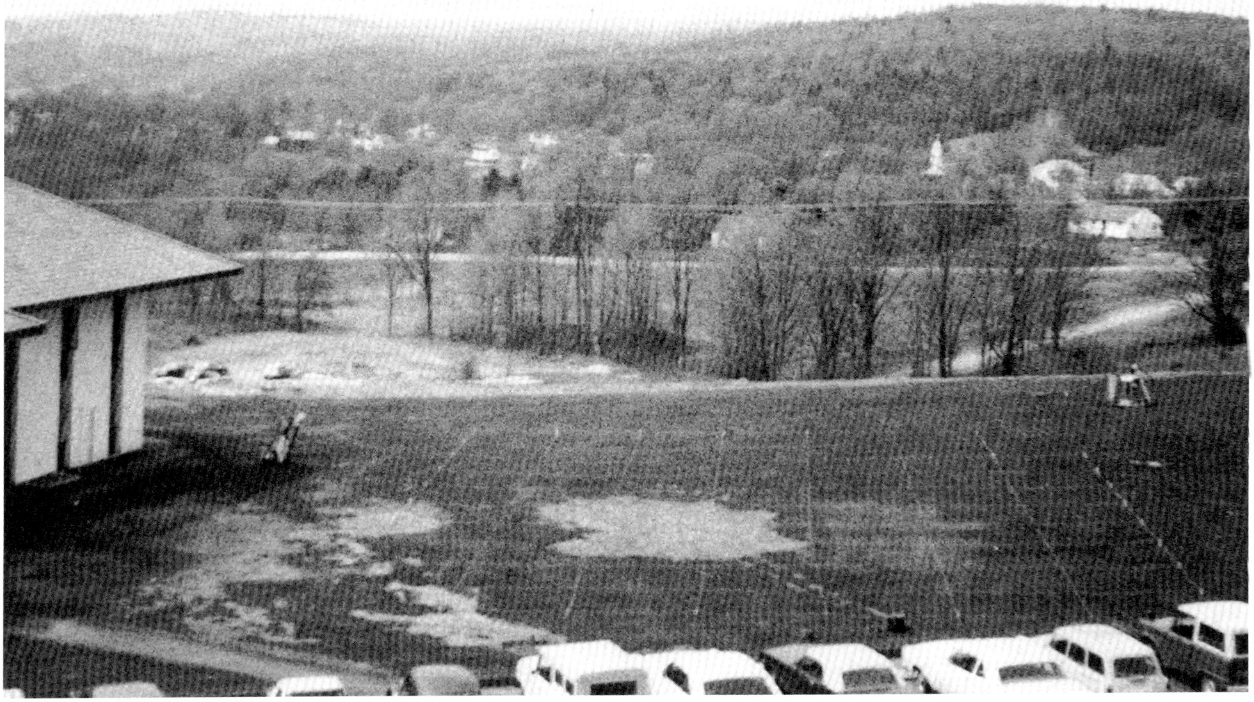

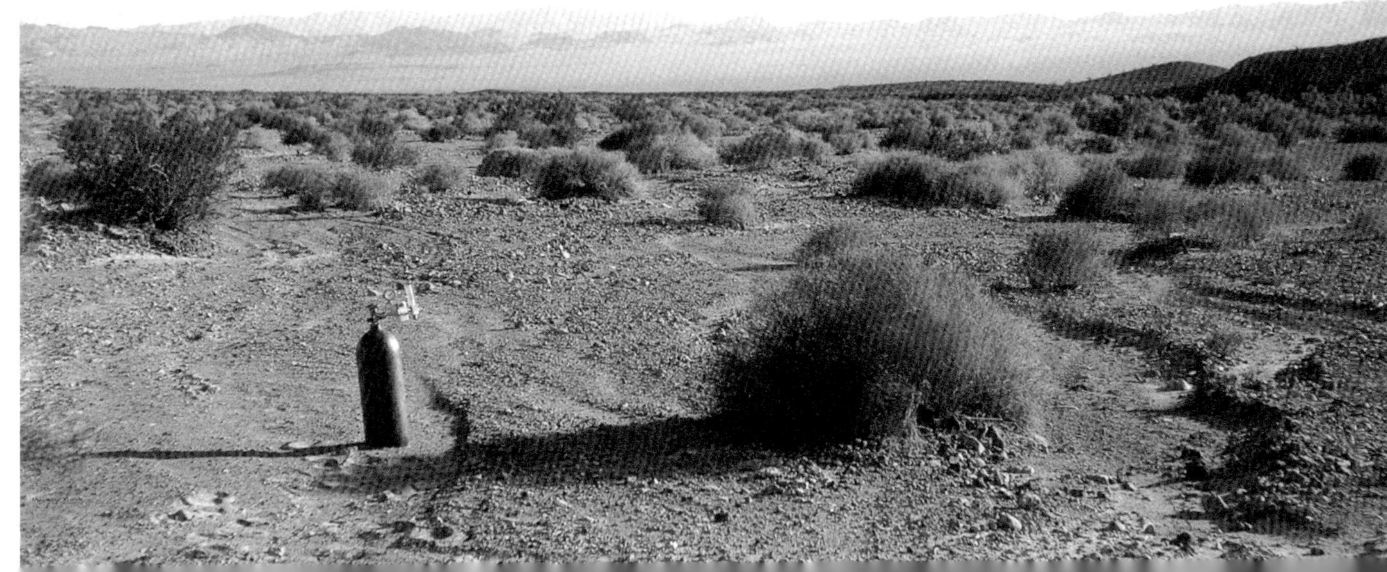

# Notes


INTRODUCTION
## Materiality in New York, 1960

1

Allan Kaprow, "The Legacy of Jackson Pollock,"
*Artnews,* October 1958, 56–57. Joan Marter, "The
Forgotten Legacy: Happenings, Pop Art, and
Fluxus at Rutgers University," in *Off-Limits: Rutgers
University and the Avant-Garde, 1957–1963,* ed.
Marter (New Brunswick, N.J.: Rutgers University
Press, 1999), 1–47, notes that Kaprow had written
the essay in 1956.

2

Barbara Rose writes of Oldenburg's meeting with
Pollock in *Claes Oldenburg* (New York: Museum
of Modern Art, 1969), 25. In *Off the Wall: Robert
Rauschenberg and the Art World of Our Time* (New
York: Penguin, 1981), 151, Calvin Tomkins reports
that Kaprow was thinking partly of a recent visit to
Rauschenberg's studio when he wrote "The Legacy
of Jackson Pollock."

3

Cunningham quoted in Susan Sontag, *Dancers on
a Plane: John Cage, Merce Cunningham, Jasper Johns*
(New York: Knopf, 1990), 22.

4

Alan R. Solomon, "The New Art," *Art International,*
25 September 1963, 39; Claes Oldenburg, "A
Statement," in *Happenings: An Illustrated Anthology,*
ed. Michael Kirby (New York: E. P. Dutton, 1965),
200–203. Fluxus, a loose global art movement, also
produced performances, publications, and "event
scores" in this period. Their focus on the banal was
very much like that of other New York avant-gard-
ists, but their works were, by design, less object-
oriented and more conceptual in nature.

5

Dore Ashton in Peter Selz, ed., "A Symposium on
Pop Art," *Arts Magazine,* April 1963, 39.

6

Rauschenberg quoted in Calvin Tomkins, *Off the
Wall* (New York: Penguin, 1981), 87; Judd in "The
New Sculpture," panel discussion, 2 May 1966, New
York, in *Minimalism,* ed. James Meyer (London:
Phaidon, 2000), 221.

7

Billy Klüver, *The International Avant-Garde: America
Discovered,* International Anthology of Contempo-
rary Engraving (Milan: Galleria Shwarz, [c. 1962]),
n.p.; *New Paintings of Common Objects,* exhibition
at the Pasadena Art Museum, 1962; *New Realists*
(New York: Sidney Janis Gallery, 1962); Lawrence
Alloway, "Junk Culture as Tradition," in *New
Forms—New Media I,* exh. cat. (New York: Martha
Jackson Gallery, 1960). Confusingly, the Martha
Jackson exhibition and its catalogue had slightly
different names.

8

Robert Rosenblum, "Castelli Group," *Arts,* May
1957, 53; "Trend to the Anti-Art: Targets and Flags,"
*Newsweek,* 31 March 1958, 96; Gerald Nordland,
"Neo-Dada Goes West," *Arts Magazine,* May–June
1962, 102–3; Barbara Rose, "Dada, Then and Now,"
*Art International,* January 1963, 23–28.

9

Alloway, "Junk Culture," n.p. In his catalogue essay
for the 1961 assemblage show at the Museum
of Modern Art, William C. Seitz underscored
Alloway's characterization: "One must agree,"
Seitz wrote, "that the proper backdrop for recent
assemblage is the multifarious fabric of the modern
city—its random patchwork of slickness and dete-
rioration, cold planning and liberating confusion,
resplendent beauty and noxious squalor." Seitz, *The
Art of Assemblage* (New York: Museum of Modern
Art, 1961), 73.

10

Many have observed parallels between Moses's
work in New York and Baron Haussmann's destruction and rebuilding of Paris in the third quarter of
the nineteenth century. T. J. Clark's work on art in
that environment, *The Painting of Modern Life: Paris
in the Art of Manet and His Followers* (New York:
Knopf, 1985), has been deeply formative to my
thinking about New York a century later.

11

John Kenneth Galbraith, *The Affluent Society* (Bos-
ton: Houghton Mifflin, 1958); Vance Packard, *The
Hidden Persuaders* (New York: David McKay, 1957);
Packard, *The Status Seekers: An Exploration of Class
Behaviour in America and the Hidden Barriers That
Affect You, Your Community, Your Future* (New York:
David McKay, 1959); Packard, *The Waste Makers*
(New York: David McKay, 1960); Daniel Boorstin,
*The Image; or, What Happened to the American
Dream* (New York: Atheneum, 1962).

12

Jasper Johns, sketchbook A, 8, c. 1960, photograph-
ically reprinted in Kirk Varnedoe, ed., *Jasper Johns:
Writings, Sketchbook Notes, Interviews* (New York:
Museum of Modern Art, 1996), 27.

13

Lucy Lippard, *Six Years: The Dematerialization of the
Art Object, 1966–1972* (New York: Praeger, 1973).

14

The works of these four artists eventually became
high luxury objects, but this fact hardly provides
adequate reason to abandon them as critical representations of their time and place.

15

"The [Marxian] sense that 'all that is solid melts
into air,'" Harvey concludes, "has rarely been
more pervasive." David Harvey, *The Condition of
Postmodernity* (Cambridge, Mass.: Blackwell, 1990),
285–86. Ernest Mandel and Fredric Jameson have
used the term *late capitalism* to refer to roughly the
same condition. Even while recognizing it as deeply
systematized, Jameson and Harvey emphasize a
fractured and heterogeneous quality in postmodernity (and especially in postmodernism). In
New York around 1960, however, it was a smooth,
generic regularity that seemed to define the new
situation. Ernest Mandel, *Late Capitalism,* trans.
Joris De Bres (London: NLB, 1975); Fredric Jameson,
*Postmodernism; or, The Cultural Logic of Late Capital-
ism* (Durham, N.C.: Duke University Press, 1991).

16

I thank David Bjelajac and Hannah Feldman for
their discussions with me on this topic.

CHAPTER ONE
## A Neo-Dada City

**1**

In addition to *The Street, Ray Gun* included Jim
Dine's environment *The House* as well as three
nights of happenings, or Ray Gun Spex. More on
these follows. The term *installation,* although   use
it here, was not yet in circulation among artists
or critics in 1960; most critics in fact struggled to
find a term for the new form. Suzanne Kiplinger,
for example, writing for the *Village Voice,* called
Oldenburg's and Dine's genre "a sort of 3-D world
which surrounds the beholder, using elements of
sculpture, Surrealism, interior decoration, analysis,
and the fun house at an amusement park." Kiplinger, "Ray Gun," *Village Voice,* 17 February 1960,
11. The first use of the word *environment* to refer to
Oldenburg's work seems to have been made by Irving Sandler in a review of *The Street* at the Reuben
Gallery, *Artnews,* Summer 1960, 16.

**2**

Oldenburg described the work as a mural in one of
his sketchbooks. See Barbara Rose, *Claes Oldenburg*
(New York: Museum of Modern Art, 1969), 41.

**3**

Barbara Rose's chapter on *The Street,* written forty
years ago, is still the most comprehensive overview
of the work. Rose, *Claes Oldenburg,* 37–50. Robert
E. Haywood analyzes *Ray Gun* (and especially Oldenburg's happening staged there) in the context of
the unusual social and religious agenda of the Judson Memorial Church in "Heretical Alliance: Claes
Oldenburg and the Judson Memorial Church in the
1960s," *Art History* 18, no. 2 (June 1995): 185–212.
Both of these accounts have been foundational to
my own thinking. Two other useful mentions of *The
Street* come in works dedicated to other concerns:
Marshall Berman, *All That Is Solid Melts into Air: The
Experience of Modernity* (New York: Penguin, 1988),
320; and Yve-Alain Bois, "Ray Guns," in *Formless:
A User's Guide,* ed. Yve-Alain Bois and Rosalind
E. Krauss (New York: Zone, 1997), 172–79. Of the
many catalogue essays that make brief mention
of *The Street,* three of the most useful are Ellen H.

Johnson, *Claes Oldenburg,* Penguin New Art Series
(Harmondsworth, U.K.: Penguin, 1971); Barbara
Haskell, "The Aesthetics of Junk," *Blam! The Explo-
sion of Pop, Minimalism, and Performance, 1958–1964*
(New York: Whitney Museum of American Art,
1984); and Germano Celant, "Claes Oldenburg and
the Feeling of Things," trans. Stephen Sartorelli, in
*Claes Oldenburg: An Anthology* (New York: Guggenheim Museum, 1995), 12–31.

**4**

The values of order, negotiability (or "flow"), and
legibility—all aspects of the drive to abstraction—
were frequently intertwined in renewal, both as it
was practiced and as Oldenburg responded to it.
The discussion that follows treats them, as necessary, sometimes singly, sometimes as a group.

**5**

Oldenburg has confirmed the identity of these
forms as a shoe-shine stand and shop window.
Letter to the author signed by Oldenburg's studio
assistant, Anu Vikram, 10 November 2000.

**6**

It is unclear to what extent and on what occasions
viewers were able to walk freely through the work.
Although Oldenburg has recently indicated that
the installation was "separated from the viewer"
(e-mail letter to the author, 30 July 2003), Suzanne
Kiplinger's review in the *Village Voice* ("Ray Gun,"
11) indicates that *The Street* "surround[ed] the
beholder," and the photograph that appeared with
her article shows visitors, along with Oldenburg,
very much at the heart of things.

**7**

These works were originally published as *Urban-
isme* (Paris: G. Crès, 1924), which was available in
English by 1929, and *Quand les cathédrales étaient
blanches* (Paris: Plon, 1937), available in English
by 1947.

**8**

Fritz Malcher, *The Steadyflow Traffic System* (Cambridge, Mass.: Harvard University Press, 1935). I
thank Paul Groth for his helpful discussion with me
on this topic.

**9**

Robert Moses's way of putting it: "You can draw
any kind of picture you like on a clean slate and
indulge your every whim in the wilderness in laying
out a New Delhi, Canberra or Brasília, but when
you operate in an overbuilt metropolis, you have to
hack your way with a meat ax." Robert A. Caro, *The
Power Broker: Robert Moses and the Fall of New York*
(New York: Vintage, 1975), 849.

**10**

These figures are reported in ibid., 2.

**11**

McCandish Phillips, "City Marks Birth of Public
Housing," *New York Times,* 4 December 1960.

**12**

Francis Bello reported that the Federal Aid Highway
Act planned to add 5,500 miles of urban highway
to the existing 1,500 miles. Bello, "The City and
the Car," in *The Exploding Metropolis: A Study of the
Assault on Urbanism and How Our Cities Can Resist It,*
ed. Editors of *Fortune* (Garden City, N.Y.: Doubleday,
1958), 34. Robert Caro (*Power Broker,* 704) puts the
total figure at 6,700 miles. On the confusion over
urban interstates, see Tom Lewis, *Divided Highways:
Building the Interstate Highways, Transforming American Life* (New York: Viking Penguin, 1997), 146.

**13**

Caro, *Power Broker,* 940. Caro mentions in the same
chapter that New York area railways did not gain
a single additional mile of track between 1933 and
1974.

**14**

The one-way traffic change is reported in Irving
Spiegel, "Two One-Way Shifts Go Smoothly," *New
York Times,* 18 July 1960. For more on this change,
see chapter 3 in the present volume. The narrowing
of sidewalks is mentioned in Jane Jacobs, *The Death
and Life of Great American Cities* (New York: Vintage,
1961), 364.

**15**

Caro, *Power Broker,* 9 (cost) and 20 (displacement).

**16**

Quotations from "City Clean-Up Begins This
Week," *New York Times,* 30 March 1959; figures
from Edmond J. Bartnett, "City Ready to Buy 14,587
Litter Cans," *New York Times,* 6 October 1959.

**17**

This history is culled from coverage in the *New York Times.* See for example articles published on 3 May, 15 June, 8 August, and 17 November 1958, and on 31 March 1959. See especially Bernard Stengren, "550 'WALK' Lights to Be Added Here," *New York Times,* 15 June 1959.

**18**

William H. Whyte Jr. and the other editors of *Fortune* in fact organized *The Exploding Metropolis,* which was subtitled *A Study of the Assault on Urbanism and How Our Cities Can Resist It.* Several of its essays had previously appeared in the magazine's pages. The book garnered prominent reviews in publications from the *New York Times,* 5 October 1958, to the Greenwich Village socialist journal the *Monthly Review,* April 1959, 476–86. Among others, Lewis Mumford (in the *New Yorker*) and Jane Jacobs (in *Architectural Forum*) had already been publishing prominent criticism of urban highways and modernist planning.

**19**

"Lindsay Acts to Take Secrecy Wrap off Title I," *Village Voice,* 1 April 1959, 1; major articles on the slum clearance scandal appeared in the *New York Times* that summer on 21, 22, 24, and 30 June; 1, 2, 4, 14, and 15 July. In the fall, a special issue of the *Nation* addressed the Title I scandal, among other controversies. Fred J. Cook and Gene Gleason, "The Shame of New York," *Nation,* 31 October 1959.

**20**

Jacobs, "Downtown Is for People," in Editors of *Fortune, Exploding Metropolis,* 168, 143 (see also Jacobs, *Death and Life*); William H. Whyte Jr., introduction to *Exploding Metropolis,* x. It was Sigfried Giedion who saw the elimination of the street as a necessity, in *Space, Time, and Architecture: The Growth of a New Tradition* (Cambridge, Mass.: Harvard University Press, 1941), 559. For a discussion of the use of modernist planning to postmodernize the city, see the introduction to the present volume.

**21**

Laura Benet, letter to the editor, *New York Times,* 7 April 1958.

**22**

Charles Grutzner, "Strategy Revamped on Washington Sq.," *New York Times,* 30 March 1958.

**23**

"Mumford Hits Plan for Washington Sq.," *New York Times,* 10 March 1958. Moody actions reported in Daniel Wolf, "Moses Hints 'Retreat' on Sq. Owing to Village Pressure," *Village Voice,* 21 May 1958, 3; "Washington Square Traffic Plea," *New York Times,* 4 February 1959; and "Close 'Square' Permanently; Take It Out of Politics," *Village Voice,* 14 January 1959, 3.

**24**

Charles G. Bennett, "'Village' Protesters Led by De Sapio," *New York Times,* 19 September 1958.

**25**

For this history, see Charles G. Bennett, "Washington Sq. Traffic to Halt While Road Issue Is Decided," *New York Times,* 24 October 1958; Bennett, "City Vote Backs a Ban on Traffic in Washington Sq.," *New York Times,* 10 April 1959; and "Villagers Celebrate Victory on Traffic; Burn Car in Effigy," *New York Times,* 13 June 1959. A recent essay by Robert Fishman, "Revolt of the Urbs: Robert Moses and His Critics," in *Robert Moses and the Modern City: The Transformation of New York,* ed. Hilary Ballon and Kenneth T. Jackson (New York: W. W. Norton, 2007), 122–29, considers the Washington Square roadway fight in some detail. Fishman credits especially the leadership of Shirley Hayes and other women from the neighborhood for the roadway's defeat.

**26**

"Statement of Robert Moses Regarding Washington Square," *Village Voice,* 1 January 1958, 15.

**27**

Robert Moses had championed the roadway project as "progress" (ibid., 15), while two *New York Times* editorials, in arguing against the road, had used the same word in distancing quotation marks: "Washington Square," *New York Times,* 5 November 1958; "Washington Square," *New York Times,* 11 April 1959.

**28**

The destruction of stores and lofts was noted in "'Village' Housing Dedicated Here," *New York Times,* 11 December 1957. The area had been home to about one thousand small businesses, mostly hat manufacturers, and about 132 families (Cook and Gleason, "Shame of New York," 295). Early

on, Washington Square Village was described as a "middle-income" project ("Washington Square Village: A Special Supplement," Village Voice, 26 March 1958, 5), but soon the *Village Voice* was characterizing it as a "luxury" development (Mary Perot Nichols, "Project Drops Expansion as Renting Slows Down," *Village Voice,* 6 January 1960, 1), and John Lindsay was charging, "The Washington Square Title I project has torn down low-rent apartments and lofts and unrooted small businesses only to build a string of luxury apartment houses renting for better than $75 per month per room" ("House OK's Lindsay Move to Spotlight Title I Projects," *Village Voice,* 27 May 1959, 3).

**29**

This change is made apparent by a comparison of the situation today with a 1955 fire insurance map: *Manhattan Land Book of the City of New York,* desk and library ed. (New York: G. W. Bromley, 1955). For an encyclopedic treatment of Washington Square Village and related development, see Ballon and Jackson, *Moses and the Modern City,* 244–48.

**30**

Ira Henry Freeman, "New Projects Will Change the Face—and the Character—of the Washington Square Area," *New York Times,* 8 December 1957.

**31**

"New Look on Washington Square South," photograph caption, *Village Voice,* 11 November 1959, 1.

**32**

"Lindsay Acts," 1.

**33**

William W. Brill, "Zoning for Survival," *Village Voice,* 29 April 1959, 4; "Vegetables and Art," photograph caption, *Village Voice,* 29 July 1959, 1; Lester Dreizen, letter to the editor, *Village Voice,* 19 August 1959, 4, 12.

**34**

"'Save the Village' Wins Sq. Association Support," *Village Voice,* 14 October 1959, 3; "'Save the Village' Drive Seeks Local Volunteers, 10,000 Petition Signers," *Village Voice,* 28 October 1959, 3. See also "'Save Village' Group Asks City Aid for Community," *Village Voice,* 30 September 1959, 3.

**35**

Freeman "New Projects Will Change the Area." This article was accompanied by the map that appears here as fig. 1.10.

**36**

Claes Oldenburg, interview by Paul Cummings, 1973–74, transcript, p. 70, Archives of American Art, Smithsonian Institution, Washington, D.C. Cooper Union's new structure was its engineering building (see the northeast corner of the map reproduced as fig. 1.2).

**37**

Fourth Street address indicated in Rose, *Claes Oldenburg,* 199; quotation from Oldenburg, interview by Cummings, 116. One particularly large project under construction near Oldenburg's home was the development planned as Franklin D. Roosevelt Houses and now called Village View Houses. It occupies nearly four city blocks along Avenue A and is pictured in fig. 1.9. Oldenburg was working at Cooper Union in Greenwich Village, right by the Bible House renewal.

**38**

Claes Oldenburg, *Injun and Other Histories, 1960* (New York: Great Bear. 1966), 13. A copy is held in the library of the Museum of Modern Art, New York.

**39**

Quoted in Barbara Rose. "The Origins, Life and Times of Ray Gun: 'All Will See as Ray Gun Sees . . . ,'" *Artforum,* November 1969, 53.

**40**

Claes Oldenburg and Emmett Williams, eds., *Store Days: Documents from The Store, 1961, and Ray Gun Theater, 1962* (New York: Something Else Press, 1967), 7.

**41**

A letter that Oldenburg wrote in the summer of 1959 to Bernard "Bud" Scott, a minister at the Judson Church who oversaw the gallery, suggests that Oldenburg had taken charge of planning shows there for the upcoming year: letter to Bud Scott, 17 August 1959, Judson Church Archives, Elmer Holmes Bobst Library, New York University, New York. Dine has compared his input into planning the exhibition to Oldenburg's by saying, "He was a mature artist; I was a young man," and, "He had a clear idea. I just knew I wanted to be famous": Dine, telephone interview with author, 15 August 2000. Julia Blaut and Ellen H. Johnson have both also suggested that Oldenburg was the primary planner of

*Ray Gun*: Blaut, "A 'Painter's Theater': Jim Dine's Environments and Performances," in *Jim Dine: Walking Memory, 1959–1969,* ed. Germano Celant and Clare Bell (New York: Guggenheim Museum, 1999), 32–45; Johnson, *Claes Oldenburg,* Penguin New Art Series (Harmondsworth, U.K.: Penguin, 1971).

**42**

"Goo" can be seen in *The Smileing* [sic] *Workman,* the film that Stan Vanderbeek made with Dine in *The House.* Prints of the film are owned by the Museum of Modern Art, New York, and by Stan Vanderbeek's widow, Johanna Vanderbeek. The Ray Gun Spex appear to have been presented, in succession, on each of three nights "and never again": 29 February, 1 March, and 2 March. Ray Gun Spex tickets, Judson Church Archives.

**43**

Kiplinger, "Ray Gun," 11.

**44**

A[nne]. S[eelye]., "Reviews and Previews: New Names this Month: Ray Gun," *Artnews,* March 1960, 18; "Up-Beats," *Time,* 14 March 1960, 80.

**45**

The word *Gun* also appeared here; it is hidden in this photograph by the sculpture of the walking figure.

**46**

The photographs and my discussions with Claes Oldenburg and Patty Mucha (formerly Pat Muschinski Oldenburg) suggest that, although "Stan's film is . . . a bit more melodramatic" (Oldenburg), the filmed and live versions were similar: Claes Oldenburg, telephone interview, 15 June 2000; Patty Mucha, e-mail letter to the author, 9 June 2000. Of the live audiences, Oldenburg said, "Not only were they in the dark, but they had a great deal of difficulty seeing, because of a small opening to the room in which it was performed. The audience was in another room, and they had to look through a doorway." The performance, Oldenburg added, was originally to have taken place on Thompson Street: "We had planned to block the street at the moment of performance by stalling a car." Oldenburg interview in Richard Kostelanetz, *The Theatre of Mixed Means: An Introduction to Happenings, Kinetic Environments, and Other Mixed-Means Performances* (New York: Dial, 1968), 137, 139. Prints of the film

are owned by the Museum of Modern Art, New York; the Film-Makers' Cooperative, New York; and Stan Vanderbeek's widow, Johanna Vanderbeek.

**47**

Oldenburg, telephone interview.

**48**

Asked if this gun was a "Ray Gun," Oldenburg responded that it was "some kind of gun . . . a bit more realistic." Ibid.

**49**

"New Uses of the Human Image in Painting" (symposium, 2 December 1959), transcript. Judson Church Archives, p. 1. For more on Oldenburg's contemporary primitivism, see Haywood, "Heretical Alliance."

**50**

Michael Leja, *Reframing Abstract Expressionism* (New Haven, Conn.: Yale University Press, 1993).

**51**

Kiplinger, "Ray Gun," 1; "Up-Beats," 80.

**52**

Haywood, "Heretical Alliance," 199; Oldenburg, "Judson Gallery," note in Oldenburg artist file, Museum of Modern Art, New York; Oldenburg, telephone interview. That the money, mostly unsigned, was Oldenburg's project has been confirmed in my interviews with Oldenburg and Dine (Oldenburg, telephone interview; Dine, telephone interview, 15 August 2000). Some of this money is held in the Judson Church Archives.

**53**

Haywood, "Heretical Alliance," 199. Ray Gun's peripheral address to consumption suggests that the emphatic materiality of *The Street* was a negative cogitation on increasing abstraction not only in the city but also in consumerism. Consumerism was the conceptual foundation for Oldenburg's next major project, *The Store.*

**54**

Oldenburg, telephone interview. Oldenburg added that this reading may have been a passage in Swedish. Oldenburg and Dine—along with Richard O Tyler, Robert Whitman, and possibly Red Grooms—also used the church's stencil machine to turn out a series of absurdist comic books. Although rendered in a variety of styles, all of the comics used chaotic, childlike line-drawing techniques and refused ordinary narrative. Oldenburg's *Ray Gun Poems,* for example, is a chaos of vague figures, empty speech bubbles, and scrawled lettering, all suspended at the edge of legibility. (Copies of these comics are held in the Judson Church Archives.)

**55**

The recent remark is from Oldenburg, telephone interview. Oldenburg made the earlier comment while speaking of the performance of his happening *Injun* in Dallas in 1962: Claes Oldenburg, interview by John Jones, 1965, transcript, p. B6, Archives of American Art.

**56**

Oldenburg and Williams, *Store Days,* 8.

**57**

Oldenburg quotation ibid., 8. Jack Kerouac, *On the Road* (New York: Viking, 1957; New York: Penguin, 1991), 194; references to the madman prophet appear on pages 35, 55, and 137. Page references are to the Penguin edition.

**58**

"Help to Stamp Out Mental Health!" advertisement, *Village Voice,* 22 April 1959, 12; J. H. Livingston, "The Search for a Way Out by a Way-Out Magazine," *Village Voice,* 29 April 1959, 3.

**59**

"Statement of Robert Moses," 1; Jean Shepherd, "Bring on the Concrete, We're Behind You, Bob," *Village Voice,* 22 April 1959, 12; John Wilcock, "All Right, Men, Go Out and Police the Area," editorial, *Village Voice,* 30 April 1958, 4.

**60**

John Wilcock, "Greenwich Village, 1927–1957: How Many Times Have They Buried Its Bohemians?" *Village Voice,* 1 January 1958, 16 (this is the same issue in which Moses extolled the "common sense" of the roadway plan); "Abrams on the Village: Sameness Is a Bore, Variety a Strength," *Village Voice,* 19 February 1958, 1 (ellipsis original to the article; even in 1958, a double entendre in "straighten out . . . Gay Street" would have been audible to many Village readers); David McReynolds, "Save the Village," *Village Voice,* 23 March 1960, 12.

**61**

Rose, *Claes Oldenburg,* 38.

**62**

Oldenburg, telephone interview; notebook as reprinted in Oldenburg and Williams, *Store Days,* 44.

**63**

"The slogan of RAYGUN is 'Annihilate-Illuminate.' RAYGUN is both destructive and creative." Jim Dine and Claes Oldenburg, "Spring Calendar at the Judson Gallery" [1960], typescript, n.p., Judson Church Archives. Ray Gun advertisement, *Village Voice,* 27 January 1960, 11. See Oldenburg notebook pages reproduced in Rose, "Origins, Life and Times," 51, 54. Jim Dine's comic called *A Ray Gun Cut Out Coloring and a Real Love Kind of Deluxe Book,* also in the Judson Church Archives, repeats the phrase.

**64**

The whiteness of the buildings had a metaphoric racial register as well. In America in the late 1950s, the population of cities was becoming darker-skinned. In New York, white flight after *Brown v. Board of Education* was accompanied by a giant migration from Puerto Rico. In at least some cases, renewal made neighborhoods whiter by pricing out old residents.

**65**

This barrier literally blocked the flow of physical movement around it: photographs reveal that Oldenburg and Muschinski, for example, had to remove it in order to perform *Snapshots from the City.* The adjacent human figure appears to have been removed for some performances but not others.

**66**

Raymond R. Rubinow, chair of the Joint Emergency Committee to Close Washington Square to Traffic, quoted in Grutzner, "Strategy Revamped"; architecture critic Douglas Haskell quoted in "Village Hears Gibe at 'Traffic Hounds,'" *New York Times,* 1 April 1958; Shirley Hayes, letter to the editor, *Village Voice,* 9 April 1958, 4.

**67**

Claes Oldenburg, typed notebook page, a copy of which is held in the Ellen H. Johnson Papers, Archives of American Art. The note was probably made in 1963. Ellipses and parentheses original.

**68**

The Judson installation was almost entirely destroyed. One small cutout of a car (visible at upper right in fig. 1.6) was reused at the Reuben show. Another small work now called *Car II (Wall Piece)* and held at the Museum Ludwig in Cologne also appears to have been part of the original Judson installation (visible in fig. 1.7).

**69**

See Rose, *Claes Oldenburg,* 41.

**70**

"Oldenburg, of Ray-Gun Fame, to Exhibit at Reuben Gallery," press release, Judson Church Archives. Ellipses original to press release. Oldenburg's description emphasizes another effect of this revisioning of *The Street,* in a concluding phrase that was excised from the press release: "All components of the Street can be purchased separately": Oldenburg's notebooks, 1960, as quoted in *Claes Oldenburg: An Anthology* (New York: Guggenheim Museum, 1995), 50. Indeed, unlike at the Judson, the sculptures at the Reuben—and they really are sculptures—were for sale. There were not many buyers: Anita Reuben, the gallery's director, remarked in a November 2000 telephone interview that, at most, they may have sold one small piece. *Street Figure in Grey Planes* still bears a label on the back pricing it at $150, although it is possible that this dates from a slightly later exhibition, such as the *New Media—New Forms* show at the Martha Jackson Gallery in June 1960, in which this work was shown separately. For more on Oldenburg's use of the word *mamagangers,* see Richard H. Axsom and David Platzker, *Printed Stuff: Prints, Posters, and Ephemera by Claes Oldenburg: A Catalogue Raisonné, 1958–1996* (New York: Hudson Hills Press, 1997), 52.

**71**

This issue of the *Voice* was the very one in which the *Ray Gun* advertisement (fig. 1.16) appeared.

**72**

A copy of this notation, dated 1963, is held in the Johnson Papers. Many of the ellipses are original to the copy in the archives.

**73**

*Manhattan Telephone Directory* (New York: New York Telephone Company, 1958–59); and "Orpheum Theatre," advertisement, *Village Voice*, 24 December 1958, 19.

**74**

*Manhattan Telephone Directory*, 483. The listings are virtually identical in the 1959–60 and the 1961–62 editions.

**75**

Rose, *Claes Oldenburg*, 43. Letter to the author from Oldenburg's studio, signed Anu Vikram, 10 November 2000: "Mr. Oldenburg found the burlap bags he used to make *Street Head* on the street, and the address '5 W 11' was already painted on them when he found them." Claes Oldenburg, letter to the author, 20 November 2000: "The burlap bags used for *Street Head* were garbage bags of that time, marked with the address where they were left to be emptied each day."

**76**

In that year, the current First Presbyterian Church of New York was built, stretching west from Fifth Avenue and occupying the place where 5 West Eleventh would lie. The first address on the odd-numbered side of West Eleventh Street is the church house at number 7. It is remotely possible that Oldenburg simply misremembered the address where he found this, and that what we see is only a fragment of 115 West Eleventh Street or some other longer address.

**77**

Oldenburg lived in 1960 at 330 East Fourth Street (Rose, *Claes Oldenburg*, 199), and the Empire Burlap Bag Company was located at 231 East Ninth (*Manhattan Telephone Directory*, 483).

**78**

Rose, *Claes Oldenburg*, 199; Oldenburg, interview by Cummings, 70–73.

**79**

David B. Sicilia, "Wanamaker's," in *The Encyclopedia of New York City*, ed. Kenneth T. Jackson (New Haven, Conn.: Yale University Press, 1995), 1235.

**80**

"New Uses of the Human Image," Judson Church Archives, pp. 6, 5, 1, 7, 4.

**81**

Haywood, noting this lineage, observes that Oldenburg later described himself as a "post-Pollock" artist. Haywood, "Heretical Alliance," 197–98.

**82**

Oldenburg has recently indicated that he made *Lady* in 1957: e-mail letter to the author, 24 July 2003. Barbara Rose, *Claes Oldenburg*, 29, notes that the work was both exhibited and destroyed in 1959.

**83**

Clement Greenberg, "Abstract and Representational," *Arts Digest*, 1 November 1954, 7. In Greenberg's view, this literalness was dialectically engaged, in the best modernist art, with a persistent (if thin) pictorial depth. See especially Greenberg, "Modernist Painting" (1960), in *The New Art: A Critical Anthology*, ed. Gregory Battcock (New York: E. P. Dutton, 1966), 100–110.

**84**

Allan Kaprow, "The Legacy of Jackson Pollock," *Artnews*, October 1958, 26, 57. By 1959, Kaprow and Oldenburg were both associated with the Judson.

**85**

As Kaprow suggests, Oldenburg and his peers inherited from Pollock not only an insistent materiality but specifically a materiality of the ordinary world. In *Full Fathom Five* (1947), for example, Pollock placed nails, cigarettes, keys, and coins into the painted surface. It is important to note here that Pollock's painting, while "abstract" in respect to its lack of figures or objects, was, in one view at least, fundamentally resistant to abstraction, asserting its own materiality over mimesis and legibility. See discussion of this terminological difficulty in the introduction to the present volume.

**86**

Quoted, without citation, in Rose, *Claes Oldenburg*, 53.

**87**

Oldenburg's debt to the literalness of Abstract Expressionist painting is what allowed him, even

as he was making the semi-mimetic sculptural reliefs for *The Store* in 1961, to remark about that previous movement, "By parodying its corn I have (miracle!) come back to its authenticity!" and to add, "I feel as if Pollock is sitting on my shoulder or rather crouching in my pants!" Quoted, without citation, ibid.

**88**

Oldenburg has admitted an interest in Marcel Duchamp, who, along with Kurt Schwitters, defined the American reception of Dada. He mentioned his discovery of Dubuffet in his interview by Cummings, 63–65. See also Sophie Berrebi, "*Paris Circus* New York Junk: Jean Dubuffet and Claes Oldenburg, 1959–1962," *Art History* 29, no. 1 (February 2006): 79–107.

**89**

*Village Voice*, 3 February 1960, 1.

**90**

J. B. Jackson, "Signs of Life," *Landscape* 14, no. 2 (Winter 1964–65): 1.

**91**

Kevin Lynch, *The Image of the City*, Publications of the Joint Center for Urban Studies (Cambridge, Mass.: MIT Press, 1960).

**92**

Kevin Lynch and Donald Appleyard, eds., *Signs in the City* (Cambridge, Mass.: MIT Press, 1963), 76, 28–30.

**93**

Choay sees modernist planning as an attempt to beat the chaos of the nineteenth-century city, but she also reads both of these urban types in opposition to preindustrial built environments, where plans coherently expressed systems of belief. Françoise Choay, "Urbanism and Semiology," in *Meaning in Architecture*, ed. Charles Jencks and George Baird (New York: George Braziller, 1970), 34.

**94**

Jackson, "Signs of Life," 1. Signs are rarely if ever visible in Le Corbusier's drawings for the city; the signification of the plan is so total and efficient, at least in its utopian conception, as to make signs nothing but excess clutter.

**95**

In the last forty years, architectural critics have pointed out that modernist architecture never really privileged function over form. Robert Venturi, Denise Scott Brown, and Steven Izenour's landmark work *Learning from Las Vegas* (Cambridge, Mass.: MIT Press, 1972) was a direct attack on modernist architecture as essentially symbolic. Peter Blake's brilliant *Form Follows Fiasco: Why Modern Architecture Hasn't Worked* (Boston: Little, Brown, 1977) criticizes modernist architecture for its failure to cope with the inevitable appearance of the unwanted porch umbrella or little scrawl of graffiti. The problem with modern architecture, we could say, was just that design was always (and against its own purported aims) in service of a total self-signification.

**96**

See especially Pamela M. Lee, *Object to Be Destroyed: The Work of Gordon Matta-Clark* (Cambridge, Mass.: MIT Press, 2000). No doubt most artists who have addressed the city over the past four decades have done so without much knowledge of *The Street*; they have simply responded to similar developments. In Oldenburg's own later works—I am thinking of the monumental sculptures—we can recognize his early desire to encourage the city's illogic. This interest is now reclothed, however, in the smooth language of commodity exchange, its playfulness having defeated its once insistent disruption.

**97**

Tom McDonough, "Situationist Space," in *Guy Debord and the Situationist International* (Cambridge, Mass.: MIT Press, 2002), 246. See also Simon Sadler, *The Situationist City* (Cambridge, Mass.: MIT Press, 1998).

**98**

Quoted in McDonough, "Situationist Space," 243.

**99**

Henri Lefebvre, *Le Droit à la ville* (Paris: Anthropos, 1968), reprinted as "The Right to the City," in *Writings on Cities*, ed. and trans. Eleonore Kofman and Elizabeth Lebas (Oxford: Blackwell, 1996), 167. Debord's own words on the city are often quite similar to Lefebvre's. Guy Debord, *La Société du spectacle* (Paris: Buchet/Chastel, 1967), reprinted as *The Society of the Spectacle,* trans. Donald Nicholson-Smith (New York: Zone, 1995).

## CHAPTER TWO
### The Disappearance of Objects

**1**

John Ashbery, "Paris Notes," *Art International*, 20 December 1962, 51 (emphasis original); F[airfield] P[orter], "Jasper Johns," *Artnews,* January 1958, 20; Stuart Preston, "Haseltine Views of Italy at Cooper Union," *New York Times,* 25 January 1958.

**2**

Leo Steinberg, "Jasper Johns," *Metro* 4–5 (May 1962): 87–109, reprinted as Steinberg, "Jasper Johns: The First Seven Years of His Art," in *Other Criteria: Confrontations with Twentieth-Century Art* (Oxford, U.K.: Oxford University Press, 1972). Alan R. Solomon's catalogue essay for Johns's first retrospective took a similar line: "The ambiguity in his sculptures," Solomon wrote in *Jasper Johns* (New York: Jewish Museum, 1964), 18, "is overwhelming." One different trend in the literature was a late formalism, which appeared primarily in the 1960s. According to this line of interpretation, Johns found a way forward from Abstract Expressionism by preserving the flatness of the canvas even while readmitting illusion. He pulled off this trick by selecting flat subjects, such as targets, maps, and flags. Greenberg himself gave grudging nods to Johns on these terms: Clement Greenberg, "After Abstract Expressionism," *Art International,* October 1962, reprinted in *Clement Greenberg: The Collected Essays and Criticism,* ed. John O'Brian (Chicago: University of Chicago Press, 1993), 4:121–34; and Greenberg, "Post Painterly Abstraction," *Art International,* Summer 1964, 63–65. It was Sidney Tillim, however, who first fully articulated this argument, in "Ten Years of Jasper Johns," *Arts Magazine,* April 1964, 22–26. Later, Rosalind Krauss—in an early mode—also found Johns interesting for formalist reasons; she added that Johns's gray paintings performed the end of pictorial illusion. Krauss, "Jasper Johns," *Lugano Review* 1, no. 2 (1965): 84–113; Krauss, "Jasper Johns: The Functions of Irony," *October* 2 (Summer 1976): 91–99.

**3**

Several of these analyses adopted semiotic language, about which I write more below. Jonathan Weinberg, "It's in the Can: Jasper Johns and the Anal Society," *Genders* 1 (March 1988): 50; Esther Levinger, "Jasper Johns: Painted Words," *Visible Language* 23, nos. 2–3 (1989): 286; Charles Harrison and Fred Orton, "Jasper Johns: Meaning What You See," *Art History* 7, no. 1 (March 1984): 81. See also Rolf-Dieter Herrmann, "Jasper Johns' Ambiguity: Exploring the Hermeneutical Implications," *Arts Magazine*, November 1977, 124–29. Starting in the 1960s, some scholars attempted to understand this resistance to representation as a Wittgensteinian exploration of the conventional quality of meanings; Johns did read Wittgenstein in the period. See, for example, Rosalind Krauss, "Jasper Johns," 1965; Peter Higginson, "Jasper's Non-Dilemma: A Wittgensteinian Approach," *New Lugano Review* 10 (1976): 53–60; and Jessica Prinz, *Art Discourse/Discourse in Art* (New Brunswick, N.J.: Rutgers University Press, 1991).

**4**

Fred Orton, *Figuring Jasper Johns* (Cambridge, Mass.: Harvard University Press, 1994), 86, 212. Orton also wrote a text to accompany a show of Johns's sculpture, *Jasper Johns: The Sculptures* (Leeds, U.K.: Centre for the Study of Sculpture at the Henry Moore Institute, 1996). For another general account linking the resistance to legibility in Johns's work with subjectivity, see Isabelle Loring Wallace, "Signification and the Subject: The Art of Jasper Johns" (Ph.D. diss., Bryn Mawr College, 1999). Kenneth E. Silver, "Modes of Disclosure: The Construction of Gay Identity and the Rise of Pop Art," in *Hand-Painted Pop: Art in Transition, 1955–1962,* ed. Paul Schimmel (Los Angeles: Museum of Contemporary Art, 1992), 179–203. Among Katz's publications on the topic, see the following: Jonathan D. Katz, "The Art of Code: Jasper Johns and Robert Rauschenberg," in *Significant Others: Creativity and Intimate* Partnership, ed. Whitney Chadwick and Elizabeth de Courtivron (London: Thames and Hudson, 1993), 189–208; Katz, "Opposition, Inc.:

The Homosexualization of Postwar American Art" (Ph.D. diss., Northwestern University, 1995); Katz, "Lovers and Divers: Interpictorial Dialog in the Work of Jasper Johns and Robert Rauschenberg," *Frauen, Kunst, Wissenschaft* 13 (June 1998): 16–31; Katz, "Dismemberment: Jasper Johns and the Body Politic," in *Performing the Body/Performing the Text*, ed. Amelia Jones and Andrew Stephenson (London: Routledge, 1999), 170–85. Katz's forthcoming book is called *The Homosexualization of American Art: Jasper Johns, Robert Rauschenberg and the Collective Closet* (University of Chicago Press).

**5**

Exceptions to this trend include Jonathan Weinberg's identification of anal references in the works, and Jonathan D. Katz's identification of references to homosexual culture and of jokes shared with Robert Rauschenberg, his partner in the years around 1960. See previous note.

**6**

Fredric Jameson as quoted in Hal Foster, "The Passion of the Sign," in *The Return of the Real* (Cambridge, Mass.: MIT Press, 1996), 77, citing Jameson, "Periodizing the Sixties," in *The 60s without Apology*, ed. Sohnya Sayers et al. (Minneapolis: University of Minnesota Press, 1984), 200.

**7**

In applying Saussurian language to consumerism, Foster runs into inevitable confusions (inherited from the hyperbolic taxonomy of the Saussurian language itself): for example, is the consumer object itself signifier or referent? One result of these ambiguities is that Foster seems to end up arguing that recent developments in capitalism have hastened the exchange of objects, while somehow leaving meanings to the side. For reasons that will become clear, it seems to me more accurate to say—almost to the contrary—that it is meanings that are exchanged with new freedom, and their material supports that have grown more incidental. (The claim that Johns's numbers and letters appear without signifieds is in any case a dubious one even within Saussurian logic: although absent any particular *referents*, the figures are still capable of signifying the concepts of enumeration or spelling.)

**8**

Dore Ashton, "New York Commentary: Acceleration in Discovery and Consumption," *Studio International*, May 1964, 212–15; "The Older, the Younger," *Newsweek*, 24 February 1964, 82–83; "Catcher of the Eye," *Time*, 4 December 1964, 84–87.

**9**

Stuart Preston, "Art: Jasper Johns Retrospective Show," *New York Times*, 15 February 1964; Greenberg, "After Abstract Expressionism," 127; "Catcher of the Eye"; Fairfield Porter, "The Education of Jasper Johns," *Artnews*, February 1964, 62. Porter, as we have seen, was thrilled at Johns's first show.

**10**

Quoted in Grace Glueck, "'Once Established,' Says Jasper Johns, 'Ideas Can Be Discarded,'" *New York Times*, 16 October 1977, reprinted in Kirk Varnedoe, ed., *Jasper Johns: Writings, Sketchbook Notes, Interviews* (New York: Museum of Modern Art, 1996), 163.

**11**

Jasper Johns, interview by David Sylvester, recorded for the BBC in June, 1965, in Varnedoe, *Jasper Johns: Writings*, 121; "His Heart Belongs to Dada," *Time*, 4 May 1959, 58.

**12**

The particularity of Johns's sculptures is one of their chief means of emphasizing their materiality: their distinguishing details underscore their status as things. For a discussion of the word *abstraction*, see the introduction to the present volume.

**13**

In *Jasper Johns' Paintings and Sculptures, 1954–1974: "The Changing Focus of the Eye"* (Ann Arbor, Mich.: UMI Research Press, 1975), 51, Roberta Bernstein has indicated that Johns had tried earlier to make a plaster sculpture of a lightbulb attached to a wire, abandoning it after finding it too fragile.

**14**

Fred Orton provides an excellent profile of Sculp-Metal in *Johns: The Sculptures*, 25–26.

**15**

It is unclear how exactly Johns made *Light Bulb I*, and the artist does not remember. Fred Orton, *Johns: The Sculptures*, 20, proposes that the Sculp-Metal was layered against a mold, while Roberta

Bernstein, in *Johns' Paintings and Sculptures*, 51, suggests that Johns coated the material over a positive replica he had built. This latter suggestion seems unlikely, given Bernstein's observation that the bulb is so light as to approximate the weight of a true lightbulb.

**16**

Some photographs, taken from above, seem to deliberately foreshorten the bulky base. The work's apparent heaviness is ironized by the bulb's actual lightness, and its separability from the base.

**17**

Harold Rosenberg, "Jasper Johns: Things the Mind Already Knows," *Vogue* 1 (February 1964): 203; Irving Sandler, "In the Art Galleries," *New York Post Magazine*, 22 December 1963, 14. It is unclear which sculpture Sandler is addressing. He mistakenly calls it *Cast Light Bulb*. Fairfield Porter, "The Education of Jasper Johns," 62. Andrew Forge, "The Emperor's Flag," *New Statesman*, 11 December 1964, 938. Roberta Bernstein (*Johns' Paintings and Sculptures*, 53) also wrote of *Flashlight I* that it is displayed "as if it were a rare, precious object, rather than a familiar, pedestrian household item."

**18**

Jasper Johns, sketchbook A, 8, c. 1960, photographically reprinted in Varnedoe, *Jasper Johns: Writings*, 27.

**19**

"I think my thinking is perhaps dependent on real things and is not very sophisticated abstract thinking," Johns remarked. "I think I'm not willing to accept the representation of a thing as being the real thing, and I am frequently unwilling to work with the representation of the thing as, you know, as standing for the real thing. I like what I see to be real, or to be my idea of what is real. And I think I have a kind of resentment against illusion when I can recognize it. Also, a large part of my work has been involved with the painting as object, as a real thing in itself. And in the face of that 'tragedy,' so far my general development, it seems to me, has moved in the direction of using real things as painting." Johns, interview by Sylvester, 18–20. Oldenburg indicated a similar "preference for the thing rather than the picture of the thing": interview in Richard Kostelanetz, *The Theatre of Mixed Means: An Introduction to Happenings, Kinetic Environments, and Other Mixed-Means Performances* (New York: Dial, 1968), 155.

**20**

Of course there is an odd contradiction between this archaeological (and synecdochical) quality of the sculptures and the literalness that seems (along with this first quality) to have so preoccupied critics. Both properties, however, are very much at work in these sculptures. It may be, in fact, that Johns's sculptures derive their funereal voice in part from the very fact of their emphatic literalness, their appearing as nothing but form and matter.

**21**

Advertisement for the Ad Council's *Miracle of America,* a publication promoting consumption, *Hardware Age: The Hardware Dealers' Magazine* 165, no. 3 (1950): 235.

**22**

On "You 'Auto' Buy," see coverage in the *New York Times* on 23, 25, and 26 April 1958; and also David Halberstam, *The Fifties* (New York: Villard, 1993). Quotation from Vance Packard, *The Waste Makers* (New York: David McKay, 1960), 17. John A. Kouwenhoven, "Waste Not, Have Not: A Clue to American Prosperity," *Harper's Magazine,* March 1959, 72–81.

**23**

See, for example, Rita Reif, "Exhibition at Coliseum Will Offer Vivid Picture of the Russian Way of Life," *New York Times,* 26 June 1959, 28; and Peter Kihss, "Soviet Fair Open; Kozlov and Nixon Stress Peace Aim," *New York Times,* 30 June 1959. See also Halberstam, *Fifties,* 723–24.

**24**

David Potter, *People of Plenty* (Chicago: University of Chicago Press, 1954).

**25**

Marguerite C. Burk, in *Consumption Economics: A Multidisciplinary Approach* (New York: John Wiley & Sons, 1968), cites the U.S. Department of Commerce's 1966 report *The National Income and Product Accounts of the United States, 1929–1965,* according to which, in 1958 dollars, per capita consumption expenditures were $1,178 in 1940, $1,520 in 1950, and $1,749 in 1960.

**26**

Vance Packard, *The Hidden Persuaders* (New York: David McKay, 1957), 20; and Packard, *Waste Makers,* 10. Consumer spending was further hastened by the arrival of bank-issued credit cards, which could be used in any number of stores. An advertisement for Chase Manhattan credit cards trumpeted them in 1958 as "a brand new way to shop without cash!": *New York Times,* 22 October 1958. See chapter 14, "Selling on the Never Never," in Packard, *Waste Makers.* For a history of credit cards, see Lendol Calder, *Financing the American Dream: A Cultural History of Consumer Credit* (Princeton, N.J.: Princeton University Press, 1999), especially 1–16.

**27**

Gilbert Burck and Sanford Parker, "What a Country!" *Fortune,* October 1956, 128, 130.

**28**

Lil Picard, "Jasper Johns," *Das Kunstwerk,* November 1963. An English translation of the article, from which this text is quoted, appears in the Leo Castelli Gallery Papers at the Archives of American Art, Smithsonian Institution, Washington, D.C. Quoted passage is from page 2 of the typescript. According to Lilian Tone, "Chronology," *Jasper Johns: A Retrospective* (New York: Museum of Modern Art, 1996), 386n127, this translation was the work of Henry F. Odell.

**29**

David Riesman, "The Nylon War," *Common Cause* 4, no. 6 (1951): 379–85, reprinted in Riesman, *Abundance for What? And Other Essays* (Garden City, N.Y.: Doubleday, 1964); Packard, *Hidden Persuaders;* Packard, *The Status Seekers: An Exploration of Class Behaviour in America and the Hidden Barriers That Affect You, Your Community, Your Future* (New York: David McKay, 1959); Packard, *Waste Makers;* John Kenneth Galbraith, *The Affluent Society* (Boston: Houghton Mifflin, 1958).

**30**

In 1956, the gross national product was about 45 percent larger than it had been in 1950: "'57: Advertising's Biggest Year Ever," *Printers' Ink,* 8 February 1957.

**31**

Ibid.; Daniel Horowitz, *Vance Packard and American Social Criticism* (Chapel Hill: University of North Carolina Press, 1994), 104.

**32**

Richard W. Pollay, ed., *Information Sources in Advertising History* (Westport, Conn.: Greenwood, 1979). The forty-three books from the 1950s represent over 40 percent of the 105 volumes listed in Pollay's accounting of all fictional books related to advertising. The popularity, in particular, of the advertising murder mystery suggests that readers understood the power of advertising as excitingly threatening.

**33**

A third, more epistemic development is the topic of the next section of this chapter.

**34**

Packard, *Waste Makers,* 42, 45, 43. Ellipses in the final quotation are original.

**35**

Joseph J. Seldin, *The Golden Fleece: Selling the Good Life to Americans* (New York: Macmillan, 1963), 146, 156.

**36**

Packard, *Waste Makers,* 68, 53.

**37**

Ibid., 120.

**38**

Johns, interview by Sylvester, 113–14.

**39**

The most useful sources in this search were *Collector's Digest Flashlights* (Gas City, Ind.: L-W Book Sales, 1995); Stuart Schneider, *Collecting Flashlights: With Value Guide* (Atglen, Pa.: Schiffer, 1996); various issues of *Hardware Age: The Hardware Dealer's Magazine;* and the N. W. Ayer Advertising Agency Collection, National Museum of American History, Smithsonian Institution, Washington, D.C.

**40**

Sears, Roebuck, & Co. catalogue, Philadelphia ed., Spring–Summer 1950, 997A; Sears, Roebuck, & Co. catalogue, Philadelphia ed., Spring–Summer 1955, 1060; Sears, Roebuck, & Co. catalogue, Philadelphia ed., Spring–Summer 1957, 1053; Sears, Roebuck, & Co. catalogue, library ed., 1961, 1411. Copies of these catalogues are held in the collection of the Smithsonian Institution Libraries Annex, Washington, D.C.

**41**

*Hardware Age: The Hardware Dealer's Magazine* 183, no. 5 (1959): 98.

**42**

The bronze version of *Flashlight III*, although usually dated 1958, was not cast until 1987. Orton, *Johns: The Sculptures,* 20; Jasper Johns, letter to the author, 5 August 2003. See the very helpful discussion of the making of these works in Orton, *Johns: The Sculptures,* 23–25; Orton notes, for example, that Johns deliberately "interrupted and distressed" the surface of *Flashlight II.*

**43**

*N.Y.C. Telephone Directory: Manhattan Yellow Pages* (n.p., 1950); *Manhattan Yellow Pages* (New York: New York Telephone Company, 1961). Surveying a sample of the twelve streets in the district most populated by hardware businesses, I discovered a decline of twenty-six listings between 1950 and 1961, a fall of 30 percent; this loss was led by an especially dramatic decline of wholesalers on Warren Street and Park Place. The streets in the sample: Broadway (to number 400), Chambers, Duane, Fulton, Greenwich, Hudson, Park Place, Park Row Reade, Walker, Warren, and West Broadway (to number 300).

**44**

In the winter of 1958, Johns was living at 278 Pearl Street; in March he moved six blocks south to 128 Front Street, where he remained until 1963: see Tone, "Chronology," 129. For a more detailed discussion of Johns's and Rauschenberg's homes, see chapter 3 in the present volume. The stores near Fulton Street had been Richard Schwimmer, at 37 Wall Street, and W & J Tiebout, at 64 Front Street. Each had been the only hardware store on its street. *N.Y.C. Telephone Directory.* The store on Park Row had been Patterson Brothers, according to "Old Hardware Store Bows to Suburban Competition," *New York Times,* 16 January 1959. Jane Jacobs was probably referring to Patterson Brothers when she wrote in *The Death and Life of Great American Cities* (New York: Vintage, 1961), 154, regarding the Wall Street area, "The district used to have one of the best hardware stores in New York, but a few years ago it could no longer make ends meet, and closed."

**45**

The figure is supplied by a hardware executive cited in "Optimism Is Voiced by Hardware Group," *New York Times,* 13 July 1960.

**46**

*N.Y.C. Telephone Directory,* 1950; *Manhattan Yellow Pages,* 1961.

**47**

Walker Evans, "'Downtown': A Last Look Backward," *Fortune,* October 1956, 157; "Wall Street's Other Boom," *Fortune,* October 1956, 163. For more on the transformation of this area, see chapter 3 in the present volume.

**48**

Packard mentions flashlights explicitly in *The Waste Makers* (60), noting that General Electric had recently deliberately shortened the lives of its flashlight bulbs. Quotations, ibid., 317, 290.

**49**

By way of comparison, note the similarity of Packard's complaints to the classical Marxist materialism of Raymond Williams, who—although almost certainly unknown to both Johns and Packard—published an essay in 1960 called "Advertising: The Magic System." Williams observed that advertising encourages consumers to buy goods not for their materially driven utility but rather to appear forward-looking, for example, or manly. The frequent claims, then, that the society is too materialist are flatly wrong: "Our society is quite evidently not materialist enough." Williams, *Problems in Materialism and Culture* (London: New Left Books, 1980), 185.

**50**

There has been a great deal of inconclusive discussion in the art-historical literature over the reasons for Johns's selection of beer cans as a subject. Often quoted is Johns's own remark that Willem de Kooning, in a moment of frustration, suggested that Leo Castelli (Johns's dealer) could sell anything—even "two beer cans." Johns claims to have been inspired by the idea, which, for reasons he did not indicate, "seemed to me to fit in perfectly with what I was doing." Gene R. Swenson, "What Is Pop Art? Part II," *Artnews,* February 1964, reprinted in Varnedoe, *Jasper Johns: Writings,* 94.

**51**

*Beer Consumption in the American Home, 1949–1958* (New York: American Can Company, c. 1959), 12 (consulted in the library of the National Museum of American History). Even bottles in the period became increasingly disposable. While no-deposit bottles represented less than 5 percent of the bottled-beer market in 1949, their share had grown by 1958 to nearly 20 percent (ibid.). One company advertised "No-Deposit, No-Return Bottles" in 1959 with the words "ALWAYS BUY BEER IN BOTTLES YOU DON'T TAKE BACK": Owens-Illinois bottle advertisement, *Brewers Digest* 34, no. 6 (June 1959): 13.

**52**

See "First Aluminum-Canned Beer," *Modern Packaging,* September 1958, 106; "Aluminum Beer Cans Make U.S. Debut," *Modern Brewery Age* 59, no. 1 (1959): 28–30; "New Advances in Aluminum-Canned Beer," *Modern Packaging,* February 1959, 90; and N. E. Coe, "Aluminum Cans, Boxes, Drums, Cylinders," *Modern Packaging Encyclopedia Issue,* 1960, 341–42.

**53**

John Kouwenhoven, "The Beer Can by the Highway; or, Whatever Became of Emerson?" in *The Beer Can by the Highway: Essays on What's 'American' about America* (Garden City, N.Y.: Doubleday, 1961), 226, 221; this essay is a revised reprint of Kouwenhoven, "Waste Not, Have Not." Johns although born in 1930 and raised by various members of his extended family, was not poor as a child. For biographical information on Johns, see Jill Johnston, *Jasper Johns: Privileged Information* (New York: Thames and Hudson, 1996), especially chapter 6.

**54**

Packard, *Waste Makers,* 195 (statistic) and 42 (discussion of advertisement).

**55**

The advent of the beer can is discussed in Will Anderson, *The Beer Book: An Illustrated Guide to American Breweriana* (Princeton, N.J.: Pine Press, 1973), 56–57. For the report on the package contest, see *Modern Packaging* 9, no. 6 (February 1936): 98.

**56**

T. Jackson Lears reproduced this same advertisement, without comment, as a visual comparandum for *Painted Bronze (Ale Cans):* Lears, "'Out of

Control': Art and Accident in a Managerial Age,"
in *Off Limits: Rutgers University and the Avant-Garde,
1957–1963,* ed. Joan Marter (New Brunswick, N.J.:
Rutgers University Press, 1999), 60. The advertisement originally appeared in *Printers' Ink,* 27 February 1936, 8–9.

**57**

Jasper Johns, interview by Sylvester, 114. The ale
can did undergo a minor design change in 1956,
when the color of the label was brightened and
when "Ballantine's" became simply "Ballantine."
The ale bottle appears to have lost its apostrophe
and S somewhat later. These changes are made
evident in a comparison of advertisements in the
J. Walter Thompson Archive, Hartman Center for
Sales, Advertising, and Marketing History, Duke
University, Durham, N.C.

**58**

It is difficult to date these design changes precisely,
but Jack Martell's *Beer Can Collector's Bible* (Mat-
teson, Ill.: Greatlakes Living Press, 1976) indicates
that the new script and label shape appeared on
Ballantine Beer cans in approximately 1958, and
that the design was further simplified around 1960.
The Ballantine advertising files from the period
suggest that the major design change in the beer
can may have happened slightly earlier, in 1955:
Thompson Archive.

**59**

This history of Ballantine Draft and Ballantine
Bock is suggested by the approximate dating of
can designs in Martell, *Beer Can Collector's Bible.*
In 1960, Ballantine claimed its two chief products
were, respectively, "America's largest selling ale,"
and "the largest selling beer from Maine to Florida."
"It's Happened Again!" Ballantine Beer and Ale
advertisement, periodical and publication date not
indicated, Thompson Archive.

**60**

In addition to the classicism of its label, Ballantine
Ale was distinguished from Ballantine Beer in its
marketing by its description as "genuine." The beer
was instead described as "lively." Ballantine advertisements from the late 1950s, Thompson Archive.

**61**

Forge, "Emperor's Flag," 938.

**62**

This work, from an edition cast in 1960, has often
been dated in that earlier year. Fred Orton, however, has indicated that Johns did not paint it until
two years later, and the artist has confirmed this
dating. Orton, *Johns: The Sculptures,* 42; Johns, letter
to the author, 5 August 2003.

**63**

Seldin, *Golden Fleece,* 163.

**64**

Ibid., 165.

**65**

Larry Dobrow, *When Advertising Tried Harder: The
Sixties, the Golden Age of American Advertising*
(New York: Friendly Press, 1984). In Dobrow's view,
this decade "changed the language and look of
advertising forever" (2). Thomas Frank's excellent
history of advertising, *The Conquest of Cool: Business
Culture, Counterculture, and the Rise of Hip Consumerism* (Chicago: University of Chicago Press, 1997),
devotes itself to a slightly later development: the
industry's successful efforts to appropriate the
(anyway never pure) anticonsumerist impulses of
the 1960s counterculture in service of encouraging
further consumption.

**66**

Packard, *Hidden Persuaders,* 47.

**67**

Ibid., 48. Among the Freudian approaches Packard
enumerates are tales of cigarette preferences predicted from Rorschach tests, air conditioners sold
to "womb-seekers," and cakes made by women
wishing to express their fertility. Ibid., 51, 73, 77.

**68**

Ibid., 121. The beer Packard discusses here is
almost certainly not Ballantine, which was brewed
in Newark, not Chicago. Interestingly, however,
Ballantine's campaign in the 1950s did include
images of golfers and sailors, as well as partygoers
in evening gowns and tuxedos. The company was
careful, however, to balance such advertisements
with images of working-class figures as well. In a
series headlined "That's Ale, Brother!" Ballantine
sometimes showed pairs of men from different
classes, toasting together: in one such ad, a man in
a tweed overcoat, tie, and fedora shares the frame

with another in a T-shirt, thick jacket, and wool
cap. Hemingway and the novelist Eugene Burdick
were also used in Ballantine advertisements, their
literary credentials matched by an evidently active
masculinity: Thompson Archive.

**69**

Packard, *Hidden Persuaders,* 9.

**70**

Daniel J. Boorstin, *The Image: A Guide to Pseudo-
Events in America,* 25th anniversary ed. (New York:
Atheneum, 1987), 3, 192–93, originally published
as *The Image; or, What Happened to the American
Dream* (New York: Atheneum, 1962). Virtually all
the writing on consumerism in the period was
marred by sex stereotyping, in which female consumers are especially irrational.

**71**

Ibid., 204. Packard, *Hidden Persuaders,* 52, cited a
Buick advertising slogan: "It makes you feel like the
man you are."

**72**

Boorstin, *Image,* 199.

**73**

Boorstin's interest in place indicates that, even at
the time, at least one writer saw the departicularization of place and the abstraction of advertising
as related phenomena. Television statistic from
William E. Leuchtenburg, *A Troubled Feast: American
Society since 1945,* rev. ed. (Boston: Little, Brown,
1979), 67.

**74**

Quotations from Boorstin, *Image,* 204, 240.
Boorstin does provide some hints of why he is
so committed to the old order, in which reality
was more prominent. God, for one, has been
increasingly, and erroneously, dethroned by
aggrandizing illusions (see especially chapters 1
and 2), and the old class distinctions are also
now blurred (see especially chapter 5, 229–32).

**75**

"Catcher of the Eye," 84.

**76**

The model for the other can was bought in New
York. Fred Orton is one of the writers to have
pointed out the differing sources for the two cans
(Orton, *Figuring Jasper Johns,* 184–85), and Jasper

Johns has confirmed the distinction (Jasper Johns, letter to the author, 10 August 2000). Art historians have enjoyed cataloguing differences between the two cans, and it has frequently been stated, too, that the cans are different sizes, although this is not true: measurement reveals that both are 2 $^{11}/_{16}$ inches (6.8 cm) across and 4 $^3/_4$ inches (12 cm) high. This assertion about the differing heights seems to have been made first by Roberta Bernstein, who must have been looking at Johns's second rendering of the sculpture, which he made for himself in 1964, three years after selling the original. The cans in this second version do indeed stand at slightly different heights, at least when placed on their pedestal. There are a few other minor differences between the two editions as well: there is none of the dry yellow overpainting on the labels in the later version, and the steel-colored seams are made less conspicuous. For discussions of the differences between the cans, see Bernstein, *Johns' Paintings and Sculptures,* 53–54; and Wendy Weitman, "Jasper Johns: Ale Cans and Art," in *American Art of the 1960s,* Studies in Modern Art (New York: Museum of Modern Art, 1991), 40.

**77**

Weitman, "Ale Cans and Art," 40, indicates that Johns did all the work positively by hand. Quotation from Jasper Johns, letter to the author, 5 August 2003. Michael Crichton, *Jasper Johns,* rev. ed. (New York: Whitney Museum of American Art, 1994), 42, quotes Johns on the making of the plaster for *Painted Bronze (Ale Cans):* "Parts were made by casting, parts by building up from scratch, parts by molding, breaking, and then restoring. I was deliberately making it difficult to tell how it was made."

**78**

*Right* and *left* in *Painted Bronze (Ale Cans)* are terms particular to individual photographs. This is not only because the sculpture can be photographed from either side but also because the cans, which are separable from the base, can be rotated and switched.

**79**

See the discussion of the terms *abstraction* and *materiality* in the introduction to the present volume.

**80**

Jasper Johns, quoted in Joseph E. Young, "Jasper Johns: An Appraisal," *Art International,* September 1969, reprinted in Varnedoe, *Jasper Johns: Writings,* 134.

**81**

Johns told Leo Steinberg that he did not know that the bronze version of this sculpture would come from the foundry in three separate parts (although he also said he was not displeased with the results). This seems unlikely, since if Johns had wanted the sculpture to be whole, he could certainly have given the technicians a single positive from which to work. Steinberg, *Other Criteria,* 32.

**82**

Boorstin, *Image,* vii, 255, 240, 250.

**83**

We can't really see anything like forty-eight stars here. We can only just make out the overall design: six rows of eight. Three additional casts of the flag sculpture—in plaster, resin, and silver—were not made until 1986 and 1987: e-mail letter to the author from Johns's studio, signed Lynn Kearcher, 9 May 2008. See also n. 88.

**84**

John Yau, *The United States of Jasper Johns* (Cambridge, Mass.: Zoland, 1996), 8. Yau also sees this embodiment of a changeless world as somehow inherent in paintings as well. This may be true for some viewers of some paintings, particularly very famous paintings that become fixed icons in a culture, but I am arguing that Johns's works, like any good art, have a far more complicated relationship to the world of which they are a part. For a reading of *Flag* (1954–55) as expressing both the coercive and solicitous faces of hegemony, see Anne M. Wagner, "According to What," *Artforum,* November 2006, 272–77, 322.

**85**

"On the Scene," *Playboy,* March 1964, 123; Picard, "Jasper Johns," 4. See also Johns, interview by Sylvester, 114. Johns continued for decades to paint the old American flag, although flags with fifty stars also began appearing by the late 1960s. In some works, such as his drawing *Two Flags* of 1980, Johns has thematized the difference between the designs, including one flag of each kind.

**86**

Irving Sandler, "In the Art Galleries," *New York Post,* 1 March 1964.

**87**

Although most flags seem to have been made of cotton well into the 1960s, nylon flags were available by 1959. Whitney Smith, the Flag Research Center, Winchester, Mass., e-mail letter to the author, August 26, 2007, citing *A Catalogue of Marine Flags* (Barrington, R.I.: Ships Store, 1959–60), 27. When Sears introduced their nylon flags in 1967, they advertised them as "lightweight"; earlier, they had sold "durable, heavyweight cotton" American flags. Sears, Roebuck & Co. catalogue, Minneapolis ed., Spring–Summer 1967, 687; Sears, Roebuck, & Co. catalogue, Philadelphia ed., Spring–Summer 1955, 929.

**88**

Fred Orton (*Johns: The Sculptures,* 27) points out that the block shapes are formed by stamp and newsprint. Johns has described the processes in this way: "I made the first plaster in a moulage that I took from the original Sculp-metal piece. It was made so that the edition of four bronzes could be sandcast from it. Later [in the 1980s], technicians took another mold from the original to make the resin version, and a wax was cast in that mold for the silver cast. The same mold was probably used for the plaster with wooden frame but I don't really remember." Johns, letter to the author, 5 August 2003. The Sculp-Metal flag is in the Rauschenberg collection, and Calvin Tomkins indicates that Johns made it for his partner. He adds that Johns has recently had the silver cast hanging in his own home in Connecticut. Calvin Tomkins, "The Mind's Eye: The Merciless Originality of Jasper Johns," *New Yorker,* 11 December 2006.

**89**

Leo Steinberg observed the object quality of the face casts early on: "They were stowed away on that upper shelf like a standard commodity." Leo Steinberg, "Contemporary Art and the Plight of Its Public," *Harper's Magazine,* March 1962, 36. Roberta Bernstein, in *Johns' Paintings and Sculptures,* 219n53, records that it was Fanny Stevenson who served as the model. Jonathan D. Katz, "Dismemberment," 183; for an argument related to Katz's, see Gavin

Butt, "Bodies of Evidence: Queering Disclosure in the Art of Jasper Johns," in *Between You and Me: Queer Disclosures in the New York Art World, 1948-1963* (Durham, N.C.: Duke University Press, 2005), 136-52.

**90**

Roni Feinstein, "New Thoughts for Jasper Johns' Sculpture," *Arts Magazine,* April 1980, 139-45. This grounding of the commodity—terrain of the newly ascendant sign—in the register of the body may be, as Hal Foster has suggested of body works by artists such as Vito Acconci, an expression of a desire to secure the sign in the real or the natural. I mean to suggest here that for Johns, the procedures have more specific engagements. Foster, *Return of the Real,* chapter 3.

**91**

Although I have been at pains in this chapter to reveal the historic specificity of Johns's materialism and his negation of language, his sculpture also owes a special debt to the example of Marcel Duchamp's readymades of 1913-17, which, as David Joselit has demonstrated, materialize language and play at becoming simultaneously pure sign and pure thing. Duchamp remade many of these works in 1964. Joselit, *Infinite Regress: Marcel Duchamp, 1910-1941* (Cambridge, Mass.: MIT Press, 1998); see especially chapter 2, "Between Reification and Regressions: Readymades and Words."

**92**

Georg Frei, Sally King-Nero, and Neil Printz, eds., *Paintings and Sculptures, 1964-1969: Warhol 02A: The Andy Warhol Catalogue Raisonné* (New York: Phaidon, 2004), 58-62, 70-86. Others of Warhol's works make more of the specific material registration of images. See the conclusion to the current volume.

**93**

Jasper Johns, quoted in Swenson, "What Is Pop Art?" 92.

**94**

Guy Debord, *The Society of the Spectacle* (1967), trans. Donald Nicholson-Smith (New York: Zone, 1995), 12.

CHAPTER THREE
## Black Market

**1**

Gene R. Swenson, "Rauschenberg Paints a Picture," *Artnews,* April 1963, 44ff.

**2**

Ibid., 45, 67. The initials on the label stand for Consolidated Telegraph and Electric Subway Company, a corporation that had ceased to exist when it was bought by Consolidated Edison in 1960; see William J. Hausman, "Light and Power," in *The Encyclopedia of New York City,* ed. Kenneth T. Jackson (New Haven, Conn.: Yale University Press, 1995), 674.

**3**

Depending on whether they were wall-mounted or more sculptural, Rauschenberg called his assemblages combine paintings or combines.

**4**

Alan Solomon had organized a contemporary art program at the Jewish Museum, and Rauschenberg's was its first exhibition, opening in March 1963. It has been claimed that this was the first museum show for any post–World War II artist from New York. Joan Young and Susan Davidson, "Chronology," in *Robert Rauschenberg: A Retrospective* (New York: Guggenheim Museum, 1997), 562.

**5**

It is not clear precisely when Johns and Rauschenberg broke up. Young and Davidson are silent on the issue, while Jonathan D. Katz reports simply that it was 1961. Lilian Tone puts the breakup at "around [the] time" of late summer 1961, arguing that Calvin Tomkins's declaration that the rupture had happened in the summer of 1962 was erroneous. Young and Davidson, "Chronology"; Jonathan D. Katz, "The Art of Code: Jasper Johns and Robert Rauschenberg," in *Significant Others: Creativity and Intimate Partnership,* ed. Whitney Chadwick and Elizabeth de Courtivron (London: Thames and Hudson, 1993), 189; Lilian Tone, "Chronology," in *Jasper Johns: A Retrospective* (New York: Museum of Modern Art, 1996), 194, 389n23; Calvin Tomkins, *Off the Wall: Robert Rauschenberg and the Art World of Our Time* (New York: Penguin, 1981), 198.

**6**

Swenson, "Rauschenberg Paints a Picture," 66-67, 45. Irving Sandler, "In the Art Galleries," *New York Post Magazine,* 26 November 1961, 12.

**7**

D[onald] J[udd], "In the Galleries: Robert Rauschenberg," *Arts Magazine,* May–June 1963, 103. *Arts Magazine* did not illustrate the Giotto. Thomas Kellein has indicated that Judd's manuscript for the review (in the Judd Foundation Archive, Marfa, Texas) opened with a sentence excised by the editors: "While Rauschenberg's work was good before, it is outstanding now." Kellein, "The Whole Space: The Early Work of Donald Judd," in *Donald Judd: Early Work, 1955-1968* (New York: Distributed Art, 2002), 40n80.

**8**

Donald Judd, "Specific Objects," *Arts Yearbook* 8 (1965), reprinted in Judd, *Complete Writings, 1959-75* (Halifax: Nova Scotia College of Art and Design, 1975), 187. (Citations are from *Complete Writings.*) Of course, Judd's own sculpture would make good on his vision for a new art "not partial or scattered." The endorsement of Rauschenberg may seem all the more paradoxical as Judd has since been credited (both for his art and for his writing) as a seminal figure in the deflection of attention in contemporary art away from the organization of the surface and toward space of the gallery. In truth, Judd's allegiance makes good sense: Rauschenberg's objects were a rejection of illusionism in favor of what Judd called "real space" (184). In fact, Judd explicitly mentioned "Johns's few cast objects [*sic*] and a few of Rauschenberg's works" as "beginnings" toward the new art (183). See also chapter 4 of the present volume.

**9**

John Cage, "On Robert Rauschenberg, Artist and His Work," in *Silence* (Middletown, Conn.: Wesleyan University Press, 1961), 100, originally published in *Metro* 1, no. 2 (1961): 36–50. Branden Joseph points out in *Random Order: Robert Rauschenberg and the Neo-Avant-Garde* (Cambridge, Mass.: MIT Press, 2003), 52, that Cage was applying words written in another context by Indian art historian Ananda K. Coomaraswamy. Leo Steinberg, "Other

Criteria," in *Other Criteria: Confrontations with Twentieth-Century Art* (Oxford: Oxford University Press, 1972), 88. Few art historians have noted the debt Steinberg owes to Cage. See, for example, Thomas Crow's otherwise excellent historiography, "This Is Now: Becoming Robert Rauschenberg," *Artforum*, September 1997, 94ff. In addition to Cage and Steinberg, others at various points have understood Rauschenberg's work along epistemological-realist terms. See, for example, Henry Geldzahler, "Robert Rauschenberg," *Art International*, 25 September 1963, 62–67. Rosalind Krauss elaborated on and revised Steinberg's formulation in her essay "Rauschenberg and the Materialized Image," *Artforum*, December 1974, 36–53.

**10**

Swenson, "Rauschenberg Paints a Picture," 46.

**11**

The critic who objected was Paul Brach, in "Rauschenberg," *Scrap: New York's Bulwark against Time*, 23 December 1960, 3. (*Scrap* was a local art journal that survived only from 1960 to 1962; its title could serve to characterize most of the art discussed in this book.) Geldzahler, "Robert Rauschenberg," 62. Judd, "In the Galleries: Robert Rauschenberg," 104. Despite their enthusiasm for the apparent independence of the objects, Judd and Geldzahler did not argue that Rauschenberg's combines lacked compositional unity. On the contrary, Judd noted that the objects were "variously related through color" (104), and Geldzahler declared that "everything is unquestionably where it belongs" (62). Like Judd and Geldzahler, Alan Solomon characterized Rauschenberg's objects as "facts offered to us without prejudice," and Brian O'Doherty noted that "they often refuse to settle in, selfishly declaring their individuality." Alan R. Solomon, *Robert Rauschenberg* (New York: Jewish Museum, 1963), n.p.; Brian O'Doherty, "Robert Rauschenberg," *New York Times*, 28 April 1963.

**12**

Allan Kaprow, "The Legacy of Jackson Pollock," *Artnews*, October 1958, 57, 56 (emphasis original). See the introduction and chapter 1 of the present volume for further discussions of Kaprow's interpretation of Pollock. Rauschenberg statement in Dorothy C. Miller, *Sixteen Americans* (New York: Museum of Modern Art, 1959), 58. Calvin Tomkins reports in *Off the Wall*, 151, that Kaprow was thinking partly of a recent visit to Rauschenberg's studio when he wrote "The Legacy of Jackson Pollock."

**13**

"Painting relates to both art and life. Neither can be made. (I try to work in that gap between the two)." Rauschenberg statement in Miller, *Sixteen Americans*, 58. Rauschenberg quoted in "The Emperor's Combine," *Time*, 18 April 1960, 92. Rauschenberg's interest, as he put it elsewhere, in making the room "become *part* of the painting," or even making the work "*be* the room itself," is an important analogue and precedent for the far more widely known phenomenological aims of Robert Morris. Quotations from Barbara Rose, *Rauschenberg* (New York: Vintage, 1987), 56.

**14**

Cage, "On Robert Rauschenberg," 108; Rauschenberg as quoted in an uncited typescript of quotations, n.d., David Bourdon Papers, Archives of American Art, Smithsonian Institution, Washington, D.C.

**15**

Kenneth Bendiner, "Robert Rauschenberg's *Canyon*," *Arts Magazine*, June 1982, 50. The most absurd of these accounts is probably that of Charles F. Stuckey, who has read *Rebus* (fig. 3.4) literally as a rebus—that is, a riddle in which pictures can be decoded into sentences—to produce the following message: "That reproduces sundry cases of childish and comic coincidences to be read by eyes opened finally to a pattern of abstract problems." Stuckey, "Reading Rauschenberg," *Art in America*, March–April 1977, 74–84. Stuckey withdrew somewhat from this reading in his later essay, "Rauschenberg's Everything, Everywhere Era," in *Robert Rauschenberg: A Retrospective*, ed. Walter Hopps and Susan Davidson (New York: Guggenheim Museum, 1998), 30–41. See also Graham Smith, "Robert Rauschenberg's *Odalisque*," *Wallraf-Richartz Jahrbuch* 44 (1983): 375–82.

**16**

Katz also notes references to gay subculture, such as the Judy Garland autograph in *Short Circuit* (1955), and points out the phallic nature of Rauschenberg's frequent use of neckties. He even identifies allusions to the artist's own gay relationships, finding torn-up letters from Jasper Johns pasted to the surface of *Untitled* (1955). Katz, "The Art of Code," 200–201; Katz, "Lovers and Divers: Interpictorial Dialog in the Work of Jasper Johns and Robert Rauschenberg," *Frauen, Kunst, Wissenschaft* 25 (June 1998): 16–31; see also Katz, letter to the editor, *Artforum International*, May 2006, 24. For a fuller mention of Katz's work, see chapter 2 of the present volume. Laura Auricchio, "Lifting the Veil: Robert Rauschenberg's *Thirty-Four Drawings for Dante's Inferno* and Commercial Homoerotic Imagery of 1950s America," *Genders* 26 (1997): 119–54; Lisa Susan Wainwright, "Reading Junk: Thematic Imagery in the Art of Robert Rauschenberg from 1952 to 1964" (Ph.D. diss., University of Illinois at Urbana-Champaign, 1993).

**17**

Solomon, *Robert Rauschenberg*, n.p.; Yve-Alain Bois, "Eye to the Ground," *Artforum International*, March 2006, 244–48, 317. Leo Steinberg loosely quoted a snide remark of Robert Motherwell's in responding to the decoding efforts: "We like to see young iconographers enjoying themselves." Steinberg, *Encounters with Rauschenberg: A Lavishly Illustrated Lecture* (Chicago: University of Chicago Press, 2000), 61.

**18**

Roger Cranshaw and Adrian Lewis, "Re-Reading Rauschenberg," *Artscribe*, June 1981, 44–51; Jonathan Fineberg, "Robert Rauschenberg's *Reservoir*," *American Art* 12, no. 1 (Spring 1998): 85–86.

**19**

Rosalind Krauss, "Perpetual Inventory," in *Robert Rauschenberg: A Retrospective* (New York: Guggenheim Museum, 1997), 209, reprinted in *October* 88 (Spring 1999): 86–113. Citations are from *Robert Rauschenberg: A Retrospective*. This essay revises some of the claims of Krauss's earlier essay "Rauschenberg and the Materialized Image." The Rauschenberg interview is by Dorothy Gees Seckler, "The Artist Speaks: Robert Rauschenberg," *Art in America*, May–June 1966, 76.

**20**

Krauss, "Perpetual Inventory," 219; Rauschenberg quotation from interview by David Sylvester, August 1964, audiotape in Chelsea School of Art Library, London. Krauss suggests that this remark reveals a shift in Rauschenberg's thinking from an earlier insistence on the literalism of things. However, it is plain that there was no such clean chronological development. The artist's remark about the associative meanings of bricks pre-dates by one year his discussion of the black paintings.

**21**

Krauss, "Perpetual Inventory," 209, 219, 223n60. Rauschenberg quotation from Tomkins, *Off the Wall*, 201. In formulating this argument, Krauss clearly draws on work by Craig Owens and Benjamin Buchloh, who in turn are indebted to Walter Benjamin's discussions of allegorical procedures in German tragic drama and in Baudelaire. Craig Owens, "The Allegorical Impulse: Toward a Theory of Postmodernism," *October* 12 (Spring 1980): 67–86, and *October* 13 (Summer 1980): 59–80; Benjamin H. D. Buchloh, "Allegorical Procedures: Appropriation and Montage in Contemporary Art," *Artforum*, September 1982, 43–56.

**22**

Joseph, *Random Order*. Joseph argues that Rauschenberg's work offers a critical intervention in the hegemonic and spectacular organization of late capitalism. This critique is roughly that of the Frankfurt school's aesthetic negation, although Joseph adds that Rauschenberg's work also opens a space of Deleuzian "difference" for the viewing subject. For their part, the combines, largely illegible, gesture toward a place outside signification, and transitively, outside the totalized reification of capitalism (see especially 163–71). Joseph's book is importantly provocative, constituting the first real effort to understand the relationship between Rauschenberg's work and late capitalism. It runs into difficulty, however, at moments of overdetermination, such as in the argument that Rauschenberg's *White Paintings* of 1951, by capturing the shadows of passing viewers, encourage a progressively transformed subjectivity in the face of a culture of mass entertainment (67–71). In my

view, these paintings could as easily be interpreted as a provocation of reactionary (or at least atomized) individualism. (Joseph does signal some doubts in his conclusion.) Joseph's more recent article on the subject, "Rauschenberg's Refusal," in *Robert Rauschenberg: Combines,* ed. Paul Schimmel (Los Angeles: Museum of Contemporary Art, 2005), 256–83, insists more unequivocally on the antihierarchical and anti-instrumental negation in the work.

**23**

In a recent essay, Thomas Crow aims to triangulate the "iconophobic" interpretations (such as Krauss's) with the "iconophilic" ones (such as Bendiner's and Katz's). He argues that Rauschenberg's work presents a "maximized proliferation and multiplicity of signs," but that, nevertheless, "regularities begin to appear." Discussing the combines of the mid-1950s in particular, Crow identifies imagery related to climbing, falling, failed flight, and beauty. These motifs, he argues, evoke a loose theme of frustrated romantic quest, parallel to the frustration of meaning. Crow, "Rise and Fall: Theme and Idea in the Combines of Robert Rauschenberg," in *Robert Rauschenberg: Combines,* ed. Paul Schimmel (Los Angeles: Museum of Modern Art, 2005), 230–55; quotations, 254. See also the discussion of this debate in Jaimey Hamilton, "Strategies of Excess: The Postwar Assemblage of Alberto Burri, Robert Rauschenberg, and Arman" (Ph.D. diss., Boston University, 2006), 150n110.

**24**

Calvin Tomkins (*Off the Wall*, 199) records the former use of this object as "a Roman religious medallion enclosing the tooth of a saint." Rauschenberg had said he owned such an object in 1958: "Is Today's Artist with or against the Past?" *Artnews*, Summer 1958, 46.

**25**

Gerald Nordland, *My Country 'Tis of Thee* (Los Angeles: Dwan Gallery, 1962), n.p.; a copy is held in the Leo Castelli Gallery Papers, Archives of American Art.

**26**

I thank my former colleagues in the fellows' office at the Smithsonian American Art Museum for

pointing out the possibility of seeing a maulstick in the Rauschenberg painting. Quotation from Kaprow, "Legacy of Jackson Pollock," 56.

**27**

If an allegory in *Co-Existence* figures the tentative nature of representation, the barricade plays a central role. Although almost a legible letter of the alphabet, the barricade operates also—as it had in Oldenburg's *Street*—as a material obstacle to interpretation; we might see it as the central figure in a blockage of possible readings. The title of this work is itself something of an enigma. Rauschenberg may have intended the name *Co-Existence* to signal the work's figuration of an escape from readings of art as either metaphoric or literal. In a 1965 interview, the artist loosely associated the word *co-existence* with an escape from binaries, while talking enigmatically about his art: "It's a combination of the necessary co-existence of the known and unknown in a positive relationship, a constructive relationship to each other. Without one or the other, the event wouldn't be possible. I guess it's a kind of a fight against dualism, using dualism as using both yes and no at the same time to say yes, I hope." Rauschenberg, interview by Dorothy Gees Seckler, 1965, transcript, p. 35, Archives of American Art.

**28**

These are *Blue Eagle, First Landing Jump, Inside-Out, Johanson's Painting, Reservoir,* and *Slow Fall.*

**29**

Solomon, *Robert Rauschenberg,* n.p.; Steinberg, *Other Criteria,* 90. Steinberg's language builds on the fact that Rauschenberg's 1959 work *Broadcast* included dials connected to unseen radios working behind the canvas. In addition to the city, Steinberg also evokes here Rauschenberg's interest in meta-material systems of monitoring and communication, about which I will say more below. In 1973, Brian O'Doherty published an essay closely following Steinberg's account, and similarly interested in the city chiefly as emblem of the contemporary mode of vision and representation at work in Rauschenberg's art. Brian O'Doherty, "Rauschenberg and the Vernacular Glance," *Art in America*, September–October 1973, 82–87.

**30**

Lawrence Alloway, "Assembling a World between Art and Life," *Second Coming Magazine,* June 1962, 52. On Alloway and "New York junk culture," see the introduction to the present volume.

**31**

Far more recently, the art historian Robert S. Mattison has devoted a chapter to characterizing Rauschenberg's downtown urban environment in the 1950s and 1960s, drawing parallels between the artist's eclectic combines and the unkempt visual diversity of the area. It is an account loaded with relevant contextual information, but one that, like the early critical mentions, takes little interest in what we might learn from the urbanism of the work, either as a fresh understanding of the city or as a cogitation on representation itself. Robert S. Mattison, "Urban Experiences," in *Robert Rauschenberg: Breaking Boundaries* (New Haven, Conn.: Yale University Press, 2003), 41–104. Thomas Crow, in "This Is Now," makes the important point that much of the writing on Rauschenberg assumes we have an interest in his references, without making any argument for their value, or that of the works.

**32**

Sandler, "In the Art Galleries," 1961, 12; Sandler, "In the Art Galleries," *New York Post Magazine,* 14 April 1963, 14; Sandler, "Robert Rauschenberg,' *Artnews,* April 1960, 14.

**33**

There is even a large metal fire bell visible at upper left in fig. 3.14.

**34**

Robert Rauschenberg, "Random Order," *Location,* Spring 1963, 27–31.

**35**

The three demolished buildings, no more than five stories each, appear in a 1957 fire insurance map: *Atlas of the City of New York,* vol. 1, *Borough of Manhattan* (Philadelphia: G. W. Bromley, 1931, updated with paste-ins to 1957), plate 30.

**36**

Ira Henry Freeman, "New Projects Will Change the Face—and the Character—of the Washington Square Area," *New York Times,* 8 December 1957.

**37**

Tomkins, *Off the Wall,* photo caption, after 290; Young and Davidson, "Chronology," 560.

**38**

Fred J. Cook and Gene Gleason, "The Shame of New York," *Nation,* 31 October 1959, 295. The fractured sign that Rauschenberg nailed across the back of *Inside-Out*—reading CLOSED in red capital letters—may, we could now say, have another meaning, and one in tension with the self-allegorical overtones I suggested above. The large-scale shuttering of Manhattan's industry meant a literal closure of buildings such as the one Rauschenberg lived and worked in and the one he imagined in this piece. For further discussion of Manhattan's deindustrialization, see chapter 4 of the present volume.

**39**

The precise date of Rauschenberg's move to Broadway is unclear. Lilian Tone indicates that it was early in the year, while Young and Davidson write that it was in July. It is likely that the move was correlated with Rauschenberg's breakup with Johns, which seems to have happened in the summer. Tone, "Chronology," 192; Young and Davidson, "Chronology," 560.

**40**

See, for example, *Atlas* (1931, updated to 1957), vol. 1, plate 4. Rauschenberg has said that he paid $10 a month for the space, and that it had neither heat nor running water, requiring him to wash with a bucket and hose in the backyard. Mattison, *Rauschenberg: Breaking Boundaries,* 45. Rauschenberg was among the first New York artists to live in an abandoned loft; Young and Davidson ("Chronology," 552) point out that John Cage, Merce Cunningham, Philip Guston, and Morton Feldman all lived nearby.

**41**

These buildings were demolished sometime between 1955 and 1957. In 1963, this vacant lot became the nine-story parking structure that stands on the lot today. *Manhattan Land Book of the City of New York,* desk and library ed. (New York: G. W. Bromley, 1955), plate 4; *Atlas* (1931, updated to 1957), vol. 1, plate 4; *Manhattan Land Book* (1955, updated with paste-ins to 1967), plate 4.

**42**

Johns's addresses are indicated in Tone, "Chronology," 123, 125; and in Young and Davidson, "Chronology," 555. The date of Johns and Rauschenberg's meeting is not known precisely: see Tone, "Chronology," 122; Young and Davidson, "Chronology," 553. Regarding the development of their relationship, see Rachel Rosenthal, interview by Moira Roth, 2–3 September 1989, transcript, pp. 23–24, Archives of American Art

**43**

Rachel Rosenthal, unpublished interview by Calvin Tomkins, 2 June 1978, quoted in Tone, "Chronology," 123. Rosenthal later noted that she and Johns had been dating when they began looking for this place, just before Johns and Rauschenberg became a couple. She added that, between the two lofts, hers had the only bathtub: "My facility was extremely popular. I remember everybody in my bathtub." Rosenthal, interview by Roth, 23, 25. Width: *Atlas* (1931, updated to 1957), vol. 1, plate 4.

**44**

*Insurance Maps of the City of New York: Borough of Manhattan,* vol. 1, *South* (New York: Sanborn Map Company, 1923, updated with paste-ins to 1951), plate 8.

**45**

Date of Third Avenue El destruction indicated in Robert A. M. Stern, Thomas Mellins, and David Fishman, *New York, 1960. Architecture and Urbanism between the Second World War and the Bicentennial* (New York: Monacelli, 1997), 840. Eviction of Rauschenberg and Johns reported in Tone, "Chronology," 129; Young and Davidson, "Chronology," 556.

**46**

Johns and Rauschenberg seem to have moved to Front Street some time in March. Tone, "Chronology," 129; Young and Davidson, "Chronology," 556. Lil Picard, "Jasper Johns." *Das Kunstwerk,* November, 1963. An English translation of the article, from which this text is quoted, appears in the Castelli Gallery Papers. Quoted passage is from page 2 of the typescript. According to Lilian Tone ("Chronology," 386–127), this translation was the work of Henry F. Odell. Picard erroneously notes that 128 Front was three stories tall, and Tone (129) follows Picard's suggestion in this regard.

**47**

Lisa Wainwright ("Reading Junk," 221) argues that the hose in the work suggests a ticker tape. Roni Feinstein, in "Random Order: The First Fifteen Years of Robert Rauschenberg's Art, 1949–1964" (Ph.D. diss., New York University, 1990), 340n39, has noted a similarity between the composition of *Wall Street* and that of Kurt Schwitters's *Merz Picture with Candle* of 1925–28. Early photographs of *Wall Street* reveal that the twisted deformation of the bracket was originally rather subtle, and that it has been exacerbated with age.

**48**

Most of the roadway demolition was undertaken between 1959 and 1961: compare *Atlas of the City of New York: Borough of Manhattan,* vol. 1, *Battery to 14th Street* (New York: G. W. Bromley, 1959), plate 1; and *City of New York* (New York: Falk-Plan, 1961). Robert A. M. Stern et al., in *New York, 1960,* 218, note that the widening project threatened "some of Manhattan's last remaining eighteenth-century houses."

**49**

By 1967, in fact, 128 Front Street was the only building in its block more than sixteen years old; it, too, was later cleared for a skyscraper. The relevant plate of the New York Public Library's 1955 map, updated until 1967, is literally stiff with pasted-in updates. *Atlas,* 1959, plate 1; *Manhattan Land Book* (1955, updated to 1967), plates 1, 4.

**50**

Chase planned the building to consolidate 8,700 employees from nine different locations. The plaza, including a garden designed by Isamu Noguchi, opened in 1962. See the detailed treatment by Stern et al., *New York, 1960,* 172–76.

**51**

This construction history is gleaned from comparisons of the Bromley fire insurance maps dating 1957 and 1967: *Atlas* (1931, updated to 1957), vol. 1, plate 1; *Manhattan Land Book* (1955, updated to 1967), plate 1.

**52**

*Land Use, 1955–56,* (New York: City Planning Commission, Department of City Planning, 1956).

**53**

*Zoning Map* (New York: City Planning Commission, Department of City Planning, 1961). The map, "effective December 15, 1961," was "based upon a comprehensive amendment of the zoning resolution adopted by the Board of Estimate on December 15, 1960 and as subsequently amended." For more on the rezoning of 1961, see chapter 4 of the present volume.

**54**

*Insurance Maps* (1923, updated to 1951); *Manhattan Land Book* (1955); *Atlas* (1931, updated to 1957).

**55**

*Nathan Nirenstein's Real Estate Atlas: New York City and Its Environs* (Springfield, Mass.: Nirenstein's National Realty Map, [1955–58]), n.p.

**56**

Ogden Tanner with David Allison, Peter Blake, and Walter McQuade, "The Chase—Portrait of a Giant," *Architectural Forum* 115 (July 1961): 94, quoted in Stern et al., *New York 1960,* 176. Daniel J. Boorstin mentioned the Chase symbol as an example of the deliberate tendency toward simplicity in new corporate logos. Boorstin, *The Image: A Guide to Pseudo-Events in America,* 25th anniversary ed. (New York: Atheneum, 1987), 193, originally published as *The Image; or, What Happened to the American Dream* (New York: Atheneum, 1962). Caroline Jones, in *Machine in the Studio: Constructing the Postwar American Artist* (Chicago: University of Chicago Press, 1996), 162–63, has compared Chase's new logo with Frank Stella's 1963 painting *Sidney Guberman.*

**57**

"Downtown: A Last Look Backward," *Fortune,* October 1956, 157–62. Walker Evans documented the old neighborhood for the article. In 1958 the *New York Times* allowed itself a lament, too, although its editorial board supported the area's redevelopment: "Close to 3,000 low, moldering architectural relics, mostly of warm red brick, of soot-covered yellow brick or of sagging clapboard with dormered top floors, will go to rubble under the wreckers' blows. . . . That lower part of town has fought against

chromium-faced, white-vested progress, and for an astonishingly long time. The area from the Brooklyn Bridge to the Battery, which has always been the market place, has maintained the pleasant blend of fish, coffee and spice smells for long years." Meyer Berger, "About New York: The Sagging Houses of the City-That-Was May Finally Yield to Progress," *New York Times*, 15 October 1958.

**58**

"I actually had a kind of house rule," Rauschenberg said. "If I walked completely around the block and didn't find enough to work with, I could take one other block and walk around it in any direction— but that was it. The works had to look at least as interesting as anything that was going on outside the window." Quoted without citation in Robert Hughes, *The Shock of the New* (New York: Alfred A. Knopf, 1981), 334.

**59**

"Most Happy Fella," *Time,* 18 September 1964, 84–87; Rauschenberg, interview by Seckler, 4–5. Rauschenberg also said, "New York is so exciting because the edges haven't got knocked off it. . . . I don't think New York is a melting pot at all. Nothing melts here; it all just stands out like a sore thumb": Mattison, *Rauschenberg: Breaking Boundaries,* 76, quoted from Calvin Tomkins, "Sistine on Broadway," in *Robert Rauschenberg: The Silkscreen Paintings, 1962–64,* ed. Roni Feinstein and Calvin Tomkins (New York: Whitney Museum of American Art, 1990), 14. Years later, Rauschenberg added, "We're going to end up with a generic world. Where everybody is going to be exactly the same. It doesn't matter about changing colors or anything. Even Africa is becoming like that. . . . I'm not going to live that long, but for me seeing everything leveled down to the same attitude is going to be the most depressing. I look forward to the differences. I need them. I respect them": Joseph, *Random Order,* quoted from Julia Brown Turrell, "Talking to Robert Rauschenberg," in *Rauschenberg Sculpture* (Fort Worth, Tex.: Modern Art Museum of Fort Worth, 1995), 68. Cézanne had once remarked, "In a few centuries it will be senseless to be alive, everything will be so flattened out. But the bit that remains is still very dear to the heart and the eye." John Rewald, *Paul Cézanne: A Biography* (New York:

Simon & Schuster, 1948), 132. Kathryn A. Tuma used this quotation as the epigraph for her essay, "The Color and Compass of Things: Paul Cézanne and the Early Works of Jasper Johns," in *Jasper Johns: An Allegory of Painting, 1955–1965,* ed. Jeffrey Weiss (Washington, D.C.: National Gallery of Art, 2007), 170.

**60**

It is possible that the flashlight was not originally part of the work; it is not visible in some early photographs. See, for example Andrew Forge, *Rauschenberg* (New York: Harry N. Abrams, 1969); and Castelli Gallery Papers.

**61**

Solomon, *Robert Rauschenberg,* n.p.; O'Doherty, "Robert Rauschenberg," 1963. Gerald Nordland, in "Neo-Dada Goes West," *Arts Magazine,* May–June 1962, 102–3, described the work of Rauschenberg and other "Neo-Dada" artists as "anthologies of obsolescence."

**62**

Vance Packard, *The Waste Makers* (New York: David McKay, 1960), 4–5.

**63**

Packard, *The Hidden Persuaders* (New York: David McKay, 1957), 46; Boorstin, *Image,* 186.

**64**

Also shown were *193466, Aen Floga, Empire I, Empire II, Pantomime, Reservoir, Slug,* and a 1959 work called *Magician.* Not all of these works were displayed during the entire exhibition, as Rauschenberg rotated some works in to replace others. The show was also installed and taken down over an extended period, with Rauschenberg's works gradually replacing those of the previous exhibition and gradually being replaced by those of the next. Young and Davidson, "Chronology," 560; advertisement for Castelli exhibition, *New York Post Magazine,* 26 November 1961, 12; installation photographs, Panza Papers, Getty Research Institute.

**65**

*First Landing Jump, Co-Existence,* and *Pantomime* were again exhibited at this show, which ran March 4–31, 1962; the other works were *Black Market, Rigger, Blue Exit. Blue Eagle, Nettle* (1960), *Navigator* (1961–62), and *Wooden Gallop* (1962). Dwan Gallery Archive, Archives of American Art.

**66**

Rauschenberg capitalized on the fact that the solvent-transfer method he had been using in his drawing resulted in the reversal of the appropriated image or text.

**67**

Alloway, "Junk Culture as Tradition," in *New Forms—New Media I* (New York: Martha Jackson Gallery, 1960), n.p. For further discussion of this essay, see the introduction to the present volume. Sandler, "In the Art Galleries," 1961, 12.

**68**

Although the National Collection of Fine Arts exhibition catalogue has claimed that *Black Market* was made for the 1961 show at Castelli, there is no evidence that it was in that show. Young and Davidson indicate that the work was made for the Stedelijk show. *Robert Rauschenberg* (Washington, D.C.: National Collection of Fine Arts, 1976); Young and Davidson, "Chronology," 559. See also the discussion at the beginning of Joseph, "Rauschenberg's Refusal." For unusually close accounts of this painting, see Jürgen Wissman, *Robert Rauschenberg: Black Market* (Stuttgart: Reclam, 1970); and Joachim Jäger, *Das Zivilisierte Bild: Robert Rauschenberg und Seine Combine-Paintings der Jahre 1960 bis 1962* (Klagenfurt, Austria: Ritter, 1999).

**69**

The likelihood that this structure was a stand for the inauguration was suggested to me by Barbara Wolanin, curator at the Architect of the Capitol, in an e-mail letter, 15 August 2001.

**70**

For more on Clement Greenberg, see chapter 1 of the present volume.

**71**

We might see these as a materialist prototype for what Benjamin Buchloh has identified, in slightly later and more abstract art, as an "aesthetics of administration." Buchloh, "From the Aesthetics of Administration to Institutional Critique: Some Aspects of Conceptual Art, 1962–1969," *October* 55 (Winter 1990): 105–43.

**72**

Young and Davidson call it a valise in "Chronology," 559. The work seems also to make a passing reference to Marcel Duchamp's 1941 *Boîte-en-Valise,* in which Duchamp rematerialized his own artworks as miniature, portable objects. Roni Feinstein has suggested in "Random Order," 330, that *Black Market* also draws on George Brecht's 1959 work *Suitcase,* in which the viewer was invited to rearrange and remove objects

**73**

Instructions in several languages were posted on cards in the suitcase. Rauschenberg suspended this practice of exchange when some viewers took objects without replacing them. *Robert Rauschenberg,* National Collection of Fine Arts, 114; Young and Davidson, "Chronology," 559.

**74**

The objects Rauschenberg contributed in 1969 were not exchanged and remain in the collection of the Museum Ludwig in Cologne. With the exception of pages on which Rauschenberg drew these late contributions, the pads in the clipboards seem to have been lost.

**75**

More precisely, each viewer would mark her contribution with one of four stamps, each bearing Rauschenberg's name, the name of the work, and a number—one through four—corresponding to the pad on which she had drawn her object. Instructions are still held at the Museum Ludwig, Cologne.

**76**

Paul Crowell, "Traffic Program Hailed by Mayor," *New York Times,* 1 January 1959. The conversion of the avenues had begun with the adoption, in 1951, of the Traffic Control Plan for Manhattan. Third, Lexington, Madison, and Fifth were the last of the avenues slated for the change. Irving Spiegel, "2 One-Way Shifts Go Smoothly," *New York Times,* 18 July 1960.

**77**

See, for example, "5th Avenue Merchant Hits One-Way Plan," *New York Times,* 2 January 1959; and Bernard Stengren, "One-Way Avenues Debated 7 Hours," *New York Times,* 22 May 1959.

**78**

Spiegel, "2 One-Way Shifts"; Joseph C. Ingraham, "One-Way Avenues in First Big Test," *New York Times,* 19 July 1960. For a discussion of "steady flow" as a traffic engineering principle, see chapter 1 of the present volume.

**79**

Light timing reported in Spiegel, "2 One-Way Shifts." Quotations from Kate P. Durrell, letter to the editor, *New York Times*, 25 July 1960.

**80**

Stanley M. Isaacs, letter to the editor, *New York Times*, 28 July 1960. In mid-1961, Commissioner Wiley declared that traffic deaths on Third and Lexington were down 60 percent since the switch. "Traffic Deaths Down," *New York Times*, 15 June 1961.

**81**

Because its economy is one of barter rather than monetary exchange, any surplus value carried by the traded objects (to put it in Marxist language) is at least materially embodied and not carried in the abstraction of money. Here again the work marks out an ambiguous relationship to systems of abstraction.

**82**

That the artist expected the object exchange not to work is reported in *Robert Rauschenberg*, National Collection of Fine Arts, 114. In reality, Rauschenberg's own exchanges were of course not money-less: by early 1961, he was already selling works for as much as $3,600 each. Panza Papers.

**83**

Quotation from "Is Today's Artist," 56.

**84**

Spoerri was the only artist given two rooms. See *Dylaby: Dynamisch Labyrint* (Amsterdam: Stedelijk Museum, 1962). Simon Sadler notes that Constant and the Situationist International proposed the idea of a labyrinth to the Stedelijk's director, Willem Sandberg, in 1959. This project, never realized, must have been the inspiration for the exhibition mounted in 1962. For more on Dylaby, see Rauschenberg, interview by Seckler; Young and Davidson, "Chronology," 561; and Meredith Malone, "Nouveau Réalisme: Exhibition Strategies and the 'Everyday' in Post-World-War-II France" (Ph.D. diss., University of Pennsylvania, 2006).

**85**

It was at *Dylaby* that Rauschenberg's work most resembled that of Tinguely, his fellow exhibitor there. Rauschenberg designed the cover for the *Dylaby* exhibition catalogue, and he borrowed for it the image of the one-way sign he had used in *Black Market*. In the hand-drawn catalogue illustration, however, the drip from the simple black arrow is made longer and messier, and the arrow's corralling function—its systematizing and uniting purpose—is defeated by its apparently nonsensical pointing in two directions at once.

**86**

Rauschenberg quoted in Young and Davidson, "Chronology," 561. Rauschenberg seems to have learned about silk screens from Andy Warhol, who had himself only just begun to use them: ibid.

**87**

It is tempting to declare, in keeping with a traditional model of art-historical narrative, that the works after 1962 are fallen—simply shadows of Rauschenberg's earlier, critically engaged works. I am trying instead to complicate the story. Nevertheless, it is striking how well Rauschenberg's silk-screen style has accommodated itself to its appropriation by advertising. The telecommunications company Sprint, for example, ran ads in 2005 that used the signature look of Rauschenberg's silk screens (overlapping images of planes, clocks, arrows, and construction sites) to promote their wireless service; see, for example, *New Yorker*, July 11 and 18, 2005. It is a style of eclecticism made seamless, and it was picked up in the early 1980s by MTV, too.

**88**

Through the remainder of the 1960s, Rauschenberg maintained a secondary interest in sculpture, of which perhaps the most probing case was *Oracle* of 1966–65. The work concealed five radios within scrap-metal objects mounted on casters. His performances, too, included incongruous objects.

**89**

Note that in *Estate*, Rauschenberg also makes use of photographs shot from the window of his Broadway studio. A one-way sign also appears in another stencil Rauschenberg used frequently in the period; it can be seen, for example, in *N.Y. Bird Calls for Öyvind Fahlström* (see fig. 3.44), where it hangs before a pedestrian whose way is blocked by a moving taxi.

## CHAPTER FOUR
### A Loft Without Labor

**1**

John Perreault, "Plastic Ambiguities," *Village Voice*, 7 March 1968, 19.

**2**

Mahonri Sharp Young, "The Great Gromboolian Plain," *Apollo*, July 1968, 65; Gordon Brown, "Month in Review: Geometry and Other Matters," *Arts Magazine*, April 1968, 53.

**3**

Elizabeth C. Baker, "Judd the Obscure," *Artnews*, April 1968, 44ff.; James R. Mellow, "Everything Sculpture Has, My Work Doesn't," *New York Times*, 10 March 1968; Jane Harrison Cone, "Judd at the Whitney," *Artforum*, May 1968, 36; Grace Glueck, "A Box Is a Box Is a Box," *New York Times*, 10 March 1968.

**4**

Barbara Rose, "Donald Judd," *Artforum*, June 1965, 32; Lucy R. Lippard, "New York Letter: Recent Sculpture as Escape," *Art International*, February 1966, 50; James R. Mellow, "Hostage to the Gallery," *New Leader*, 14 March 1966, 32. On the occasion of Judd's retrospective at the National Gallery of Canada in Ottawa, Dudley Del Balso, Roberta Smith, and Brydon Smith compiled the catalogue raisonné, assigning a number to every work made since August 1960. Brydon Smith, *Donald Judd: Catalogue Raisonné of Paintings, Objects, and Wood-Blocks, 1960–1974* (Ottawa: National Gallery of Canada, 1975). It is surprising, given this effort, how infrequently art historians uniquely identify Judd's Minimalist works, generally preferring instead to assume that his seriality was total.

**5**

Hilton Kramer, "Display of Judd Art Defines an Attitude," *New York Times*, 14 May 1971; Robert Hughes, "Exquisite Minimalist," *Time*, 24 May 1971, 68; Richard Shiff, "Donald Judd, Safe from Birds," in *Donald Judd*, ed. Nicholas Serota (New York: Distributed Art, 2004), 61, 33.

**6**

Robert Hughes, "Exquisite Minimalist," 68.

**7**

Michael Fried, "Art and Objecthood," *Artforum,* June 1967, reprinted in Gregory Battcock, ed., *Minimal Art: A Critical Anthology* (Berkeley: University of California Press, 1968), reprinted in Fried, *Art and Objecthood* (Chicago: University of Chicago Press, 1998), reprinted in James Meyer, ed., *Minimalism* (London: Phaidon, 2000). Citations below are from Battcock, *Minimal Art.* I will return to Fried's view of Minimalism, and to the canonical account of Judd's work as literalist, in the conclusion to this chapter.

**8**

Glueck, "Box Is a Box"; "Exhibitions: Mathman's Delight," *Time,* 22 March 1968, 54; Barbara Rose, "Don Judd: The Complexities of Minimal Art," *Vogue,* March 1969, 105.

**9**

Stuart Preston, "Art: Jasper Johns Retrospective Show," *New York Times,* 15 February 1964; John Ashbery, "Paris Notes," *Art International,* 20 December 1962, 51 (emphasis in the original). See chapter 2 in the present volume.

**10**

John Coplans, "Don Judd: An Interview with John Coplans," in *Don Judd,* ed. Coplans (Pasadena, Calif.: Pasadena Art Museum, 1971), 30.

**11**

Harold Rosenberg, "Defining Art," *New Yorker,* 25 February 1967, reprinted in Battcock, *Minimal Art,* 303, 298. Looking back at the artistic environment from which critics and art historians have plucked the canonical Minimalists, one indeed finds a telling obsession with architecture. Books and exhibitions included explicitly architectural works by artists such as William Anastasi, Richard Artschwager, John F. Bennett, Mel Bochner, Anthony Caro, Tom Doyle, Dan Flavin, Judy Gerowitz, Dan Graham, Patricia Johanson, Sol LeWitt, Robert Mangold, Robert Morris, Richard Van Buren, and Lawrence Weiner.

**12**

"Mathman's Delight," 54.

**13**

Rosalind Krauss, "Allusion and Illusion in Donald Judd," *Artforum,* May 1966, 24–26, reprinted in Meyer, *Minimalism,* 2000, 212; Clement Greenberg,

"Recentness of Sculpture," in *American Sculpture of the Sixties* (Los Angeles: Los Angeles County Museum of Art, 1967), reprinted in Battcock, *Minimal Art,* 186.

**14**

Jonathan Flatley, "Allegories of Boredom," in *A Minimal Future? Art as Object, 1958–1968,* ed. Ann Goldstein (Los Angeles: Museum of Contemporary Art, 2004), 63. Flatley's is an unusually subtle account, arguing that Judd's art delivers to the attentive viewer, in the face of contemporary overstimulation and boredom, a means of contemplation. In the best-known account, Anna Chave, while disavowing the work's literalism altogether, has argued that Minimalism recapitulates the rigid forms of patriarchy. Chave, "Minimalism and the Rhetoric of Power," *Arts Magazine,* January 1990, 44–63. See also Chave's important essay on the interpersonal aspects of some of the Minimalists' success, "Minimalism and Biography," *Art Bulletin* 82, no. 1 (March 2000): 149–63. Other accounts of the referentiality of the works include Charles Reeve, "Cold Metal: Donald Judd's Hidden Historicity," *Art History* 15, no. 4 (December 1992): 486–504; David Batchelor, "Everything as Colour," in Serota, *Donald Judd,* 65–75; and Josiah McElheny, "Invisible Hand," *Artforum,* Summer 2004, 209–10.

**15**

Batchelor, "Everything as Color," 75.

**16**

Donald Judd, "Specific Objects," *Arts Yearbook* 8 (1965), reprinted in Judd, *Complete Writings, 1959–1975* (Halifax: Nova Scotia College of Art and Design, 1975), 184. Judd said that he wrote "Specific Objects" in 1964; see, for example, James Meyer, *Minimalism: Art and Polemics in the Sixties* (New Haven, Conn.: Yale University Press, 2001), 134. It invites confusion that, in this essay, Judd used the word *literal* disparagingly, denoting not an absence of extrinsic reference but rather the act of faithful transcription of the world. In "The New Sculpture," Clement Greenberg had used this word with both these meanings: "The New Sculpture" (1948, rev. 1958), in *Art and Culture: Critical Essays* (Boston: Beacon Press, 1961), 139–45. Bruce Glaser, "Questions to Stella and Judd," originally broadcast

as "New Nihilism or New Art?" WBAI-FM, New York, February 1964, Pacifica Radio Archive number BB3394, first published (edited by Lucy Lippard) in *Artnews,* September 1966, reprinted in Battcock, *Minimal Art,* 155. Dan Flavin participated in this interview; it appears that Lippard edited out his comments. A recording of the interview (mistakenly dated December 1965) is held in the Lucy Lippard Papers, Archives of American Art, Smithsonian Institution, Washington, D.C.; the recording reveals that a woman, almost certainly Lippard, also participated in the original interview.

**17**

Donald Judd, "In the Galleries," *Arts Magazine,* September 1963, reprinted in Judd, *Complete Writings, 1959–1975,* 93; "The New Sculpture," panel discussion, 2 May 1966, New York, in Meyer, *Minimalism,* 2000, 221.

**18**

Glaser, "Questions to Stella and Judd," 156, 157; "Is Easel Painting Dead?" panel, New York University, 10 November 1966, transcript, p. 34, Archives of American Art; Donald Judd, interview by Barbara Rose and Frank Stella, [1966 or 1967 (mistakenly dated 1965)], transcript, pp. 35, 16, Jeffrey Kopie Archives, Brooklyn. See similar remarks in Donald Judd, interview by Lucy Lippard, 1968, transcript, Archives of American Art; and Donald Judd, "In the Galleries," *Arts Magazine,* September 1964, reprinted in Judd, *Complete Writings, 1959–1975,* 133.

**19**

Judd, interview by Lippard, 27. Decades later, Judd bemoaned the falsity of even the rudiments of linguistic representation: "The Don Quixote of our time would be against all stories and words. We're brought up on stories: children's stories, literature, movies, trite expectations, if this then that." Donald Judd in unpublished note, 15 November 1988, quoted in David Raskin, "Judd's Moral Art," in Serota, *Donald Judd,* 91.

**20**

Donald Judd, "In the Galleries," *Arts Magazine,* February 1962, reprinted in Judd, *Complete Writings, 1959–1975,* 44.

**21**

Donald Judd, interview by Bruce Hooton, transcript, p. 7, Archives of American Art.

**22**

Roberta Smith indicated that Judd was inspired to make this freestanding object because he liked the way that *Untitled (DSS 29)* (see fig. 4.14), an earlier boxlike work made as a relief, looked when left on the floor. Roberta Smith, "Donald Judd," in Brydon Smith, *Donald Judd,* 21.

**23**

Roberta Smith refers to the metal part of *DSS 36* as a "wire mesh insert," while the entry in the catalogue raisonné calls it a "metal lathe," clearly intending to identify a lath, a sheet made as a support for plaster. Brydon Smith, *Donald Judd,* 23, 54, 112.

**24**

Brian O'Doherty, "Recent Openings: Don Judd," *New York Times,* 21 December 1963; Barbara Rose, "New York Letter," *Art International,* 15 February 1964, 41. A year later, thinking in part of Judd, Rose would comment that the works of "'object' sculpture" "appear to be functionless objects rather than sculpture as we know it": Rose, "Looking at American Sculpture," *Artforum,* February 1965, 34. Sidney Tillim, "The New Avant-Garde," *Arts Magazine,* February 1964, 20.

**25**

Roberta Smith, "Donald Judd," 21.

**26**

Coplans, "Don Judd," 23. Judd said, "I didn't really care if the wood was sloppy or bad. And I still don't care the way some people care. . . . I want my work well made, but I don't necessarily want it made with a great deal of precision." Coplans asked, "You mean industrial precision?" Judd replied, "Yes, a certain amount of variation doesn't detract from them." Judd kept for decades a fourth plank, clearly from the same pallet. It now sits at the back of the Safeway Building in Marfa, Texas, which Judd used as an art studio late in life.

**27**

Lease for a loft at 53 East Nineteenth Street, Kopie Archives. The lease indicates that the space was "the loft, three flights up." This lease, for a two-year term, is dated to begin August 1, 1960. Judd may have held an earlier lease on the same space; in his recent chronology of Judd's life, Kopie indicates that Judd moved to this location on August 1, 1959. Jeffrey Kopie, "Chronology," in Serota, *Donald Judd,* 248. The 1975 catalogue raisonné indicates that Judd arrived at East Nineteenth Street in 1960 (Brydon Smith, *Donald Judd,* 92, 40), while Thomas Kellein, in "The Whole Space: The Early Work of Donald Judd," *Donald Judd: Early Work, 1955–1968* (New York: Distributed Art, 2002), 34, has erroneously written that Judd moved to the loft in 1961. Kellein also writes that Judd had previously lived on Eighty-fifth Street, and, indeed 326 East Eighty-fifth Street is entered in the 1960 lease as Judd's home address. This entry may have been a cover, however, intended to hide the fact that Judd was in fact living, as well as working, on East Nineteenth Street; I know of no other evidence suggesting that Judd in fact ever lived on the Upper East Side.

**28**

*Manhattan Address Directory,* January 1962. Among the listings were, for example, "Atlee Printing Corp.," "Efficient Litho Inc.," "Neotype Co type founders," and "US Dye Wks Inc."

**29**

*Manhattan Address Directory,* January 1955. Photographs of buildings near 53 East Nineteenth Street in New York City photographic tax survey, 1939–41, Municipal Archives, New York City Department of Records and Information Services.

**30**

Statistics according to Arthur L. Sheer, president of an industrial leasing company, quoted in "Increase Is Noted in Movement of Related Trades to Same Area," *New York Times,* 18 November 1962.

**31**

Charles R. Simpson, *SoHo: The Artist in the City* (Chicago: University of Chicago Press, 1981), table A2 on 248, 130–31.

**32**

Simpson, *SoHo,* 117. The art historian Julia Bryan-Wilson, writing chiefly about the sculptor Robert Morris, has observed that the United States lost one million manufacturing jobs between 1953 and 1965, adding, "It was precisely at this moment that artists became interested in factory work themselves." See her excellent article "Hard Hats and Art Strikes: Robert Morris in 1970," *Art Bulletin* 89, no. 2 (June, 2007): 333–59 (quotation 344); and her related book, forthcoming from the University of California Press. For one contemporary report on the causes of the shift, see Walter H. Stern, "Industrial Parks Change Suburbs," *New York Times,* 2 July 1961; for an early general discussion of deindustrialization, see Daniel Bell, *The Coming of Post-Industrial Society: A Venture in Social Forecasting* (New York: Basic Books, 1973).

**33**

Simpson, *SoHo,* table A3 on 249.

**34**

*Manhattan Address Directory,* January 1955; and *Manhattan Address Directory,* January 1962. Although no telephone was registered in Judd's name, there was a listing in the building that year for Yayoi Kusama. The Judd literature has ignored the personal relationship between the two artists, but scholarship on Yayoi Kusama acknowledges it directly: "Let's say it like it is: Judd was Yayoi Kusama's first lover." Eric Troncy, biographical text, *Yayoi Kusama,* trans. Simon Pleasance (Dijon: Les Presses du Réel, 2001), 60. According to Troncy, the idea of making box sculptures came to Judd when Kusama kicked over a cardboard box that the two had been using as a coffee table. Judd admired Kusama's work, moderately, in reviews written in 1959 and 1964: see Judd, *Complete Writings, 1959–1975,* 2, 134–35, 189.

**35**

Nancy L. Green, *Ready-to-Wear, Ready-to-Work: A Century of Industry and Immigrants in Paris and New York* (Durham, N.C.: Duke University Press, 1997), 2.

**36**

Judd claimed that he liked the way the signature color of his early oeuvre, light cadmium red, made the shapes of his works stand out in high definition. Coplans, "Don Judd," 25. Peter Ballantine, who worked as Judd's studio assistant from around 1969 until Judd's death in 1994, said in a conversation with the author, 9 January 2006, that the canvas of *DSS 29* was stapled to the wood, and that a previous blue painting lies underneath the one now visible.

**37**

"Designs for New Skyscraper Show Zoning Impact," *New York Times,* 17 September 1961. Buildings could grow even taller if developers included public space at ground level.

**38**

"New Name Helps Fourth Avenue Segment," *New York Times,* 6 September 1959.

**39**

*Land Use, 1955–56* (New York: City of New York, City Planning Commission, Department of City Planning, 1955–56), map 8. *Zoning Maps* (New York: City of New York, City Planning Commission, Department of City Planning, 1961), map 8d. Machine shops and automobile mechanics could operate in some commercial zones, although this appears not to have been the case on Park Avenue South, which was coded C5–2 for "restricted central commercial." See Thomas W. Ennis, "New Zoning Laws in Effect Friday," *New York Times,* 10 December 1961.

**40**

"Mall on Park Ave. South Advances," *New York Times,* 16 March 1962.

**41**

Judd had praised Pollock's materialism ("I think Pollock's a greater artist than anyone working at the time or since. . . . The dripped paint . . . is dripped paint"), and *DSS 29* extrapolates from this materialism, resulting not only the abstraction of pictoriality but also that of the city itself. Donald Judd, "Jackson Pollock," *Arts Magazine,* April 1967, reprinted in Judd, *Complete Writings, 1959–1975,* 195. Judd's longtime studio assistant, Peter Ballantine, has said that Judd mixed cigarette butts into the painted surface of *DSS 29,* as Pollock famously did in *Full Fathom Five* (1947), but my own visual inspection of the surface could not confirm this claim. Ballantine, conversation with the author, 9 January 2006.

**42**

The copper disk, now dented, appears smooth in the photograph used for the catalogue raisonné in 1975: Brydon Smith, *Donald Judd,* 110. The bulging gobs of material on the surface of this work, while shaped irregularly by hand, are located at holes that the artist drilled through the surface at precise intervals.

**43**

Donald Judd, interview by Paul Cabon, 1989 or after, transcript, pp. 11–12, Judd Foundation Archive, Marfa, Texas. Judd suggests that he is speaking of a different and slightly later sculpture, *Untitled (DSS 47)* (1964). It seems, however, that the artist was confusing the two works; *DSS 47* is not perforated, while *DSS 43* has 780 holes in a grid of 30 by 26.

**44**

For a discussion of Judd's use of sketches toward sculpture, see *Donald Judd: Zeichnungen/Drawings* (Basel: Kunstmuseum Basel, 1976), 8. Judd did make two wooden floor boxes in 1963, *Untitled (DSS 39)* and *Untitled (DSS 41),* but these had strong compositional asymmetry and parts with curved edges.

**45**

Although it proved less directly influential for his later work than *DSS 64,* Judd had already made a totally rectangular box for the floor, *Untitled (DSS 53)* (1964). Other works had included rectangles as parts of larger shapes. *DSS 64* clearly came out of thinking related to *Untitled (DSS 47)* (1964), which, although it had a trough like some of the early floor boxes, also measured 6 x 27 x 24 inches (15 x 69 x 61 cm) and was mounted on the wall. Judd was invoiced for *DSS 64,* together with several other pieces, on 22 June 1965; his previous bill had been dated 24 May. Brydon Smith, *Donald Judd,* 94, 126–28. The artist's single-unit wall pieces are installed so that their upper edges hang just over five feet (61 to 63 inches, he stipulated) above the floor. Ibid., 93.

**46**

Galvanized iron is now sometimes used for expressive purposes, as in counters for hip boutiques.

In 1965, however, postindustrial chic had not yet blossomed.

**47**

The prominence of these stripes varies among different examples of *DSS 64,* as it does in Judd's other galvanized iron sculptures.

**48**

Jane Gollin, "Donald Judd," *Artnews,* April 1966, 17.

**49**

Fabrication records for some of Judd's works are held by the Judd Foundation (New York and Marfa, Texas) and by Richard Bernstein of Bernstein Sculpture Restoration (Deer Park, New York), but these are not now available to scholars. The method by which Bernstein Brothers made Judd's sculpture was reconstructed by Richard Bernstein, son of Edward Bernstein, in conversation with the author, 8 June 2006. The shop obtained its sheets of metal ready-made from foundries in Pennsylvania. Late in his life, Judd told an interviewer that Otero had been his favorite technician at the shop: Judd, interview by Cabon, 9. The early fabricated works in iron cost Judd about $80–$100 apiece. See the invoices reproduced in Sertoa. *Donald Judd,* 251; and Kopie Archives. See also a costlier 1966 invoice in Meyer, *Minimalism: Art and Polemics,* 177.

**50**

Although his cataloguers identified only one example each of *DSS 63* and *DSS 66,* Judd may have ordered two of these as well. A very slightly misshapen object in the form of *DSS 66* now sits in the back of Judd's Safeway Building in Marfa, Texas. its face labeled "NG" in black marker; the letters were the artist's notation for an attempt at a work that was "no good." In 1970, Judd had Bernstein Brothers build six additional examples of *DSS 64.* (He had kept all of the 1965 examples for himself.) The artist first combined steel and Plexiglas in a floor box in 1964.

**51**

Judd lived at 304 East Twenty-seventh Street for about seven years; Eagle Sheet Metal was at number 306, while A & A and Vanderleenden shared an address and a phone at number 309. These shops probably occupied the only storefronts at Judd's end of the block. At the other end, by First Avenue, the block accommodated shops for textile printing, cabinetmaking, and lumber, as well as two companies selling lasts, foot-shaped forms for the making and repairing of shoes. See Jeffrey Kopie, "Chronology," 247; and *Manhattan Address Directory,* January 1955. Judd discusses this home in Judd, interview by Lippard, 144.

**52**

Judd, interview by Cabon, 5–6. Bernstein Brothers invoice, reproduced in Serota, *Donald Judd,* 251.

**53**

The firm had been founded by Ignatz Weiss. By 1940, it seems to have been called Weiss and Bernstein. One ninety-three Third Avenue had once been the home of J. Unterman Trusses and Braces. Richard Bernstein, conversation with the author, Long Island City, N.Y., 8 June 2006; *Manhattan Land Book of the City of New York,* desk and library ed. (New York: G. W. Bromley, 1955), plate 44; New York City photographic tax survey.

**54**

According to the several "sheet metal" headings in Manhattan telephone directories, the borough housed 299 such shops in 1950 and 238 in 1961. The loss may in fact have been heavier; changes in the listing of "sheet metal specialties" make it difficult to know for sure. Of the firms on Judd's block in the mid-fifties, only one, Eagle Sheet Metal Works, survived to 1961. *N.Y.C. Telephone Directory: Manhattan Yellow Pages,* 1950; *Manhattan Yellow Pages* (New York: New York Telephone Company, 1961).

**55**

All these buildings were located in the twenty blocks north of Fourteenth Street, along Second and Third Avenues. Any projects planned under the old zoning law needed approval by October. Thomas W. Ennis, "Housing Chasing 3d Ave. 'El' Ghost: High-Rent Apartments Are Changing the Scene from 14th to 34th Street," *New York Times,* 22 January 1961. On East Twenty-seventh Street, Judd had also lived just three blocks down from what was to become the ten-acre, three-block, 1,136-unit project by I. M. Pei called Kips Bay Plaza. Although construction didn't begin until 1961, planning had

begun in 1957. Pei Cobb Freed & Partners Web site, www.pcfandp.com/a/p/5705/s.html, accessed 12 June 2006. This new development typified the smoothing and lightening of Manhattan's visual texture: "With their boldly scaled concrete grids and extensive glazing, the buildings [of Kips Bay Plaza] were a deliberate departure from the prevailing neighborhood fabric of brownstones and tenements." Robert A. M. Stern, Thomas Mellins, and David Fishman, *New York, 1960: Architecture and Urbanism between the Second World War and the Bicentennial* (New York: Monacelli, 1997), 288.

**56**

Judd first contracted with Bernstein Brothers to help execute a work in March 1964: dissatisfied with the look of *Untitled (DSS 47),* which he had made in wood (probably with the help of his father), he had Bernstein coat it in a fitted sheet of galvanized iron. Following this job, the artist immediately moved most of his fabrication out of his own studio and into the shop. On Judd's first use of Bernstein Brothers, see Brydon Smith, *Donald Judd,* 24, 92, 118; Serota, *Donald Judd,* 183–84, 250; and Judd, interview by Cabon, 11–12. For discussion of fabrication at Bernstein Brothers, see Ann Temkin, "Wear and Care: Ann Temkin Charts the Complicated Terrain Surrounding the Preservation of Donald Judd's Work," *Artforum,* Summer 2004, 204–8, 289. Bernstein Brothers appears to have moved in October or November 1964: an invoice of October 2 still shows the Manhattan address, while one from November 4 has this old address lined out and the new one hand-stamped in its place. See Kopie Archives and Serota, *Donald Judd,* 251.

**57**

Richard Bernstein discussed the payment in a telephone conversation with the author, 4 January 2006. The new building, occupying the full length of the block along Third Avenue, was not completed until after 1970, when several remaining buildings had been cleared. *Manhattan Land Book of the City of New York,* desk and library ed. (New York: G. W. Bromley, 1970), plate 44.

**58**

Invoice reproduced in Serota, *Donald Judd,* 251. *Insurance Maps of the Borough of Queens, City of*

*New York* (New York: Sanborn Map Company, 1915, reprinted 1948, updated to 1964), vol. 1. Today, this area is still dominated by light industry, even by a kind of activity that seems in some ways beneath the systematized legibility of international late capitalism. Sounding like a page out of Oldenburg's notebooks, the businesses remaining on this block include Michael Mazzeo Electrical Corp., Municipal Electrical Company, and Liberty Construction Supply and Material Corp.

**59**

In a recent publication, this photograph has been dated 1968, but it seems more likely that the work being assembled is *Untitled (DSS 79),* 1966.

**60**

Coplans, "Don Judd," 37.

**61**

"I've had a tinsmith make a few when I've gotten hold of some money": Judd, interview by Hooton, 10. "He may go to Long Island City and have the Bernstein Brothers, Tinsmiths, put 'Pittsburgh' seams into some (Bethcon) iron boxes": Robert Smithson, "Donald Judd," *7 Sculptors* (Philadelphia: Institute of Contemporary Art, 1965), reprinted in Meyer, *Minimalism,* 2000, 210. Smithson seems to suggest, with his use of the word *Bethcon* (for Bethlehem Consolidated) that he understood that the metal was not rolled, in fact, in New York City. For Judd's use of the word *factory* see, for example, "From New Materials, a Dynamic Sculpture," *National Observer,* 20 February 1967, 22; Robert Hughes, "Exquisite Minimalist"; and Judd, interview by Cabon.

**62**

Judd, interview by Cabon, 13. The artist Josiah McElheny has recently observed that while Judd's sculptures look mass-produced, "the reality . . . is that Judd's work was made in a setting much closer to the average person's picture of a wood shop in a garage." McElheny, "Invisible Hand," 209.

**63**

For accounts of the increasing automation, see articles in *Factory* magazine, such as "Robots: From Fantasy to Fact," *Factory,* January 1964, 76–79; and "Plant of 1970 Is Here in '64" *Factory,* February 1964, 62–65 (as in fig. 4.33).

**64**

Marc Levinson indicates that the Port of New York and related businesses employed 100,000 people in 1951, and that 90,000 manufacturing jobs were "fairly directly" tied to the port in 1956. Levinson, *The Box: How the Shipping Container Made the World Smaller and the World Economy Bigger* (Princeton, N.J.: Princeton University Press, 2006), 78–79. Witold Rybczynski, in a review of Levinson's book, "Shipping News," *New York Review of Books,* 10 August 2006, 22, writes that ships often spent as much time in port as at sea.

**65**

On standardization, see especially Marc Levinson, "Setting the Standard," in *Box,* 127–149. Reduction of necessary labor: ibid., 91; and Jacques Nevard, "Trailership Cutting Pier-Loading Time," *New York Times,* 23 November 1958. Nevard claimed that cost savings could run as high as 95 percent.

**66**

Meanwhile, the Matson company containerized much of the West Coast, while also building container cranes at dock—McLean had had them on board—creating the first dedicated container ports. Frank Broeze, *The Globalization of the Oceans: Containerization from the 1950s to the Present,* Research in Maritime History (St. John's, Newfoundland: International Maritime Economic History Association, 2002), 33-34.

**67**

New Jersey governor Hughes declared that the transformation of the port "would not have been possible if an 'adequate' network of highways had not first been constructed." George Cable Wright, "Authority Spurs Port Elizabeth," *New York Times,* 23 March 1962

**68**

Marc Levinson, *Box,* 94. The *New York Times* suggested that the containerized portion of the area's shipping was higher—perhaps representing 20 percent of its cargo. Werner Bamberger, "Progress Report Given on Harbor," *New York Times,* 26 April 1964.

**69**

Farnsworth Fowle, "Container Port Marks Fifth Year," *New York Times,* 20 August 1967.

**70**

"Planners' Stand on Piers Backed," *New York Times,* 24 September 1964. Shipping historian Frank Broeze put it simply in *Globalization of the Oceans,* 32: "Manhattan would play no role in containerization."

**71**

The International Longshoremen's Association had initially resisted containerization, but the union struck a deal with shippers in 1959, agreeing to handle the new boxes in exchange for increased pay and other benefits. Containerization was so successful that overall port employment in the region as a whole actually increased in some early years. Figures cited from "Port of New York Made Gains in '66," *New York Times,* 24 June 1967; and George Horne, "Dockers Critical of Plans for Port," *New York Times,* 23 October 1966. For a history of labor's response to containerization, see Marc Levinson, *Box,* 101-26. It is Levinson who argues that industry followed shipping out of town; "the local economy," he adds, "was left devastated as new technology made the nation's largest port obsolete" (76). See also "Jobs on Local Waterfront Rose to 392,672 in May," *New York Times,* 11 June 1962; Charles G. Bennett, "Longshoreman Picket City Hall," *New York Times,* 10 November 1964; and Werner Bamberger, "2,500 Quit Docks to Prod City on Pier Revival," *New York Times,* 19 September 1967. Witold Rybczynski ("Shipping News," 23) has claimed that the volume handled by New York City docks fell fully 98 percent between 1960 and 1970.

**72**

The sheer scale and number of the containers should remind us that New York's transformation in this period hardly meant that materiality itself disappeared; the new landscape of things, rather, was more modular than the older city being scrapped, smoother and less palpable. For contemporary reportage on the dereliction of the piers, see, for example, "Planners Stand on Piers Backed"; "Progress Report Given on Harbor"; and McCandlish Phillips, "Seaport Museum Urged Downtown," *New York Times,* 15 May 1967. A group of large, untitled Judd sculptures from around 1989–90 took on roughly the dimensions of a container, at about half scale. See for example Serota, *Donald Judd,* cat. no. 37. Paul Katz's photographs of Judd at Spring Street have been dated 1970 in *Donald Judd: Selected Works from the Judd Foundation* (New York: Christie's, 2006), 36. Gordon Matta-Clark's 1975 work *Day's End* operated in the space proffered by the decline of Manhattan's piers. Matta-Clark spoke about the "containerization of space" in a 1974 interview by Liza Bear: "Gordon Matta-Clark: Splitting the Humphrey Street Building," in *Gordon Matta-Clark,* ed. Corinne Diserens (London: Phaidon, 2003), 164.

**73**

Judd explicitly associated his stacks with architectural elevations in a schematic sketch, drawn in 1968 or 1969, of the five floors of his new home and studio at 101 Spring Street. The floors are given the shape of Judd's boxes, and they are spaced one from the other as in the sculptures. See *Donald Judd: Architecture* (Ostfildern-Ruit: Hatje Cantz, 2003), 43.

**74**

It was Reinhold Martin's book, *The Organizational Complex: Architecture, Media, and Corporate Space* (Cambridge, Mass.: MIT Press, 2003), that drew my attention to the System/360, and to its visual assonance with Minimalist sculpture. The text from *Fortune* is quoted, undated, in Emerson W. Pugh, Lyle R. Johnson, and John H. Palmer, *BM's 360 and Early 370 Systems* (Cambridge, Mass.: MIT Press, 1991), xi. Pugh, Johnson, and Palmer make their claim for the importance of the System/360 on p. xv and cite sales statistics on 174. Westinghouse was advertising office cubicles at the time; see, for example, *Architectural Record,* January 1964, 234. Information about the fair is drawn from *New York World's Fair 1964/65. Official Souvenir Book* (New York: Time-Life Books, [1964]). In addition to corporations, nations and states of the United States had pavilions at the fair.

**75**

William H. Whyte Jr., *The Organization Man* (New York: Simon & Schuster, 1956).

**76**

John Perreault, "Minimal Abstracts" (1967), in Battcock, *Minimal Art,* 259; Perreault, "Plastic Ambiguities," 19; "Mathman's Delight," 54.

**77**

Indeed it is not just in their abstraction that Judd's sculptures pick up the new logic of their world. They also mimic, for example, the shipping container's everyday workings. A container conceals the specificity and diversity of its cargo, effectively reducing it to a few variables (hardly more than how much it is worth, where it is bound, and what it weighs). Similarly, Judd's boxes—on the level of their first apprehension—work to bracket or suspend content, measuring out a blank, enclosed space on the gallery wall. I thank Jennifer L. Roberts for proposing this idea.

**78**

Ogden Tanner with David Allison, Peter Blake, and Walter McQuade, "The Chase—Portrait of a Giant," *Architectural Forum,* July 1961, 94, quoted in Stern et al., *New York 1960,* 176. Note that Peter Blake, one of the authors of this laudatory review, would later become a major critic of the false functionality of the International Style: see the end of chapter 1 in the present volume. For further mention of Chase Manhattan Plaza, see chapter 3 in the present volume. We now know that computers operate (and sell) perfectly well in curved housings emblazoned with perky logos, but in the early 1960s, IBM's president claimed that the design of their machines was dictated simply by "what they are." Martin, *Organizational Complex,* 174.

**79**

The age of the International Style corporate skyscraper may have been the world historical zenith of the rooting of authority in appeals to mechanistic efficiency. Quite soon, abiding inequalities of class, race, gender, and sexual orientation dramatically cracked the face of this ideology, and not long after, postmodernist styles of architecture and design cheerfully (and compensatorily) began claiming to embody difference.

**80**

Donald Judd, "Art and Architecture," lecture at Yale University, 20 September 1983, in *Donald Judd: Complete Writings, 1975–1986* (Eindhoven: Stedelijk van Abbemuseum, 1987), 33. In distinguishing between truth and rationality here, I follow Judd's insistence that he eschewed the human order that earlier artists had imposed on their world. (Such a distinction, however, shows us that Judd shared one of the central dreams of the new economy itself: the fantasy of a place where the shapes of things were dictated by physics rather than by whim, style, or desire.) I should add that, however deep the assonance between Judd's works and, say, International Style office buildings, his sculptures are never images of those buildings. I owe thanks to Huey Copeland and to Matthew Witkovsky for their conversations with me on the nature of representation in Judd's work. David Batchelor argues explicitly that we should think of representation as "pointing in certain directions rather than stating a finite set of things." Batchelor, "Abstraction, Modernism, Representation," in *Thinking Art: Beyond Traditional Aesthetics,* ed. Andrew Benjamin (London: Institute of Contemporary Arts, 1991), 55.

**81**

Perreault, "Minimal Abstracts," 259.

**82**

Judd mentioned this as a reason for setting the top surface below the upper edge. See Coplans, "Don Judd," 41–44.

**83**

My mention of the Manufacturer's Trust building relies on Stern et al., *New York 1960,* 372–75. The quotation is from Ada Louise Huxtable, "Bankers' Showcase," *Arts Digest*, 1 December 1954, 12–13. Another critic added, "Banks used to sell *security.* But now, with their deposits federally insured, they are selling *service.*" "Big Banking and Modern Architecture Finally Connect," *Architectural Forum*, September 1953, 134–37. Perreault may also have been thinking of more contemporary filmic images of the future, in which stand-alone objects are few, and work is accomplished by push button rather than by tool or winch. Although it was released a year after Perreault's review, Stanley Kubrick's 1968 film *2001: A Space Odyssey,* for example, explicitly used the forms of rectilinear abstraction to link the prehistoric past with the technologized future. A simple black monolith—looking very much like a model of the Seagram Building stripped of its fenestration—appears both at "the dawn of man" and at a futuristic lunar excavation site.

**84**

Note the thick Pittsburgh seams in *To Susan Buckwalter* (1964). Judd made a notation rejecting the Pittsburgh method in a 1965 drawing; see *Donald Judd: Zeichnungen,* cat. no. 105.

**85**

DiSuvero famously declared, while on a symposium panel with Judd, "I think that my friend Don Judd can't qualify as an artist, because he doesn't do the work." "The New Sculpture," panel discussion, 2 May 1966, New York, in Meyer, *Minimalism,* 2000, 220. For his part, Judd praised DiSuvero's sculpture, while acknowledging its distance from his own work: Judd, *Complete Writings, 1959–1975,* 22, 91, 112–13, 177. Public sculpture was rapidly filling the new plazas spawned by the 1961 zoning law, and it is little wonder that it usually looked very little like Judd's. The softly biological forms of Isamu Noguchi (666 Fifth Avenue, 1957; Chase Manhattan Plaza, 1960; 140 Broadway, 1967), for example, or Jean Dubuffet (Chase Manhattan Plaza, 1972) provided an inoculating "garnish," as Barbara Kruger would later put it, for the corporations in the new towers, proposing an indemnifying harmony between the body and the society of abstraction. W. J. T. Mitchell, "An Interview with Barbara Kruger," in *Art and the Public Sphere,* ed. Mitchell (Chicago: University of Chicago Press, 1992), 234.

**86**

The longer quotation here is drawn from Glueck, "Box Is a Box." The other words Judd used frequently; all appear, for example, in "Specific Objects."

**87**

Mellow, "Hostage to the Gallery," 33.

**88**

The major accounts attributing a radical criticality to Judd's works are Rosalind Krauss, "Double Negative: A New Syntax for Sculpture," in *Passages in Modern Sculpture* (Cambridge, Mass.: MIT Press, 1977); Hal Foster, "The Crux of Minimalism" (1986), in *The Return of the Real* (Cambridge, Mass.: MIT Press, 1996); Yve-Alain Bois, *Donald Judd: New Sculpture* (New York: Pace Gallery, 1991); and David Raskin, "Specific Opposition: Judd's Art and Politics," *Art History* 24, no. 5 (November 2001): 682–706. Foster's article expresses ambiguity,

Bois's misgivings. Krauss later declared, along with Benjamin H. D. Buchloh, that Judd's work participated woefully in the spectacularization of culture and in capitalist modes of production; see "The Cultural Logic of the Late Capitalist Museum," *October* 54 (Fall 1990): 3–17; and Krauss et al., "The Reception of the Sixties," *October* 69 (Summer 1994): 3–21. The major accounts of the complicity of Judd's art are Karl Beveridge and Ian Burn, "Don Judd" ("What would you say," they asked Judd, "if people started referring to you as the first *complete* capitalist artist?"), *Fox* 2 (1975): 129–42, reprinted in Meyer, *Minimalism*, 2000, 260–64; and Chave, "Minimalism and the Rhetoric of Power." In his introduction to *Minimalism: Art and Polemics in the Sixties*, the major history of the movement, James Meyer states that Minimalism holds an "irresolvable position of conformity and critique within the New York art world and late capitalist society from which it emerged." Meyer, *Minimalism: Art and Polemics*, 3. Later, however, Meyer goes on to offer an account of Minimalism as a dialectical negation in Adorno's sense. It is an art, he writes, that offers a critique by "desemanticization," by "resisting interpretation" and "refus[ing] to signify" (185, 187). Jonathan Flatley and Alex Potts have offered accounts of Judd's work that speak with unusual subtlety to the ambiguities in the work. Potts, *The Sculptural Imagination: Figurative, Modernist, Minimalist* (New Haven, Conn.: Yale University Press, 2001); Potts, "Minimalism and Junk," transcript of lecture, 2004, Getty Research Institute; Flatley, "Allegories of Boredom." Thomas Crow has importantly argued that much of modernism is both critical and complicit: Crow, "Modernism and Mass Culture in the Visual Arts," in *Modern Art in the Common Culture* (New Haven, Conn.: Yale University Press, 1996), 3–37.

**89**

James R. Mellow, "Everything Sculpture Has"; Judd, interview by Cabon, 1, 3. Of 101 Spring Street, Judd later wrote, "There had been a separate business on each floor, most with machines leaking oil. The trash was so much that Arman could have bought the building and left it alone": Donald Judd, "101 Spring Street," in *Donald Judd: Architektur* (Münster,

Germany: Westfälischer Kunstverein, 1989), 18. Specifically, the 1962 occupants had been A & F Envelope Co., J. P. Carmel Hardware, Jehm Sportswear, L. D. Swiss Embroidery Works, Lanigan & Cross Inc. machinists, New Mtn. Offset Supply Co., and Trevi Fountain Mfg. Corp: *Manhattan Address Directory*, January 1962. Around 1940, H. H. Silverman & Sons Hardware, Tools and Factory Supplies had operated at 101 Spring; Judd found and kept one of their business cards. New York City photographic tax survey; Kopie Archives. Originally, 101 Spring Street had probably housed a garment factory and showroom. Serota, *Donald Judd*, 99; Joyce Gold, "SoHo," in Jackson, *Encyclopedia of New York City*, 1088. As New York's transformation continued in the 1970s, Judd complained, "Several hundred thousand more office workers mean the end of everything in Manhattan but business. Manhattan's one big local business, incidentally, is real estate." "General Statement," *Newspaper-Lower Manhattan Township*, January 1971, reprinted in Judd, *Complete Writings, 1959–75*, 204. Eventually, Judd more or less abandoned New York for his remote home in Marfa, Texas, where he spaciously elaborated his imagined alternative to urban expedience.

**90**

Fried, "Art and Objecthood"; see especially 135, 147. More recently it is Hal Foster's "Crux of Minimalism" that has perpetuated the centrality of Fried's terms to the discourse on Minimalism. Both of these essays implicitly privilege Robert Morris's works and writings over Judd's, which leads them to emphasize the phenomenological aspect of Minimalism—an aspect in which Judd did not, at least in the 1960s, take interest.

**91**

The major essays of Greenberg's mature theory of modernism, in which materiality is forever entangled with the pictorial, appeared in these years. See, for example, "Abstract and Representational" (1954), reprinted as "Abstract, Representational, and So Forth," in Clement Greenberg, *Art and Culture* (Boston: Beacon, 1961), 133–38; and "Modernist Painting" (1960), reprinted in Clement Greenberg, *The Collected Essays and Criticism.*, ed. John O'Brian, vol. 4 (Chicago: University of Chicago Press, 1993),

85–93. For a different account of the historicity of Greenberg's formalism, see Caroline A. Jones, *Eyesight Alone: Clement Greenberg's Modernism and the Bureaucratization of the Senses* (Chicago: University of Chicago Press), 2005, especially chapter 5, "The Modernist Sensorium."



CONCLUSION

## Into Air: The Late 1960s and After

**1**

Marx and Engels. "Manifesto of the Communist Party" (1848, 1888), in *The Marx-Engels Reader*, ed. Robert C. Tucker, 2nd ed. (New York: W. W. Norton, 1978), 476. Marshall Berman of course draws on this source in titling his important book *All That Is Solid Melts into Air: The Experience of Modernity* (New York: Penguin, 1988). For Berman, Marx and Engels's formulation expresses the rapid and disorienting change endemic to modernity. Applying it here to a slightly later moment, I mean to draw out specifically its suggestion of etherealization.

**2**

Warhol addressed the news media just as James Rosenquist addressed billboards and Allan D'Arcangelo addressed American roadways. The whole American Pop art movement was driven by the increasingly departicularized look of the United States, but it was Warhol—the one to train his focus most relentlessly on media images—who has proved by far the most revealing of these artists. He recognized in TV and magazines what Judd recognized in architecture.

**3**

Lucy Lippard's landmark record of the movement was in fact titled *Six Years: The Dematerialization of the Art Object, 1966–1972* (New York: Praeger, 1973). It has been argued that conceptual art, taking a bare minimum of material form, imitated Madison Avenue's pursuit of the salable idea, and also that it imagined a radical alternative to consumerism. I would claim instead that conceptual art richly represented the persistently awkward relationship between abstraction and materiality, just as that relationship seemed everywhere to be shifting.

For consideration of these problems see especially
Benjamin H. D. Buchloh, "From the Aesthetics of
Administration to Institutional Critique: Some
Aspects of Conceptual Art, 1962–1969," *October* 55
(Winter 1990): 105–43; and Alexander Alberro, *Conceptual Art and the Politics of Publicity* (Cambridge,
Mass.: MIT Press, 2003).

**4**

Robert Smithson was obsessed at the end of the
1960s with the tensions between physical things
and images of them. For an excellent analysis of
this strain in Smithson's work, and of its relationship to a similar problem in the work of Carl Andre,
see Alex Potts, "The Minimalist Object and the
Photographic Image," in *Sculpture and Photography:
Envisioning the Third Dimension,* ed. Geraldine A.
Johnson (Cambridge: Cambridge University Press,
1998), 181–98. See also Potts, "Tactility: The Inter-
rogation of Medium in the Art of the 1960s," *Art
History* 27, no. 2 (April 2004): 282–304.

# Index

**Y**



**Z**

## Illustration Credits



© 2008 The Andy Warhol Foundation for the Visual Arts/Artists Rights Society (ARS), New York (fig. 2.42); The Andy Warhol Foundation, Inc./Art Resource, NY/© The Andy Warhol Foundation for the Visual Arts/Artists Rights Society (ARS), New York (figs. 5.1, 5.2); Courtesy of Art Institute of Chicago/Art © Jasper Johns/Licensed by VAGA, New York, NY. Photograph by Jamie M. Stukenberg (fig. 2.38); Photograph L2(14)46, © 2008 Artists Rights Society (ARS), New York/ADAGP, Paris/FLC (fig. 1.8); Photo courtesy of Richard Bernstein (fig. 4.28); © Christie's Images Limited/Art © Judd Foundation. Licensed by VAGA, New York, NY (fig. 4.20); © 2008 Jim Dine/Artists Rights Society (ARS), New York (fig. 1.13); Photo: Estel/Klut 2004 © SKD (fig. 3.10); Art © Jasper Johns/Licensed by VAGA, New York, NY (figs. 2.9, 2.10, 2.17, 2.31–2.35, 2.37, 2.39, 2.40, 2.41); Art © Jasper Johns/Licensed by VAGA, New York, NY. Photo by Richard Carafelli (fig. 2.4); Art © Jasper Johns/Licensed by VAGA, New York, NY. Photo by Graydon Wood (figs. 2.28, 2.29); Art © Jasper Johns/Licensed by VAGA, New York, NY. Photo © Dorothy Zeidman 1989 (figs. 2.2, 2.18, 2.27); From K. Varnedoe, *Jasper Johns: A Retrospective* (New York: Museum of Modern Art, 1996) (figs. 3.22, 3.27); Ellen Johnson (fig. 4.13); Art © Judd Foundation. Licensed by VAGA,

New York, NY (figs. 4.21–4.26, 4.36–4.38, 4.41); Art © Judd Foundation. Licensed by VAGA, New York, NY. Photo by Geoffrey Clements (fig. 4.1); Art © Judd Foundation. Licensed by VAGA, New York, NY. Photo by Flavin Judd (fig. 4.3); Art © Judd Foundation. Licensed by VAGA, New York, NY. Photo by Craig Rember (figs. 4.5, 4.6, 4.14, 4.19, 4.27); Art © Judd Foundation. Licensed by VAGA, New York, NY. Photo by Nick Tenwiggenhorn (figs. 4.8, 4.15, 4.16); The Estate of André Kertész/Higher Pictures (fig. 1.2); Kunstmuseum Basel, Martin Bühler/© Judd Foundation. Licensed by VAGA, New York, NY (figs. 4.7, 4.9); Photographer Arthur Lavine (fig. 3.34); Wendy Marech (figs. 4.29, 4.30); Photograph © Fred W. McDarrah, all rights reserved. Member New York Press Club, New York Photographers Association, ASPP (figs. 1.17, 3.39); Art © Robert R. McElroy/Licensed by VAGA, New York, NY (fig. 1.28); Digital Image © The Museum of Modern Art/Licensed by SCALA/Art Resource, NY/Art © Jasper Johns/Licensed by VAGA, New York, NY (figs. 2.3, 2.6); Digital Image © The Museum of Modern Art/Licensed by SCALA/Art Resource, NY/Art © Robert Rauschenberg/Licensed by VAGA, New York, NY (fig. 3.7); Photo © National Gallery of Canada, Ottawa/Canadian Museum of Contemporary Photography/Art © Judd Foundation. Licensed by VAGA, New York, NY (figs. 4.4, 4.6); New York Public Library (fig. 1.3); Copyright 1959. The New York Times Company. Reprinted by Permission (fig. 2.19); Copyright 1960. The New York Times Company. Reprinted by Permission (figs. 1.9, 1.10, 3.53); Copyright 1961. The New York Times Company. Reprinted by Permission (fig. 4.17); Copyright 1962.

The New York Times Company. Reprinted by Permission (fig. 4.18); Copyright 1967. The New York Times Company. Reprinted by Permission (fig. 4.34); NYU Archives (figs. 1.11, 1.12); Oldenburg van Bruggen Foundation (figs. 1.1, 1.4–1.7, 1.8, 1.9, 1.26, 1.27, 1.31); Art © Robert Rauschenberg/Licensed by VAGA, New York, NY (figs. 3.1–3.4, 3.6, 3.9, 3.13, 3.30, 3.41–3.44, 3.46–3.50, 3.54, 3.55); Art © Robert Rauschenberg/Licensed by VAGA, New York, NY, Photo by Ben Blackwell (fig. 3.40); Art © Robert Rauschenberg/Licensed by VAGA, New York, NY Photo by Graydon Wood, 1994 (fig 3.58); © Rheinisches Bildarchiv (fig. 1.23); © Rheinisches Bildarchiv/Photo: Britta Schlier (figs. 1.22, 4.46); © Rheinisches Bildarchiv/Photo: Britta Schlier/Art © Jasper Johns/Licensed by VAGA, New York, NY (fig. 2.5); © Rheinisches Bildarchiv/Art © Jasper Johns/Licensed by VAGA, New York, NY (fig. 2.21); © Rheinisches Bildarchiv/Art © Robert Rauschenberg/Licensed by VAGA, New York, NY (figs. 3.5, 3.29, 3.45); Rachel Rosenthal (fig. 3.20); Scala/Art Resource, NY (fig. 3.9); from T. Scullin, *United States Beer Cans: The Standard Reference of Flat Tops and Cone Tops* (Fenton, Mo.: Beer Can Collectors of America, 2001) 34 (fig. 2.26); © The Solomon R. Guggenheim Foundation, New York/Art © Judd Foundation. Licensed by VAGA, New York, NY. Photograph by David Heald (fig. 4.39); © The Solomon R. Guggenheim Foundation, New York/Art © Robert Rauschenberg/Licensed by VAGA, New York, NY. Photograph by Ellen Labenski (fig. 3.57); 2008 State Russian Museum, St. Petersburg/Art © Jasper Johns/Licensed by VAGA, New York, NY (fig. 2.1); Photo Stedelijk Museum, Amsterdam/Art © Robert